AF704058

LAW AND JEWISH DIFFERENCE

After centuries of persecution and discrimination, Jews are today often seen as a successful and well-integrated religious minority group in a 'Judeo-Christian West'. This book qualifies this narrative by exploring the legacy of Christian ambivalence towards Jews in contemporary secular law. By placing disputes over Jewish practices, such as infant male circumcision and the construction of eruvin, within a longer historical context, this book traces how Christian ambivalence towards Jews and Christianity's narrative of supersession became secularised into a cultural repertoire that has shaped central ideas and knowledge underpinning secular law. Christian ambivalence, this book argues, continues to circumscribe the rights of Jews and to shape contemporary debates about religious difference. In considering the interaction between law and Christian ambivalence towards Jews, this book engages with broader questions about the cultural foundations of Western secular law, the politics of religious freedom, the racialisation of religion, and the ambivalent nature of legal progress.

MAREIKE RIEDEL is Lecturer at Macquarie Law School at Macquarie University in Sydney and Visiting Fellow at the School of Regulation and Global Governance at the Australian National University. Drawing on her background in both law and the humanities, her research examines the intersections of law, religion, and race and the history of secular law. Before joining Macquarie University, she has held research fellowships at the Max Planck Institute for the Study of Religious and Ethnic Diversity, at the Australian National University, and at the Max Planck Institute for Social Anthropology.

CAMBRIDGE STUDIES IN LAW AND SOCIETY

Founded in 1997, Cambridge Studies in Law and Society is a hub for leading scholarship in socio-legal studies. Located at the intersection of law, the humanities, and the social sciences, it publishes empirically innovative and theoretically sophisticated work on law's manifestations in everyday life: from discourses to practices, and from institutions to cultures. The series editors have longstanding expertise in the interdisciplinary study of law, and welcome contributions that place legal phenomena in national, comparative, or international perspective. Series authors come from a range of disciplines, including anthropology, history, law, literature, political science, and sociology.

Series Editors

Mark Fathi Massoud, *University of California, Santa Cruz*

Jens Meierhenrich, *London School of Economics and Political Science*

Rachel E. Stern, *University of California, Berkeley*

A list of books in the series can be found at the back of this book.

CAMBRIDGE
STUDIES IN
LAW AND SOCIETY

LAW AND JEWISH DIFFERENCE

Ambivalent Encounters

Mareike Riedel

Macquarie University

CAMBRIDGE
UNIVERSITY PRESS

CAMBRIDGE
UNIVERSITY PRESS

Shaftesbury Road, Cambridge CB2 8EA, United Kingdom

One Liberty Plaza, 20th Floor, New York, NY 10006, USA

477 Williamstown Road, Port Melbourne, VIC 3207, Australia

314–321, 3rd Floor, Plot 3, Splendor Forum, Jasola District Centre, New Delhi – 110025, India

103 Penang Road, #05–06/07, Visioncrest Commercial, Singapore 238467

Cambridge University Press is part of Cambridge University Press & Assessment, a department of the University of Cambridge.

We share the University's mission to contribute to society through the pursuit of education, learning and research at the highest international levels of excellence.

www.cambridge.org
Information on this title: www.cambridge.org/9781316514870

DOI: 10.1017/9781009091213

© Mareike Riedel 2024

This publication is in copyright. Subject to statutory exception and to the provisions of relevant collective licensing agreements, no reproduction of any part may take place without the written permission of Cambridge University Press & Assessment.

When citing this work, please include a reference to the DOI 10.1017/9781009091213

First published 2024

A catalogue record for this publication is available from the British Library

Library of Congress Cataloging-in-Publication Data
Names: Riedel, Mareike, 1984– author.
Title: Law and Jewish difference : ambivalent encounters / Mareike Riedel, Macquarie University.
Description: Cambridge, United Kingdom ; New York, NY : Cambridge University Press, 2024. | Includes bibliographical references and index.
Identifiers: LCCN 2024002959 | ISBN 9781316514870 (hardback) | ISBN 9781009091213 (ebook)
Subjects: LCSH: Religion and law. | Religious law and legislation. | Law – Religious aspects – Judaism. | Jewish law. | Law – Religious aspects – Christianity. | Orthodox Judaism.
Classification: LCC KB270 .R54 2024 | DDC 342.08/5296–dc23/eng/20240129
LC record available at https://lccn.loc.gov/2024002959

ISBN 978-1-316-51487-0 Hardback

Cambridge University Press & Assessment has no responsibility for the persistence or accuracy of URLs for external or third-party internet websites referred to in this publication and does not guarantee that any content on such websites is, or will remain, accurate or appropriate.

CONTENTS

ACKNOWLEDGEMENTS

The seeds for this book were sown several years ago when I received a scholarship to spend some time at the Hebrew University in Jerusalem during my final years of law school. Amidst the noise and bustle of the city's streets, my taken-for-granted assumptions about law, religion, and secularism slowly started to unravel and led me to formulate some of the questions that I try to answer in this book. Many of the answers to those questions have been forged in conversations with colleagues, friends, and family who have generously given their time to discuss ideas with me, to read my drafts, to listen to my presentations, and to offer comfort and support. I am immensely grateful for their challenging questions and critical comments, all of which have enriched my thinking and writing in so many ways. I hope their contributions are reflected in this book even though I may not have been able to answer all their questions. All mistakes and shortcomings remain of course mine.

Hilary Charlesworth has been a generous reader, careful interlocutor, and calm guide through the formative stages of this project. Thank you, Hilary, for inspiring me in so many ways, academically and personally, and for offering me an intellectual home when I had been uprooted. Kim Rubenstein's enthusiasm for this project has been a constant source of encouragement. Thank you, Kim, for your academic support, for welcoming us to your Shabbat table, and for sharing your advice on all things legal and Jewish with me. Kate Henne's truly interdisciplinary mind and unbelievable knowledge of a wide array of literatures have challenged me to see things in new light. Thank you, Kate, for prompting me to think further and for offering me an academic landing pad when I returned to Australia in the midst of a pandemic. With a keen eye for law's pluralism, Miranda Forsyth has acted as a wise reminder to think carefully about the many manifestations of law. Didi Herman and Margaret Davies provided detailed comments and insightful suggestions as they read and examined an earlier iteration of this work when it was still a PhD thesis. Their critical sociolegal scholarship has been a huge inspiration, and I am very grateful for their thoughtful feedback. A heartfelt thank you also goes to Anne Macduff and Marie-Eve Loiselle who provided not only warm encouragement but also crucial last-minute comments that helped me to clarify my arguments.

The Australian National University's School of Regulation and Governance (RegNet) has been a vibrant intellectual home while this project began its life as a PhD thesis. I am grateful to my RegNet colleagues and friends for keeping me company as I went on this intellectual journey. Thank you, John and Valerie Braithwaite, Christoph Sperfeldt, Julia Wee, Dang-Ni (Janice) Lee, Emma Nyhan, Ibi Losconz, and Lia Kent for many conversations, morning teas, and Tuesday seminars. During my first steps as a post-doc, I was fortunate to be based at the Max Planck Institute for the Study of Religious and Ethnic Diversity. My sincere thanks to Ayelet Shachar and Ran Hirschl for their support of my work, their encouragement to pursue this topic, and their insightful feedback on my ideas. A huge thank you also to Lisa Harms, Vanessa Rau, Alex Hudson, Barbara von Rütte, Derek Denman, Benjamin Boudou, Martijn Van den Brink, and Samuel Schmid, my colleagues and friends in the Department of Ethics, Law and Politics and beyond who not only read and commented on many drafts but also shared the joys and anxieties of post-doc life with me. Macquarie Law School has become an exciting academic home, and I am grateful to my colleagues for their warm welcome.

I have presented parts of this research at conferences, workshops, and talks in a variety of places and have benefitted a lot from these conversations. The members of the Religion and Politics Reading Group shared kind and insightful feedback, and I want to thank in particular Kate Gleeson and Ryan Williams for their detailed comments. A thank you also to the members of the Human Rights Reading Group at the Lichtenberg Kolleg in Göttingen and to the participants at the Abraham Bar Menachem Talks and at the Religion after Marriage Equality workshop. Finally, I thank Jeremy Farrall and Therese MacDermott for their generous advice on how to navigate the academic world. This project took shape at the Max Planck Institute for Social Anthropology, and I thank my colleagues and friends in the Department of Law and Anthropology for their help in shaping early ideas and arguments. Thank you, Bertram Turner, Kalindi Kokal, Katrin Seidel, Larissa Vetters, Markus Klank,

Beate Anam, and Jutta Turner. Geoffrey Levey hosted me generously for a two-months stint at the University of New South Wales and did not only draw my attention to the St Ives eruv but also helped me to formulate important ideas.

Importantly, I want to thank all my Jewish and non-Jewish interlocutors who have taken the time to ponder questions of identity, difference, and the law with me. I cannot name you all, but your contributions have inspired my thinking in so many ways, and I am very grateful for your time and generosity. At Cambridge University Press, I thank Finola O'Sullivan for her interest in my manuscript and Marianne Nield and Toby Ginsburg for their patience as the completion of this manuscript got delayed several times as I moved between countries, cities, and institutions and dealt with the challenges of a pandemic. My thanks also to the anonymous readers for insightful feedback that has helped me to strengthen and clarify my ideas and arguments. Benyamin Reich's artistic work on the complexities of Jewish identity and history has been a great inspiration, and I am grateful that he agreed to have his photograph 'Peyes' on the cover of this book. For generous financial support of portions of this research, I want to thank the Max Planck Society, the Australian National University, and Macquarie University.

A book manuscript has the habit of invading one's life beyond the university and I cannot thank my friends and family enough for their support and patience as I spent countless hours working on this book and what probably felt for them like countless hours talking about it. Thank you, Melanie Pescud, for your unwavering support, for your wisdom and warmth, and for always reminding me of the blue sky. Thank you, Jacqui Lavis and Russell Watkinson, for making me feel at home far away from home. A huge Dankeschön to Karin, Wolfgang, and Marlene Riedel. Without you I would not have made it that far. Finally, Jay Watkinson. Thank you for helping me craft and refine my ideas, for polishing my language, for cheering me on, for going above and beyond, and for always believing in me – even when I had my doubts. You have made this book possible in so many ways that appropriately thanking you would require its very own little book.

Parts of this research have appeared in different forms in the following publications: an early version of Chapter 4 was published as 'An Uneasy Encounter: Male Circumcision, Jewish Difference, and German Law' in *Studies of Law, Politics and Society*. Chapter 6 draws on revised material published in 'The Difference a Wire Makes: Planning Law, Public Orthodox Judaism, and Urban Space in Australia' in *International Journal of Law in Context*. My article 'Law and the Construction of Jewish Difference' in the *Journal of Law and Society* presents an earlier iteration of different arguments that I develop further across various chapters of this book.

CHAPTER ONE

INTRODUCTION

Jewish Questions Past and Present

Once one of Christian Europe's most paradigmatic Others, Jews are now mostly seen as a well-integrated and successful religious minority group. For centuries, Jews faced political, social, and legal exclusion from the societies in which they lived. Today, politicians proudly invoke the West's shared 'Judeo-Christian' heritage, suggesting the unity and parity of Jews and Christians as founding members of 'Western civilisation'. Compared to the past, Jews have seemingly moved from being the paradigmatic outsiders to accepted and even embraced insiders. However, despite this undoubted success, there are still moments when this narrative can become suddenly unsettled. By this, I do not refer to the terrible attacks on Jewish life, such as the synagogue shootings in Halle in 2019 and in Pittsburgh a year earlier in 2018, the still alarming rates of antisemitic violence, the groups of White supremacists chanting in the streets that Jews will not replace them, or the flourishing antisemitic conspiracy theories in the online and offline world. Uneasiness with Jews and Judaism also still manifests in less extreme and less overtly hostile ways in the midst of society on the terrain of liberal law, suggesting that the relationship between law and Jewishness is more complicated than the Judeo-Christian parity narrative suggests.

The practice of shechita, the slaughter of animals without prior stunning, for example, has been the subject of numerous controversies, regulations, and bans over many decades, such as in Sweden, Denmark, Switzerland, Belgium, and New Zealand. Supporters of such a ban claim the welfare of animals as their primary concern, accusing Jews alongside

Muslims of cruelty and insisting that state law must prevail over 'medieval' religious custom. Infant male circumcision, long an accepted and even promoted surgery in some Western societies, such as the United States and England, is now increasingly discussed alongside such practices as female genital cutting as a pre-modern and barbaric violation of a child's bodily integrity that oversteps the limits of religious freedom. In 2018, both Iceland and Denmark discussed draft bills criminalising male circumcision and in 2017, one of Norway's ruling parties called for a ban on the practice. Earlier in 2012, a German court declared the practice a criminal assault, arguing that neither parental rights nor religious freedom can trump the rights of the child. Similarly, the practice of the eruv, an inconspicuous installation of wires and poles in public space allowing Orthodox Jews to transport objects on Shabbat, has turned into a thorny issue for residents in Canada, the United Kingdom, Australia, South Africa, and the United States. Neighbours opposing this almost invisible installation in the name of the secularity of public space warn against a Jewish take-over of their neighbourhood, claiming the eruv would turn their locality into a religious 'ghetto' and impose Jewish law on secular citizens.

At first sight, these cases may appear unconnected, a collection of temporary and geographically dispersed disturbances of the general acceptance of Jews and Judaism in Western societies. These cases cover an array of legal concerns, including the built environment, children's rights, and the welfare of animals. Yet, reading under the surface of each of these cases reveals something similar that extends beyond the narrow legal issue in question. These disputes are often not only about foreskins, wires, or butcher knives, but about the difference these things signify; a difference some find so troubling that it has to be contained by law.

This book takes these 'disturbances' as a vantage point to explore the question of Jewish difference in Western secular liberal law.[1] My argument is that contemporary legal responses to Jews, Judaism, and Jewishness reveal a persistent ambivalence about the place and belonging of Jews and Judaism in Western societies. I use the term 'ambivalence' deliberately instead of antisemitism. An analytical focus on antisemitism conceals more than it reveals, potentially narrowing the

[1] I use the terms 'the West' and 'Western' to refer to the societies of Western/Latin Christendom in Western Europe and settler societies of Western European descent, such as Australia, Canada, and the United States.

analysis to questions of hatred, hostility, and violence that still dominate approaches to antisemitism.[2] However, reading legal debates about Jews and Judaism both past and present reveals a more complex set of dynamics and interactions that cannot be reduced to hatred, hostility, or enmity alone. In using the concept of ambivalence, I draw from work in the Jewish studies that uses the notion of ambivalence to capture a more complex set of attitudes and responses to Jews and Judaism beyond antisemitism. Ambivalence, as Tony Kushner notes, can take the 'form of praising westernized, assimilated Jews and rejecting those who were deemed foreign'.[3] Ambivalence assigns Jews a liminal position in the dominant cultures of the West by constructing Jews 'as *both* anti-Christs *and* potential converts as *both* inherently Other or as potential citizens'.[4]

In law and legal conflict, ambivalence towards Jews and Judaism manifests as a contradictory pattern of arguments: On the one hand, there is the promise of inclusion, incorporation, and equality. However, this inclusion is rarely ever unconditional and hinges upon the remaking and transformation of Jewishness in line with dominant cultural and religious norms. Inclusion and equal rights are often still predicated on assimilation, which is to be enforced through the law to ensure that Jews adhere to values presented as secular, and universal – sometimes even as 'Judeo-Christian'. On the other hand, there remains a profound suspicion and anxiety of Jewish difference. This line of legal arguments often rests on a racialising and essentialising logic that casts doubt on the possibility of a successful assimilation and defers equality. In oscillating between conditional inclusion and exclusion, between incorporation and differentiation, and between proximity and distance, ambivalence creates a tension around the belonging of Jews that is never fully resolved.

Sociolegal scholarship and critical legal analyses have long been concerned with how Western law has been implicated in maintaining social hierarchies and inequality along various lines of difference, such

[2] See, for example, Robert S. Wistrich, *Antisemitism: The Longest Hatred* (London: Thames Methuen, 1991). For a detailed critique of antisemitism as under-theorised, see Jonathan Judaken, 'AHR Roundtable: Rethinking Anti-Semitism. Introduction', *American Historical Review* 123, no. 4 (2018): 1122–38.

[3] Tony Kushner, 'Anti-Semitism in Britain: Continuity and the Absence of a Resurgence?', *Ethnic and Racial Studies* 36, no. 3 (2013): 434–49, p. 441. For an extensive discussion of 'ambivalence' as a force in modernity, see Zygmunt Bauman, *Modernity and Ambivalence* (Ithaca: Cornell University Press, 1991).

[4] Bryan Cheyette, 'English Anti-Semitism: A Counter-Narrative', *Textual Practice* 25, no. 1 (2011): 15–32, p. 22. (Italics in original.)

as gender, race, and sexuality. However, the question of Jewish difference and issues of antisemitism more broadly have to date received little attention. There are of course notable exceptions, such as Didi Herman's excellent work on representations of Jewishness in modern English judicial discourse and Stephen Feldman's critical history of the American constitutional separation of state and church 'from the viewpoint of an American Jew'. Their work reveals that the belonging of Jews to the imagined communities of the West is far from settled and that the law remains implicated in the cultural domination of Jews.[5] Apart from these studies, however, Jews, Judaism, and antisemitism have remained largely absent from critical sociolegal scholarship. The reasons for this lacuna are diverse and complex, perhaps partly owing to perceptions of Jews as members of a privileged Western 'White Judeo-Christian' mainstream and understandable concern with more overt forms of legal oppression and domination.[6] This lacuna, however, is a missed opportunity, not only because, as Didi Herman has already pointed out in the context of England, our understanding of identity and difference in Western law must remain incomplete without considering Jews and Judaism.[7] The legal encounter with Jewish difference, I argue in this book, also offers an opportunity to critically engage with the religious-cultural foundations of Western secular law by examining how the historical relationship between Christianity and one of its most significant Others has shaped central ideas, knowledge, and meanings in secular liberal law.

The significance of Christian theology and Christian attitudes towards Judaism for not only the history of Jews but also for the development

5 Didi Herman, *An Unfortunate Coincidence: Jews, Jewishness, and English Law* (Oxford: Oxford University Press, 2011); Stephen M. Feldman, *Please Don't Wish Me a Merry Christmas: A Critical History of the Separation of Church and State* (New York: New York University Press, 1998) (quote at p. 9).

6 See also Bryan Cheyette, 'Postcolonialism and the Study of Anti-Semitism', *American Historical Review* 123, no. 4 (2018), p. 1238. A note on the spelling of White in this book: spelling 'Black' with a capital letter has become increasingly common to account for the fact that 'Black' is a constructed racial identity. There remains debate whether 'white' too should be spelled with a capital letter to highlight its constructed and artificial nature. Those against such a spelling worry that it would elevate White Supremacists. For an argument in favour of capitalising both 'Black' and 'White', see, for example, Kwame Anthony Appiah, 'The Case for Capitalizing the B in Black', *The Atlantic*, 20 June 2020. In this book, I follow Appiah's argument by spelling 'White' with a capital letter when referring to a racial category rather than a colour.

7 Herman, *An Unfortunate Coincidence*, pp. 174–75.

of foundational categories of thought in Western Christendom or what today is often called 'the West' is well-known to scholars in the humanities. David Nirenberg, for example, has shown how thinking about Jews and Judaism and engaging the question of Jewish difference allowed Christian and Western thinkers to make sense of their own identities and histories as well as of broader questions of their times.[8] These 'Jewish questions', Nirenberg contends, shaped fundamental categories and habits of Western thought by mobilising a figure of 'the Jew' and of 'Judaism' as a foil and this thinking could often have profound consequences for actual living Jews. The societies of Greek and Roman antiquity of course thought about Jews too, but the question of Jewish difference became a particularly troubling and irritating issue with the rise of Christianity. For Christianity, Jews constituted unstable 'figures of difference' that have reinforced but also continuously troubled Christian identity by challenging its central narratives of universalism and truth.[9] Ideas about Jewish difference, therefore, have profoundly shaped the Christian tradition and, as I seek to show in this book, continue to reverberate in modern liberal law.

My aim in this book is to bring sociolegal studies into conversation with this work in the humanities to offer a critical perspective on secular law and Jewish difference that foregrounds the role of Christian ambivalence for shaping foundational categories and assumption in secular law and legal thinking. That the tradition of Western Christendom has left an imprint on secular liberal law is not a novel claim in sociolegal scholarship and in the critical study of religion and secularism. However, the central argument that I advance in this book is that we cannot understand contemporary legal responses to Jews, Judaism, and Jewishness – and indeed, to other non-Christians – without considering the legacy of *Christian ambivalence* towards Jews and Judaism in Western secular law.[10] By Christian ambivalence, I refer to a set of secularised Christian discourses and ideas about Jews and Judaism that

[8] David Nirenberg, *Anti-Judaism: The Western Tradition* (New York; London: WW Norton, 2013). See also Sander L. Gilman, *The Jew's Body* (New York; London: Routledge, 1991); Jeremy Cohen, *Living Letters of the Law: Ideas of the Jew in Medieval Christianity* (Berkeley and Los Angeles: University of California Press, 1999).

[9] Jonathan Boyarin, *The Unconverted Self: Jews, Indians, and the Identity of Christian Europe* (Chicago; London: University of Chicago Press, 2009).

[10] See also Zygmunt Bauman, 'Allosemitism: Premodern, Modern, Postmodern', In *Modernity, Culture, and 'The Jew'*, eds., Bryan Cheyette and Laura Marcus (Cambridge: Polity Press, 1998), 143–56, p. 148.

emerged from Christian theology and its attempts to make sense of its Jewish origins. Christian ambivalence, as I explore in this book, has shaped both policies and laws towards Jews in ways that rejected Jews but also desired and even required Jewish inclusion, yet rarely ever unconditional. However, Christian attitudes towards Jews and Judaism did not only shape the lives of Jews in Western societies in a myriad of ways but also established ways of thinking and reasoning that continue to underpin modern secular law – with consequences not only for the equality and rights of Jews but also for other non-Christians. This book is, therefore, at one level a study of how Christian ambivalence has shaped legal responses towards Jews and Judaism, yet it is also a study of the often-unstated assumptions and biases about religion and religious difference and about some of their roots in Christian ambivalence towards Jews. These assumption and biases entrench and reproduce the dominance of Christian normativity in law and society, perpetuate Christian privilege, and contribute to the assimilation, racialisation, and marginalisation of not only Jews but also other non-Christians.[11] This book is thus also an attempt to engage through the lens of Jewish difference more broadly with the issue of Christian privilege and its impact on religious equality in Western law at a time when a populist and nationalist backlash against diversity and multiculturalism increasingly involves the mobilisation of Christianity as a central element of an allegedly beleaguered and threatened 'Western civilisation' that secular law is called upon to defend.[12]

Moreover, this book contends that taking note of the Christian underpinnings of Western secular law and legal thought must also grapple with questions of race. To date, the critical sociolegal analysis of religion in law and of race in law has not always occurred in tandem, reflecting how there has often been little conversation between

[11] Work on Christian privilege and the law has largely focused on the United States, see, for example, Khyati Y. Joshi, *White Christian Privilege: The Illusion of Religious Equality* (New York: New York University Press, 2020); Caroline Mala Corbin, 'Justice Scalia, the Establishment Clause, and Christian Privilege', *First Amendment Law Review* 15, no. 22 (2017): 185–220. On Christian privilege in Western Europe more generally albeit not focused on law specifically, see A. Sophie Lauwers, 'Religion, Secularity, Culture? Investigating Christian Privilege in Western Europe', *Ethnicities* 23, no. 3 (2023): 403–25.

[12] Rogers Brubakers speaks of 'Christianism' as a part of the shift from nationalism to civilizationism: Rogers Brubakers, 'Between Nationalism and Civilizationism: The European Populist Moment in Comparative Perspective', *Ethnic and Racial Studies* 40, no. 8 (2017): 1191–1226.

theories of race and theories of religion more broadly.[13] However, I would suggest that a critical consideration of contemporary debates about religious difference needs to attend to the racialisation of religious difference, which renders religious differences insurmountable and therefore unassimilable. This dynamic has been particularly salient in relation to Islam but, as I will show, also still permeates responses to Jewish practices, such as infant male circumcision and the eruv. The intersection of religion and race in legal and political responses to religious difference is, I suggest neither accidental nor novel but reflects how the modern problem of what is termed cultural racism finds some of its roots in the Christian attempt to distance itself from its Jewish origins. The question of Jewish difference in secular law therefore also offers a vantage point from which to examine the interplay between Christian ambivalence, the racialisation of religious difference, and Western law in both contemporary and historical perspectives. Before setting out the approach this book takes in more detail, this introductory chapter will proceed by locating Jews, Judaism, and Jewishness in the interdisciplinary scholarly debates about religion, secularism, and the law on the one hand as well as the literature on law and the racialisation of religion on the other.

SECULAR LAW AND CHRISTIAN NORMATIVITY

Religious symbols and practices remain the source of much public debate, litigation, and legislation across Western liberal democracies. In these debates and conflicts, secular law is tasked with drawing the

[13] On this lack of conversation in legal scholarship, see also Nomi Maya Stolzenberg, 'Righting the Relationship between Race and Religion in Law', *Oxford Journal of Legal Studies* 31, no. 3 (2011): 583–602. For example, Stephen Feldman's otherwise excellent study of Christianity's influence on the development of contemporary US constitutional law does not mention race, although it identifies religious antisemitism as an important factor in this history, see Feldman, *Please Don't Wish Me*. Didi Herman's *An Unfortunate Coincidence* work is highly attentive to processes of racialisation in judicial discourses but does not centre on the historical relationship between Christianity, Jewishness, and race. For a cultural legal history of religion and race as overlapping and intersecting forces in the development of Western law, see Eve Darian-Smith, *Religion, Race, Rights: Landmarks in the History of Modern Anglo-American Law* (Oxford; Portland: Hart Publishing, 2010). On the racialisation of Muslims in American law, see, for example, Neil Gotanda, 'The Racialization of Islam in American Law', *Annals of the American Academy* 637, no. 1 (2011): 184–95; Margaret Chon and Donna E. Arzt, 'Walking While Muslim', *Law and Contemporary Problems* 68, no. 2 (2005): 215–54.

appropriate line between religion and the public sphere and with protecting the right to religious freedom for minorities and majorities alike in a way that reflects secular and not religious values. The secularity of law implies that state law remains largely unencumbered by religious particularities. This view underpins the term 'law and religion' that describes a field of scholarly inquiry in which law and religion are largely seen as two separated realms, mirroring an understanding of 'the secular' and 'the religious' as distinct and separate. However, as critical studies of secularism have shown, the relationship between 'the religious' and 'the secular' is not one of simple opposition. Instead, the secular state and its law remain deeply involved in defining and shaping religion.[14] Secularism as both a regime of governance and an ideology does not just draw a line of separation between religion and state to enable tolerance of difference and diversity but also involves 'remaking certain kinds of religious subjectivities'.[15] In doing so, secularism constructs and produces that which is 'religious' as well as that which is 'secular', delineating 'religion' from other spheres of life and from other aspects of identity and community attachment.[16]

Secular law as a key site for instituting secular rule participates in constructing 'religion' and in drawing the boundaries of religious difference and religious freedom. In defining and regulating religion, secular liberal law does not operate from an entirely neutral standpoint. Instead, by being embedded in historical power relations, secular law often reflects majoritarian norms, expectations, and biases about what constitutes 'proper religion', which, in a Western context, remain indebted to the tradition of Western Christianity. Even if the influence of Christian religious institutions in public life has changed compared to the past, affiliation with institutional Christianity is in decline, and religious diversity has increased, Christian culture and traditions remain ubiquitous in Western secular societies. The secular calendar of the year reflects the Christian calendar, while the rhythm of the week follows the Christian rhythm of the week that designates Sunday as the central day of rest. Many Christian holidays are nationally recognised holidays, Christian symbols, such as Christmas decorations but

[14] See, for example, Talal Asad, *Formations of the Secular: Christianity, Islam, Modernity* (Stanford: Stanford University Press, 2003).

[15] Saba Mahmood, 'Secularism, Hermeneutics, and Empire: The Politics of Islamic Reformation', *Public Culture* 18, no. 2 (2006): 323–47, p. 328.

[16] Mayanthi L. Fernando, *The Republic Unsettled: Muslim French and the Contradictions of Secularism* (Durham; London: Duke University Press, 2014), 22.

also crucifixes remain common sights in public spaces, and Christian prayers open the sittings of parliaments, such as in Australia. The Christian tradition maintains a dominant and hegemonic *cultural* presence, which also manifests in and through secular law.

There remains a Christian residue in secular law that reflects and reproduces Christian normativity, values, and knowledge. In making this argument, I build on a body of interdisciplinary scholarship that explores the influence of Christian knowledge and thought, particularly in its Protestant variant, on Western formations of secularism and secular law.[17] This influence is most evident in the way that Western law often privileges a notion of religion as private, voluntary, individual, autonomous faith. This liberal notion of religion is presented as a religiously neutral, ahistorical, and universal category of secular law. Yet, in privileging subjective and individual interior belief, this notion of religion marginalises religion's outward manifestation. Indeed, most other religious traditions, such as Judaism, Islam, or Hinduism, do not fit as easily within such limited notion of 'religion' as private, individual, and voluntary faith.[18] Instead, these religions often value and privilege other elements of identification and attachment, such as community, public religiosity, descent, and ritual practice. Indeed, as Robert Yelle points out, there are few traditions in which such an 'antiritualistic' notion of religion makes sense.[19]

This mismatch is not just an epistemic problem. Once constituted as the legal benchmark for religion, this Christo-centric notion of religion is deployed to regulate other traditions by turning them 'from

[17] See, for example, Suhraiya Jivraj, *The Religion of Law: Race, Citizenship and Children's Belonging* (Basingstoke: Palgrave Macmillan, 2013); Feldman, *Please Don't Wish Me*; Winnifred Fallers Sullivan, *The Impossibility of Religious Freedom* (New Haven: Princeton University Press, 2005); Herman, *An Unfortunate Coincidence*; Winnifred Fallers Sullivan, Robert A. Yelle, and Mateo Taussig-Rubbo, eds., *After Secular Law* (Stanford: Stanford University Press, 2011); Wendy Brown, 'Civilizational Delusions: Secularism, Tolerance, Equality', *Theory & Event* 15, no. 2 (2012). Practices of separating religion and state are not unique to Western Christian societies. On Jewish approaches to secularism, see, for example, Suzanne Last Stone, 'Religion and State: Models of Separation from within Jewish Law', *International Journal of Constitutional Law* 6, no. 3–4 (2008): 631–61.

[18] See, for example, Lena Salaymeh and Shai Lavi, 'Religion Is Secularised Tradition: Jewish and Muslim Circumcisions in Germany', *Oxford Journal of Legal Studies* 41, no. 2 (2021): 431–58.

[19] Robert Yelle, 'Imagining the Hebrew Republic: Christian Genealogies of Religious Freedom', in *Politics of Religious Freedom*, eds., Winnifred Fallers Sullivan et al. (Chicago: University of Chicago Press, 2015), 17–28, p. 25.

public actors of communal traditions into individual believers of private choice'.[20] However, much like in relation to gender and race, law's biased religious benchmark is rendered invisible and normal, even though this benchmark privileges and universalises one religion over others in ways that marginalise non-Christian religions and impacts on their rights and citizenship. Despite the diverse manifestations of secularism and the variety of legal frameworks of state–church relations, the privileging of Christian normativity in and through secular law runs like a common thread through Western jurisdictions.[21]

A growing body of work documents the various ways in which the law remains complicit in reproducing and protecting Christian values across different Western legal systems. 'Christianity', Suhraiya Jivraj notes in the context of English law, 'has had and continues to have, an embedded, dominant and regulatory role within juridical state discourse, even despite the different theological and cultural forms it takes in particular contexts'.[22] Christian values and sensibilities, Jivraj observes, have become associated with the secular values of the English state and its institutions in both judicial and policy discourse where these secularised Christian values provide both a lens and a point of – often – negative comparison for assessing non-Christian religions who are presented as uncivilised and potentially dangerous. Didi Herman too highlights the influence of the Christian tradition on secular legal reasoning and argues that secularism serves 'as a term that facilitates judicial Christian thinking'.[23] Christian values and norms circulates through English law masked as supposedly universal and secular values and norms despite their religious particularity. Analysing court cases involving Jewish litigants, Herman how this judicial thinking leads to Christian impositions

[20] Shai Lavi and Lena Salaymeh, 'Secularism', in *Key Concepts in the Study of Antisemitism*, ed. Sol Goldberg, Scott Ury, and Kalman Weiser (London: Palgrave, 2021), 257–72, p. 267.

[21] Lena Salaymeh argues that there is no authentic form of secularism, only a fluctuating and diverse ideology albeit with a Eurocentric bend, see Lena Salaymeh, 'The Eurocentrism of Secularism', *West Windows*, 14 September 2020. On remarkable similarities between the legal responses of different European countries to the issue of religious symbols despite significant differences of state–church relationships, see also Susanna Mancini, 'The Power of Symbols and Symbols as Power: Secularism and Religion as Guarantors of Cultural Convergence', *Cardozo Law Review* 30, no. 6 (2009): 2629–68.

[22] Jivraj, *Religion of Law*, p. 10.

[23] Herman, *An Unfortunate Coincidence*, p. 16.

onto Jewish litigants, such as in the case of a Jewish school case in which the UK Supreme Court imposed a Christian understanding of religion as belief onto the Jewish Orthodox school that disregards Jewish self-understanding and the complexity of Jewish identity that cuts across notions of religion, ethnicity, and culture.[24] In applying a Christo-centric notion of religion to non-Christians, the Court, a secular legal institution, engages in their assimilation to a majoritarian religious norm.

In the United States, Khyati Joshi makes a similar observation and describes the relationship between Christianity and law as institutional and structural despite the legal line that the Constitution's First Amendment seeks to draw between church and state: 'Christian privilege is built into the edifice of American law'.[25] Due to the social and historical power of Christianity, American law and public institutions reflect the 'accretion of Christian privilege and Christian normativity into an infrastructure of Christian hegemony'.[26] For Joshi, the First Amendment is shaped by a profoundly Protestant view of religion that prioritises belief over action and that provides the 'face' for when courts assess the impact of 'facially neutral' laws on other traditions, rendering Christianity the implicit benchmark.[27] Despite the state's supposed religious neutrality and the separation of state and church, the law fails to deliver equality for all religions. Stephen Feldman's critical history of the separation of state and church supports this argument by showing how the core secular principle of separation and its constitutional enactment and interpretation is an outgrowth of the history of Christianity and continues to entrench Christian privilege. Contemporary judicial interpretation of the First Amendment manifest and reinforce Christian cultural and political dominance at the expense of non-Christian groups.[28] In a predominantly Christian society, Stephen Feldman concludes, a 'neutral' standpoint equals a Christian standpoint, allowing Christian practices a pass whereas non-Christian practices are scrutinised and constrained.[29]

Even nominally Catholic states, Winifred Fallers Sullivan observes, can rely on a Protestant-Christian notion of religion as voluntary,

[24] See the discussion in Herman, *An Unfortunate Coincidence*, pp. 168–69.
[25] Joshi, *White Christian Privilege*, p. 33.
[26] Joshi, *White Christian Privilege*, p. 4.
[27] Joshi, *White Christian Privilege*, pp. 33–36.
[28] Feldman, *Please Don't Wish Me*.
[29] Feldman, *Please Don't Wish Me*, pp. 275–76.

individual, and private, which does not make them Protestant but small-p 'protestant' in their religio-politico-legal arrangements.[30] An example is predominantly Catholic France where in contemporary debates about the Muslim headscarf private faith has been constituted as the most authentic site of religion.[31] However, this 'small-p Protestantism' does nonetheless accommodate the majoritarian religion of Catholicism. Similarly, in Germany's mixed Protestant-Catholic setting, small-p 'protestant' notions of religion remain influential in secular legal thinking, as I explore in Chapter 4.[32]

The Protestant-Christian influence on secular understandings of religion is also apparent in international human rights law, such as in Article 9 of the *European Convention on Human Rights* that reflects the split of religion into a spiritual/belief and a ceremonial/practice/exercise component. Article 9 distinguishes between a *forum internum* and a *forum externum*. The *forum internum* is conceptualised as absolute, whereas the *forum externum* is subject to legal regulation, a view that elevates private faith over practice, but fails to capture how Judaism, Islam, and other religions view this relationship.[33] 'Belief' is seen as a private matter and therefore largely out of the reach of the state and its law, while 'practice' as the outward manifestation of religion is subject to legal regulation. Lena Salaymeh and Shai Lavi argue that in the caselaw of the European Court of Human Rights on the headscarf, practice is construed as 'belief-based choice'. This approach renders practices discretionary, such as when the headscarf is treated like an optional piece of clothing in cases such as *Dogru* v. *France* or *Kervanci* v. *France*.[34] The practice-belief distinction acts as an assimilatory device that can be deployed to remake non-Christians in line with majoritarian expectations about what constitutes 'religion', while ostensibly guaranteeing religious freedom.

However, the emphasis on belief is not always deployed in the same way to Christian practices. The privatisation of non-Christian

[30] Sullivan, *Impossibility of Religious Freedom*, p. 7.

[31] See the analysis in Fernando, *The Republic Unsettled*, pp. 132–33.

[32] See also Salaymeh and Lavi, 'Religion Is Secularised Tradition'.

[33] For a critique of this distinction, see, for example, Saba Mahmood and Peter G. Danchin, 'Immunity or Regulation? Antinomies of Religious Freedom', *South Atlantic Quarterly* 113, no. 1 (2014): 129–59.

[34] Salaymeh and Lavi, 'Religion Is Secularised Tradition', p. 446 (discussing *Dogru* v. *France* (App no. 27058/05) ECtHR 4 December 2008 and *Kervanci* v. *France* (App no. 31645/04) ECtHR 4 March 2009).

religions intersects with the legal accommodation of Christian symbols and practices in public. Case law reveals a tendency to associate Christianity with national culture and heritage and thereby to withdraw the public elements of Christianity from the legal mandates of separation that underpin the public–private distinction. Most notably, Christmas trees maintain a pervasive presence in public spaces across the West and courts have given crucifixes[35], crosses[36], and crèches[37] in public spaces a pass. Moreover, in distinguishing between symbols deemed inconspicuous and conspicuous, secular law accommodates Christian symbols, such as the wearing of a crucifix, whereas non-Christian symbols, such as the headscarf or the kippah, have been seen as threatening values of state neutrality.[38] Christian privilege thus operates not only through marginalising and assimilating non-Christian religions. Law also maintains Christian privilege by legitimising and naturalising the public presence of Christianity through a different process of secularisation that turns Christian symbols into *non-religion*.[39] Christianity therefore continues to slip through the cracks of the private sphere's boundaries, rearticulated as 'culture', 'national heritage', and 'shared tradition', and thereby legitimised as areligious representations of the shared identity and history of *all* citizens in a given national context.

The critique of secular law's biases does not mean that secular law is just Protestant Christianity in disguise or that the institutions of Christianity or certain Christian groups still yield overwhelming power in Western law.[40] The critical inquiry into secular law's biases

[35] See, for example, *Lautsi and Others* v. *Italy*, European Court of Human Rights (Grand Chamber), 18 March 2011, Appl. No. 30814/06.

[36] See, for example, *American Legion v. American Humanist Association*, 139 S. Ct. 2067 [2019].

[37] See, for example, Conseil d'Etat, decision of 9 November 2016, no. 395122.

[38] On the legal distinction between conspicuous and non-conspicuous symbols and how this distinction privileges Christianity in France, see Ratna Kapur, 'Secularism's Others: The Legal Regulation of Religion and Hierarchy of Citizenship', in *Constitutions and Religions*, ed. Susanna Mancini (Cheltenham: Edward Elgar, 2020): 41–48. On the kippah, see the decision in *Goldman v. Weinberger*, 475 U.S. 503 (1986).

[39] I consider this legal strategy in Chapter 5. See also Lori G. Beaman, *The Transition of Religion to Culture in Law and Public Discourse* (London: Routledge, 2020).

[40] While related, my line of analysis is different from the conversation about 'Christian Human Rights'. This conversation, on the one hand, explores the influence of Christian ethics as well as of Christian groups and individuals on the formulation of the right to religious freedom in international human rights law

is instead concerned with the unstated assumptions that continue to underpin influential secular legal discourses and reasoning that *if not always consciously* but *in effect* can privilege a (Protestant) Christian normativity. This Christian normativity in law is not the same as Christian theology. Secularised Christianity normativity emerged out of the traditions of Christian thought that have been transformed, modified, adapted, and secularised over time and become embedded in central categories of liberal thought. This point has been made by many scholars, including Gil Anidjar, who, paraphrasing Carl Schmitt, notes that 'all significant concepts of the modern world are *liquidated* theological concepts'.[41] Similarly, as Elizabeth Mensch has shown, modern liberal thought and liberal law derive much of their foundational categories from Christianity.[42] Christian normativity, therefore, refers to a set of discourses, values, and preferences that have been secularised into a cultural repertoire.

Approaching Christianity in this way is neither meant to essentialise Christianity nor to homogenise what is an internally diverse and often contested tradition. As a cultural repertoire, manifestations of Christian normativity in law also may not necessarily align with how confessional Christians see themselves and their own faith. Many groups of the Christian Right in fact would argue that they too are marginalised by secular law.[43] Indeed, Christians have been among

and examines, on the other, how Christian groups mobilised religious freedom to push back against what they perceived as a threatening form of secularism. See, for example, Samuel Moyn, *Christian Human Rights* (Philadelphia: University of Pennsylvania Press, 2015). On Jewish contributions to this history, see, for example, James Loeffler, 'The Religions of Human Rights', *Harvard Theological Review* 116, no. 1 (2023): 147–71.

41 Gil Anidjar, *Blood: A Critique of Christianity* (New York: Columbia University Press, 2014).

42 Elizabeth Mensch, 'Christianity and the Roots of Liberalism', in *Christian Perspectives on Legal Thought*, ed. Robert F. Cochran, Michael W. McConnell, and Angela C. Carmella (New Haven: Yale University Press, 2001), 54–72. See also Brown, 'Civilizational Delusions'. Emphasising the role of Christianity in shaping categories of Western thought does not mean that the relationship between Christianity and liberal secularism is a one-way street. Clearly, liberal secularism has shaped and continues to shape Christianity in profound ways too. On this dialectical relationship, see, for example, Sarah Shortall, 'From the Three Bodies of Christ to the King's Two Bodies: The Theological Origins of Secularization Theory', *Modern Intellectual History* (2022): 1–23, https://doi.org/10.1017/S147924432200035X.

43 Elenie Poulos, 'Protecting Freedom/Protecting Privilege: Church Responses to Anti-Discrimination Law Reform in Australia', *Australian Journal of Human Rights* 24, no. 1 (2018): 117–33.

the staunchest critics of secularism. 'Christianity', Elizabeth Mensch observes in the US context, 'finds in liberalism both its own reflection, and, simultaneously, a starkly conceived and alien antagonist'.[44] Indeed, not all Christians will benefit equally from Christian privilege given that privilege is always intersectional, contextual, historically contingent, and nationally as well as locally specific. Depending on its context, Christian privilege will be more beneficial to some Christians than to others. For example, depending on the legal and political context, it might be more beneficial to those whose Christian identity – be it confessional or cultural only – fits more easily with the idea of a private and autonomous faith.[45] Despite these complexities and tensions, I believe that it is not only possible but also crucial to acknowledge how the Christian tradition as one of 'the most powerful hegemonic cultural systems in the history of the world'[46] has influenced ways of seeing, knowing, and approaching 'difference' in Western law and society in ways that render some religions the natural and desirable norm, while treating others as in need of legal reform.

CHRISTIAN AMBIVALENCE TOWARDS JEWS

Critical studies of secularism identify the Protestant Reformation as a crucial moment for the formation of Western notions of secularism and their association with Protestant values. During the Reformation, the Protestant rejection of Catholic ritualism gave rise to a crucial set of distinctions between belief and reason, thought and action, and body and mind that came to underpin the emerging secular order.[47]

[44] Mensch, 'Christianity and the Roots of Liberalism', p. 54.

[45] However, even non-mainstream Christians will benefit from Christian privilege not only because it affords a 'basic' privilege but also because it renders their practices and traditions more palatable to the state. See the discussion of the US Supreme Court's treatment of the Amish in Feldman, *Please Don't Wish Me*, pp. 246–47. On secular Christians as 'main recipients' of Christian privilege, see also Lauwers, 'Religion, Secularity, Culture?', p. 411. Political and therefore legal landscapes also shift and thereby change the contours of Christian privilege. On the legal protection of conservative Christians in US law and possible implications for liberal Jews, see, for example, David H. Schraub, 'Liberal Jews and Religious Liberty', *New York University Law Review* 98 (2023): 1–72.

[46] Daniel Boyarin, *A Radical Jew: Paul and the Politics of Identity* (Berkeley: University of California Press, 1994), 9.

[47] Talal Asad, *Genealogies of Religion: Discipline and Reasons of Power in Christianity and Islam* (Baltimore; London: Johns Hopkins University Press, 2009). See also

After the Reformation, the modern notion of religion gained further contours in the writings of Protestant writers and in the academic study of 'world religions' that further entrenched the blueprint of what constitutes proper religion.[48] Influential thinkers, such as John Locke, for example, argued that toleration necessitated a personalised notion of religion, a privately held, non-political, and spiritual belief, to enable loyalty to the law of the nation state in the public sphere. Yet, many of these ideas about what is 'good' and 'true' religion and what is not have been forged even earlier – in Christianity's encounter with Jews. Ari Joskowicz and Ethan Katz draw attention to this genealogy by highlighting that

> many of the key dichotomies underpinning secularist discourse evolved from the oppositions that Christian thinkers historically constructed to juxtapose Christianity and Judaism. Indeed, the idea that a forward-looking Christianity had superseded an archaic Judaism established patterns of thinking about time and meaning in history that shaped notions of progress among religious, non-religious, and anti-religious thinkers alike.[49]

From its early days, ambivalence towards Jews has been a crucial component of Christian identity formation in which Christianity struggled with its Jewish roots. Christian attitudes towards Jews were marked by a profound ambivalence that affirmed the inferiority of Jews alongside their necessity. The production of Christian identity needed Jews, so Christianity could not outright reject them. Jews were seen as a cursed community to be punished for their rejection of the gospel and the death of Jesus. But they were also witnesses to the Christian truth and their conversion in large numbers would signal the second coming of Jesus. In constructing its identity in relation to Jews, Christianity

Cécile Laborde, 'Rescuing Liberalism from Critical Religion', *Journal of the American Academy of Religion* 88, no. 1 (2020): 58–73, pp. 60–61; Darian-Smith, *Religion, Race, Rights*, ch. 1.

48 See, for example, Janet R. Jakobsen and Ann Pellegrini, 'Introduction: Times Like These', in *Secularisms*, ed. Janet R. Jakobsen and Ann Pellegrini (Durham: Duke University Press, 2008), 1–35, pp. 7–9; Tomoko Masuzawa, *The Invention of World Religions. Or, How European Universalism Was Preserved in the Language of Pluralism* (Chicago: University of Chicago Press, 2005).

49 Ari Joskowicz and Ethan B. Katz, 'Introduction: Rethinking Jews and Secularism', in *Secularism in Question. Jews and Judaism in Modern Times*, ed. Ari Joskowicz and Ethan B. Katz (Philadelphia: University of Pennsylvania Press, 2015), 1–22, p. 2. See also the contribution by Amnon Raz-Krakotzkin in the same volume.

created what Jeremy Cohen termed the 'hermeneutical Jew'. However, the images of this 'hermeneutical Jew' and therefore of 'Jewish difference' often clashed with what Jews in real life did, which could make those real Jews who did not properly perform this ideological role less deserving of protection in Christian eyes.[50] Jews, of course, did not constitute Christianity's only Other. Muslims, in particular, also played an important role in Christianity's identity formation, and my focus in this book on Jewish difference is not meant to deny this significance. Thinking and discourses about Jews and Muslims in fact often intersected and occasionally converged in Christian polemics and church legal theory and continue to do so today in secular legal debates – a point to which I will return in Chapters 4 and 7. But Jews and Muslims also figured differently in the self-understanding of the Christian world. Whereas Muslims, often also called Saracens, were perceived as external Others and political enemies that were seen as beleaguering and threatening lands claimed by Christians, Jews constituted theological and internal enemies, living among Christians and through their continued existence also challenging Christianity's claim to truth and unity.[51]

Supersessionist thinking has constituted a central feature of Christian ambivalence towards Jews and established ideas and knowledge about progress, history, and time that remain relevant today as ideas and assumptions underpinning secular legal thinking and secular legal reasoning. Supersessionism forms what Jeremy Cohen calls a 'replacement theology' in Latin Christendom:

> From apostolic times until our own, Christian believers and teachers have held that the Passion of Christ inaugurated a new covenant of grace that superseded the old covenant of Mosaic law. Christians had come to constitute a new Israel of the spirit; they had replaced the Jews, Israel of the flesh, as God's chosen people. Christianity now offered the only viable path to salvation.[52]

The idea that true religion is first and foremost a matter of the spirit and not of law, ritual, or ceremony became the Christian founding

[50] Cohen, *Living Letters*, p. 2.

[51] Gil Anidjar, *The Jew, the Arab: A History of the Enemy* (Stanford: Stanford University Press, 2003), p. 38.

[52] Jeremy Cohen, 'Supersessionism, the Epistle to the Romans, Thomas Aquinas, and the Jews of the Eschaton', *Journal of Ecumenical Studies* 52, no. 4 (2017): 527–53, p. 528.

narrative in the writings of Paul who distinguished between Jewish 'law' and 'flesh' and Christian 'grace' and 'spirit'.[53] Paul's writing, Daniel Boyarin notes, was underpinned by an interlinked set of binaries and relations, such as literal–figurative, circumcision–baptism, and Israel–Church, all of which elevated Christianity and assigned Jews to an earlier time that had been overcome.[54] When Jews failed to accept the Gospel, they found themselves taken out of progress, out of time and history.[55] Their laws with their ritual orientation were seen as holding Jews back and tied to this past. In Christian thought, Jewish rituals merely foreshadowed what was to come and Christ's sacrifice on the cross made them obsolete. Christianity saw itself as removing Judaism's 'marks of an external discipline',[56] replacing and thereby perfecting them through a superior spiritual discipline. One consequence of this turn from law to spirit was then the denigration of the ceremonial aspect of Judaism that Christian thinkers viewed as a veil that left Jews in darkness and in separation from other peoples.[57] It is therefore no surprise that embodied rituals, such as infant male circumcision, became the topic of much Christian polemics, as I explore in Chapter 3. Moreover, for Christian thinkers, Jewish ritual law, such as the dietary laws of kashrut or the practice of circumcision, signified the particularistic and therefore exclusionary ethno-religious character of Jews that had been replaced by Christian universalism that could encompass all of humanity. As Paul stipulated, 'there is neither Jew nor Greek, there is neither slave nor free, there is no male and female, for ye are all one in Christ Jesus'.[58]

Supersessionary thinking not only matters for understanding the place of Jews in Western thought. In attempting to distance itself from Jews, Christian Europe developed a vocabulary of difference that it applied, refined, and modified not only in relation to Jews but also

[53] Robert A. Yelle, 'Moses' Veil. Secularization as Christian Myth', in *After Secular Law*, ed. Winnifred Fallers Sullivan, Robert A. Yelle, and Mateo Taussig-Rubbo (Stanford: Stanford University Press, 2011), 24–42, p. 24.

[54] Boyarin, *A Radical Jew*, p. 31.

[55] Amnon Raz-Krakotzkin, 'Secularism, the Christian Ambivalence toward the Jews and the Notion of Exile', in *Secularism in Question*, ed. Ari Joskowicz and Ethan B. Katz (Philadelphia: University of Pennsylvania Press, 2015), 276–98, p. 282.

[56] Yelle, 'Moses' Veil', p. 26.

[57] Yelle, 'Moses' Veil', p. 25.

[58] Galatians 3:28. Boyarin reads Paul as a Jewish cultural critic who was motivated by a 'Hellenistic desire for the One … beyond difference and hierarchy'. Boyarin, *A Radical Jew*, p. 7.

in encounters with other Others.[59] European Christian expansion brought ideas about the proper religion to the colonies and extended them to other religions that they perceived as ritualistic, such as Islam or Hinduism. For example, the British in colonial India perceived of the Hindu rituals of purification much like Christianity perceived of the Jewish rituals: As unnecessary signs of social separation that clashed with Christian universalism and as primitive signs of an earlier stage of the development of law and religion.[60] In India, the British colonial administration relegated Hindu ritual law to the private sphere but also marginalised the legal significance of rituals for areas of law governing areas such as contracts and succession.[61] The mission of civilising colonised populations of Muslims and Hindus redeployed ideas that had been forged earlier to assure an anxious Christian self vis-à-vis its Jewish Other and now became embedded and further developed in an broader Orientalist discourse that positioned European Christian culture as the beacon of process and colonised people at a lower stage of civilisation.[62] European secular rule, Amnon Raz-Krakotzkin argues, can therefore be seen as 'the expansion of the Christian ambivalence towards the Jews, to include also other non-Christians'.[63] These ideas and arguments also influenced evolving secular categories that helped to delineate the religious from the legal and religion from state. As Robert Yelle argues, in carving out a space for religion, secular law eventually employed similar supersessionary strategies that Christianity had already used to distinguish itself from Judaism. 'Religion' became spiritual in opposition to law that was redefined as a 'disenchanted, bureaucratic technology', an opposition that once more mirrored the exclusion and rejection of Jewish ritual law.[64]

59 Boyarin, *The Unconverted Self.*

60 Robert Yelle, 'The Hindu Moses: Christian Polemics against Jewish Ritual and the Secularization of Hindu Law under Colonialism', *History of Religions* 49, no. 2 (2009): 141–71.

61 Yelle, 'The Hindu Moses', pp. 147–49. See also Leora Batnitzky, 'Between Ancestry and Belief: "Judaism" and "Hinduism" in the Nineteenth Century', *Modern Judaism – A Journal of Jewish Ideas and Experience* 41, no. 2 (2021), 194–219.

62 In his study of orientalism, Edward Said notes that he has found himself studying 'the history of a strange, secret sharer of Western anti-Semitism'. Edward Said, *Orientalism*, 25th ed. (New York: Vintage Books 1994 [1979]), at 27.

63 Raz-Krakotzkin, 'Secularism', p. 279.

64 Yelle, 'Moses' Veil', pp. 34–35. See also David Kennedy, 'Images of Religion in International Legal Theory', in *Religion and International Law*, ed. Mark Janis and Carolyn Evans (The Hague: Martinus Nijhoff, 1999), 145–53, pp. 151–52.

The privileging of the spirit over the body in Paulinian thought does not mean that the body became irrelevant in Christian thought and practice. Christianity has of course maintained its own corporeal practices, such as the communion or Christian asceticism, but there has been a correct hierarchy assumed between the two.[65] With the Reformation, Protestant Christianity deepened the critique of rituals when it wrestled with Catholicism. As Protestants expressed their aversion for rituals as 'either "empty works" or outright idolatry',[66] their main target was the Catholic Church, yet their arguments reiterated older Christian engagements with Jews – whom they also did not spare from criticism, as the writings of Luther for example show. Remarkably, even though the suspicion of ritual and devotional practices became further entrenched through Protestantism's critique of Catholicism and remains a key issue in secular legal Christian normativity, today, secular law has largely shed its bias towards Catholics. As Udi Greenberg notes, from the mid-twentieth century, the small-p Protestant secularism prevalent in many Western societies became more inclusive of Catholic practices in favour of a pan-Christian identity as a bulwark against the perceived threat of communist secularism, affording protections to Catholic practices previously shunned.[67] Yet, despite numerous references to the narrative of Judeo-Christianity that emerged at around the same time and purported to include Jews into this pan-Christian identity, the acceptance of Jews and Judaism has remained much more ambivalent, conditional, and incomplete.

The strange narrative of Judeo-Christianity also alludes to the fact that the history of Jewish difference in the Christian West is not only a story of rejection, exclusion, or distance but has also involved various acts of not only toleration but also incorporation and inclusion as another facet of Christian ambivalence. These acts of incorporation

[65] Boyarin, *A Radical Jew*, p. 15.

[66] Yelle, 'Moses' Veil', p. 28.

[67] Udi Greenberg, 'Is Religious Freedom Protestant? On the History of a Critical Idea', *Journal of the American Academy of Religion* 88, no. 1 (2020): 74–91. In this regard, Christianity as a dominant identity operates in somewhat comparable ways to Whiteness that has over time become more expansive and inclusive of groups previously not always considered White, such as Jews, the Irish, or Southern Europeans. See, for example, David R. Roediger, *Working towards Whiteness. How America's Immigrants Became White. The Strange Journey from Ellis Island to the Suburbs* (New York: Basic Books, 2005).

and inclusion, however, were not necessarily unconditional but often required the remaking or even abandonment of Jewish identity either via conversion or assimilation. The desire and in fact the necessity that Jews would convert eventually to attest to the truth of Christianity have been a central feature of Christian ambivalence, which translated into attempts by both church and secular authorities to convert Jews to Christianity, sometimes by nudging them, sometimes through more coercive means, even though Church doctrine was sceptical of forced conversions. As Julia Tartakoff notes, converting Jews was a 'Christian desideratum' because 'for Christianity to be true, Judaism had to be misguided'.[68] The period of emancipation during the eighteenth and nineteenth centuries that would gradually grant Jews legal equality did not expect Jews to convert in exchange for equal rights but still required the transformation of Jews into citizens of the Mosaic faith. Access to legal equality frequently hinged upon the remaking of Jewishness into a de-politicised and de-nationalised private belief through a process of secularisation driven as much by law as by social and cultural pressures and expectations emanating from both non-Jews and Jews. However, in light of the Christian history of the prevailing notion of religion, it is perhaps more apt to use the term 'Christianisation' to highlight how secularisation and assimilation expected Jews to become a 'religion' in a Christian sense, thereby creating an unresolved tension in post-emancipatory times around the more complex nature of Jewish identity and community that transcends a narrow category of private faith.[69]

By contextualising contemporary secular legal attempts to ban or restrict Jewish practices (and thereby to properly 'secularise' Judaism) in this longer history, my aim in this book is to show how today's legal dynamics reflect and echo this longer history of attempts to 'Christianise' Jews in post-emancipatory times. This may appear like a

[68] Paola Tartakoff, 'Testing Boundaries: Jewish Conversion and Cultural Fluidity in Medieval Europe, C. 1200–1391', *Speculum* 90, no. 3 (2015): 728–62, p. 736.

[69] Leora Batnitzky, *How Judaism Became a Religion: An Introduction to Modern Jewish Thought* (Princeton: Princeton University Press, 2011). Assimilation has been a complex process in which Jews have been active agents. My focus in this book here is primarily on the role of law as a force for assimilating Jews to majoritarian norms. For a critical discussion of 'assimilation' in the context of Jewish history, see Todd M. Endelman, 'Assimilation and Assimilationism', in *The Cambridge History of Judaism. Volume Eight: The Modern World 1815–2000*, ed. Mitchell B. Hart and Tony Michels (Cambridge: Cambridge University Press, 2017).

stark statement, but I agree here with Didi Herman who argues that the secular legal imposition of Christian norms can be seen as 'de-facto conversions' that seek to de-Judaise Jews.[70] There is, as I will discuss in in this book, a lingering assimilationism that often hides behind the language of secularism, of liberal rights, of religious freedom, of multiculturalism, and of tolerance that masks how the colonialist relationship between Christianity and Judaism endures in a language of secularism and liberal values. In making this point, I do not suggest that the pressure to assimilate today is the same as the pressure to assimilate during emancipation or earlier Christian attempts to convert Jews when lives would be at stake. However, it is important to remain attentive to the ways in which assimilatory and conversionary processes morph over time to tell a more nuanced story of legal progress and unmask how pressures to 'convert', to change one's identity in order to fully benefit from citizenship and equality in all its dimensions, can underpin seemingly more benign assimilatory or even tolerating strategies of secular law in dealing with difference.[71] These processes have become more subtle over time, yet as I hope to show in the in this book, there is still an assimilating Christianising logic that pervades contemporary encounters with Jewish difference in secular law. Moreover, attending to this ambivalent dynamic is an important step towards unmasking how such partial Jewish inclusion has served as a vehicle for hiding Christian privilege behind a supposed pluralism.

THE RACIALISATION OF RELIGIOUS DIFFERENCE IN LAW

Contemporary secular legal discourses not only produce and regulate 'religion', but in the process also distinguish 'good religion' from 'bad religion' in ways that are often racialised and that render non-Christian traditions foreign, backward, and uncivilised when they fail to fit a Christo-centric notion of 'religion'. Racialisation essentialises and solidifies religious differences, making them innate to certain cultures, and creating hierarchies of civilisation. While 'good religion' conforms to majoritarian expectations, 'bad religion'

[70] Herman, *An Unfortunate Coincidence*, p. 17.

[71] On lingering assimilationism and conversion demands in liberal law, see Kenji Yoshino, 'Covering', *Yale Law Journal* 111, no. 4 (2002): 769–940. I return to Yoshino's framework in the conclusion.

is construed as in need of reform through the law but also the subject of racialised suspicion about the effectiveness of reform. In this book, I therefore consider secularisation *and* racialisation as intersecting techniques for explaining, constituting, and regulating Jewish difference in law. To grapple with the intersection of religion and race in law, it is necessary to go beyond accounts of race that privilege biology, skin colour, and/or phenotype. In approaching race and racialisation in this book, I draw on the work of Geraldine Heng who resists a definition of race that prioritises biology and somatic features to excavate the longer history of race and its intersection and co-constitution with religion in Christian Europe, a history that predates secular modernity. Heng approaches race as 'a structural relationship for the articulation and management of human differences, rather than a substantive content'.[72] For Heng, race-marking or racialisation works through 'strategic essentialisms' that demarcate human beings through the selective essentialising of differences as 'absolute and fundamental' for the allocation of powers, rights, privileges, and positions. These 'strategic essentialisms' construct hierarchies of human beings through a multitude of interlocking discourses and practices that have shifted and changed across time and space, attaching to bodies and somatic features here, and to social, cultural, and religious practices elsewhere.[73] As Anne Stoler and Frederick Cooper observe, racism has never relied on phenotype alone but 'depended on hierarchies of civility, on cultural distinctions of breeding, character, and psychological disposition'.[74]

Such hierarchies of civility also underpin much contemporary discourse about religious difference in the West, in particular in relation to Muslims and Islam. Legal and political debates posit forms of Muslim religiosity, such as the headscarf as worn by Muslim women, as a problem for secular legality.[75] While framed as protecting gender

[72] Geraldine Heng, *The Invention of Race in the European Middle Ages* (Cambridge: Cambridge University Press, 2018), p. 19.

[73] Heng, *Invention of Race*, p. 27.

[74] Laura Ann Stoler and Frederick Cooper, 'Between Metropole and Colony. Rethinking a Research Agenda'. In *Tensions of Empire*, ed. Laura Ann Stoler and Frederick Cooper (Berkeley: University of California Press, 1997), 1–56, p. 34.

[75] Susanna Mancini, 'Patriarchy as the Exclusive Domain of the Other: The Veil Controversy, False Projection and Cultural Racism', *International Journal of Constitutional Law* 10, no. 2 (2012): 411–28. On the racialisation of Muslims, see also Suhraiya Jivraj, 'Interrogating Religion: Christian/Secular Values, Citizenship

equality, female autonomy, secular neutrality, or *vivre ensemble*, the various laws and court decisions attempting to ban this piece of clothing have often relied on a logic of cultural racism that renders Muslim men inherently patriarchal and Muslim women inherently oppressed yet also dangerous.[76] Drawing on the work of Etienne Balibar on cultural racism, Susanna Mancini observes that

> [i]rrespective of whether Muslims are depicted as 'black sheep', as uncivilized and barbarian, or just as not liberal enough to successfully integrate in Western societies, the crux of the matter is the 'insurmountability of cultural differences' between us and them.[77]

The production of religion, Suhraiya Jivraj observes in the context of English law, involves 'a value judgement that is often racialized in being deemed a form of non-acceptable religion'.[78] The racialisation of non-Christians presents their traditions as static and intrinsic but also as potentially culturally contaminating. Law's notion of religion, Jivraj notes, 'comes to circulate as a signifier of belonging, community and nationhood in ways that distinguish and demarcate the secular Christian West from (uncivilized) racialized non-Christian Others'.[79] Didi Herman and Davina Cooper make a similar observation, noting that English legal discourses depict Jews as 'people joined by culture, ancestry and blood ... according to a racialised discourse of difference'.[80] At the same time, Englishness is constructed as White and Christian, but remains unremarked upon and is thereby constituted as the invisible, yet privileged religio-racial identity. However, cultural racism towards non-Christian religious difference holds the promise of what Jivraj terms 'racial upliftment'. Educating non-Christian

and Racial Upliftment in Governmental Education Policy', *International Journal of Law in Context* 9, no. 3 (2013): 318–42; Sherene H. Razack, *Casting Out: The Eviction of Muslims from Western Law and Politics* (Toronto: Toronto University Press, 2008).

76 Mancini, 'Patriarchy as the Exclusive Domain of the Other'.

77 Mancini, 'The Tempting of Europe, the Political Seduction of the Cross: A Schmittian Reading of Christianity and Islam in European Constitutionalism', 115. Mancini refers to Etienne Balibar, 'Is There a "Neo-Racism"?', in *Race, Nation, Class. Ambiguous Identities*, ed. Etienne Balibar and Immanuel Wallerstein (London; New York: Verso, 1991), 17–36, p. 22.

78 Jivraj, *Religion of Law*, p. 42.

79 Jivraj, *Religion of Law*, p. 11.

80 Davina Cooper and Didi Herman, 'Jews and Other Uncertainties: Race, Faith and English Law', *Legal Studies* 19, no. 3 (1999): 339–66, p. 340.

children in secularised Christian values functions not only as a remaking of their religiosity but also as a promise to shed the stigma of race, akin to colonial practices of 'civilising' natives by encouraging their conversion and cultural assimilation – only now that this process takes place in the metropole instead of in the colonies.[81] Yet, the promise of upliftment never fully materialised as the stigma of race remained, thereby maintaining the superiority of the colonial culture.

In Australia too, the racialisation of religious differences shapes legal norms and the protections afforded to different religious groups. Margaret Thornton and Trish Luker observe how Christianity provides the unstated norm in in law, whereby non-Christian Others are constructed in racialised terms as 'the unknown, the exotic and the dangerous'.[82] This implicit norm for what constitutes appropriate religious behaviour impacts in particular on Muslims whose identity and experiences are assessed through an Islamophobic lens that perpetuates representations of Muslims as threatening and suspicious. Instead of acknowledging experiences of discrimination, the law participates in the racialisation of Muslim religiosity and identity and thereby shifts the blame for discrimination onto Muslims as threatening and foreign.[83]

Even in the United States where the colour line has often been more significant than in Europe where religious difference has loomed large, religion continues to intersect with race in a myriad of ways, impacting on the rights and equality of both non-Christians and those racialised as non-White. Kyathi Joshi argues that contemporary US constitutional law still remains implicated in constituting American national identity as both White *and* Christian.[84] Joshi writes against treating questions of religious equality in the United States in isolation from race given that Christian and White superiority have intersected and amplified each other in the history of the US and its European heritage. Religious equality is an 'optical illusion', Joshi contends, given that

81 Jivraj, *Religion of Law*, p. 143.

82 Margaret Thornton and Trish Luker, 'The Spectral Ground: Religious Belief Discrimination', *Macquarie Law Journal* 9 (2009): 71–91, p. 74.

83 Mareike Riedel, 'Studying While Muslim: Anti-Discrimination Law, Countering Violent Extremism, and Suspect Youth', *Griffith Law Review* 31, no. 2 (2022): 193–216. See also Margaret Thornton and Trish Luker, 'The New Racism in Employment Discrimination: Tales from the Global Economy', *Sydney Law Review* 32, no. 1 (2010): 1–28.

84 Joshi, *White Christian Privilege*.

US law and policy remain imbued with a racialised Christian normativity that renders certain expressions of Christianity normal, ordinary, invisible, and therefore privileged. Moreover, this Christian privilege is stratified along racialised lines with White Protestantism at the top of the hierarchy and non-White Christians marginalised.[85] This intimate connection between Whiteness and Christianity in the United States, legal scholar Khaled Beydoun argues, denies non-Christians full equality and rights.[86] Religious minority groups, such as Jews and Muslims, may be formally classified as White by the state but need to 'exercise and perform their religious identities against negative racial meanings assigned to their faith by law, political and popular discourse' in order to avoid losing their racial privilege.[87] Commonly assumed White, Beydoun argues, '[f]ormal whiteness hardly insulated Jewish Americans from the violent reminders, echoed by state and private actors, that *Jews weren't really white*'.[88]

These contemporary dynamics point to the historical significance of both Whiteness *and* Protestant Christianity in constituting US American notions of national identity. In her study of the rhetorics of religious freedom in the United States from the end of the nineteenth century to the Second World War, Tisa Wenger observes that those who appealed to this ideal often linked it to Protestant Christianity, racial Whiteness, and American national identity. As a tool of imperial categorisation and control, the idea of religious freedom served to delineate 'good religion' from 'bad religion' but also to assert racial superiority.[89] Wenger notes that Anglo-Americans believed in their 'racial-religious propensity for freedom'.[90] For them, their racial superiority rested in part on their possession of the truly modern religion of Protestant Christianity, the rational, ethical, and free religion, which imbued them with the values of modernity, freedom, and civilisation. Being Protestant-Christian associated them with values that rendered them White and racially superior. Those racialised as non-white, such

[85] Joshi, *White Christian Privilege*, p. 17.

[86] Khaled A. Beydoun, 'Faith in Whiteness: Free Exercise of Religion as Racial Expression', *Iowa Law Review* 105, no. 4 (2020): 1475–1536.

[87] Beydoun, 'Faith in Whiteness', p. 1481. By formal Whiteness, Beydoun refers to the categories of the US census.

[88] Beydoun, 'Faith in Whiteness', p. 1493.

[89] Tisa Joy Wenger, *Religious Freedom. The Contested History of an American Ideal* (Chapel Hill: University of North Carolina Press, 2017), p. 3.

[90] Wenger, *Religious Freedom*, p. 6.

as African Americans, or those with a more precarious Whiteness, such as Catholics and Jews, sought to escape racial stigma and redefine their identities in religious terms by appealing to religious freedom too. While US American Jews, particularly those with fair skin, were able to apply this strategy with success and thereby to access Whiteness and shed some of the racial stigma of antisemitism, African Americans however could not overcome the entrenched racial boundaries of religious freedom given the deep association of Christianity with Whiteness.[91] However, as scholars such as Beydoun and those working in Jewish studies note, US American (fair-skinned) Jews may be White but remain ambivalently positioned in a context of racialised Christian dominance. Not only does is access to Whiteness premised on assimilation. Conceiving Jewish difference only in terms of religion also veils how racialised ideas about Jews continue to regulate the boundaries of acceptable Jewish difference in the name of secular legal values and how the problem of cultural racism remains connected to Christian supersessionism and supremacy.

JEWS, RACE, AND THE LIMITS OF LIBERAL ASSIMILATION

While there remains a lively debate about the origins of race and, relatedly, the exact definition of race, studies of pre-modern race-making emphasise the role of Christian supersessionism and ambivalence towards Jews in shaping ideas about racial difference and in laying the groundwork for the emergence of modern forms of racism and the contemporary racialisation of religion. '[M]odernity's racial imagination', J. Kameron Carter observes, 'has its genesis in the theological problem of Christianity's quest to sever itself from its Jewish roots'.[92] Similarly, Magda Teter argues that the 'modern rejection of equality of both Jews and Black people in the West is the legacy of Christian supersessionism' – and, Teter notes, law was crucial for this process by

[91] See Chapter 5 in Wenger, *Religious Freedom*. On the erasure of Jews of Colour and Jews of African descent in perceptions of *all* Jews as White, see also Lewis R. Gordon, 'Rarely Kosher: Studying Jews of Color in North America', *American Jewish History* 100, no. 1 (2016): 105–16.

[92] J. Kameron Carter, *Race: A Theological Account* (Oxford: Oxford University Press, 2008), at 4. On the role of Christian intellectual history for the development of racial thought, see also Terence Keel, *Divine Variations: How Christian Thought Became Racial Science* (Stanford: Stanford University Press, 2018).

reifying these supersessionist narratives and ideas.[93] Even though early Christianity constituted itself as the universal and egalitarian faith in opposition to the perceived particularism of Jews, Denise Kimber Buell argues, ethno-racial ideas have formed part of Christianity's rhetorics and self-understanding of peoplehood from its early beginnings. Ethno-racial reasoning offered early Christians a tool to 'demarcate the limits of authentic Christianness'.[94] Different to modern biological accounts of race, early Christians understood race and ethnicity to be both fluid and fixed. Fluidity enabled the making of universalising arguments, that everyone could become Christian via conversion. Fixity constructed others as particular(istic) while also ascribing an essence to Christians.[95] In late antiquity, '[b]y collapsing Christianity with humanity, early Christians could argue that Christians constitute the ideal form of the human race, whereas all other peoples (and their forms of piety) fall short'.[96]

Early Christians, Buell suggests, resorted to ethno-racial reasoning as a rhetorical strategy to justify Christianity as 'the universal, most authentic manifestation of humanity' but also to affirm their superiority in relation to others, including Jews.[97] As Jonathan Boyarin notes, this Christian argument that associated Christianity with humanity was 'more than garden variety ethnocentrism. It depended … on the potential of Christianity to include all of humanity; but it also left plenty of space for rhetorics that treated non-Christians as not quite human'.[98] By denigrating or even denying the humanity of non-Christians who failed to see its truth, Christianity could re-assert its superiority. Indeed, in the twelfth century, the failure of Jews to convert became attributed to their lack of reason, with reason constituting the hallmark of humanity.[99] If Christianity's truth was accessible

[93] Magda Teter, *Christian Supremacy: Reckoning with the Roots of Antisemitism and Racism* (Princeton: Princeton University Press, 2023), p. 3.

[94] Denise Kimber Buell, *Why This New Race. Ethnic Reasoning in Early Christianity* (New York: Columbia University Press, 2008), 165.

[95] Buell, *Why This New Race*, p. 3. On the significance of fluidity and fixity for race, see Laura Ann Stoler, 'Racial Histories and Their Regimes of Truth'. *Political Power and Social Theory* 11 (1997): 183–206

[96] Buell, *Why This New Race*, pp. 77–78.

[97] Buell, *Why This New Race*, p. 2.

[98] Boyarin, *The Unconverted Self*, p. 72.

[99] Julia Costa Lopez, 'Beyond Eurocentrism and Orientalism: Revisiting the Othering of Jews and Muslims through Medieval Canon Law', *Review of International Studies* 42, no. 3 (2016): 450–70, p. 466.

to all humans, then failure to accept this truth could only mean that someone lacked a capacity that made one human. The existence of such racial ideas does not imply that early Christians were racist or that Christian thought is inherently racist but highlights how conceiving of Christianity in racial terms as a people helped Christians at times to assure themselves of their own identity and boundaries vis-à-vis others, such as Jews whom they accused of ethnic particularism and exclusionism.[100] Buell's work suggests that despite its ostensible universalism, there has been an exclusionary streak to Christianity that at times deployed proto-racial ideas as a means to re-assert boundaries and secure an emerging Christian identity.

Focusing on inferiority instead of biology or culture as a defining feature of an emerging race concept, Lindsay Kaplan argues that the medieval Christian theological discourse of the 'cursed inferiority' of Jews eventually created 'a racial status that functions like and anticipates modern racism'.[101] Although much Christian writing on Jewish difference was directed towards the self-assurance and identity formation of Christians, with the consolidation of Christian political power in the medieval period, this theological discourse about Jewish inferiority began entering and shaping both canon and secular laws. Albeit often erratically and unevenly, medieval law and policy slowly entrenched increasingly racialised religious hierarchies that affirmed Christian supremacy. The interplay between religious laws, secular laws, and theological discourses about 'the Jew' gradually solidified social and economic boundaries between Jews and Christians and provided ideological justifications for the exclusion and subordination of actual living Jews, even though these images of 'the Jew' sometimes clashed with the reality of medieval societies in which Jews and Christians lived side by side and interacted in a myriad of ways.

Christian theology of course did not alone give rise to racial thought and practices, and it is important to acknowledge the internal heterogeneity of Christian thought, Christian resistance to racism, and the role of Christianity and Black theology as a source of empowerment for People of Colour. Moreover, there have been many ruptures

[100] Buell argues that acknowledging the existence of such ideas is also important to work against tendencies within Christianity to locate the unrealised but potential ideal of racial inclusiveness within Christianity against the implicit racial and ethnic exclusiveness of Judaism, see Buell, *Why This New Race*, p. 12.

[101] M. Lindsay Kaplan, *Figuring Racism in Medieval Christianity* (Oxford: Oxford University Press, 2018), 1.

and transformations along the way to modern racism through the Reformation, colonial expansion, the Atlantic slave trade, and the modern emphasis on phenotypical markers of difference as well as the renewed turn to culture in contemporary racism. However, what this body of work on premodern race highlights is the significance of the narrative of Christian superiority vis-à-vis Jews and other non-Christians for supplying crucial arguments and patterns of thinking that continue to justify the subordination and exclusion of not only Jews but also other non-Christians, of Black People, and of People of Colour in law and society today.[102]

Over the course of history, the racialisation of Jewish difference has ebbed and flowed, changed its logic and language, singled out certain Jewish groups over others, and served many different purposes. The prospect of Jewish equality and therefore proximity – via conversion or via assimilation – arguably constituted one of the moments when racialisation became salient. While many Jews converted successfully in the medieval period, there remained at times doubts about the efficacy of conversion in eliminating Jewish difference such as in medieval England or early modern Spain. These doubts expressed not only an ambivalence about the 'true nature' of Jews and, by extension, what it meant to become and be Christian. While a variety of factors have contributed to the racial formation of Jews, it also enabled, as Geraldine Heng notes, the perpetual delay of equality that conversion promised.[103] Race made a forceful return during and shortly after the period of emancipation that had granted Jews legal equality. While this period saw the rise of racial antisemitism that entrenched Jewish difference in biological and allegedly scientific terms, there was also a more subtle form of antisemitism that Bryan Cheyette and Nadia Valman call 'liberal antisemitism'.[104] Writing against accounts that locate antisemitism outside or in opposition to liberalism, Cheyette and Valman focus on ambivalence towards Jews within nineteenth-century liberal thought and politics. The liberal support for rights and universal citizenship for Jews remained coupled with liberalism's enduring attachment to the idea of the homogenous nation, which rendered the particularity of Jews and other

102 See also Teter, *Christian Supremacy*, p. 3.

103 Heng, *Invention of Race*, p. 39.

104 Bryan Cheyette and Nadia Valman, 'Introduction: Liberalism and Anti-Semitism', *Jewish Culture and History* 6, no. 1 (2003): 1–26.

ethno-religious groups inherently problematic. The liberal view of Jews expected them to assimilate to majoritarian norms, but there was a limit to this liberal tolerance, surfacing in

> discourses of religious and/or secular conversion which only 'tolerates' Jews when they are seen to be good citizens who have transcended their difference. But this liberal formulation of anti-semitism always has a Jewish Other in reserve (in contrast to 'his' benevolent counterpart) who is deemed not to conform to the dominant norms of society.[105]

This unassimilated Jewish Other was constituted as one that either cannot be assimilated or that embodies the failure of assimilation. Thus, in this liberal antisemitism, assimilation intersected with a process of dissimilation that delineated and affirmed difference in frequently racialised terms.

Scholars studying the past and present of Jewish assimilation suggest that this process of 'dissimilation' or differentiation is not the accidental by-product of liberal assimilation but that the logic of assimilation in fact produces this difference.[106] Writing about the period of Jewish emancipation during the eighteenth and nineteenth centuries, Yolande Jansen refers to this problem as the 'paradox of assimilation'. She argues that the demand of assimilation 'causes its own impossibility' by enabling cultural majorities 'to focus on the detection of deviance, especially in times of conflict'.[107] One of the responses to this suspected 'deviance' is racialisation. 'Racialization', Wendy Brown explains, 'facilitated the coexistence of pressure to assimilate, on the one hand, and the marking of Jews as an object of surveillance to ensure conformity with the terms of their emancipation on the other'.[108] Racialisation enabled the policing of the acceptable boundaries of Jewish difference and maintained the idea of Jews as naturally linked, even though the terms of emancipation had involved their secularisation with the aim of dissolving the communal elements that suggested Jewish nationhood. This interplay of assimilation and dissimilation has also allowed

105 Cheyette and Valman, 'Liberalism and Anti-Semitism', p. 5.

106 Other scholars suggest that acts of exclusion, including through race, are an inherent element of liberalism, see, for example, Uday Mehta, 'Liberal Strategies of Exclusion', *Politics & Society* 18, no. 4 (1990): 427–54.

107 Yolande Jansen, *Secularism, Assimilation and the Crisis of Multiculturalism: French Modernist Legacies* (Amsterdam: Amsterdam University Press, 2013), p. 278.

108 Wendy Brown, *Regulating Aversion: Tolerance in the Age of Identity and Empire* (Princeton: Princeton University Press, 2006), p. 69.

to make Jews complicit in policing their difference. By constituting Jews in racial terms, non- or less-assimilated Jews are rendered a threat to assimilated Jews because, as Zygmunt Bauman summarises, 'the collective maturity of acceptance … would be measured by the quality of its weakest section'.[109] The persistence of non-conforming Jewish difference threatened the 'racial upliftment' of assimilated Jews, thereby undermining the solidarity of assimilated Jews with their less assimilated kin[110] – a dynamic that still surfaces in contemporary eruvin controversies in which Jews of different levels of observance have at times mobilised the law to 'discipline', 'secularise', and 'modernise' other Jews, as I discuss in Chapters 5 and 6.

Laura Levitt similarly notes that the paradigm of liberal assimilation via secularisation still creates Jewish Otherness post-emancipation. By expecting Jews to fit into a Christian category of religion, liberal assimilation 'produces a subject who is almost but not quite dominant'.[111] This misfit leads to a constant excess. On the one hand, there is the excess of 'too much' Jewishness through public expressions of Jewishness that transgress the category of private faith. On the other hand, there is an excess of 'too little religion' given that Jewishness is more than just a religious identity, instead encompassing a myriad of identifications, including but not limited to ethnicity and culture that cannot be captured by private faith.[112] However, by containing Jewishness in the category of religion, these identifications cause

[109] Zygmunt Bauman, 'Modernity and Ambivalence', *Theory, Culture & Society* 7, no. 2 (1990): 143–69.

[110] Cynthia Levine-Rasky describes how North American Jews paid a similar price for their access to Whiteness by becoming involved in distinguishing 'acceptable' from 'less acceptable' forms from Jewishness, see Cynthia Levine-Rasky, 'White Privilege. Jewish Women's Writing and the Instability of Categories', *Journal of Modern Jewish Studies* 7, no. 1 (2008): 51–66. On this topic, see also Eric L. Goldstein, *The Price of Whiteness: Jews, Race, and American Identity* (Princeton: Princeton University Press, 2006).

[111] Laura Levitt, 'Other Moderns, Other Jews: Revisiting Jewish Secularism in America', in *Secularisms*, ed. Janet R. Jakobsen and Ann Pellegrini (Durham: Duke University Press, 2008), 108–38, at 111. Levitt's and Jansen's analysis of liberal assimilation shares elements with Homi Bhaba's idea of colonial mimicry: Homi Bhaba, 'Of Mimicry and Man. The Ambivalence of Colonial Discourse', in *Tensions of Empire*, ed. Laura Ann Stoler and Frederick Cooper (Berkeley: University of California Press, 1997), 152–60.

[112] Levitt, 'Other Moderns, Other Jews', p. 110. On the diversity of definitions of Jewish identity, see, for example, Susan A. Glenn and Naomi B. Sokoloff, *Boundaries of Jewish Identity* (Seattle: University of Washington Press, 2011).

confusion, including in the realm of law.[113] Assimilation, Levitt concludes, does not so much achieve sameness but creates 'an excess that always marks this subject as other'.[114]

Although Levitt's analysis relates to the situation of American Jews, my aim in this book is to show that this analysis is also relevant for understanding contemporary legal conflict over Jewish practices in other Western societies. As I go on to discuss in this book, these paradoxes and tensions of assimilation still weave through contemporary secular legal discourses and debates on Jewish difference, suggesting a persistent suspicion and anxiety around 'excesses' of Jewishness even in post-emancipatory times. Visible signs of Jewish identity in particular, such as the eruv and male circumcision, that do not fit the prevailing paradigm of 'religion' thereby turn into racialised attributes. Scholars studying the racialisation of Islam have highlighted how cultural traits read as Muslim, including 'customs and costumes' as Junaid Rana put it,[115] have been essentialised in negative terms as inferior, barbaric, patriarchal, disloyal, terrorist, and foreign, as non-White and non-Western.[116] Saher Selod argues that Muslim religious signifiers, such as the hijab, come to stand as racialised symbols of an imagined cultural conflict, signifying support for misogyny and a conflict with national values.[117] Racialised meanings, buttressed by ideas about national character and civilisation, are also projected onto signifiers of Jewish 'excess', such as infant male circumcision and the eruv. These racialised projections echo older Christian devaluations of the public elements of Judaism and together with secularisation circumscribe the boundaries of acceptable Jewish difference while maintaining the superiority of Christian culture and its distance from Jewishness.[118]

113 Susanna Mancini, 'To Be or Not to Be Jewish: The UK Supreme Court Answers the Question; Judgement of 16 September 2009, R v. Governing Body of JFS UKSC 2015', *European Constitutional Law Review* 6 (2010): 481–502. I also briefly discuss the JFS case in Chapter 4.

114 Levitt, 'Other Moderns, Other Jews', p. 11.

115 Junaid Rana, *Terrifying Muslims. Race and Labor in the South Asian Diaspora* (Durham; London: Duke University Press, 2011), p. 28.

116 Saher Selod and David G. Embrick. 'Racialization and Muslims: Situating the Muslim Experience in Race Scholarship'. *Sociology Compass* 7/8 (2013): 644–55, p. 649.

117 Saher Selod, *Forever Suspect: Racialized Surveillance of Muslim Americans in the War on Terror* (New Brunswick: Rutgers University Press, 2018).

118 By drawing this parallel, my point is not that Jews experience the same amount of racialisation as Muslims in law and society. Instead, these dynamics unfold within a hierarchy of *Semitic difference*, a point to which I will return in the conclusion.

A CULTURAL STUDY OF LAW: A NOTE ON METHODOLOGY

In tracing the interplay between law and Christian ambivalence, this book follows the circulation of a set of discourses in and through law. I am not a theologian, and this book is not meant as a study of Christian theology. Instead, my analysis is indebted to a rich and insightful body of writing in Jewish studies and on the history of Christian attitudes towards Jews in Europe/the West, which I aim to bring into conversation with a long tradition of sociolegal analysis that seeks to understand the unstated norms and assumptions of law. In doing so, this book pursues a critical cultural study of law. A cultural study of law views the relationship between law and culture as co-constitutive, dynamic, and dialectical. 'To focus on culture', Eve Darian-Smith writes, 'is to locate the ways in which law influences who we are and who we aspire to be, and moves beyond the standard critique of what the law is and what we want it to be'.[119] A cultural study of law centres on how law shapes the identity of groups and individuals, of cultural meanings, and of social practices, which in turn shape legal meanings and what is seen as lawful, desirable, and acceptable.

This book is therefore, at once, a study of discourses and representations, which I described as the secularised cultural repertoire of Christian ambivalence. Thus, when I speak of Jewish difference, I do not refer to some reality that law and legal discourse simply reflect, and in many ways, this is a book much more about the 'us' from which Jews have been imagined to be different in so many profound and often deeply consequential and tragic ways. Christian ambivalence, as noted earlier, has produced its own 'hermeneutical' or 'theological Jew' that may have very little to do with what actual Jews think and do.[120] Similarly, the law, legal discourses, and cultural debates surrounding legal conflict constitute and regulate 'Jewish difference', but there is a limit to the power of law to create social realities. Thinking in terms of images and representations also highlights how Jewish questions have offered societies a forum to debate the larger questions of their time. As James Shapiro points out in the context of England, 'the English turned to

[119] Eve Darian-Smith, *Laws and Societies in Global Contexts: Contemporary Approaches* (Cambridge: Cambridge University Press, 2013), p. 72.

[120] For a study of the 'hermeneutical Jew' in medieval Christian thought, see Cohen, *Living Letters*.

Jewish questions in order to answer English ones'.[121] While Jews and Judaism sometimes took on the role of a metaphorical reference point in these debates, the answers that Western societies found to these questions could have significant consequences for real living Jews.

This book is thus not only a study of discourses and representations. It is also a study of what kind of legal work these discourses perform. I therefore consider, on the one hand, how 'law's often abstract and indeterminate form'[122] enables the importation and reproduction of elements of Christian ambivalence and, on the other, how legal form, categories, and structures reflect but also adapt and transform Christian normativity and ambivalence towards Jews.[123] In following the interplay between Christian ambivalence and the law, I draw on critical race theorist Ian Haney López's approach to the interaction between law and race to explore how the law constructs Jewish difference both formally through legislation and litigation but also informally 'by relying on, promulgating, and giving force … to particular ideas' about Jewish difference and its place in the Christian West.[124] Moreover, I also explore how the law participates in defining 'the spectrum of domination and subordination'[125] that reflects a Christian view of its own superiority vis-à-vis Jews and supersession of Judaism, while requiring their however partial inclusion and toleration.

Tracing the interplay between law and Christian ambivalence does not assume an unchanged continuity or causality between past and present, for example, between the thinking of Paul to the Holocaust or today's contemporary legal challenges to Jewish practices. Instead, I understand the career of Christian ambivalence and its translation and adaptation into a secular legal vocabulary in terms of a legacy in which categories, concepts, and ideas are, to some extent, shaped by

[121] James Shapiro, *Shakespeare and the Jews* (New York: Columbia University Press, 2016), p. 1.

[122] Marlee Kline, 'The Colour of Law: Ideological Representations of First Nations in Legal Discourse', *Social & Legal Studies* 3 (1994): 451–76, p. 452.

[123] In analysing these two dimensions, I draw on Marlee Kline's conceptualisation of these two types of relations between law and racist ideologies, which she described as 'interdependent and mutually reinforcing'. See Marlee Kline, 'Child Welfare Law, "Best Interests of the Child" Ideology, and First Nations', *Osgoode Hall Law Journal* 30, no. 2 (1992): 375–426, p. 381, note 20.

[124] Ian Haney López, *White by Law. The Legal Construction of Race* (New York; London: New York University Press, 10ed., 2006), pp. xv–xvi.

[125] López (2006), p. 8.

remnants of their previous deployments and use but also adapted and transformed by them. To use Paul Kahn's words:

> The remnants of past meanings endure not because they are included in dictionary definitions, but because we find ourselves responding to them. They are drawn up into claims, narratives, and arguments. They remain as long as they persuade us, that is, as long as we respond to them. They become linked to other meanings as they are deployed in new contexts. In time, they may simply fail to move us.[126]

Thinking in terms of legacy does not imply that certain ideas or representations mean the same across time and space or that they serve the same purpose. Although the basic structure of the discourse of Christian ambivalence remains somewhat stable in its oscillation between inclusion and exclusion, it manifests and matters differently in different contexts, accentuates inclusion over exclusion at certain times and vice versa at others, and reflects prevailing concerns of a period such as religion, nation, and race. My inquiry therefore takes inspiration from Talal Asad's call to shift the analysis away from seeking to prove the Christian origins of secularism – and by extension, the Christian origins of secular law, but to 'identify elements of a tradition that have been retrieved, reorganized, and put to modern use in contemporary formations'.[127] I aim to explore how these ambivalent ideas and discourses have been mobilised *both for and against* certain legal arrangements and reforms but also how they sit within larger local debates about rights, citizenship, belonging, and national identities.

In identifying elements of the tradition of Christian ambivalence in the realm of law, this book is organised around select case studies and iconic events that cast light on dynamics and patterns, tendencies and strategies, continuities, and changes in the interplay between Christian ambivalence and law. The narrative I tell in this book is by no means exhaustive and I do not provide a comprehensive account of the interaction between Christian ambivalence and the genealogy of what would be called 'secular law'. My aim is also not to tell a complete history of Jews in Christian Europe/the Christian West – I refer

[126] Paul Kahn in Daniel Bonilla Maldonado, 'The Cultural Analysis of Law: Questions and Answers with Paul Kahn', *German Law Journal* 21 (2020): 284–98, p. 294.

[127] Talal Asad, 'Thinking about the Secular Body, Pain, and Liberal Politics', in *Living and Dying in the Contemporary World: A Compendium*, ed. Veena Das and Clara Han (Oakland: University of California Press, 2015), 337–53, p. 251.

to scholars who have written these kinds of studies throughout this book. Moreover, as I explain further below, I do neither suggest that this has been the only force at play nor that these events have been exemplary for the whole of Jewish history in the Christian West. The dichotomies and binaries but also the contradictions of Christian ambivalence reflect only part of the worlds that Jews and Christians have shared and continue to share.

Chapter 2 traces Christian ambivalence from a theological position into the secular legal imagination by discussing historical events and turning points drawn from Western Europe and settler societies of European descent.[128] Beginning in the late medieval period, I explore the role of law in reifying and promulgating ideas of Christian supersessionism and pf the role of Jews in the Christian salvation story. I am conscious that a discussion of different events could produce an alternative yet not entirely different narrative, but I believe that these events are significant in illuminating and illustrating some of the features of the complex interplay between Christian ambivalence and Western law. Chapters 3 and 4 as well as Chapters 5 and 6 form pairs. These chapters focus on infant male circumcision and the eruv, respectively, and track their journey from both cherished Jewish practices and Christian theological issues into problems of secular law. I have chosen these practices given that the body and space have been paradigmatic sites for the construction, regulation, and negotiation of Jewish difference.[129] Practices such as circumcision and the observance of Shabbat, to which the eruv relates, have been seen as 'emblematic' of Jewish difference in Western Christian thought.[130] Historically, they have often served as tropes for the imagined deficiencies of Judaism, as indicators of Jewish assimilability or lack thereof, and as reference points to shore up anxieties about Jewish equality and influence. In modern times, they have become increasingly the subject of legal regulation.

128 There has been criticism of the Eurocentric focus of much Jewish history that marginalises Jews in other parts of the world. My focus in this book reflects my interest in the role of Jewish difference for a Western legal vocabulary.

129 Shechita and the laws of kashrut would have offered another obvious case study. I discuss religious slaughter and the intersection of the othering of Jews in Muslims in Mareike Riedel, '"They Are from Mars": The Othering of Jews and Muslims in European Legal Debates', in *Religious Othering. Global Dimensions*, ed. Mark Juergensmeyer, Kathleen Moore, and Dominic Sachsenmaier (Abingdon, Oxon: Routledge, 2022), 77–93.

130 Boyarin, *A Radical Jew*, p. 53.

Both practices take Jewish difference into the public, even if only in the most inconspicuous ways. Moreover, infant male circumcision as an almost universally practiced Jewish rite and the eruv as a distinctly Orthodox Jewish practice allow me to consider with more nuance how the boundaries of acceptable Jewish difference are drawn in specific local contexts and in relation to different kinds of Jewishness. Importantly, the boundaries of 'acceptable Jewish difference' shift and change and are often contingent on prevailing majoritarian norms and interests in law and society. The two practices also serve as reminders that a simple binary of majority – minority, of domination and subjugation, can be insufficient for capturing Jewish-Christian dynamics given the ambiguous and complex positionality of Jews and of different Jewish groups in different contexts. As I discuss in Chapter 3, circumcision has a different meaning in a context where Christians circumcise too, such as in the US, as compared to a context where Jews and Muslims are the main circumcising groups, such as in continental Europe. Similarly, as I explore in Chapter 5, the eruv complicates a simple Jewish-Christian binary when other Jews join the legal case for opposition and mobilise what may seem at first sight like the rhetorical repertoire of Christian ambivalence to resist a public expression of Jewishness through the eruv.

I then devote a chapter each to a close reading of a particular contemporary case – the German circumcision controversy in 2012 (Chapter 4) and the dispute about an eruv in an Australian suburb between 2008 and 2016 (Chapter 6). While the selection of these cases is partly pragmatic given that I understand both languages and the events were unfolding as I was conducting this research, this selection also allows me to undertake a more fine-grained analysis of how contemporary secular law participates in managing Jewish difference according to local grammars of religion and race, different legal traditions, and particular national anxieties against the broader backdrop of persistent ideas about 'Christian Europe' as a hegemonic and privileged identity of Western liberal societies. While Germany remains heavily associated with the Holocaust and its relationship with its Jewish population remains complicated, Australia has often been seen, much like the United States, as a Jewish success story. However, placing these two contemporary instances side-by-side enables me to tell a more nuanced story of success and legal progress and to illustrate how Christian ambivalence manifests in different national and legal contexts. There is a further advantage of selecting these two cases. The small but insightful body of work on the politics of Jewish difference in law has to date largely focused on the United States, reflecting the prominence of Jewish studies in the American academy. Focusing on Germany and Australia offers an opportunity to add other countries and contexts to an emerging 'map'.[131]

It is worth repeating that in discussing these two particular cases, my intent is not to declare any of these cases as paradigmatic for how contemporary Western secular law responds to Jewish difference or for how Christian ambivalence manifests in particular secular legal settings. Instead, this book is an attempt to begin mapping the persistence of Christian ambivalence and of supersessionary thinking in law and to examine the ways in which Christian ambivalence has been mobilised and embedded in law, legal discourse, and legal reasoning. Through this analysis, I hope to shed light on what these events may tell us about the enduring influence of our Christian past on the way we think about Jewish questions and difference more broadly today and to invite others to consider how my observations might play out in other contexts. Tracing how secularised Christian ambivalence manifests in law and legal discourses does therefore neither imply that individuals or institutions subscribe to an ideology of Christian superiority nor that they are antisemitic. It also does not deny the genuine nature of concerns about children's rights, the limits of religious freedom, or the use of city space. Instead, my aim is to cast some light on the manifestations of Christian ambivalence and Christian normativity as the product of the particular histories of Western societies and the resulting pervasiveness and dominance of certain perceptions, values, and habits of mind that are seen as the natural and normal state of being and doing despite their particularistic origins.

Two further caveats are necessary. First, I am conscious of the problems of focusing on one particular set of ideas and patterns of thought, as this focus means that I can pay less attention to other

131 I discussed some of this work earlier in this chapter, including Feldman, *Please Don't Wish Me*; Beydoun, 'Faith in Whiteness'. See also Annalise Glauz-Todrank, *Judging Jewish Identity in the United States* (Lanham: Lexington Books, 2022); Schraub, 'Liberal Jews'; Nomi M. Stolzenberg and David N. Myers, *American Shtetl: The Making of Kiryas Joel, a Hasidic Village in Upstate New York* (Princeton: Princeton University Press, 2022); Naomi W. Cohen, *Jews in Christian America: The Pursuit of Religious Equality* (Oxford; New York; Toronto: Oxford University Press, 1992). On representations of Jewishness in English law, see Herman, *An Unfortunate Coincidence*.

relevant and influential concerns. Clearly, gender, class, sexuality but also broader structures and forces such as capitalism, imperialism, and the state's pursuit of sovereignty and power have influenced and still influence legal responses to Jewish difference. For example, as I discuss in Chapter 2, the economic, cultural, and political usefulness of Jews for secular rulers has tempered, amplified, sidelined, and modified pursuits of Christian dominance. Therefore, my focus on the role of Christian ambivalence does not suggest that this is the only way that this history and these present legal conflicts should be read or that there is a singular causal relationship between Christian ambivalence and certain legal outcomes. The power and persuasiveness of Christian ambivalence depend on local historical and legal contexts and will therefore play out differently for Jews and for other non-Christian groups in different national and local contexts. Indeed, as I noted earlier and as I will discuss in throughout this book, Christian ambivalence does not automatically lead to particular material effects, such as the denial of rights, but involves sometimes seemingly contradictory practices of inclusion and assimilation. Moreover, I agree with Robert Hefner that specific systems of religious governance, including particular legal ideas, emerged from 'a more diverse assortment of actors, discourses, and powers, and more varied array of ethicoreligious imaginaries'.[132] Nonetheless, I believe it is worth focusing on this part of the story given that the dominant popular narrative still appears to be that 'we' and 'our' law are secular, having moved beyond our religious particularities, whereas 'they' have either too much religion or the wrong kind of religion, a narrative not only countlessly repeated in the various accusations levelled against Islam as insufficiently secularised but also resonating in contemporary backlash against Jewish religious practices.

Second and related to this, I therefore also do not suggest that secular law is the product of a coherent ideological formation and reflects only one clear set of values, ideas, and meanings. Instead, I understand secular law as inherently plural and as the product of ongoing struggles over meaning and power. Here, I draw on Margaret Davies account of law as plural. Law is, as Davies observes, 'fragmented and complex' as well as 'full of gaps, contradictions, unresolved histories,

[132] Robert A. Hefner, 'Varieties of Religious Freedom and Governance: A Practical Perspective', in *Politics of Religious Freedom*, ed. Winnifred Fallers Sullivan et al. (Chicago; London: University of Chicago Press, 2015), 127–34, p. 128.

counter-narratives and, most pertinently, composed of multiple dimensions and layers'.[133] I thus analyse the interaction between legal categories and the narratives of those who appeal to the law's authority and explore how the law absorbs, values, and authorises some these narratives in ways that reproduce and reflect Christian ambivalence. However, understanding law as reflecting plural concerns is necessary to avoid painting a picture of Christian ambivalence in Western secular law as all-dominating. Such an approach would write out the agency and contributions of Jews, Judaism, and Jewishness as well as of those who supported them, suggesting a history of eternal Jewish victimhood. As noted above, a purely binary approach to Jewish-Christian legal interactions does not fully capture the complexity of Jewish-Christian interactions, even though the reality of unequal power must be acknowledged.

Jews, alongside other marginalised and non-dominant groups, including other non-dominant Christians, have actively resisted pressures of assimilation, challenged Christian cultural hegemony, appropriated, subverted, and contested categories of difference, and advanced their own visions of identity and belonging in the secular nation state by means of law. Jewish resistance has constrained and shaped Christian ambivalence and Jews in all their diversity themselves have been agents in and of secular law, challenging an account of the relationship between Western law and Jewish difference as one-directional domination. As Austin Sarat and Thomas Kearns note, legal meaning-making is a multi-directional process because legal subjects 'deploy and use meanings strategically to advance interests and goals. They press their understandings in and on law and, in so doing, invite adaptation and change in the practices of law. Law thus exists as what Raymond Williams called "moving hegemony"'.[134] Part of the problem of ambivalence then also hints at the futile struggle of maintaining and policing boundaries and categories of identity and difference, of 'Jewish' and 'Christian', of 'White' and 'non-White', of 'Europe' and 'the West' that in reality are always permeable, contested, precarious, entangled, and inherently unstable.

133 Margaret Davies, 'The Ethos of Pluralism', *Sydney Law Review* 27, no. 1 (2005): 87–112, pp. 93 and 96.

134 Austin Sarat and Thomas R. Kearns, 'The Cultural Lives of Law', in *Law in the Domains of Culture*, ed. Austin Sarat and Thomas R. Kearns (Ann Arbor: University of Michigan Press, 2009), 1–20, p. 8.

Although not the primary focus of this book, in the debates and events analysed here, Jews have been active participants, contesting, appropriating, subverting, and resisting but also promoting and endorsing specific legal arrangements by leveraging dominant legal discourses as well as ideas about religion and race to carve out a space for Jewish identity in societies dominated by Christianity. In their struggle for legal equality, Jews have successfully manipulated and leveraged the dominant structures of law and deployed secularisation and racialisation as powerful rhetorical strategies for their own purposes to carve out space for Jewish particularism in the face of an assimilating universalism, thereby leaving an imprint on secular legal meanings and ideas.[135] Of course, discerning what makes an imprint 'Jewish' is difficult given the diversity of Jewish identifications, interests, and aspirations,[136] but this difficulty should not prevent us from acknowledging the existence and significance of these interactions. While it often required Jewish individuals and institutions to engage with a restrictive majoritarian framing and to potentially reinforce the problematic assumption of Christian ambivalence, their wrestling with the law nonetheless opened opportunities for alternative meanings and therefore legal outcomes. Hence, Jewish responses to the pressures and expectations of assimilation and their own cultural, social, legal, and political aspirations have left a mark too, thereby contributing to the discourses of secular law. I will return to the significance of Jewish engagements with secular law as a challenge to the hegemonic and universalising legal impulses of the Christian West in the final Chapter 7.

135 There is a growing body of literature that examines Jewish engagement with Western law, particularly in the international sphere, see, for example, James Loeffler, *Rooted Cosmopolitans. Jews and Human Rights in the Twentieth Century* (New Haven; London: Yale University Press, 2018); Reut Yael Paz, *A Gateway between a Distant God and a Cruel World: The Contributions of Jewish German-Speaking Scholars to International Law* (Leiden: Brill, 2012).

136 On this difficulty, see, for example, James Loeffler and Moria Paz, 'Introduction', in *The Law of Strangers. Jewish Lawyers and International Law in the Twentieth Century*, ed. James Loeffler and Moria Paz (Cambridge: Cambridge University Press, 2019), 1–20.

CHAPTER TWO

FROM JEWISH OTHER TO CITIZEN OF THE MOSAIC FAITH

A Brief Legal History of Christian Ambivalence

After the destruction of the Second Temple in 70 CE (common era), Jews found themselves dispersed in diaspora. For Jews, this raised complicated questions about cultural survival under the rule of non-Jews, who were suspicious and often hostile to their presence. Western Christendom wrestled with the question of how to deal with Jews, a group so closely tied to Christianity through origin, yet a theological puzzle because of their continuous existence. Alongside the writings of Paul, the teachings of Augustine of Hippo (354–430) shaped Christian attitudes towards Jews in profound ways, particularly during the medieval period. Wrestling with Roman legal precedent that recognised Jews as a lawful religion and further developing Paul's ideas about Christian supersessionism, Augustine formulated his 'witness doctrine'. The witness doctrine holds that Jews as a collective are responsible for the death of Jesus and their punishment was the loss of their national home, their dispersal, and their subjugation to Christians.[1] The subjugation of Jews became encapsulated in the concept of *servitus Judaeorum* that assigned an inferior spiritual status to Jews.[2] Through their dispersal and subjugation, Jews bore witness to their own blindness and disbelief, which confirmed biblical prophecy and therefore Christian truth. Moreover, they kept the Old Testament for Christians

[1] On Augustine's witness doctrine Jews, see Cohen, *Living Letters*, ch. 1.

[2] On the notion of *servitus Judeaorum* in Christian texts, see also Kaplan, *Figuring Racism*. The spiritual notion of servitude does not mean that Jews were in fact servants or enslaved.

which contained the Christian prophecies and truth. Augustine also stipulated that Jews would convert eventually, even if hope for conversion had to be postponed. The witness role in Christianity's salvation story required the toleration of Jews as Jews, even if this meant the toleration of infidels. For Christian theology, Jews therefore constituted an inferior yet necessary Other, a perpetual servant that was not to be harmed or prevented from observing Judaism.

What Christian theologians, such as Augustine, thought and wrote did neither convert immediately nor directly into law. Rather, ideas would take time to mature into church policy and it could take even longer for these policies to impact on the everyday affairs of Jews. Here, these policies would intersect with the policies of secular rulers with their own ambitions and ideas about the usefulness of Jews. The witness doctrine laid some groundwork for the conditional toleration of Jews based on the idea of Jewish usefulness. What constituted usefulness, however, was interpreted in a flexible way by secular and ecclesiastical authorities and involved not only theological but also political, economic, and legal ideas of usefulness.[3] Moreover, Christian theological ideas and papal legislation interacted with existing legal precedents, such as Roman law and the messy everyday realities of Jewish-Christian co-existence. Christian ambivalence did therefore not simply translate into policies of exclusion. Instead, Christian attitudes towards Jews would animate a complex set of policies and laws that spanned a variety of practices of toleration and co-habitation, separation and segregation, and, in extreme cases, expulsion and extermination.[4]

This chapter explores the interplay between Christian ambivalence and the law from the late Middle Ages to the period of emancipation. There are of course already many excellent studies of the history of Jews in Christian Europe that fill the shelves of libraries, and this chapter does not tell this entire history.[5] Instead, my ambition is more modest. In focusing on key moments and turning points in this history, this chapter aims to canvass the shifting role of law in reproducing and entrenching Christo-centric assumptions about Jews, including their inferiority but also conditional toleration, and to trace some of the

[3] Anna Sapir Abulafia, 'Response to "the Gifts and the Calling of God Are Irrevocable"', *European Judaism* 50, no. 1 (2017): 92–98, pp. 93–94.

[4] See also Lopez, 'Beyond Eurocentrism'.

[5] On Jews in medieval Europe, see, for example, Robert Chazan, *The Jews of Medieval Western Christendom 1000–1500* (Cambridge: Cambridge University Press, 2006). On Jewish emancipation, see Sorkin (2019).

enduring tensions these assumptions have created around Jewish difference. I begin my discussion by exploring how theological arguments about Jewish inferiority and difference entered both canon law and secular laws during the late medieval period, turning Christian supersessionism into Christian domination in the sociolegal realm. I then consider the increasing racialisation of Jewish difference through the purity of blood doctrine that solidified boundaries between Jews and Christians on the Iberian Peninsula at a time when masses of Jews had converted to Christianity. Focusing on the crucial period of Jewish emancipation, I then trace how these ideas eventually seeped into the secular legal imagination, shaping ideas about what constitutes the proper 'religion' in the modern secular nation state and how the law was used to remake Jews into such a religion. Throughout this chapter, I consider some of the shifting dynamics of conversion and assimilation as two important historical pathways for Jews to achieve social and legal equality with Christians through the remaking of their identities. These promising pathways could, however, at times turn into dead ends as Jewish equality was met with suspicion and fears of upsetting an entrenched idea of Christian superiority, suspicion and fears that have often drawn on a racialising register. By retracing these particular moments of conversion and assimilation, my aim is to shed light on some earlier precedents for contemporary cultural racism towards religious minorities that continues to challenge their belonging and equality in the Christian West.

MANAGING JEWISH DIFFERENCE IN THE MEDIEVAL AND EARLY MODERN PERIOD

During the medieval period, narratives of Christian superiority and Jewish inferiority had remained largely in the realm of theology where the 'theological Jew' had more often served to reassure an anxious Christian self than to deal with actual living Jews. In the social and professional realm, there was often a complex web of interactions between Jews and Christians that cannot be reduced to a narrative of exclusion. As Robert Chazan notes, the status of Jews as the only legitimate dissenting religious minority group in Western Christendom was precarious, but there was also cooperation that benefited both Jews and Christians.[6] However, beginning in the late medieval period and

[6] Chazan, *Jews of Medieval Western Christendom*, pp. 8–9.

leading into the early modern period, the status of Jews deteriorated in Christian thought and the Augustinian position that had afforded Jews a limited tolerance became gradually reconceptualised in Christian thought. As Robert Chazan observes, the Augustinian witness doctrine required a balance of protection and limitation but beginning in the eleventh century, the balance tilted more and more towards limitation and efforts to convert Jews.[7] The crusades led to escalating violence against Jews across Europe, and during the twelfth century, the terms 'leper', 'heretic', and 'Jew' became almost interchangeable in Christian writing to denote an impurity that threatened Christendom.[8] The reasons for these developments are complex and embedded in larger transformations and changes brought about by the consolidation of the power of the Church and its pursuit of Christian unity, Christian territorial expansion, and the ongoing reconquest of Spain from Muslims who had ruled parts of the Iberian Peninsula since the eighth century.[9] Moreover, Jewish questions were not necessarily the primary concern in these larger theological transformations. The treatment of Jews in Christian thought has to be understood as just one 'cog in a larger wheel' of theological and political issues.[10] Yet, these questions continued to offer a site to debate and conceptualise identity and difference in Christian Europe and impacted on the lives of Jews in Europe even if Jewish resistance constrained and shaped the 'imaginary field' of Christian ambivalence.[11] What is noteworthy is that the gradual deterioration of the Jewish position in Christian thought now migrated into medieval canon legislation and also began providing an ideological justification for secular local laws that regulated the status of Jews as well as relationships between Jews and Christians in ways that often sought to entrench Jewish inferiority to Christians.[12]

Canon law was a crucial vehicle for injecting Christian supersessionism into the social realm. As a central source of church law, derived from legislation made by church councils, local clergy, and

[7] Chazan, *Jews of Medieval Western Christendom*, p. 52.

[8] Cohen, *Living Letters*, p. 157.

[9] The reasons for this change are complex and manifold, see Cohen, *Living Letters*, pp. 147–66.

[10] Cohen, *Living Letters*, p. 4.

[11] See also Boyarin, *The Unconverted Self*, pp. 22–25.

[12] Scholars have begun to pay more attention to law and policy alongside theology and culture to investigate how these ideas gained political and social relevance, see, for example, Kaplan, *Figuring Racism*; Teter, *Christian Supremacy*.

certain papal letters, canon law also played an important role for discussing and transmitting political ideas in the medieval period, in which canon lawyers occupied important positions in ecclesiastical and secular administrations and courts of law in which they drew on their knowledge of canon law.[13] Canon law, therefore, constituted a conduit for disseminating ideas about Jews and Jewish difference beyond the immediate realm of the Church. The Third Lateran Council in 1179, for example, abolished the practice of allowing Jews to testify against Christians and vice versa in secular courts because, as Canon 26 explained, 'the only fitting condition is that Jews be placed below Christians, and that they be treated kindly by the latter solely because of humanitarian reasons'.[14] The same canon also stated that Jews were not to employ Christian slaves and servants and that converts were to be treated better than Jews, thereby maintaining an inferior status for Jews as compared to Christians.[15] The Third Lateran Council reflected an anxiety about the social significance of Jewish theological subordination.

Responding to complaints about Jews exercising authority and power over Christians whom they employed as servants or testified against in court, Pope Innocent III reiterated the need to protect Jews from physical violence so they could attest to the truth of Christianity and eventually convert. Yet, in his letters to kings and local clergy, the Pope also reminded Christians of Jewish servitude. Until their conversion, they were to be subjugated to Christians – not only theologically but also socially. Previously, anxieties about Christian and Jewish interaction in the household had often circled around the potential of Jews converting their Christian servants and separation was the response to a threatening proximity. Now the Pope's concern was also about the correct social order: Christians should not be subordinated to Jews in the social realm, as this would upset the necessary hierarchy between Christians and Jews as set out by Christian theology.[16]

[13] Lopez, 'Beyond Eurocentrism', pp. 453–54. James Muldoon, too, notes the significance of canon law in shaping medieval intellectual life and beyond, including in countries affected by the Reformation, see James Muldoon, *Popes, Lawyers, and Infidels: The Church and the Non-Christian World, 1250–1550* (Philadelphia: University of Pennsylvania Press, 1979), p. ix.

[14] Quoted in Kaplan, *Figuring Racism*, p. 20.

[15] Kaplan, *Figuring Racism*, p. 56, fn. 3.

[16] Magda Teter, 'The Catholic Church', in *Key Concepts in the Study of Antisemitism*, ed. Sol Goldberg, Scott Ury, and Kalman Weiser (Cham: Palgrave Macmillan, 2021), 65–78, pp. 69–70.

The preoccupation of canonists with the matter of Jews having or owning Christian servants did not in fact reflect social realities, Lindsay Kaplan notes. Instead, it was a testament to the growing fears and anxieties of Christians being subordinated to Jews that led to legislative action.[17] Under the leadership of Innocent III, the Fourth Lateran Council in 1215 sought to further reinstate this hierarchical order by legislating on the relationship between Christians and Jews. One of the most well-known rules that came out of the Fourth Lateran Council was the requirement that Jews had 'to be distinguished in public from other people by the character of their dress',[18] mainly to prevent sexual intercourse between Christians and non-Christians and which often became translated into the requirement to wear a badge. Many of these provisions also applied to Muslims, called Saracens, given that medieval canon law now often treated Jews and Muslims together, two Others that were increasingly seen as a 'joint threat to the Christian faith'.[19] The Fourth Lateran Council, Jonathan Boyarin observes, constituted a key attempt in constituting an idea of Europe as 'monolithically Christian'.[20]

The stubborn persistence of Jews but also the presence of Muslims turned into a particularly troubling issue that had to be contained by law. Yet, Jews seemed to arouse particular anxieties given their proximity to Christians. The Fourth Lateran Council also banned Jews from holding public office 'since under cover of them they are very hostile to Christians'[21] and restricted the movement of Jews during the Christian Holy Week. Moreover, the Fourth Lateran Council also held that converts must abstain 'from observing their old rite, so that those who freely offered themselves to the Christian religion may be kept to its observance by a salutary and necessary coercion'.[22] Finally, the Church also asserted jurisdiction over the interpretation of Jewish doctrine. Innocent IV, who was Pope from 1243 until 1254, affirmed the toleration of Jews but also held that it was the right of the Pope and not that of Jewish authorities to adjudicate Jewish belief and practice according to what Christians held to be the correct interpretation of the Old Testament as per their witness doctrine.[23]

[17] Kaplan, *Figuring Racism*, p. 46.

[18] In Jeffrey M. Wayno, 'Rethinking the Fourth Lateran Council of 1215', *Speculum* 93, no. 3 (2018): 611–37, p. 634.

[19] Muldoon, *Popes, Lawyers, and Infidels*, p. 52.

[20] Boyarin, The Unconverted Self, p. 63

[21] In Wayno, 'Rethinking the Fourth Lateran Council', p. 634.

[22] In Wayno, 'Rethinking the Fourth Lateran Council', p. 634.

[23] Muldoon *Popes, Lawyers, and Infidels*, pp. 30–31.

The Church stipulated these decrees at a time when Europe had become thoroughly Christianised and European identity was increasingly viewed as synonymous with being Christian. By the thirteenth century, the Church had consolidated its power to an extent that permitted it to not only legislate on Jewish-Christian relations but also expect the implementation of such decrees by local secular rulers.[24] Despite this expectation, the influence of these decrees was often erratic, uneven, and limited. Their implementation was hampered by existing legal arrangements on the ground and by the interests and ambitions of secular rulers. These could be reluctant to endanger a community on which they often relied for economic reasons and to interfere with the complex web of every-day commercial and social relations between Christians and Jews. However, their conditional toleration rendered Jews vulnerable. The perception of Jews as an asset to rulers could quickly change depending on local politics and power struggles, such as in the case of England during the thirteenth century. Here, the theological idea of Christian superiority and its codification in canon law became embroiled in the re-ordering of power between Kings and Barons and a fledgling medieval English nationalism that mobilised Christianity as a unifying force.[25]

Jews had settled in England from 1066 on the invitation of William the Conqueror until their expulsion by Edward I in 1290. The Crown defined their legal status, which was different from the rest of the Christian population. Jews, including their property, were property of the King, who acknowledged them as a self-governing religious community.[26] Across Europe, the legal status of Jews was that of serfs, which does not mean that Jews were slaves but that they were property of the ruler. They therefore lacked status as actual persons, different to the rest of the Christian population.[27] Though small in numbers – estimates put them at 3,000 to 5,000 – English Jews played, as elsewhere in Europe, an important role in securing the wealth of the Crown.

[24] Boyarin, *The Unconverted Self*, p. 7.

[25] On Jewish racialisation and 'embryonic' English nationalism, see Matthea Westerduin, 'Questioning Religio/Secular Temporalities: Mediaeval Formations of Nation, Europe and Race', *Patterns of Prejudice* 54, no. 1 (2020): 136–49.

[26] H. S. Q. Henriques, 'The Jews and the English Law. IV', *Jewish Quarterly Review* 14, no. 4 (1902): 653–697. See also Karen Barkey and Ira Katznelson, 'States, Regimes, and Decisions: Why Jews Were Expelled from Medieval England and France', *Theory and Society* 40, no. 2 (2011): 475–503, p. 482.

[27] Thomas, 'Racial Formation of Medieval Jews', pp. 1245–46.

Jews contributed a disproportionate amount of income for the King's expenses through their taxation and moneylending. As the position of Jews in Christian Europe began to worsen during the twelfth and thirteenth centuries, so too did the position of English Jews for a melange of economic, political, and ideological reasons. Although English Christians engaged in moneylending too, it was Jews who drew the ire of the population. A small number of English Jews had acquired a position of economic superiority, yet this superiority was ascribed to *all* Jews by the Christian population. Jews were associated with usury qua their Jewishness. This perceived economic dominance of all Jews stood in tension with the theological mandate of subordination. At the same time, Jews became associated with sovereign power as Christians were well aware that the King benefited from Jewish money-lending and attacking Jews and Jewish money-lending became a means of resisting sovereign power.[28] Moreover, efforts of the English Crown to mobilise Christianity for an 'embryonic' medieval nationalism as a glue in an 'otherwise fragmented community'[29] not only accentuated the difference of Jews but also found in Jews a useful Other.

Anti-Jewish measures began emanating from both the Crown and the English church. The English church was one of the first in Europe to require the wearing of the badge in 1218, and almost a third of its canons between 1208 and 1290 concerned Jews.[30] At the same time, shifting power relations between the English King and Barons changed the utility of Jews to the Crown. The Magna Charta from 1215, a celebrated milestone in the history of the rule of law in Western societies, constrained absolute royal power yet also indirectly led to the demise of the Jewish position in England. The Magna Carta granted inter alia greater jurisdictional autonomy to towns that beginning in the 1230s used this opportunity for self-government to expel Jews, which was followed by a period of escalating violence against Jews. Beginning in 1215, badge laws were introduced to distinguish Jews through clothing as required by Lateran IV – an imposition that English Jews often resisted. Authorities who were in charge of enforcing the badge laws allowed Jews to avoid wearing the badge upon payment of a fine, which ensured further income to the Crown. Although this practice

[28] Nirenberg, *Anti-Judaism*, pp. 197–200. For a discussion of the complex political, social, and fiscal reasons that led to the expulsion of English Jews, see Barkey and Katznelson, 'States, Regimes, and Decisions'.
[29] Westerduin, 'Questioning Religio/Secular Temporalities', p. 142.
[30] Heng, *Invention of Race*, p. 73.

created frictions between secular and religious authorities, it enabled the exploitation of papal restrictions for financial gain.[31] At the same time, the Crown increased the taxation of Jews.[32] Between 1240 and 1255, Jews were taxed at a rate 100 times higher than in proportion to their numbers in the population, rapidly deflating the wealth of Jews and in turn also their economic value to the Crown.[33]

In 1253, King Henry III gave an ordinance to the Exchequer for Jews that further entrenched the legal subjugation and differentiation of Jews from the rest of English society by implementing measures of the Fourth Lateran Council through secular law. The Exchequer for Jews was a department of the Great Exchequer that exercised jurisdiction over civil and criminal matters involving Jews and oversaw the taxation of Jews. The ordinance given by King Henry III to the Exchequer emphasised the usefulness of Jews to the English Crown as a precondition of their tolerance by stipulating that 'no Jew remain in England unless he do the King service'.[34] It also restricted the rights of Jews, including by stating that 'there be no synagogues of the Jews in England save in those places in which synagogues were in the time of King Johns', and that 'no Jew or Jewess eat or buy meat in Lent'. The ordinance further ordered that 'no Jew disparage the Christian Faith' and held that Jews were to practice their worship quietly so that they would not disturb Christians. The decree also banned Jews from employing Christian servants, prohibited 'secret familiar intercourse' between Jews and Christians, and disparaged Christians from eating with Jews. To avoid misidentifications, it was also decreed that 'every Jew wear his badge conspicuously on his breast'. In 1275, Henry's son Edward I required in his *Statutum the Judeismo* the badge to be increased in size by one and a half times and also extended the obligation to Jewish children aged seven and older.[35]

Geraldine Heng argues that these legal changes did not merely differentiate between Jews and Christians as a matter of religious difference but instituted a social differentiation that produced Jews as an

[31] Nicholas Vincent, 'Two Papal Letters on the Wearing of the Jewish Badge, 1221 and 1229', *Jewish Historical Studies* 34, no. 1994–1996 (1994–1996): 209–24, p. 215.

[32] Barkey and Katznelson, 'States, Regimes, and Decisions', p. 488.

[33] Robert Stacey, 'The Conversion of Jews to Christianity in Thirteenth-Century England', *Speculum* 67, no. 2 (1992): 263–83, p. 270.

[34] For the complete decree, see James Macmullen Rigg, *Select Pleas, Starrs, and Other Records from the Rolls of the Exchequer of the Jews: A.D. 1220–1284*. (London: Quaritch, 1902), p. xlix.

[35] Heng, *Invention of Race*, p. 75.

'ethnoracial constituency'.[36] Despite ongoing debate about the origins of race, scholars such as Heng but also James Thomas and Lindsay Kaplan contend that the racialisation of Jewish difference began during the late medieval period and spread across Europe as the power of the Church took hold. 'While Jews were not yet essentialised as innately inferior', James Thomas notes about this period, 'everything about their body is marked as "less than Christian" as long as they deny the Christian saviour'.[37] Through its decrees that instigated social separation and differentiation, the Church treated Jews as a 'physical threat to Christendom'.[38] Alongside these legal declarations, Christian polemics perpetuated images and narratives about Jewish bodies as defective, unclean, and diseased, whereas Christian bodies were seen as healthy and increasingly as White[39]:

> Scientific, medical, and theological treatises ... argued that the bodies of Jews differed in nature from the bodies of Western Europeans who were Christians: Jewish bodies gave off a special fetid stench (the infamous foetor judaicus), and Jewish men bled uncontrollably from their nether parts, either annually, during Holy Week, or monthly, like menstruating women. Some authors held that Jewish bodies also came with horns and a tail, and for centuries popular belief circulated through the countries of the Latin West that Jews constitutionally needed to imbibe the blood of Christians, especially children, whom they periodically mutilated and tortured to death, especially little boys.[40]

The legal construction and regulation of Jewishness as an inferior social status through both canon law and local secular law, such as in England, did not only restrict the socioeconomic rights of Jews as compared to Christian subjects, it also seems to have contributed to entrenching social views of Jews as inherently different and untrustworthy. Restrictive laws and perceptions of Jews became mutually constitutive and reinforced one another.[41] The ways in which negative views

[36] Heng, *Invention of Race*, p. 66.

[37] James M. Thomas, 'The Racial Formation of Medieval Jews: A Challenge to the Field', *Ethnic and Racial Studies* 33, no. 10 (2010): 1737–55.

[38] Thomas, 'Racial Formation of Medieval Jews', p. 1744.

[39] Thomas, 'Racial Formation of Medieval Jews', p. 1745.

[40] Heng, *Invention of Race*, at 15–16. See also Kaplan, *Figuring Racism*; Thomas (2010).

[41] See also Thomas, 'Racial Formation of Medieval Jews'. Thomas further notes that the 'denial of socio-economic rights of Jews through Church doctrine must also be seen as congruent with the emergence of the nation state, gaining status as the sociopolitical entity, but one still not separated in theory or practice from the Church's influence' (p. 1748).

of Jews solidified become also apparent in the problem of conversion. In Christian thought, Jews would be able to leave their cursed inferior status behind as soon as they converted. Medieval church authorities tended to celebrate the conversion of Jews and while forced conversions went against official papal policy that stressed the voluntariness of conversion and therefore the freedom of belief, a firm 'nudging' was deemed permissible.[42] During the thirteenth century, the legal restrictions placed on English Jews, their heavy taxation, and escalating Christian violence had created an environment that forced Jews to consider conversion to escape their dire conditions. Certainly, some converts had genuine religious reasons. Others wanted to flee from problems in the Jewish community. Yet many others hoped to escape poverty as well as the massacres that had continued despite papal direction against persecution.[43] While Jewish communities developed strategies to prevent conversion, these external social and legal pressures rendered conversion as a means to escape a legal and social status of inferiority and to acquire rights and status in English Christian society.[44]

During the thirteenth and fourteenth centuries, a 'conversionary fervor' swept across Europe, in which Christian authorities welcomed Jewish converts with favourable policies and thereby promised them a better life.[45] In England, it was indeed Crown policy to improve the status of Jewish converts to Christianity. The royally sponsored *Domus Conversorum* was an institution that housed new converts, educating them in their new faith and providing them with skills to enable their integration into Christian society. The *Domus* was funded by a special tax levied on English Jews and it is estimated that it housed hundreds of converts over the period from 1232 until 1500.[46] While set up as an institution of transition, many converts and their descendants remained in the *Domus* even after Jews had been expelled from England in 1290. Robert Stacey suggests that this decision reflects

[42] It is difficult to estimate the number of European Jews who converted in Christian Europe during this period. On the prevalence and dynamics of conversion in Europe between 1200 and 1391 as well as Jewish resistance to conversion, see Tartakoff, 'Testing Boundaries'.

[43] Stacey, 'Conversion of Jews'. In Italy too, heavy increases in taxation led to a mass conversion of Jews at the end of the thirteenth century, see Tartakoff, 'Testing Boundaries', p. 742.

[44] Tartakoff, 'Testing Boundaries', p. 732.

[45] Tartakoff, 'Testing Boundaries', pp. 735–36. For quote, see fn. 21 on p. 735.

[46] Lauren Fogle, 'Between Christianity and Judaism: The Identity of Converted Jews in Medieval London', *Essays in Medieval Studies* 22 (2005): 107–16, p. 109.

at least in part the difficulties of converts to find full acceptance in the Christian mainstream society that remained suspicious about the power of conversion to eradicate Jewish difference[47]:

> By the middle of the thirteenth century in England, there was clearly an irreducible element to Jewish identity in the eyes of many Christians, which no amount of baptismal water could entirely eradicate, at least from a layman. Through baptism, converts from Judaism became Christians, but this did not mean that they had entirely ceased to be Jews in the eyes of their brothers and sisters in Christ.[48]

Despite the aim to affirm Christian superiority by improving the status of converts, socially entrenched views of Jewish untrustworthiness and innate difference as well as doubts about the motivations of converts undermined conversion's promise of social and legal equality with Christians. Christians remained suspicious of Jewish converts, a fate that Jews not only encountered in England but also elsewhere in Europe.[49] During the second half of the thirteenth century, Pope Clement IV expressed concerns about Jews converting Christians and about relapsing Jewish converts to Christianity, particularly in Spain. Constant pressure to prevent such a relapse was necessary as well as vigilance to contain the threat of Jews for Christian souls.[50] Geraldine Heng argues that the conversion of Jews, despite its significance and desirability in medieval Christian theology, created a category crisis for Christians by raising doubts about the nature of Jewish and Christian identity.[51]

This crisis was particularly acute when converts entered positions of power and influence, therefore upsetting the social order between Jews and Christians, such as when the royally favoured convert Henry of Winchester was to be made a justice in a coin-clipping trial. Members of the King's council reiterated the idea of Jewish subordination to Christians and rejected that a convert should have legal authority over a Christian, citing 'Jewish perfidy and the ancient hatred of the Jewish people for Christians'.[52] The emerging racial formation of Jews as it became visible in the problem of conversion allowed for the

[47] Stacey, 'Conversion of Jews', p. 274.
[48] Stacey, 'Conversion of Jews', p. 278. See also Tartakoff, 'Testing Boundaries'.
[49] Tartakoff, 'Testing Boundaries', pp. 744–47.
[50] Muldoon, *Popes, Lawyers, and Infidels*, pp. 50–51.
[51] Heng, *Invention of Race*, p. 77.
[52] Quoted in Stacey, 'Conversion of Jews', p. 278.

'perpetual deferment' of equality by essentialising Jewish difference and by re-asserting boundaries between Jews and Christians.[53]

A century later in Spain, an even larger group of Jewish converts to Christianity faced similar suspicion and here law played an even more prominent role in producing Jewish difference in not merely religious but increasingly racial terms as hereditary and rooted in blood. On the Iberian Peninsula, fuelled by the Christian reconquest of Spain from Muslim ruler and by accusations of Jewish responsibility for the plagues, violence against Jews escalated during the fourteenth century, with many Jews massacred, forced to flee, or to accept baptism. These events led to both mass conversions and a huge exodus of Sephardic Jews in 1391.[54] While conversion set those New Christians on equal legal footing with Old Christians and removed restrictions on occupations and property ownership, the Christian status of the *conversos* was not stable either, a suspicion that also affected Muslim converts to Christianity who were called *moriscos*.[55] Soon Old Christians began to view New Christians with doubt, fear, and suspicion, accusing them of secretly 'Judaising'.[56] Some Old Christians even interpreted conversion as a sinister Jewish plot to infiltrate the Spanish state.[57] Anxieties grew around crypto-Jews, or so-called *marranos*, New Christians who maintained their Jewishness in private while presenting to the outside world as true Christians. As earlier in England, for some converts, conversion had been a genuine desire; for others, it had been a matter of necessity. It is difficult to estimate the numbers of these secret Jews that in fact continued to practice Judaism – to the dismay of Old Christians:

> Many people suspicious of Marranos, no doubt quite shocked to learn that holy water was less powerful than they had believed, looked back with nostalgia to the good old days when Christians

[53] Heng, *Invention of Race*, at 39.

[54] Jerome Friedman, 'Jewish Conversion, the Spanish Pure Blood Laws and Reformation: A Revisionist View of Racial and Religious Antisemitism', *Sixteenth Century Journal* 18, no. 1 (1987): 3–30.

[55] See L. P. Harvey, *Muslims in Spain 1500 to 1614* (Chicago; London: University of Chicago Press, 2005).

[56] On the different terms used to describe Jewish converts to Christianity in Spain and associated assumptions, see Friedman, 'Jewish Conversion', pp. 5–6. Marranos (literally 'pigs') or crypto-Jews often refer to those Jews who maintained their Jewishness in secret, while conversos and New Christians refer to converts who embraced their new faith.

[57] Friedman, 'Jewish Conversion', p. 17.

> were Christians and Jews were Jews and everyone know their place. Clearly, repressive legislation aimed at eliminating a non-Christian Jewish minority had not succeeded. There were still Jews and, worse, Christians who were Jews.[58]

While elsewhere, these New Christians faced fewer issues and often became an important part of local economies and trading networks, in Spain, they began to constitute a social problem as *all* New Christians started to be seen as secret Jews. While the reasons for this change of attitude remain a puzzle, perhaps it had something to do with their numbers. By 1492, when Spain expelled its remaining Jews, some estimates suggest that there were between 250,000 and 600,000 conversos.[59] These conversos also played a significant role in Spanish economic, institutional, and religious life, including in discussions about Christian theology. In 1480, courts of inquisition began operating in Spain to deal with heresy and the question of crypto-Jews with the inquisitors chosen by the Crown.[60] Being Jewish could be a matter of not behaving properly Christian. Inquisition authorities convicted New Christians of being Jews in secret based on evidence such as the changing of sheets on Friday, refusing to buy an apple on Saturday, or using olive oil instead of lard.[61] These cultural habits that sometimes could have been mere coincidences, such as not buying an apple on a Saturday, were seen as remnants of Jewishness and therefore of an inauthentic Christian identity, despite converts affirming the sincerity of their faith. Even Old Christians could find themselves accused of Judaising behaviour if they were suspected to engage in practices deemed Jewish.

Alongside the purity of faith that testified to pure Christian origins, purity of blood became another marker of Christianness.[62] Following the mass conversions, the belief took hold that Jews and Muslims constituted *razas*, who possessed different blood that could not be

[58] Friedman, 'Jewish Conversion', p. 11.

[59] Friedman, 'Jewish Conversion', p. 8.

[60] For the political, economic, and religious context of the operation of this 'first proto-national institution', see María Elena Martinez, *Genealogical Fictions: Limpieza De Sangre, Religion, and Gender in Colonial Mexico* (Stanford: Stanford University Press, 2008), 34–35.

[61] Friedman, 'Jewish Conversion', p. 15; David Nirenberg, 'Was There Race before Modernity? The Example of "Jewish" Blood in Late Medieval Spain', in *The Origins of Racism in the West*, ed. Eliav-Feldon, Benjamin Isaac, and Joseph Ziegler (Cambridge: Cambridge University Press, 2013), 232–64, p. 242.

[62] Martinez, *Genealogical Fictions*, p. 83.

transformed through conversion to Christianity and that transmitted such Jewish practices. After insisting on their assimilation via conversion, Old Christians now rejected the idea that Jews and Muslims could be turned into true Christians. David Nirenberg observes that Spanish Christians became convinced that '[b]aptism could not alter the fact that the converts' blood was corrupted by millennia of mixture and debasement, indelibly saturated with a hatred of everything Christian'.[63] *Raza* in fact meant a 'defect' or 'blemish', implying that Jewish and Muslim blood was tarnished.[64] Judaising was not merely the secret practice of a different religion but a matter of contaminated blood. As a Spanish commentator wrote in 1604:

> Who can deny that in the descendants of the Jews there persists and endures the evil inclination of their ancient ingratitude and lack of understanding, just as in Negros [there persists] the inseparability of their blackness. For if the latter should unite themselves a thousand times with white women, the children are born with the dark color of the father. Similarity, it is not enough for the Jew to be three parts aristocrat or Old Christian for one family-line alone defiles and corrupts him.[65]

To protect Christians from 'biological' Jews, converts were forced to wear badges and hats so 'true' Christians could identify Jews.[66] Invisible from the outside, race had to be inscribed and marked onto the body, testifying to 'the Jew' as untrustworthy and unassimilable. Law was instrumental in constructing Jews in such racial terms. The doctrine of *limpieza de sangre* (purity of blood) held that the blood of Jews and Muslims was inferior to that of Christians and prone to heresy as well as moral corruption.[67] The so-called 'purity of blood' laws were in fact not a single piece of legislation but a collection of local statutes, regulating the conduct of specific corporate entities, such as cathedrals, guilds, and university colleges, but also towns towards New Christians.[68] The underlying doctrine implemented the distinction

[63] David Nirenberg, 'Enmity and Assimilation: Jews, Christians, and Converts in Medieval Spain', *Common Knowledge* 9, no. 1 (2003): 137–55.
[64] Harvey, *Muslims in Spain*, p. 7 (n. 4).
[65] Quoted in Friedman, 'Jewish Conversion', pp. 16–17.
[66] David Nirenberg, 'Enmity and Assimilation', p. 142.
[67] David Nirenberg, 'Was There Race before Modernity?', p. 242.
[68] John Edwards, 'Race and Religion in 15th and 16th Century Spain: The "Purity of Blood" Laws Revisited', *Proceedings of the World Congress of Jewish Studies*, Division B, Volume II: The History of the Jewish People (1989): 169–66.

between Old Christians and New Christians of Jewish and Muslim descent through a strict policy of segregation by legally banning intermarriage between the two groups and by preventing New Christians from holding positions of power in church or secular institutions as well as from accessing guilds and professions.[69] In 1451, the *Sentencia-Estatuto* in Toledo, perhaps the first of these statutes, made all converts and their descendants ineligible for public office, based on the idea that conversos could not be trusted due to their 'deep hatred of *christianos viejos lindos* ("clean/beautiful Old Christians")'.[70] Although Pope Nicholas V was critical of the statute due to its impact on baptism and the unity of the Church, King Juan II eventually approved it. *Limpieza de sangre* spread across Spain and further statutes followed, such as the statutes of the candlemakers and the surgeons' guild in Barcelona that excluded anyone who descended from 'infected persons' and thereby depicted Jewish blood and bodies as diseased and blemished.[71] The purity of blood doctrine held that all descendants of Jews were still Jews no matter how much they had assimilated to Christianity. These laws therefore reconstructed both what it meant to be Christian and what it meant to be Jewish. Conversion, according to the doctrine, could not cure Jewish blood and any drop of Jewish blood made a person 'liable to heresy and moral corruption', reflecting old Christian fears of Jewish contamination.[72] However, despite this biological justification, there also remained the view in the Inquisition that faith could overcome nature, allowing extraordinarily dedicated converts to cure these 'spiritual "maladies"'.[73]

Neither Jews nor converts were entirely passive victims of Christian exclusion. New Christians in Spain too mobilised the racialising purity of blood discourse to distance themselves from Jews and thereby to protect their own status. These converts lobbied for their own inclusion with all its associated social and legal privileges based on arguments about their own biological difference from other Jews, a difference that enabled them to truly become Christians as it had enabled the earlier Jews, such as Paul, to become true Christians. Rabbinic authorities, in turn, also benefited from the purity of blood discourse as it held that Jews always remained

69 Nirenberg, 'Was There Race before Modernity?', p. 242.
70 Martinez, *Genealogical Fictions*, p. 29.
71 Edwards, 'Race and Religion'.
72 Nirenberg, 'Was There Race before Modernity?', p. 242.
73 Martinez, *Genealogical Fictions*, p. 83.

Jews, therefore providing an incentive for New Christians to return to their Jewish kin outside of Spain but also enabling rabbis to exert disciplinary power over their communities by stoking fears of Christians.[74] Yet, while Jews and New Christians engaged in the purity of blood discourses too, they often lacked the institutionalised power of Old Christians. Race became a legal and social wedge between Jewish converts to Christianity and those born with 'Christian blood', providing the justification for the reversal of legal rights and privileges from conversos who had acquired them only a few decades earlier. It enabled the pursuit of the 'purification' of the Spanish population by discouraging intermarriage and by regulating access to power and privilege against a larger backdrop of social and political transformation, including Spain's expanding overseas empire and struggles between Crown and nobility. In practice, the implementation of these statutes often proved difficult. Many New Christians indeed assimilated quietly into Spanish society. After centuries of co-existence and intermarriage, confirming the 'pure origins' of applicants was not easy to achieve and other considerations, such as nobility or social class, could easily trump any consideration of racial and religious origin.[75]

The suspicion towards converts, such as in late medieval England and early modern Spain, can be seen as anticipating some of the problems and tensions around assimilation as it emerged following Jewish emancipation by marking a moment in which 'sameness rather than difference became suspect'.[76] For both English and Spanish Christians, the conversion of Jews that set them socially and legally *en par* with Christians seemed to have been a source of anxiety. Both religious and secular authorities desired the conversion of Jews, yet soon their conversion aroused fears about sincerity and authenticity, of relapse and recidivism – about the true nature of Jews and therefore also the true nature of Christians. My point is not to suggest a structural affinity between conversion and racialisation. Plenty of Jews converted and integrated successfully into Christian societies. However, these episodes suggest

[74] Friedman, 'Jewish Conversion', at 25. New Christians countered these exclusionary ideas by developing their own genealogies that suggested that Old Christians descended from idol-worshipping gentiles. Others suggested that descent from the chosen people ennobled the New Christians, see Nirenberg, 'Was There Race before Modernity?', pp. 253–54.

[75] Edwards, 'Race and Religion'.

[76] Westerduin, 'Questioning Religio/Secular Temporalities', p. 140.

that some of our modern anxieties about Jewish and more broadly religious difference may find echoes in older histories. As Geoffrey Galt Harpham has pondered, 'the triumph of the Enlightenment might not, after all, have eradicated, but simply continued by other means, the poignantly specific dilemma of the *conversos*'.[77]

The Protestant Reformation led to a decline in the power of the Catholic Church and set in motion a complex process of separating church and state. Although the Protestant Reformation could be seen as an intra-Christian divide between Catholics and Protestants, it did not do away with the view of Jews as a problematic presence in Europe that was splitting into two confessions but remained predominantly Christian. The anti-Jewish views of Luther, particularly in his later life, are well known. Disappointed by the Jews' failure to convert, one of the key figures of the Reformation, Martin Luther lamented Jewish stubbornness and suggested in his writing on 'this insufferable devilish burden' to solve Europe's Jewish problem by burning down their synagogues, destroying their houses, taking away their Talmud, and preventing rabbis from teaching by threat of death so that Christian Europe would be protected from Jewish contamination.[78] Moreover, Luther harboured suspicion towards converts, doubting the sincerity of their conversion, and considered the religious contributions of New Christians as potentially deceptive and dangerous 'Judaising'.[79] Importantly, Luther and post-Reformation thinkers laid significant groundwork for the modern liberal notion of religion that would provide the normative benchmark for the regeneration of Jews as a precondition for their legal emancipation. In his writings, Luther attacked the Catholic church as 'Jewish' for its literalism and ritualism and emphasised private faith over ritual practice that he condemned as ceremonial and external.[80]

RELIGION OR NATION? THE CONDITIONS OF JEWISH LEGAL EQUALITY

The period of the Enlightenment and the American and French revolutions in 1775–83 and 1789 brought the idea of universal human rights, equality, and liberty to political fruition but also saw science

77 Geoffrey Galt Harpham, 'So … What Is Enlightenment? An Inquisition into Modernity', *Critical Inquiry* 20, no. 3 (1994): 524–56, p. 551.
78 In Thomas, 'Racial Formation of Medieval Jews', p. 1749.
79 Friedman, 'Jewish Conversion', pp. 24–26.
80 Nirenberg, *Anti-Judaism*, ch. 7.

and reason replace theology as the authoritative sources of knowledge, the question of Jewish difference and the legal and social status of Jews took on a new tone. All across Europe, societies began debating the Jewish question – that is, whether Jews should be granted equal political and civil rights and access to citizenship in predominantly Christian states. These debates were not just the result of a benevolent acknowledgment of the humanity of Jews that would bestow them with equality and rights. Indeed, as Salo Baron noted, Jewish emancipation was as much a necessity for Jews as it was for the modern state.[81] With the consolidation of modern state power, corporate communities, such as Jews, with their special status and differentiated rights, became an anomaly and disturbance. However, the corporate organisation of Jews, their perceived 'oriental and superstitious' practices, their alleged hostility to Christians, and their tendency to engage in trade, commerce, and petty peddling rendered Jews a particular problem.[82] To join the modern nation state as equals and as useful citizens, Jews had to change.

While the economic activities of Jews, their association with usury and petty trade, played a central role in their alleged need of transformation, here I focus on the interlinked concerns about the public aspects of Jewish identity and therefore the national character of Judaism as a problem for the legal equality of Jews. Different to the medieval and early modern society, most participants in the debate about emancipation did not see conversion as a necessary requirement of legal equality and social integration. Jews could remain Jewish, but their current state was nonetheless seen as deficient and hence in need of transformation, improvement, and regeneration before Jews would be able to join the modern state as useful citizens.[83] Thus, even though baptism was not seen as necessary, among emancipation theorists there still was the hope that the assimilation of Jews would eventually weaken the authority of the Jewish community in such a way that it would 'in due course end in conversion to Christianity'.[84]

[81] Salo W. Baron, 'Newer Approaches to Emancipation', *Diogenes* 8, no. 29 (1960): 56–81, p. 57.

[82] James Pasto, 'Islam's "Strange Secret Sharer": Orientalism, Judaism, and the Jewish Question', *Comparative Studies in Society and History* 40, no. 3 (1998): 437–74, p. 450.

[83] David Sorkin, *Jewish Emancipation. A History across Five Centuries* (Princeton and Oxford: Princeton University Press, 2019), p. 62.

[84] Reinhard Rürup, 'The Tortuous and Thorny Path to Legal Equality: "Jew Laws" and Emancipatory Legislation in Germany from the Late Eighteenth Cent', *Leo Baeck Institute Year Book* 31, no. 1 (1986): 3–33, p. 23.

While the pathway to legal equality differed from state to state and was a tumultuous and meandering affair rather than straightforward, the idea that Jews had to transform themselves to become citizens wove like a common thread through the project of emancipation across Western European states. The question of whether Jews formed a religion or a nation took centre stage – a debate, as Amnon Raz-Krakotzkin notes, also played 'a critical role in the construction of the Western secular order' by providing a site for establishing the distinction between private religion and public politics.[85] The point of contention was whether only Jews as a religion could claim legal equality and join the nation state as citizens on equal footing with Christians. However, as Leora Batnitzky notes, the problem was that before modernity, Jewish identity had been neither a religion, a culture, nor a nationality, but all of these at once.[86] Jewish life had been governed by Jewish law, and 'adherence to law … is at least partially, if not largely, public in nature'.[87] Judaism's claim to the public identity of Jews was perceived by some as advancing a 'state within a state'[88] and therefore as an obstacle to Jewish integration as citizens into the modern nation state. German Orientalist Johann David Michaelis, for example, argued in 1782 that Jewish law was about maintaining Jews as a separate nation. Taking aim at Jewish dietary laws, he claimed that halakhic rules were designed

> to preserve the Jews as a people separated from all other peoples … and as long as the Jews retain the laws of Moses, as long as they for example do not dine with us … they will never melt with us – like the Catholic and Lutheran, the German, Wend and Frenchman, who all live in a single state.[89]

Disdain for the difference of Jews and for the political nature of Jewish ritual observance was not only the result of the consolidation of the modern secular liberal state and a romantic idea of a homogenous nation. The juxtaposition of religion and politics, as Robert Yelle observes, also harked back to an older distinction: 'that between

85 Raz-Krakotzkin, 'Raz-Krakotzkin', p. 286.
86 Batnitzky, *How Judaism Became a Religion*, p. 2.
87 Batnitzky, *How Judaism Became a Religion*, p. 1.
88 Batnitzky, *How Judaism Became a Religion*, p. 16.
89 Quoted in Jonathan M. Hess, 'Johann David Michaelis and the Colonial Imaginary: Orientalism and the Emergence of Racial Antisemitism in Eighteenth-Century Germany', *Jewish Social Studies* 6, no. 2 (2000): 56–101, p. 58.

Protestantism, or rather the ideal image of apolitical religion … and other traditions that failed to keep religion free from politics'.[90] In this tradition of Protestant thought, political religions included Roman Catholicism, Islam, and Judaism. Protestant thinkers saw the Gospel as freeing religion from 'the "carnal" worship of Mosaic ritual and, on the other, from mundane and irreligious politics'.[91] English Protestants, for example, criticised Jews for their failure to understand this separation, labelled Islam an 'imposture' due to its mixing of spiritual and political aspirations, and also used this argument to attack the Catholic Church.[92] The notion of religion as a private and individual belief also underpins John Locke's *Letter Concerning Toleration* in which he explains that a church is a 'voluntary society of man' who for the purpose of salvation join 'themselves together of their own accord, in order to the public worshipping of God'.[93] For Locke, worship is public but forming a church is a free and voluntary decision because '[n]o body is born a member of any church'.[94] His view thereby reflected a Christian view of religious belonging that emphasises choice over genealogy and descent as defining membership in a religious community.

In both continental Europe and England, Protestant liberal thought separated ritual and belief, and often arguments for this separation rehearsed a supersessionary logic. Indeed, David Nirenberg has called it 'one of the greatest ironies of the Enlightenment' that most of its central writings on freedom and toleration relied on the denigration of Jews and Judaism and its association with an archaic past.[95] German philosopher Immanuel Kant accused Judaism of not being a true religion but a political entity due to its concern with outward actions and conformity instead of moral dispositions.[96] Kant also stated that the Jewish belief in being the chosen people implied disregard for or even

90 Robert A. Yelle, '"By Fire and Sword": Early English Critiques of Islam and Judaism as "Impostures" or Political and "Unfree" Religions', *Patterns of Prejudice* 54, no. 1–2 (2020): 91–108, p. 93.

91 Yelle, "By Fire and Sword", pp. 91–92.

92 Yelle, "By Fire and Sword", p. 95.

93 John Locke, 'A Letter Concerning Toleration' [1689] in: John Locke, *Letters Concerning Toleration* (London: Printed for A. Millar et al., 1765), pp. 37–38.

94 Locke, 'A Letter Concerning Toleration', p. 38.

95 Nirenberg, *Anti-Judaism*, p. 357.

96 Immanuel Kant, *Religion within the Boundary of Pure Reason*, translated by J. W. Semple (Edinburgh: Thomas Clark, 1838), p. 165. See also Sidney Axinn, 'Kant on Judaism', *The Jewish Quarterly Review* 59, no. 1 (1968): 9–23.

hatred towards all other people.[97] The outward elements of Judaism rendered it an improper religion and prevented Jews from being loyal to their nations and from fully accepting the authority of the secular nation state. Christianity, on the other hand, was a rational religion and therefore the ideal religion for a moral community based on reason.[98] For Enlightenment thinkers, such as Kant, Judaism, with its alleged coercive legalism and clannishness, provided a perfect foil to envision a secular legal order based on universalism and rationalism[99] and to carve out a notion of religion compatible with this order. In contrast to the alleged deficiencies of Judaism, 'religion' came to be understood as a separate sphere of life, mainly private and not public, disembodied and non-political, non-coercive and voluntary, and therefore compatible with the modern liberal state.[100] Belief thereby became constituted as the most authentic site of religion.[101]

The consolidation of the modern secular nation state, in which the public realm of politics and the private realm of religion were to be separated, often relied on this Protestant notion of religion as the benchmark to implement the appropriate separation between state and religion. At the same time, this notion of religion was seen as universal and rational, so other 'deficient' religions such as Judaism could be reformed to comply with this idea of religion and therefore join the modern nation state as equal citizens. As a condition of legal equality, Jews therefore had to be secularised, to be transformed into a true religion, which was presented as universal even though it essentially required Jews to mimic a certain version of Christianity.[102] 'Secularization, from the Jewish point of view', Amnon Raz-Krakotzkin argues, 'means self-denial and integration

97 Kant, *Religion*, p. 168.

98 For a critical analysis of supersessionism in Kant's reasoning, see Terence Keel, 'Blumenbach's Race Science in the Light of Christian Supersessionism', in *Johann Friedrich Blumenbach. Race and Natural History, 1750–1850*, ed. Nicolaas Rupke and Gerhard Lauer (Abingdon, Oxon: Routledge, 2019), 123–41, at 129–32.

99 See Jonathan M. Hess, *Germans, Jews and the Claims of Modernity* (New Haven; London: Yale University Press, 2002), p. 6.

100 Batnitzky, *How Judaism Became a Religion*, p. 13.

101 On this history, see Asad, *Formations of the Secular*.

102 Susannah Heschel, 'Revolt of the Colonized: Abraham Geiger's Wissenschaft Des Judentums as a Challenge to Christian Hegemony in the Academy', *New German Critique*, no. 77 (1999): 61–85, at 61–62. See also Gil Anidjar, 'Secularism', *Critical Inquiry* 33, no. 1 (2006): 52–77, p. 62.

into the Christian perception of history. Hence, the Jews had to be emancipated from themselves in order to become citizens'.[103]

Law was crucial for this transformation, even though proponents of emancipation disagreed on how to achieve this transformation. Some saw assimilation as the prerequisite of equality and rights. Jews had to improve themselves and assimilate first in order to be worthy of legal equality. Others believed that equality under the law itself would lead to the transformation of Jews. A famous proponent of the first view was Joseph II in Austria who issued several laws allowing Jews to gain admission to education and to trades and professions. While these laws removed some legal disabilities, they did not turn Jews into citizens of the state. Instead, by removing these legal disabilities, Jews were to be set on a path of civic improvement so they could eventually turn into 'useful citizens' after their successful transformation.[104]

A famous proponent of the second view was the Prussian civil servant Christian Wilhelm Dohm, a friend of Jewish philosopher Moses Mendelssohn. In his book *Über die Bürgerliche Verbesserung der Juden* ('On the Civic Improvement of the Jews'), Dohm stipulated a model of unconditional emancipation.[105] For him, not Judaism but oppression and legal disabilities had corrupted Jews morally.[106] By granting Jews equal rights, Jews would be cured of their negative traits. The 'ennobling power of freedom and equality'[107] would help Jews lose their particularities and turn them into useful citizens of the state. Thus, legal assimilation would lead to sociocultural assimilation. The law would work its civilising magic and prove the power and superiority of the secular state. Of course, turning Jews into citizens nonetheless required a helping hand from the state to support their acculturation to the majority culture. Jews would be expected to agree to government-sponsored moral education and the restructuring of their occupations.[108] Dohm also qualified his model of unconditional emancipation, suggesting that Jews should not be admitted immediately to the civil service and therefore his model deferred full legal equality.[109] However, no matter the pathway, both

103 Raz-Krakotzkin, 'Secularism', p. 283.

104 Rürup, 'Tortuous and Thorny Path', p. 10.

105 Christian Wilhelm Dohm, *Über Die Bürgerliche Verbesserung Der Juden* (Berlin; Stettin: Friedrich Nicolai, 1781).

106 Dohm, *Bürgerliche Verbesserung der Juden*, p. 109.

107 Sorkin, *Jewish Emancipation*, p. 63.

108 Dohm, *Bürgerliche Verbesserung der Juden*, p. 111 and following.

109 Dohm, *Bürgerliche Verbesserung der Juden*, pp. 118–19.

models of emancipation still rested on the premise that Jews required improvement and reform and therefore the ultimate goal of both models was the same: Jews were 'to lose all their characteristics which made them recognisable as Jews outside the religious sphere'.[110]

LAW'S 'CIVILISING MAGIC': TRANSFORMING JEWS INTO A RELIGION

States pursued this transformative project in different ways, moving between and mixing the two models, and often withdrawing legal rights from Jews who had acquired them only recently before re-granting or modifying them through different legislation. The rapid succession of laws and sometimes contradictory legal changes reflected as much the often-tumultuous domestic political conditions, shifting European power landscapes as well as disagreement about the proper responses to these Jewish questions. France, for example, initially pursued a model of unconditional emancipation.[111] In 1889, the National Assembly debated the status of Protestants but soon veered onto the terrain of the status of Jews. In his famous speech, Stanislas Marie Adélaïde Compte de Clermont-Tonerre made clear that Jews could only be emancipated as individuals of a religious confession and that the state had to ensure this process:

> But they say to me the Jews have their own judges and laws. I respond that this is your fault and you should not allow it. We must refuse everything to the Jews as a nation and accord everything to Jews as individuals. We must withdraw recognition from their judges; they should only have our judges. We must refuse legal protection to the maintenance of the so-called laws of their Judaic organization; they should not be allowed to form in the state either a political body or an order. They must be citizens individually.[112]

Not everyone agreed with Clermont-Tonerre's motion. While supportive of the rights of Protestants, a Christian creed, Abbé Jean-Siffrein Maury, a defender of the Catholic Church and existing social hierarchies, argued against citizenship for Jews because

[110] Rürup, 'Tortuous and Thorny Path', p. 8.

[111] Scholars emphasise the role of French imperialism on domestic debates, see, for example, Ethan B. Katz, Lisa Moses Leff, and Maud S. Mandel, eds., *Colonialism and the Jews* (Bloomington; Indianapolis: Indiana University Press, 2017).

[112] In Lynn Hunt, *The French Revolution and Human Rights. A Brief Documentary History* (Boston; New York: Bedford, 1996), p. 88.

> the word *Jew* is not the name of a sect but of a nation that has laws which it has always followed and still wishes to follow. Calling Jews citizens would be like saying that without letters of naturalization and without ceasing to be English and Danish, the English and Danish could become French.... They should not be persecuted: they are men.... Let them be protected therefore as individuals and not as French for they cannot be citizens.[113]

The assembly did not settle the question of Jewish equal citizenship until late 1791 when Jews were granted full citizenship. However, under Napoléon, France reversed back to a model of conditional emancipation fuelled by perceptions of insufficient Jewish regeneration and usury accusations against Alsatian Jews. In 1806, the French state called an Assembly of Jewish Notables, composed of more than 100 rabbinical leaders and Jewish lay people, to Paris. They were asked to answer twelve questions in order to eradicate any doubts about Jewish loyalty to the French nation and Napoléon's Code Civil. These questions concerned the compatibility of Jewish law with French civil law, polygamy, intermarriage, relationships with Christians, usury, and the authority of rabbis.[114] The questions of polygamy and intermarriage linked the private realm of the family with French citizenship. Polygamy was seen as a violation of the French Code Civil and its notion of morality, and its rejection therefore as an indicator of the assimilability of Jews to French law and morals.[115] Intermarriage, on the other hand, related to the willingness of Jews to join the French nation that was defined through blood, that is, *jus sanguinis*. Adamant about breeding out any national aspirations among Jews, Napoléon even considered the introduction of legislation that would have required every marriage out of three to be an intermarriage to ensure that Jewish blood would lose its particular character.[116]

The Assembly considered these questions, seeking to balance the pursuit of Jewish emancipation with the desire to maintain Jewish culture and the integrity of Jewish law, and carefully answered them in

[113] In Hunt, *French Revolution and Human Rights*, p. 89.

[114] For a list of all questions, see Sorkin, *Jewish Emancipation*, pp. 120–24.

[115] Not only in France but also in its colonies, such as Algeria, polygamy was central to debates about Muslim and Jewish difference and their ability to obtain citizenship, see Judith Surkis, *Sex, Law, and Sovereignty in French Algeria, 1830–1930* (Ithaca; London: Cornell University Press, 2019), p. 57 and following.

[116] Sorkin, *Jewish Emancipation*, p. 126. Napoléon in fact instructed his commissioners to implement this requirement but without success.

the affirmative by invoking the halakhic dictum *dina de-malkhuta dina* ('the law of the land is the law'). The Assembly confirmed that '[our] religion orders that the law of the prince be regarded as the supreme law in civil and political matter'.[117] Moreover, the Assembly redefined Jewishness as a matter of private and voluntary faith to alleviate Napoléon's suspicion of the Jews' national character:

> By declaring their primary identification was with their fellow Frenchmen – asserting that a Jew in England felt himself a stranger though among Jews – the delegates to the assembly formally split the religious and ethnic elements subsumed within traditional Jewish identity. By validating only the ritual aspects of Jewish law, they admitted their Jewishness to be partial and theoretically limited to voluntary membership in a religious community alone. They declared their nationality to be equivalent to their citizenship. In their view, the Jews no longer constituted a nation.[118]

Satisfied by the Assembly's reassurance, Napoléon's answer to the Assembly in return echoed the words of Stanislas Clermont-Tonnerre. They were to be a religion first and foremost, and to dismantle their communalist institutions, including the judicial powers of rabbis that were now restricted to providing spiritual welfare and administering religious rites – but only after the state's administration of civil marriage and divorce. To make these rules legally binding, Napoléon established a modern Sanhedrin, a body composed of primarily rabbis that was modelled on the ancient Sanhedrin, a Jewish high court, to purport Jewish autonomy and generate Jewish commitment to Napoléon's terms. After the successful conclusion of the Sanhedrin, the *Consistoire*, a centralised legal status was created similar to that for Protestants. The *Consistoire Central Israélite* brought together all Jews in France in a centralised fashion and elevated the rabbi to a similar position as Christian clergy: 'Like Christian religious leaders, the modern rabbi was to be a preacher and pastor rather than a judge'.[119] 'Religion' became privatised, while 'law' became the public power of the state, reflected in the primacy of French civil law in governing affairs previously assigned to rabbis. However, even though the state

117 Quoted in Esther Benbassa, *The Jews of France. A History from Antiquity to the Present*, trans. M. B. DeBevoise (Princeton: Princeton University Press, 1999), p. 88.

118 Paula E. Hyman, *The Jews of Modern France* (Berkeley; Los Angeles; London: University of California Press, 1998), p. 43.

119 Hyman, *Jews of Modern France*, p. 42.

had committed to paying clergy salary for other confessions organised in similar fashion, such as Protestants, it did not do so for Jews.[120] This inequality was only resolved in 1831 under the July Monarchy, when Catholicism ceased to be the French state religion and became 'only' the majority religion in France.[121]

In Germany, emancipation was an even less linear process, reflecting the patchwork of German lands and laws. In March 1812, Prussia declared Jews citizens of the state after abolishing the category of *Schutzjuden*.[122] The *Edikt betreffend die bürgerlichen Verhältnisse der Juden in dem Preußischen Staate* (11. März 1812) ('Edict concerning the civic relations of the Jews in the Prussian state') granted all Prussian Jews the status of 'natives and citizens of the Prussian state' (section 1) and gave them the 'same civic rights and liberties as those enjoyed by Christians' (section 7). The Prussian state lifted several occupational restrictions (sections 8, 11, and 12) as well as special taxes levied on Jews (section 14) and granted Jews the right to settle in both towns and the country (section 10). These changes were not simply the success of Prussian advocacy for Jewish emancipation, rather they resulted from Napoléon's defeat of Prussia in 1806.

Yet, the Prussian edict did not grant Jews the same full or equal civil status as in France. While it permitted them to access academic positions (section 8), it did not allow them to hold government office (section 9). Moreover, as a precondition of citizenship, Jews were required to take on hereditary family surnames and only use German as a language and font for official legal documents (sections 2, 3, and 4). The Prussian edict relied on a similar notion of nationality as its French counterpart, requiring the subordination of communal identity and the privatisation of religion. The edict abolished in section 30 the judicial functions of rabbinical authorities, brought Jewish marriage and divorce under German secular civil law (sections 25–27), and thereby repeated the dictum of Count Clermont-Tonnerre, laying down a vision of Judaism as a religion that does not conflict with the sovereignty of the modern secular nation state and its legal authority in all matters except for inner belief and worship.

120 Benbassa, *The Jews of France*, p. 89.
121 Benbassa, *The Jews of France*, p. 91.
122 *Schutzjuden* refers to a status for German Jews granted to them by the imperial and royal courts that included both imperial protection and the right of the emperor to levy special taxes on Jews, an important source of income for the ruler. Jews had no right of residence, unless granted by imperial decree, and thus faced a constant threat of expulsion. I return to this spatial management of Jews in Chapter 5.

Jews were active participants in the debates about the nature of Jewishness and their access to citizenship. An early famous interlocutor was the philosopher Moses Mendelssohn, an important member of the Haskalah, the Jewish Enlightenment movement, and, as Leora Batnizky has shown, a crucial Jewish actor in presenting a notion of Judaism as a religion.[123] In his 1783 text *Jerusalem: Or on Religious Power and Judaism*, Mendelssohn formulated his own vision of Judaism, a Judaism that resembles Protestant Christianity and is therefore compatible with the secular order of the modern state. The question with which Mendelssohn grapples in this text is how Judaism, as a religion of law, can be reconciled with the demands of secular rule, which requires religion to be a voluntary and private matter. As Mendelssohn had already asserted in an earlier work, '[t]rue, divine religion needs neither arms nor fingers to be effective. It is all mind and heart'.[124] The vision of Judaism that Mendelssohn then presented in his text is a Judaism without coercive power – a power unique to the state – in which the corporate status of Judaism is dismantled, and Judaism thereby denationalised. This means, for example, that rabbis are not able to excommunicate members – a power they had held within the *kehilah*, the Jewish community, in order to enforce compliance with Jewish law. For Mendelsohn, Jewish law's coercive character was grounded in the social contract of the Jewish state, but in diaspora, Jews had to obey the law of the land.

Jewish traditionalists rejected the view that Judaism was a religion in this sense and thereby laid the foundations for what is today known as Orthodox Judaism. Samson Raphael Hirsch, one of the most important proponents of this Orthodox view, argued in 1854, in opposition to the Jewish Reform movement, which had been inspired by Mendelssohn's ideas,[125] that

[123] Batnitzky, *How Judaism Became a Religion*, p. 15, notes that when Mendelssohn made his intervention, as a Jew, he had no civil rights. Walking from Dessau to Berlin, he had to enter the city through the Rosenthaler gate, the only gate through which Jews and cattle were allowed to enter at the time.

[124] Quoted in Alexander Altmann, 'Introduction', to *Jerusalem. Or on Religious Power and Judaism*, by Moses Mendelssohn (Waltham: Brandeis University Press, 1983), 1–29, p. 5.

[125] Mendelssohn is sometimes heralded as the founder of Reform Judaism, although he himself followed an observant lifestyle. Formed during the time of Jewish emancipation, Reform Judaism is a liberal strand of Judaism that regards Jewish law as non-binding and places less emphasis on ritual observance compared to Orthodox Judaism.

> Judaism is not a religion, the synagogue is not a church, and the Rabbi is not a priest. Judaism is not a mere adjunct to life: it comprises all of life. To be a Jew is not a mere part, it is the sum total of our task in life. To be a Jew in the synagogue and the kitchen, in the field and the warehouse, in the office and the pulpit, as father and mother, as servant and master, as man and as citizen, with one's thought, in word and in deed, in enjoyment and privation, with the needle and the graving-tool, with the pen and the chisel – that is what it means to be a Jew.[126]

Although Hirsch rejected Mendelssohn's view of Judaism, Leora Batnitzky points out, he still emphasised the apolitical nature of Judaism by stressing the 'purely spiritual nature of Israel's nationhood' which allowed Jews to 'tie themselves fully to the various states in which they live'.[127] While Hirsch disagreed with Reformist Jews, he nonetheless advanced a vision of Judaism that would be compatible with the modern secular state. The period of emancipation thus not only gave rise to the notion of Judaism as a religion in a Protestant sense, but also to modern Jewish sectarianism with both Orthodox and Reform Judaism offering different answers to how Jews should relate to the demands of the secular state, yet without ever completely resolving the tensions that result from the fashioning of Judaism as a religion.[128] However, neither Mendelssohn's nor Hirsch's intervention should be seen as a simple Christianising of Judaism given that both Jewish thinkers had to carefully navigate Christian dominance, while maintaining a notion of Jewishness that would discourage conversion and preserve Jewish identity.[129] It is also important not to overstate the power of law or of social expectations of assimilation to remake Jewish identity and to ignore Jewish agency in reshaping their own identities and traditions. As Susannah Heschel notes, even if Jews reformed their religious practices against the backdrop of Christianity, introduced music into services, and installed organs in synagogue, they did so with 'a tone of rebellion'

[126] Quoted in Batnitzky, *How Judaism Became a Religion*, p. 41.

[127] Batnitzky, *How Judaism Became a Religion*, p. 41.

[128] Thus, despite its self-understanding as continuity, Orthodox Judaism is in fact a modern phenomenon – although, as we will see in the case of eruv, it becomes associated with pre-modernity by non-Jews who see Orthodoxy as a backward version of Judaism.

[129] Susannah Heschel, 'Jews and Christianity', in *The Cambridge History of Judaism. Volume Eight: The Modern World 1815–2000*, ed. Mitchell B. Hart and Tony Michels (Cambridge: Cambridge University Press, 2017), 1038–62, p. 1066.

by presenting Judaism as 'the "mother" religion of Christianity, which they portrayed in turn as derivative and unoriginal'.[130]

Official German documents reiterated the view of Jews as a religious community, referring to Jews as 'citizens of the Mosaic confession', 'Mosaic co-religionists', 'Israelites', and 'adherents of the Jewish faith',[131] thereby expressing the expectation that Jews would regenerate themselves 'in the image of German Protestantism'.[132] However, doubts remained among the German authorities. In Prussia in 1836, King Frederick William III opposed the idea of Jews as a purely religious community, arguing that Jews should be described just as what they were: Jews.[133] His comment reflected a reversal of Prussia's emancipation policy between the 1830s and 1840s. In Prussia, as elsewhere in European lands, the Jewish pathway to legal equality was not linear but marked by the repeated loss of legal rights. Incomplete implementation went hand in hand with administrative practices that undermined the rights of Jews in everyday life, while new legislation withdrew earlier-won rights. Moreover, there was a patchwork of different so-called 'Jew laws' applying to different territories that Prussia acquired up until 1847, such as the 1833 regulation for the formerly Polish Province of Poznań in which a model of civic improvement underpinned a legal regime that treated the majority of Jews as merely 'tolerated Jews' (sections 21–23).[134] Tolerated Jews, those who were not yet 'suitable for naturalisation' (section 21), were subject to a number of restrictions, such as prohibition on having Christian apprentices and servants (section 25e) and not being allowed to marry before the age of 24 (section 25a). The regulation also required them to first assimilate via work in certain professions as a precondition of naturalisation (Section 17). Yet, even naturalised Jews were excluded from a number of public offices (Section 20).

At the same time, different Prussian rulers repeatedly affirmed Prussia as a Christian state, relegating Jews to an inferior status as

130 Heschel, 'Jews and Christianity', p. 1065.

131 Rürup, 'Tortuous and Thorny Path'.

132 Pasto, 'Strange Secret Sharer', p. 450.

133 Rürup, 'Tortuous and Thorny Path', p. 24.

134 *Vorläufige Verordnung wegen des Judenwesens im Großherzogthum Posen v. 1. Juni 1833* ('Provisional Regulation Regarding Jewish Affairs in the Grand Duchy of Poznań'), in Ludwig von Rönne and Heinrich Simon, *Die Früheren und Gegenwärtigen Verhältnisse der Juden in den Sämmtlichen Landestheilen des Preußischen Staates* (Breslau: Aderholz, 1843), pp. 305–09.

compared to Christians. The term Christian state already constituted a shift from the confessional state and signalled a level of impartiality, although it did not deny the state's Christian character. Stephan Wendehorst argues that the Christian state created an ideological coherence for populations consisting of Catholics and Protestants. Yet, this coherence relied once again on the exclusion of Jews, who could not enjoy full political rights in a state understood as Christian.[135] The law reflected this view. For example, the Prussian *Gesetz über die Verhältnisse der Juden* ('Law on the conditions of the Jews') from July 1847 granted Prussian Jews (except for those in Poznań) full civic rights but still excluded them from holding positions in any state offices that would involve 'exercise of judicial, policing or executive authority' as well as from the position of dean and rector at universities (section 2). The law therefore granted Jews rights to an extent that it was understood to be possible in a 'Christian state' where they could have civil yet not political rights.[136] It took until 1869 for Jews to achieve full legal equality in Prussia.

Even in the absence of explicit more formal legal interventions, the period of emancipation saw the transformation of Jewish communities in line with majoritarian norms, such as in England (which I briefly discuss in Chapter 3) but also in the European settler colonies.[137] Although the state and its law had an important role to play, assimilation was a socially complex process, driven by a multitude of actors, including Jews themselves who aspired to integrate into European societies, and a multitude of factors, such as the Jewish Enlightenment movement, the *Haskalah*. In some European settler societies, such as in the United States and Australia, Jewish settlers did not have to undergo a formal process to acquire rights.[138] Instead,

135 Stephen Wendehorst, 'Emancipation as Path to National Integration', in *The Emancipation of Catholics, Jews and Protestants. Minorities and the Nation State in Nineteenth Century Europe*, ed. Rainer Liedtke and Stephen Wendehorst (Manchester; New York: Manchester University Press, 1999), 188–206, at 203. On the Jewish question and the negotiation of secularism in the German Reich, see Todd H. Weir, 'The Specter of "Godless Jewry": Secularism and the "Jewish Question" in Late Nineteenth-Century Germany', *Central European History* 46 (2014): 815–49.

136 Rürup, 'Tortuous and Thorny Path', p. 26.

137 Sorkin's magisterial study of emancipation covers a wide array of countries and their legal reforms, including Italy, Britain, and European settler-states: Sorkin (2019). I return to this period in England in Chapter 5 where I discuss the so-called Jew Bill.

138 The situation was different again for Jews living in Muslim countries, see the contributions in Katz, Leff, and Mandel, *Colonialism and the Jews*.

as European Jews, they were often able to benefit from their fair skin in societies more pre-occupied with the colour line than with religious difference.[139] Jews became useful for economic and political reasons as they boosted the number of White settlers in these societies, allowing them access to legal and social privileges denied to Indigenous populations and those racialised as non-White. In Australia, for example, Jews were able to secure legal and political emancipation by virtue of their arrival.[140] On board of the First Fleet, alongside other British convicts, a handful of Jews landed on Australian shores in January 1788. In Australia, no settler was able to claim a genuine connection to the land that could have served as a base for national identity. Australian Jews were eligible to stand for office, even before they were able to do so in England.[141] Jewish equality was not legislated in the early days of the colonies, but it appears that the *Plantation Act* from 1740 that had enabled the naturalisation of Jews in the English colonies formed the basis to naturalise Jews in Australia.[142] The only inequality Jews in the colonies faced was the lack of legal equality for their religion. Several of the colonies denied state aid to Jewish communities and in their struggle for religious equality, Jews also had to confront the idea of the Christian state. In the colony of New South Wales, the *Church Act* from 1836 dismantled the status of the Anglican Church as the privileged though not established church and put all Christian denominations on equal legal footing with regard to accessing land grants for religious buildings. The Act's preamble stated 'the advancement of the Christian religion' as its objective, thereby excluding Jews.[143] The exclusion of Jews may have

139 This history was not free of antisemitism and ambivalences. On the Jewish pathway to Whiteness in the United States, see, for example, Goldstein, *Price of Whiteness*; Karen Brodkin, *How Jews Became White Folks and What That Says about Race in America* (New Brunswick: Rutgers University Press, 1998).

140 Ira Katznelson, 'Between Separation and Dissappearance: Jews on the Margins of American Liberalism', in *Paths of Emancipation. Jews, States, and Citizenship*, ed. Pierre Birnbaum and Ira Katznelson (Princeton: Princeton University Press, 1995), 157–205, p. 158.

141 In England, Jews were gradually freed from their civil disabilities during the 1830s. In 1858, the *Jews Relief Act* finally removed the barriers that had prevented Jews from entering Parliament, see also my discussion in Chapter 4.

142 Israel Getzler, *Neither Toleration nor Favour. The Australian Chapter of Jewish Emancipation* (Melbourne: Melbourne University Press, 1970). I discuss the *Plantation Act* in more detail in Chapter 3.

143 Getzler, *Neither Toleration nor Favour*, p. 12.

been the result of a political compromise to appease the Anglican Church who already saw the inclusion of the Catholic Church as a threat. Extending equality to Jews appeared too radical, so the compromise left at least the primacy of Christianity formally intact.[144] In practice, Jews generally succeeded in their requests for land for synagogues and cemeteries, despite the legislation. The only difference was that Jewish clergy did not receive a stipend, something that Christian ministers received. Resistance to change this inequality did not come from New South Wales authorities but instead from the Colonial Office in London where the emancipation of Jews was still unfinished business. However, as Israel Getzler notes, Australian Jews believed in the 'magic wand of legislation'; they pushed hard and with success to remove any legal impediment to their formal equality in 1862.[145]

Despite few legal impediments, Jews in the Australian colonies still followed the conventional path that Jews had taken in other countries, whereby emancipation demanded that Jews become citizens of the Jewish faith – or rather 'British subjects' of the Jewish faith before the introduction of Australian citizenship. This was less a matter of legal regulation but of social expectation. Jewish settlers in Australia labelled Jewishness as a matter of personal belief while regarding themselves primarily as British subjects – Jews only on Shabbat and members of the general population on all other days of the week, as Suzanne Rutland describes.[146] Historians have noted the significant 'Anglicisation' of British Jews, which has been attributed to the pressures emanating from the dominant liberal culture and British Jewish attempts to prove their deservingness of emancipation by highlighting their attachment to 'British civilisation'.[147] Downplaying their differences to the Christian British settlers proved a successful strategy for Jews in Australia. The peculiar context of the colony enabled Jews

144 Getzler, *Neither Toleration nor Favour*, p. 20.

145 Getzler, *Neither Toleration nor Favour*, p. 51. The situation for Jews in Van Diemens Land, now Tasmania, was different. There, Jews faced more open discrimination from government authorities.

146 Suzanne D. Rutland, 'Reflections on "Culture Mavens" from an Australian Jewish Perspective', in *Jews at Home. The Domestication of Identity*, ed. Simon J. Bronner (Oxford; Portland: Littman Library of Jewish Civilization, 2010), 307–15, p. 307.

147 David Cesarani, 'British Jews', in *The Emancipation of Catholics, Jews and Protestants: Minorities and the Nation State in Nineteenth-Century Europe*, ed. Rainer Liedtke and Stephan Wendehorst (Manchester: Manchester University Press, 1999), p. 34.

from Britain to claim Whiteness, thereby strengthening the number of White colonists and helping to cement the European claim over colonised lands. Hence, the integration of Jews in Australia, it seems, perhaps depended not so much on the noble benevolence of settlers but on the usefulness of Jews to the colonial project and its racial underpinnings.[148]

The reluctance to grant Jews full legal equality in Europe and its colonies can of course not be attributed to Christian bias alone.[149] Indeed, the Jewish questions during the high period of emancipation dwelled on a more complex set of concerns, in which the role and status of Christianity as a source of national identity in the modern state was only one among many other concerns, such as the consolidation of state power and sovereignty, conceptions of civil society, the rapid transformation of the economy, and social changes brought about by modernity. The anticlericalism of the French Revolution sought to limit not only the influence of Catholicism but also of religion in general in the public sphere and therefore expand the power of the state over its citizens. In Prussia, emancipation meant initially emancipation into an only partially emancipated society.[150] In Australia, on the other hand, religious differences between European settlers became marginalised by the alleged threat that non-European Others, both within and from outside, would pose to a colony imagined as a White European outpost in the Southern hemisphere. However, Christianity as a tradition of thought and knowledge nonetheless influenced terms of Jewish integration. In debating the emancipation of Jews, Germans were grappling with the legacy of Christian supersessionism and Christianity's normative status,[151] whereas in France, secular universalism borrowed 'its ambition from the Catholic tradition'[152] in aiming to spread its

148 On the relationship between and role of Jews in colonialism, see, for example, Katz, Leff, and Mandel, *Colonialism and the Jews*.

149 On this issue, see Paul Mendes-Flohr, 'The Emancipation of European Jewry. Why Was It Not Self-Evident?' *Studia Rosenthaliana* 30, no. 1 (1996): 7–20.

150 Werner E. Mosse, 'From "Schutzjuden" to "Deutsche Staatsbürger Jüdischen Glaubens": The Long and Bumpy Road of Jewish Emancipation in Germany', in *Paths of Emancipation: Jews, States, and Citizenship*, ed. Pierre Birnbaum and Ira Katznelson (Princeton: Princeton University Press, 1995), 59–93, p. 71.

151 See Hess, *Germans, Jews and the Claims of Modernity*, p. 11.

152 Maurice Samuels, *The Right to Difference: French Universalism and the* Jews (Chicago: Chicago University Press 2016), p. 3. Samuels provides an account of the different understandings of universalism in French history and the role of Jews in shaping the shifting meanings of French universalism.

message to the world via a civilising mission that, as Lisa Mosses Leff has argued, shared, despite its anticlericalism, remarkable similarities in tone, though not necessarily always in content with the Catholic sacred mission.[153] Moreover, regardless of disagreements about its precise role and content, there was little doubt about Christianity as an important cultural element of European national identities and for defining the boundaries of belonging as well as the evolving concept of citizenship.[154] Importantly, habits of thought developed in Christianity's quest to distance itself from its Jewish roots helped to establish religion as the most acceptable category for Jewish difference, therefore offering a normative, albeit secularised stratum for liberal legislation that would reshape the legal status of Jews. Enlightenment ideas of progress, as Amnon Raz-Krakotzkin and various others have shown, remained indebted to Christian ambivalence towards Jews.[155]

RACIAL BACKLASH AGAINST EQUALITY

The period of emancipation did not only invent Judaism as a religion, it also saw the inventing or rather reinventing of Jewishness as a matter of race. Assimilation intersected with a process of dissimilation and distancing that reconstructed Jewish difference after Jews had obtained legal equality. Once more, not only difference but also sameness became problematic. On the one hand, there were doubts that Jews would not be willing or in fact able to assimilate because of the inherent qualities of Jewishness. On the other hand, there were anxieties that assimilation would render Jews invisible and therefore undetectable. Patchen Markell speaks here of a constitutive contradiction at the heart of the project of Jewish emancipation that involves an act of inclusion that is followed by 'vigilant surveillance' to ensure that Jews are complying with the conditions of their inclusion. To see whether Jews comply with these conditions required Jews to remain

[153] Lisa Moses Leff, 'Jews, Liberals and the Civilizing Mission in Nineteenth-Century France', in *The Jews of Modern France*, ed. Zvi Jonathan Kaplan and Nadia Malinovich (Leiden: Brill, 2016), 129–153, p. 129. Lisa Moses Leff describes how Jews aligned themselves with the civilising mission in order to secure equality and thereby even used Christian language in their efforts to support the 'sacralising' of an anti-clerical yet not irreligious secular mission.

[154] Sorkin argues that the formation of citizenship involved a 'procession of hierarchically arranged religions'. Sorkin, *Jewish Emancipation*, p. 7.

[155] See, for example, Raz-Krakotzkin, 'Secularism'; Hess, *Germans, Jews and the Claims of Modernity*.

recognisable: 'The imperative of emancipation becomes, paradoxically, that *the state must see at all times that each Jew has ceased to be Jewish*'.[156] For Markell, this contradiction is rooted in the state's futile pursuit of sovereignty, yet the blame is put on Jews, who are seen as always 'on the edge of slipping back into rootlessness and parochialism'.[157] Jews, it was feared, could easily relapse into their dangerous habits, no matter how hard they tried to assimilate and how hard the state tried to assimilate them. There remained an anxiety that the true essence of the Jews was hiding behind an assimilated façade – that Jewish difference was a problem that assimilation, much like previously conversion, could not cure.

Racial antisemitism gained strength during the 1870s, yet racial ideas about Jewish difference had already figured in the debate about Jewish emancipation. Whereas proponents of Jewish emancipation believed that legal equality and state-driven assimilation would overcome the imagined deficiencies of Jews, including their alleged clannishness and subversiveness, as well as their political and national aspirations, others cast doubt on the effectiveness of such attempts. For them, Jewish difference ran too deep and no legal or social attempt at reform could change that. Jews had been spoiled by their Judaism and by their foreign genes. An orientalist discourse underpinned opposition to Jewish emancipation by referring to Jewish Otherness as a matter of national and racial origin. Commentators described Jews in orientalist terms as 'Asiatic refugees',[158] locating their racial origins outside of Christian Europe. The Protestant theologian and orientalist Michaelis, who had not only declared Jewish law an obstacle to Jewish integration, also maintained that Jews were an 'unmixed race of a more Southern people'.[159] As an innate difference, no attempt at assimilation could eradicate it. To grant Jews equal rights required, in German philosopher Fichte's words, 'to cut off all their heads one night and replace them with others that do not contain a single Jewish idea'.[160]

[156] Patchen Markell, *Bound by Recognition* (Princeton; Oxford: Princeton University Press, 2003), 146.

[157] Markell, *Bound by Recognition*, p. 146.

[158] Jonathan M. Hess, 'Johann David Michaelis and the Colonial Imaginary: Orientalism and the Emergence of Racial Antisemitism in Eighteenth-Century Germany', *Jewish Social Studies* 6, no. 2 (2000): 56–101.

[159] Hess, 'Johann David Michaelis', p. 86.

[160] Quoted in and translated from German by Markell, *Bound by Recognition*, p. 138.

Anxieties about assimilated Jews becoming invisible continued to accompany emancipation, justifying changes in law or legal practices of differentiation. In Prussia, after decreeing that Jews had to take German names, Friedrich Wilhelm soon worried about this practice and asked the Minister of Interior and Police to intervene, noting in 1825 that '[f]or some time the Jews have been adopting names which mean that they can no longer be recognized as Jews. This must be prevented, if possible, since I do not want to permit Jews to pretend to be Christians'.[161] In France, ambivalences about Jews remained too. While the *Consistoire* was created as a religious institution, it was thought to represent all Jews in France, including those who did not identify as religious, therefore constituting Jewishness ambivalently as something more than just a religion. This ambivalence was reflected in the supervision of the *Consistoire* that fell both to the Minister of Cults, responsible for *religious* groups, and to the Ministry of Interiors, responsible for *foreign* groups.[162]

The continuing existence of Jews as Jews remained a puzzle for those who had hoped that assimilation into the nation would eliminate all traces of Jewishness: 'How could Jewish law and ritual practice, rabbinic authority, belief and attachment to the Jewish nation decline or vanish altogether without taking the Jew with it?'[163] Race provided an answer to the puzzle about 'the Jew's' continuous existence despite the mandate of assimilation that many Jews had indeed taken up. While feeding from earlier racial formations of Jews, antisemitism of the nineteenth century was embedded in a broader pseudo-scientific discourse of biological racism that presented the idea of different human races as a matter of scientific fact. Fusing anthropology, biology, and statistics, racial antisemitism found proof of Jewish racial difference in Jewish noses, Jewish gait, the Jewish voice, and of course the circumcised penis. Others traced Jewish difference back to Africa in order to explain the putative blackness of the Jew as 'a sign of racial mixing and, so, racial degeneration',[164] while other racial thinkers saw Jews as demonstrating the 'perils of *in*breeding'.[165]

161 Quoted in Markell, *Bound by Recognition*, p. 146.

162 Sorkin, *Jewish Emancipation*, p. 127.

163 Brown, *Regulating Aversion*, p. 54.

164 Ann Pellegrini, 'Whiteface Performances: "Race," Gender, and Jewish Bodies', in *Jews and Other Differences. The New Jewish Cultural Studies*, ed. Daniel Boyarin and Jonathan Boyarin (Minneapolis; London: University of Minnesota Press, 1997), 108–49, p. 111.

165 Pellegrini, 'Whiteface Performances', p. 112. Italics in original.

Despite numerous 'scientific' explanations, the conclusion was always the same: Jews were a different race, alien and inferior to a White Christian Europe, and therefore unassimilable, as neither assimilation nor conversion could overcome this difference, as nothing could 'wipe away the taint of race'.[166]

Although biology and science provided the foundation for the more modern secular notion of race based on biology, racial arguments rehearsed older tropes about the diseases and deficiencies of Jewish bodies that had already reverberated through medieval and early modern depictions of Jews. What was different, however, was that scientists now claimed to have found a rational and scientific proof for these earlier speculations about Jewish racial difference. Secularisation, however, Terence Keel cautions, should not simply be understood 'in terms of a rupture from the past but instead as a transference of religious forms into non-religious spaces of thought and practice'.[167] Old theological ideas merged with new forms of (pseudo-)scientific knowledge, such as in the work of anthropologist Johan Friedrich Blumenbach. Blumenbach's vision of race, Keel notes, drew on Christian intellectual history and the theology of supersessionism to craft a theory of race that saw Jews as White yet as possessing stable racial traits that prevent them from yielding new racial forms. The white Caucasian, on the other hand, emerges as 'the patriarch of all races'.[168]

This period also saw the invention of the 'Semites' in the work of philologists, such as Ernst Renan, who drew on the study of language and religion to classify world religions and perceived of both Jews and Muslims as at once religion *and* race.[169] Semites, such as Jews and Muslims, were race-religions and inferior to Aryan culture. For Renan, race was not so much a biological matter but a matter of linguistics and culture. He ascribed similar religious tendencies to both Semitic races – Muslims and Jews. The Israelites, Renan argued, were prone to 'moral extremism' and their religion 'deadly literal, monolithic, fanatic'.[170] Although critical of Christianity, Renan nonetheless tapped into the classic Christian narrative when he described Judaism as 'a withered trunk beside one fertile branch' and

166 Gilman, *The Jew's Body*, p. 179.
167 Keel, *Divine Variations*, p. 15.
168 Keel, 'Blumenbach's Race Science', pp. 133–36.
169 See Gil Anidjar, *Semites. Race, Religion, Literature* (Stanford: Stanford University Press, 2008).
170 See Masuzawa, *Invention of World Religions*, p. 175.

Christianity as 'the masterpiece of Judaism, its glory and the fulness of its evolution'.[171]

Jews too at times appropriated the discourse of race for their own causes, including to resist a growing antisemitism. Jewish social scientists, for example, contended that the Jews' racial make-up made them particularly suited for integration in liberal societies, such as in Victorian Britain or in France. In Germany, Austria, and Russia, Jewish scientists and anthropologists mobilised racial science to fend off the threat of antisemitism by presenting Jews as a pure and therefore 'good race' but also to re-assert a sense of identity threatened by assimilation.[172] Zionists but also antisemites referred to race for anti-emancipatory purposes to reject the liberal notion of Jews as a faith group as insufficient and to advocate for a national Jewish home.[173] However, as a minority, the power of Jews to resist their intense negative racialisation as Others in the European imagination was limited.[174]

Scholars suggest that the growth of racial antisemitism from the 1870s onwards was in part an attempt to reconstruct and reassert social hierarchies that had been rapidly disintegrating. Indeed, by the late nineteenth century, many Jews had become almost indistinguishable from non-Jews. They dressed and spoke like Christians, had obtained a secular education, and engaged in professions previously forbidden to them. Instead of their difference, now their sameness was problematic. Casting Jews as racially, and thereby eternally different sought to rebuild and reinforce the porous boundaries that had kept the Jewish Other at bay.[175] The social mobility and success that Jewish equality before the law had enabled challenged deeply entrenched views of Jewish subordination embedded in Christian thought and premodern laws.[176] In France, the social mobility of Jews and their successful integration into state institutions for example sparked antisemitic backlash: 'Despite the acquisition of citizenship and political participation, the Jew was still widely viewed as the quintessential foreigner

[171] In Masuzawa, *Invention of World Religions*, p. 177.

[172] John M. Efron, *Defenders of the Race. Jewish Doctors and Race Science in Fin-De-Siècle Europe* (New Haven; London: Yale University Press, 1994).

[173] Cheyette and Valman, 'Liberalism and Antisemitism', pp. 12–13.

[174] On Jewish self-racialisation as the Hebrew race in the United States, see Goldstein, *Price of Whiteness*.

[175] Neil MacMaster, *Racism in Europe 1870–2000* (Basingstoke; New York: Palgrave, 2001), p. 96.

[176] Teter, *Christian Supremacy*, p. 182.

who promoted new ideas that clashed with French tradition'.[177] At the centenary of the Revolution, those critical of the changes brought about by the Revolution mobilised old tropes of Jewish subversiveness and accused Jews of orchestrating the Revolution as an attempt to gain control over the country with the Catholic newspaper *La Croix* calling it 'the Semitic centenary'.[178] While the Catholic Church resented Jewish equality as a challenge to its dominance, for others, Jews embodied capitalism and the unsettling challenges of modernity.[179] The infamous Dreyfus Affair placed Jews at the centre of a debate about the national identity of France with antisemites distributing imagery of Jews as hook-nosed foreigners and capitalists.[180]

Antisemitism in France, much as elsewhere in Europe, enabled the contradictory projection of all kinds of ills and anxieties of modernity onto Jews who became associated simultaneously with capitalism and socialism, with rootless cosmopolitanism and national particularism, but also with 'godless' secularism by the Christian confessions who saw their influence dwindling.[181] For some French thinkers, Magda Teter notes, modernisation constituted the Judaization of French society.[182] Germany took the racial politics to a horrendous extreme, enshrining a racial notion of Jewishness into the infamous Nuremberg laws, and murdering more than six million Jews and millions of other people deemed inferior. Pseudoscientific racism, Neil MacMaster argues, offered the lure of a rational technique to identify the disguised Other who was masquerading as one of 'us' through assimilation, conversion, and economic integration – 'but his true nature was irrevocably stamped in biology, to be revealed by the scalpel, the microscope and the anthropologist's callipers'.[183]

Even in the colonies where their fair skin allowed Jews to enjoy most if not all of the legal and social privileges of Whiteness, race

177 Hyman, *Jews of Modern France*, p. 96.

178 Hyman, *Jews of Modern France*, p. 96.

179 Hyman, *Jews of Modern France*, pp. 96–97.

180 For a summary of the events of the Dreyfus Affair, see Hyman, *Jews of Modern France*, chapter 6.

181 Weir, 'The Specter of "Godless Jewry"', pp. 821–22. Protestants and Catholics did not only accuse Jews of promoting secularism to the detriment of Christians. For example, Catholics accused Protestants of promoting a dangerous secularism, see Greenberg, 'Is Religious Freedom Protestant?'.

182 Teter, *Christian Supremacy*, p. 190.

183 Neil MacMaster, *Racism in Europe 1870–2000* (Basingstoke; New York: Palgrave, 2001), p. 96.

continued to haunt them. In Australia, attempts to strengthen a fledgling national identity by tying it to a racial notion of 'Britishness' began to challenge the status of Jews, whose identity did not easily fit into categories of race and descent that came to underpin Australia's migration regime. In the late nineteenth century, fear of an influx of impoverished Russian Jews led to a surge of antisemitic discourse and marked the beginning of an ambivalent racialisation of Jews that reflected the racialisation of Eastern European Jews in Europe. While the highly assimilated Anglo-Jewry were accepted as White and British, the less-assimilated Jews from Eastern Europe seemed to constitute a different case. Although they shared the same faith as Anglo-Jews, racially they were viewed as somewhere in between 'Asiatic' and 'European'.[184] The intersection of religion and race in constructions of Jewishness also troubled the so-called White Australia Policy that underpinned Australia's migration law regime. The White Australia Policy describes a set of policies that, since the introduction of the *Immigration Restriction Act* in 1901, effectively prevented persons of non-European descent from migrating to Australia until these policies were gradually dismantled by 1973.[185] The policy's aim was to legally secure Australia's identity as a predominantly White nation by preserving an Anglo-Celtic majority and thereby raising complicated questions about the Whiteness of Jews from Russia and the Middle East. Were those Jews as White as their British kin? Or were those Jews in fact 'Asiatic' who just happened to share the same faith as Australian Anglo-Jewry? Under the White Australia Policy, Jews posed a racial conundrum.[186]

Ambivalences about Jewish migration surged when European Jews sought refuge in Australia from Nazi Germany. Many Australians were highly wary of Jewish migration to the country, which they saw as threatening the Australian way of life and as unwanted competition in the labour and housing markets. The media fuelled anxieties over Jewish refugees taking away jobs from returning ex-servicemen[187] and

184 Jon Stratton, *Coming Out Jewish* (London: Routledge, 2000), pp. 195–219.

185 The German Jewish journalist Egon Kisch was a prominent 'victim' of the policy that was not only deployed to bar non-Wwhite people from entering but also to prevent politically undesired visitors. Kisch eventually managed to enter Australia.

186 The relationship between Jewishness and Whiteness has been studied in much more detail in the context of the United States where Jews became 'White by law' and therefore citizens. See, for example, Goldstein (2006).

187 Suzanne D. Rutland, 'Postwar Anti-Jewish Refugee Hysteria: A Case of Racial or Religious Bigotry?', *Journal of Australian Studies* 27, no. 77 (2003): 69–79, pp. 72–73.

portrayed Jews as unable to integrate, as sticking together, and 'clannish in their behaviour'.[188] Moreover, fears radiated that Jewish migration would undermine Australian culture and its ties to Christianity. Media and public discourse depicted Jews as 'godless people, lacking in moral principles and threatening to Christianity'.[189] Australia's anglicised Jewish community too was sceptical of the newly arrived, seeing them as a threat to their own assimilated yet somewhat precarious status.[190] At the same time, Jewish welfare organisations resisted any government attempts to define Jews as a race for the purpose of migration law as it would have closed the gates of Australian Whiteness to Jewish migrants.[191] Between 1939 and 1953, quotas were placed on Jewish passengers travelling to Australia, with the quota affecting anyone belonging to the 'Hebrew race' and 'Hebrew faith'.[192] By collapsing race and religion in definitions of Jewishness, the quota overcame the uncertainties around Jewish identity in order to restrict the migration of both religious and secular Jews. Despite these suspicions, Australia accepted more Holocaust survivors per capita than any other nation apart from Israel.[193]

AMBIVALENCE POST-EMANCIPATION

During the period of emancipation, Susannah Heschel writes, Jewish thinkers were well aware that 'the "secularization" of Europe was a modernization of Christian commitments, not a repudiation of them'.[194] As this chapter has explored, the modern debate about Jewish equal rights and citizenship did indeed not only draw from older theological narratives about the inferior nature of Jews and their lack of trustworthiness and loyalty but also reflected a deep-seated anxiety and suspicion towards the assimilability and, ultimately, equality of Jews. This anxiety and suspicion echoed the ambivalent construction of 'the

188 Rutland, 'Postwar Anti-Jewish Refugee Hysteria', p. 76.
189 Rutland, 'Postwar Anti-Jewish Refugee Hysteria', p. 76.
190 Suzanne D. Rutland, *Edge of the Diaspora: Two Centuries of Jewish Settlement in Australia* (Rose Bay: Brandl & Schlesinger, 1997), 184–85.
191 Jon Stratton, 'Whiteness, Morality and Christianity in Australia', *Journal of Intercultural Studies* 37, no. 1 (2016): 17–32, p. 60.
192 Rutland, 'Postwar Anti-Jewish Refugee Hysteria', p. 78.
193 International Holocaust Remembrance Alliance, www.holocaustremembrance.com/news-archive/reflecting-holocaust-remembrance-australia.
194 Heschel, 'Jews and Christianity', p. 1065.

Jew' at the intersection of religion and race that had already begun during the late medieval period when Western Christendom had consolidated its power and influence over Western Europe. During the late medieval and early modern periods, both canon and secular laws contributed to gradually turning the theological argument of Jewish inferiority into a social status that sought to ensure the subordination of Jews vis-à-vis Christians. Even if the implementation of such laws remained at times uneven and limited, Christian ambivalence thereby entered a mutually constitutive relationship with law, in which prior religious ideas and a legislated social status began to amplify and transform each other, such as when secular laws implemented the papal requirement to wear the badge and to physically segregate Jews and Christians, which emphasised Jewish untrustworthiness and danger to the rest of the population. Certainly, Christian ambivalence was never the only ideological force as it intersected with the political ambitions of secular and ecclesiastical authorities and met the complex realities of Jews and Christians living alongside each other on the ground, yet it offered a powerful ideological narrative for these and other pursuits.

Over time, this interaction between law and the ideas of Christian superiority created a cultural repertoire that underpinned not only social perceptions of Jews but also bled into the secular legal imagination and gained normative force, such as through legislation during the period of emancipation. The influence of the Church had waned in comparison to earlier periods, yet essential elements of Christian ambivalence that constituted Jews as inferior and problematic presence continued to underpin the emancipation debate as a cultural repertoire and rendered Judaism in need of civilising reform. Even if this often legally mandated transformation was not called conversion, it still expected Jews to accept Christo-centric norms and therefore affirmed the idea of Christianity as superior by setting the benchmark for 'religion'. Moreover, this imposition created tensions around Jewishness that have endured into post-emancipatory times and play out in our present when the public aspects of Jewishness are rendered problematic. Indeed, as David Sorkin argues, emancipation is an 'interminable process'[195] that remains ongoing even today.

At first glance, it may seem that questions of religious difference have now moved from Jews to Muslims. The period after 1945 not

[195] Sorkin, *Jewish Emancipation*, p. 12.

only saw the founding of the state of Israel but also a gradual shift in state and social attitudes towards Jews. Western states began committing to the fight against antisemitism, public expression of antisemitic resentment has become increasingly taboo, and major challenges to Jewish legal equality have subsided. Instead, the focus has shifted to another religious Other – Muslims. Contemporary debates about the presence of Islam in the West now rehearse many of the earlier arguments made against the emancipation of Jews by presenting Islam as an illegitimate political religion and Muslim religiosity as backward and incompatible with liberal values and hence in need of reform and secularisation.[196] However, contemporary Muslim questions have not simply succeeded Jewish questions. In France, Ethan Katz for example observes how in conversations about Muslims – the country's 'current, undisputed ethnic and religious Other' – Jewish difference resurfaces too. It is Jews' alleged communitarianism, their supposed loyalty to another nation state, and their insistence on 'outmoded, embodied religious rituals'.[197] These embodied rituals mark Jews as different from Christians and as more than just a 'Mosaic faith'. As suspicious 'excesses' of Jewishness, these embodied practices point to the unresolved tensions of the conditional integration of Jewishness as a private faith and the challenges that Jewish difference still poses for hegemonic projects as they play out in Western law.

[196] For a discussion of some of the similarities, see, for example, Sara R. Farris, 'From the Jewish Question to the Muslim Question. Republican Rigorism, Culturalist Differentialism and Antinomies of Enforced Emancipation', *Constellations* 21, no. 2 (2014): 296–307.

[197] Ethan B. Katz, 'Where Do the Hijab and the Kippah Belong? On Being Publicy Jewish or Muslim in Post-Hebdo France', *Jewish History* 32, no. 1 (2018): 99–114, p. 100.

CHAPTER THREE

CONTENTIOUS CUT

Male Circumcision, Christian Ambivalence, and Children's Rights

In December 2012, a group of men, dressed in white suits and blood-stained pants, gathered in Berlin. In the previous weeks, posters had appeared at bus stops and other public sites in the city, showing a little boy crossing his hands across his pants. The emotive image was accompanied by the text, 'My body belongs to me! Forced circumcision is wrong – also when it concerns boys.' The posters and the men expressed their discontent with a recently passed amendment to the German Civil Code that affirmed parents' right to circumcise their sons for non-medical reasons. The German parliament had drafted the new provision to remedy an earlier court decision, in which a judge had found religious male circumcision to constitute a criminal assault. The Berlin protest forms part of a growing movement of activists who protest against what they perceive to be a mutilation of a non-consenting boy's body. In the United States, an anti-circumcision movement formed during the 1980s in order to challenge the positive views held about the procedure. The so-called 'intactivists' rally against the practice, urging to 'accept the intact male body as the normal body'.[1] In 2011, an American intactivist group called MGM *Bill* (Male Genital Mutilation Bill) brought a ban to the ballot in San Francisco after collecting 12,000 signatures. But the measure had to be withdrawn from the ballot as it did not fall within the jurisdiction of the city to regulate medical procedures.[2]

[1] See www.intactamerica.org.

[2] Mikaela Conley, 'Proposed Circumcision Ban Struck from San Francisco Ballot', *ABC News*, 29 July 2011.

In several continental European countries, political parties have joined activists in demanding a ban on the practice. In 2018, both Denmark[3] and Iceland[4] discussed possible laws that would criminalise the actions of parents who have their sons circumcised. A year earlier, one of Norway's governing parties called for a ban on circumcision for boys under sixteen years old.[5] In 2013, the Parliamentary Assembly of the Council of Europe issued a resolution that stressed the right of children to physical integrity, listing the circumcision of young boys for religious reasons as a violation of that right.[6] Earlier in 2011, the Dutch Royal Society of Medicine urged politicians to end the practice, and in 2019, the country's Health Ministry accused two popular circumcisers of breaking the law when performing circumcisions.[7] In Australia, several state law commissions have suggested a stricter legal approach to circumcision, albeit to date unsuccessfully.[8] Although none of these legal initiatives has so far led to a ban, they indicate a shifting climate for a practice that for a long time had either been embraced, as in the United States, or tolerated, as in continental Europe.

This is the first of two chapters concerned with the Jewish practice of infant male circumcision. In this chapter, I trace the history of circumcision as a trope for Jewish difference in European Christian thought and consider its symbolic role in debates about the legal equality of Jews. Christian thinkers spent much time pondering Jewish circumcision and what it told them about what they saw as the carnal, particularistic, and anachronistic nature of Jews. Apart from constituting a trope for what differentiated Jews from Christians, the

[3] Associated Press, 'Danish Parliament to Consider Becoming First Country to Ban Circumcision of Boys', *Independent*, 3 June 2018.

[4] Harriett Sherwood, 'Iceland Law to Outlaw Male Circumcision Sparks Row over Religious Freedom', *The Guardian*, 18 February 2018.

[5] Rachel Revesz, 'Norwegian Ruling Party Votes to Ban Circumcision for Men under 16 Years', *Independent*, 8 May 2017.

[6] Parliamentary Assembly of the Council of Europe, Res. 1952 (2013), available from https://assembly.coe.int/nw/xml/XRef/Xref-XML2HTML-en.asp?fileid=20174&lang=en.

[7] Cnaan Liphshiz, 'Netherlands Health Ministry Says Jewish Cirucmcisers Are Breaking the Law', *The Times of Israel*, 31 May 2019.

[8] Roger Collier, 'Tasmania Moving toward Circumcision Ban', *CMAJ: Canadian Medical Association Journal*, 184, no. 13 (2012): E690. Queensland Law Reform Commission, 'Circumcision of Male Infants. Research Paper', December 1993, available from www.qlrc.qld.gov.au/__data/assets/pdf_file/0008/372068/mp06.pdf.

bodily sign eventually became enmeshed in discussions about the possibility of Jewish emancipation where it offered a site to debate the fitness of Jews to become citizens. However, regardless of how much Christians disdained circumcision, they mostly respected the Jewish right to circumcise and due to a curious twist of history some Western societies eventually even embraced circumcision themselves. Today, circumcision has emerged as a contemporary human rights issue and I explore the legacy of Christian ambivalence in contemporary calls for a ban on the practice in the name of children's rights and gender equality.[9]

CIRCUMCISION IN THE JEWISH TRADITION

For millennia, societies have engaged in the practice of male circumcision, making it one of the oldest and most common surgeries worldwide. The Greek historian Herodotus, who lived in the fifth century BCE (before the Common Era), assumed its origins in ancient Egypt. Artwork in Egyptian tombs dating back to around 2,400 BCE indeed shows a circumcision being performed on a standing adult man. It is estimated that today around 30 per cent of men worldwide are circumcised. While circumcision can be performed for therapeutical reasons, such as for treating phimosis (the non-retractability of the foreskin), the vast majority of circumcisions occur for non-medically indicated reasons such as religion, culture, social norms, aesthetics, and ideas about general health and hygiene. Muslims, who form the largest circumcising group, derive their obligation to circumcise from the Sunnah, the sayings and teachings of the Prophet Mohammed. In Africa, many ethnic groups, such as the Xhosa, practise circumcision as a rite of passage into manhood. For a number of Australian indigenous communities, circumcision has also been an important cultural ceremony. The procedure is also popular in South Korea, where

[9] Another set of cases involving the practice concerns parental disputes about the circumcision of their children, especially in the context of interfaith couples. These cases concern the best interest of individual children and do not necessarily question its compatibility with human rights. However, as Didi Herman and Suhraiya Jivraj have shown, ideas of racialised difference and non-Christian Otherness remain part of the judicial reasoning even if the legality of the practice itself is not in question; see Suhraiya Jivraj and Didi Herman, 'It Is Difficult for a White Judge to Understand: Orientalism, Racialisation, and Christianity in English Child Welfare Cases', *Child and Family Law Quarterly* 21, no. 3 (2009): 283–308.

it became associated with economic progress,[10] and in the United States, where it has been one of the most frequently performed surgeries since the early twentieth century.[11]

In the Jewish tradition, circumcision holds a central place: 'The sign of circumcision is, as I think so important, that I could persuade myself that it alone would preserve the [Jewish] nation forever', wrote Baruch Spinoza.[12] The Jewish philosopher who lived in seventeenth-century Amsterdam was well aware of the unifying nature of male circumcision, the rite that held together the dispersed Jewish communities all over the world across space and time outside a national home. Until today, it is one of the few, if not the only, commands that even non-observant Jews almost universally still observe. While no exact numbers exist, it is estimated that around 98 per cent of Jewish Israeli men are circumcised.[13] Estimations are similar for Great Britain, with 99 per cent of Jewish males circumcised[14] and 98 per cent in the United States.[15] Jews trace their obligation to circumcise back to Abraham, the first Jewish man to undergo the procedure in the Jewish tradition. In Genesis 17: 9–14, the Torah tells that

> God said to Abraham, As for you, you are to keep my covenant, you and your seed after you, throughout their generations. This is my covenant that you are to keep, between me and you and your seed after you: every male among you shall be circumcised. You shall circumcise the flesh of your foreskin, so that it may serve as a sign of the covenant between me and you. At eight days old, every male among you shall be circumcised, throughout your generations, including one who is born in the house, or acquired with money from any foreigner, who is not of your seed. One who is born in your house, and one who is acquired with

[10] Myung-Geol Pang and DaiSik Kim, 'Extraordinarily High Rates of Male Circumcision in South Korea: History and Underlying Causes', *British Journal of Urology International* 89, no. 1 (2008): 48–54.

[11] David L. Gollaher, 'From Ritual to Science: The Medical Transformation of Circumcision in America', *Journal of Social History* 28, no. 1 (1994): 5–36, p. 5.

[12] Benedictus Spinoza, *The Chief Works of Benedict De Spinoza: Volume I: Introduction, Tractatus Theologico-Politicus, Tractatus Politicus*. Translated by Robert Harvey Monro Elwes (London: George Bell & Sons, 1891), 12.

[13] Ilan Youngster and Ben Z. Katz, 'Tradition … Tradition', *Journal of the Pediatric Infectious Diseases Society* 4, no. 2 (2014): 132–33, p. 132.

[14] Sangeeta S. Dave et al., 'Male Circumcision in Britain: Findings from a National Probability Sample Survey', *Sexually Transmitted Infections* 79, no. 6 (2003): 499–500.

[15] UNAIDS and WHO, *Neonatal and Child Male Circumcision: A Global Review* (Geneva, 2010), p. 3.

> your money, must be circumcised; and my covenant shall be in your flesh for an everlasting covenant. But a foreskinned male who does not circumcise the flesh of his foreskin, that person shall be cut off from his people, he has violated my covenant.

In the biblical story, Abraham fulfils God's command immediately. After swiftly circumcising himself, he cuts the foreskin of all male members of his household, which was said to have numbered more than 300 members. The cutting of the foreskin sealed the covenant – hence the Hebrew name, brit milah, with 'brit' meaning 'covenant' and 'milah' meaning 'circumcision': The covenant of circumcision. The Yiddish shorthand 'bris' is also often used to refer to the practice.[16]

The Torah itself does not state any other reason for circumcision other than that it is the sign of the covenant. Jewish thinkers throughout the time have discussed this question and arrived at a number of different, sometimes contradictory, explanations for this divine command. Many medieval Jewish thinkers, much like their Christian counterparts, were rather sceptical about sexuality, and they tried to make sense of the practice as a way to foster sexual modesty. In his *Guide for the Perplexed*, Moses Maimonides, a Sephardic Torah scholar and physician who lived and worked in the twelfth century in Morocco and Egypt, notes that circumcision brings 'about a decrease in sexual intercourse and a weakening of the organ in question, so that this activity be diminished and the organ be in as quiet a state as possible'.[17] According to this view, the purpose of circumcision was to reduce the faculty for sexual excitement and pleasure and to prevent desire and lust that go beyond what is necessary for procreation. Human intervention was necessary to achieve sexual moderation. Other Talmudic interpretations of circumcision understand the cutting of the foreskin as a way to create further perfection. A midrashic anecdote recounts how Turnus Rufus, the Roman Governor of Palestine, once challenged Rabbi Akiba with this question: 'If God dislikes a man having a foreskin, why did He create him with one in the first place?'[18] Rabbinic reasoning

[16] Brit is the Sephardic pronunciation, but the Ashkenazi pronunciation *bris* is also common, in particular in the United States.

[17] Moses Maimonides, *The Guide of the Perplexed*. Translated by Shlomo Pines (Chicago: University of Chicago Press, 1963), p. 609.

[18] Louis Jacobs, *The Jewish Religion: A Companion* (Oxford; New York: Oxford University Press, 1995), 81. The Midrash is a genre of rabbinic literature containing early commentaries on and interpretations of the Written Torah and the Oral Torah.

compares the foreskin to a stalk on a fig or a fingernail in need of a manicure.[19] The penis needs some human intervention by cutting off the foreskin as much as the fig needs the plucking off the stalk in order to be enjoyed: 'Whatever was created in the first six days requires further preparation, for example mustard needs sweetening, vetches need sweetening, wheat needs grinding, and man too needs improvement.'[20]

Theological explanations alone cannot account for the remarkable commitment that Jews have shown towards the practice of circumcision over the course of time. Rather, the experience of minority existence and life in the diaspora where Jewish cultural survival was often threatened or precarious, facing pressure to assimilate, strengthened the status of the practice. Circumcision marked Jews as different in non-circumcising societies, a mark that was often the target of scorn, derision, and ridicule. Instead of surrendering to cultural pressure, the rite came to signify perseverance and pride, as Elizabeth Wyner Mark suggests: 'There is an element of defiance, a refusal to feel ashamed, a proud proclamation of Jewish difference that disempowers the mockers and the Jew-haters.'[21]

CIRCUMCISION IN THE CHRISTIAN TRADITION

The Jewish body has figured prominently in the non-Jewish Western imagination. There have been myths about the Jewish nose and the Jewish voice, about the Jew's feet and gait, about Jewish male menstruation, about Jewish odour, about the Jewish mind, about Jewish sickness, and of course, about the Jew's circumcised penis. Although circumcision is not unique to Jews, the body of the circumcised male Jew has always been an image that is 'crucial to the very understanding of the Western image of the Jew at least since the advent of Christianity'.[22] Even before the rise of Christianity, the absence of the foreskin had already functioned as a rich metaphor for the difference

[19] Shaye J. D. Cohen, *Why Aren't Jewish Women Circumcised? Gender and Covenant in Judaism* (Berkeley; Los Angeles; London: University of California Press, 2005), p. 149.

[20] In Cohen, *Why Aren't Jewish Women Circumcised?*, p. 149.

[21] Elizabeth Wyner Mark, 'Crossing the Gender Divide: Public Ceremonies, Private Parts, Mixed Feelings', in *The Covenant of Circumcision: New Perspectives on an Ancient Jewish Rite*, ed. Elizabeth Wyner Mark (Hanover; London: Brandeis University Press, 2003), xiii–xxvi, p. xxiv.

[22] Gilman, *The Jew's Body*, p. 5.

of the Jewish male in Greek and Roman societies. Circumcision is an ambivalent sign. It signifies 'the positive assertion of a Jewish refusal to surrender to antisemitism', while also constituting a 'physical marking of possibly stigmatizing difference' for Jews living among non-circumcising societies.[23]

Not all non-Jewish perceptions of circumcision were derogatory or hostile. Rather, non-Jewish attitudes towards circumcision often reflected broader social, cultural, and political relationships between Jews and the societies in which they lived. Pressure to assimilate was nonetheless often directed at this visible and overt sign of Jewish collective identity that marked Jews as a people 'out of their correct "space" and "time"'.[24] Christianity has not been the only cultural force in shaping Western attitudes towards circumcision. As early as in Greco-Roman antiquity, circumcision was seen as one of the Jews' most distinctive practices and functioned as a visible mark of their cultural and political particularity. For Roman satirists during the first century, circumcision became a synonym for Judaism. While Horace spoke of the 'circumcised Jews', Persius called Jews 'the circumcised'.[25] The missing foreskin inscribed the Jews' Otherness into the body at a time when societies valued public nudity and the perfection of the unaltered body.[26]

Whereas Romans seemed to have perceived of the practice as strange or odd, for Greeks, the sign of the Jewish male had a stronger political symbolism. The First Book of Maccabees records how Greek emperor Antiochus Epiphanes sought to Hellenise ancient Judea under his rule during the earlier part of the second century BCE. In order to promote Hellenic culture among Jews through the spreading of Hellenic standards of beauty in which a cut foreskin was the source of scorn and ridicule, nude physical exercise was encouraged in Judean lands as a way to assimilate Jews. The strategy had

23 Éva Kovács and Júlia Vajda, 'Circumcision in Hungary after the Shoa', in *The Covenant of Circumcision. New Perspectives on an Ancient Jewish Rite*, ed. Elizabeth Wyner Mark (Hanover; London: Brandeis University Press, 2003), 177–87, p. 187.

24 Gilman, *The Jew's Body*, p. 91.

25 John G. Gager, *The Origins of Anti-Semitism. Attitudes toward Judaism in Pagan and Christian Antiquity* (New York; Oxford: Oxford University Press, 1985), p. 56.

26 Ra'anan Abusch, 'Circumcision and Castration under Roman Law in the Early Empire', in *The Covenant of Circumcision. New Perspectives on an Ancient Jewish Rite*, ed. Elizabeth Wyner Mark (Hanover; London: Brandeis University Press, 2003), 75–86, pp. 75–76.

some success. The First Book of Maccabees tells how a gymnasium in the Hellenic fashion was installed in Judea's capital Jerusalem by 'wicked men' who 'made themselves uncircumcised, renounced the holy covenant, intermingled among the heathen and became the slaves of wrongdoing'.[27] But the undoing of the foreskin by a couple of aspiring Jewish athletes was not enough for Hellenic political aspirations and social pressure gave way to the force of law. Antiochus eventually banned the observance of Jewish law, such as the laws of Shabbat and circumcision, by threat of death in the hope to ultimately control the Jews who continued to follow their own laws and thereby challenged the sovereignty of the Hellenic ruler. Banning circumcision amounted to a 'symbolic denial of Judaism'.[28] Those who resisted the Greek ruler's command paid a terrible price, as told in I Maccabees, 1: 60–61:

> The women who had their sons circumcised they put to death according to decree, hanging their babes from their mothers' necks and executing also their husbands and the man who had performed the circumcision.

In the Roman Empire, the mark of circumcision was not a target of assimilatory pressure but rather served as a convenient indicator of tax duties. Roman authorities inspected the genitals of some Jewish men to collect the *fiscus Judaicus*, a tax specifically aimed at Jews that was introduced following the Jewish-Roman War from 64 until 73 CE, during which Jews had rebelled against the Roman Empire. While perhaps administratively convenient, Romans nonetheless regarded circumcision as suspect. The increased popularity of eunuchs and the practice of castration in the Roman Empire drew attention to Jewish circumcision, which the Roman elites understood *on par* with genital mutilation.[29] Whether Jewish circumcision was later banned alongside castration under the Roman ruler Hadrian remains a contested issue among historians.[30] For those in favour of such an interpretation, the Jewish Bar Kokhba revolt under the messianic military leader Simon Bar Kokhba between 132 and 135 CE

[27] I Maccabees, 1:11–15.

[28] Lawrence Hoffman, *Covenant of Blood. Circumcision and Gender in Rabbinic Judaism* (Chicago; London: University of Chicago Press, 1996), p. 9.

[29] Abusch, 'Circumcision and Castration', p. 76.

[30] Alfredo M. Rabello, 'The Ban on Circumcision as a Cause of Bar Kokhba's Rebellion', *Israel Law Review* 29, no. 1–2 (1995): 176–214.

was a direct response to the alleged ban on brit milah and the revolt aimed at the restoration of Jewish legal authority, including the obligation to circumcise. Far from a purely private sign, circumcision also symbolised Jewish sovereignty and self-determination.

Circumcision had also been the dividing symbol in early Christendom's attempt to distinguish itself from Judaism. The letters of Paul set the tone for centuries of Christian ambivalence towards the practice, which was seen as a powerful boundary marker between Jews and early Christians.[31] Paul was disturbed by the insistence of historical Judaism on bodily difference. For him, true Jewishness – what would later be called Christianity – was about spirituality and inwardness and not about corporeal signs. Jonathan Boyarin argues that 'the true cultural issue dividing Christians from Jews by the second century was the significance of bodily membership in a kin-group for religious life'.[32] Emphasising the significance of spiritual circumcision, Paul wrote in Romans 2:28–29:

> For he is not a real Jew who is one outwardly, nor is true circumcision something external and physical. He is a Jew who is one inwardly, and real circumcision is a matter of the heart, spiritual and not literal. This praise is not from men but from God.

While the shunning of circumcision was partly pragmatic as it could discourage potential converts to Christendom, it also served as a symbolic boundary marker between Jews and Christians. By the end of the eleventh century, the growing association of Europe and Christianity imagined Christendom as a society that transcended ethnic and regional differences. Jewish refusal to accept the Christian truth rendered them increasingly problematic in this unified vision – and circumcision embodied this refusal. Medieval Christian thinkers conceptualised circumcision as proof of Judaism's incompatibility with reason and its preoccupation with material over spiritual matters.[33] The denigration of circumcision served to affirm the Christian truth.

The sign of circumcision that marked the Jewish body as distinct also featured in the medieval racialisation of Jews that pictured

[31] Cohen, *Why Aren't Jewish Women Circumcised?*, pp. 68–69; see also Boyarin, *A Radical Jew*.

[32] Boyarin, *A Radical Jew*, p. 36.

[33] Leonard B. Glick, *Marked in Your Flesh. Circumcision from Ancient Judea to Modern America* (Oxford; New York: Oxford University Press, 2005), pp. 86–90.

Jews as possessing 'diseased and debased bodies' and 'inferior bloodlines'.[34] Circumcision as an embodied religious rite was perceived as polluting and undermining the physical and collective wholeness of Christian Europe.[35] Not all Christian representations of circumcision, however, were negative. Christian theology for example grappled with the meaning of Jesus' circumcision, a rite that signified Jewish particularism and Jewish inability to understand true spirituality. For Christian thinkers, the circumcision of Jesus had to be different: It foreshadowed the pain and sacrifice of his Crucifixion but also testified to his humanity.[36] Some Christian medical practitioners pondered circumcision's usefulness for personal hygiene, sometimes even recommending the procedure to Christian men afflicted with disease. However, these interpretations did not displace theological interpretations of circumcision as evidence of the Jewish man's carnality and sensuality.[37]

When Spain expelled its remaining practising Jews in 1492, the Edict of Expulsion also referred to circumcision as one of the intolerable 'Judaising' behaviours that was seen as causing 'great damage to the Christians'. Justifying their expulsion from the Spanish Kingdom, the Edict complained about 'Jews, who try to always achieve by whatever ways and means possible to subvert and to draw away faithful Christians from our holy Catholic faith and to separate them from it … trying to circumcise them and their children…'.[38]

Disappointed in the failure of Jews to convert, Martin Luther in his Pamphlet *On the Jews and Their Lies* from 1543 also attacked Jewish circumcision as a symbol of ethnic pride and Jewish arrogance towards uncircumcised Christians, arguing that Jews 'disdain, despise, and curse the foreskin on us as an ugly abomination, which prevents us from becoming God's people, while their circumcision, they claim, effects all'.[39] However, Jews are 'blind, ignorant miserable people' who 'do not see that God condemns their uncircumcised heart … and thereby condemns their physical circumcision with

[34] Thomas, 'Racial Formation of Medieval Jews', p. 1745.

[35] Westerduin, 'Questioning Religio/Secular Temporalities'.

[36] Glick, *Marked in Your Flesh*, pp. 93–95.

[37] Irven M. Resnick, *Marks of Distinction. Christian Perceptions of Jews in the High Middle Ages* (Washington, DC: Catholic University of America Press, 2012), p. 78.

[38] In Jane S. Gerber, *Jews of Spain. A History of the Sephardic Experience* (New York: The Free Press, 1994), p. 286.

[39] In Glick, *Marked in Your Flesh*, p. 92.

their boasting and their prayer'.[40] Luther rearticulates the Genesis narrative through a Christian lens, accusing Jews of failing to see what God truly had in mind: That spiritual circumcision had long replaced physical circumcision.[41]

Circumcision also linked Jews, the enemy within, with Muslims, the enemy outside. Medieval Christian thinkers perceived of both Jews and Muslims as people who favoured the carnal over the spiritual in both belief and practice, thereby asserting the superiority of Christian Europe vis-à-vis its two Others.[42] Circumcision became enmeshed in a broader project of constructing distinctions between Christians on the one hand and Jews and Muslims on the other, between Occident and Orient. Christians feared forced circumcisions. As early as in the eleventh century when the crusades sought to conquer Jerusalem, Pope Urban alleged that the Muslims, who were in control of Jerusalem at the time, would 'circumcise the Christians, and the blood of the circumcision they either spread upon the alters or pour into the vases of the baptismal font'.[43] Circumcision spread polluted blood into sacred Christian spaced, thereby defiling them.[44] The blood libel also involved fantasies about circumcision, suggesting that Jews first circumcised their innocent Christian victims before murdering them.[45] In Christian belief, both Jews and Muslims were bloodthirsty Others and the supersessionary tropes of Jewish carnality also became applied to Muslims.[46] In his 1589/1590 play, Christopher Marlowe's Jew of Malta explains the Jewish–-Muslim fellowship to his Muslim slave Ithamore by reference to their shared bodily mark:

Make account of me
As of thy fellow; we are villains both:
Both circumcised, we hate Christians both.[47]

[40] In Glick, *Marked in Your Flesh*, p. 92.
[41] Glick, *Marked in Your Flesh*, pp. 92–93.
[42] Suzanne Conklin Akbari, 'Placing the Jews in Late Medieval English Literature', in *Orientalism and the Jews*, ed. Ivan Davidson Kalmar and Derek Jonathan Penslar (Hanover; London: Brandeis University Press, 2005), 32–50.
[43] In Suzanne Conklin Akbari, *Idols in the Past. European Representations of Islam and the Orient 1100–1450* (Ithaca; London: Cornell University Press, 2009), p. 237.
[44] Westerduin, 'Questioning Religio/Secular Temporalities', p. 147.
[45] Glick, *Marked in Your Flesh*, pp. 98–105.
[46] Boyarin, *The Unconverted Self*, p. 39.
[47] In Julia Reinhard Lupton, 'Othello Circumcised: Shakespeare and the Pauline Discourse of Nations', *Representations*, no. 57 (1997): 73–89, p. 83.

FROM THE 'THREAT OF CIRCUMCISION' TO 'GOOD SANITARIANS' IN THE ANGLO-WORLD

As European societies began debating Jewish emancipation and Jewish access to equal rights, they also turned their attention to circumcision – a mark that came to embody many of the concerns and anxieties but also the hopes this period aroused. While the right of Jews to circumcise their children was never really up for debate, the practice nonetheless offered European societies a site to discuss the feasibility, desirability, and conditions of Jewish integration into secular nation states still understood to be Christian, such as during the English Jew Bill debate in 1753 and the German circumcision debate in the 1840s. Yet, while in the German lands as in much the rest of continental Europe, circumcision maintained its status as a sign of Jewish religious and racial Otherness, in the English-speaking world, circumcision would go on an unlikely trajectory given the history of Christian disdain for circumcision and soon turn into an increasingly endorsed and celebrated practice, stripping the practice of its foreign character and thereby flattening differences between Jews and Christians.

During the debate about the naturalisation of wealthy foreign-born Jews in mid-eighteenth-century England, circumcision became served as a recurring motif in anti-Jewish media propaganda, predicting forced circumcisions of innocent English men once Jews had been naturalised and knife-yielding Jews slicing 'through the manhood of their English political allies'.[48] In the debates about the *Jewish Naturalization Act*[49] or, as it was known to its contemporaries, the so-called 'Jew Bill' in 1753, opponents of Jewish naturalisation invoked the rite of circumcision as a threatening symbol of Jewish political claims and national aspiration that would dispossess and emasculate Englishmen.[50] The Bill had been introduced to naturalise

[48] Madge Dresser, 'Minority Rites: The Strange History of Circumcision in English Thought', *Jewish Culture and History* 1, no. 1 (1998): 72–87, p. 74.

[49] An Act to Permit Persons Professing the Jewish Religion, To Be Naturalized by Parliament and for Other Purposes Therein Mentioned (1753), in: Paul Mendes-Flohr and Jehuda Reinharz (eds.), *The Jew in the Modern World. A Documentary History*, 2nd ed. (Oxford: Oxford University Press, 1995), pp. 27–28.

[50] The term 'Jew Bill' is not only derogatory but also misleading given that a bill refers to a proposal for a piece of legislation. The bill in question was in fact passed but contemporaries continued to refer to the Act by this name. I continue to use the name here as it is revealing about attitudes at the time.

the Sephardic merchants residing in England, who contributed significantly to its economy but due to their lack of naturalisation faced several legal disabilities, such as being unable to own land or ships and having to pay 'alien duties' on all imports that usually amounted to twice the standard tax rate.[51] Those born outside of England had two options: The Crown could grant them a status as denizens that freed them from some legal disabilities but still required them to pay the alien duties.[52] Full naturalisation was possible through a private Act of Parliament. However, a law from 1606 required communion in the Church of England and the swearing of an oath referring to the established religion as a prerequisite of naturalisation.[53]

The *Jewish Naturalization Act* was introduced to ease naturalisation and to catch up with naturalisation legislation in the British colonies in America by building on the *Plantation Act* from 1740. This Act had enabled all colonists, 'Foreign Protestants and Others', to become 'his Majesty's natural born subjects' after seven years of residency in English colonies without having to refer to Christianity in swearing their oaths.[54] Jews naturalised in the colonies under the *Plantation Act* were recognised as British subjects in England but faced the same disabilities as other non-Anglicans who were not allowed to vote or hold public office. The 'Jew Bill' only made a minor change to the requirements of naturalisation for Jews living in England and would have only affected a small number of Jews who would be able to apply to Parliament for naturalisation 'without receiving the Sacrament of the Lord's Supper'. Yet the reform elicited a host of larger questions about immigration in general but also about the legal status of Jews, their place in a Christian commonwealth, and whether they should be permitted to worship freely, a right at the time denied to Catholics and Protestant dissenters, such as Quakers and Baptists.[55]

[51] Alexander James Edmund Cockburn, *Nationality: Or the Law Relating to Subjects and Aliens, Considered with a View to Future Legislation* (London: William Ridgway, 1869), p. 151.

[52] Daniel Statt, 'The City of London and the Controversy over Immigration, 1660–1722', *The Historical Journal* 33, no. 1 (1990): 45–61.

[53] Sorkin, *Jewish Emancipation*, p. 382, fn. 16.

[54] An Act for Naturalizing Such Foreign Protestants and Others Therein Mentioned, As Are Settled, or Shall Settle, in Any of His Majesty's Colonies in America (19 March 1740), in: Mendes-Flohr and Reinharz, *The Jew in the Modern World*, pp. 21–22; see also the discussion in Sorkin, *Jewish Emancipation*, p. 72.

[55] Shapiro, *Shakespeare and the Jews*, p. 118.

Opponents feared that naturalised Jews would dominate the English economy and fantasised about the devastating impact the Bill would have on England's sovereignty and freedom, warning of a Jewish state run by the Sanhedrin that punished those who resisted circumcision with crucifixion.[56] Post-reformation England was well aware about what Paul had thought about circumcision, thanks to the efforts of Calvin and Luther to explain Paul's commentary. Moreover, rejecting Jewish circumcision had also allowed English Protestants to reject Catholicism because, as James Shapiro explains, '[b]y equating circumcision with the Law and its supersession by faith, English Protestants drew an analogy between Paul's rejection of circumcision and their repudiation of Catholicism's emphasis on justification through good work'.[57] Circumcision stood for the foreign nature of Jews and their unassimilability, and therefore gestured towards the larger question of the place of Jews in a Christian society.[58]

Both proponents and opponents of the Jew Bill also invoked political philosopher John Locke and his writings on toleration and Christianity for their purposes. In his *Letter of Toleration* from 1689, John Locke had expressed support for the integration of Jews into the Christian state. For some participants in the Jew Bill debate, defending Jews was a matter of defending a general principle of toleration, as postulated by Locke in his earlier writings. Yet, others invoked the association of England with Christianity, arguing that the common law required the English to be Christian and that 'our common law has all along from the beginning looked upon the Jews as aliens and incapable of being otherwise while Jews'.[59] In his later writings, influenced by his biblical studies, Locke's call for toleration turned into the hope of their conversion and restoration to Palestine because England could not be their home given its Christian character.[60] Indeed, other voices in the debate expressed concerns about the Bill and the naturalisation of Jews through the lens of England's role in aiding or undermining the fulfilment of biblical prophecy. Whereas some opponents of the Jew Bill feared that naturalisation would confirm Jewish unbelief and contradict their biblically demanded

[56] Dresser, 'Minority Rites', p. 76.

[57] Shapiro, *Shakespeare and the Jews*, p. 118.

[58] Glick, *Marked in Your Flesh*, p. 109.

[59] Quoted in Shapiro, *Shakespeare and the Jews*, p. 207.

[60] For a discussion of Locke's shifting attitude towards Jews, see Nabil I. Matar, 'John Locke and the Jews', *Journal of Ecclestial History* 44, no. 1 (1993): 45–62.

separation from Christians, some proponents saw the Bill as a catalyst for the conversion of Jews and their return to Palestine.[61]

Scholars such as Michael Ragussis and David Cesarani have emphasised the centrality of Protestant conversionism for England's often seemingly more favourable treatment of Jews compared to continental Europe.[62] From a conversionist perspective, welcoming Jews was a necessary first step towards their eventual conversion to Christianity. 'Protestant England, which was the bearer of the true form of Christianity', Cesarani writes, 'would welcome the Jews and, by exposing them to pure Christian forms, would win them over'.[63] The toleration of Jews also served to affirm notions of English-Protestant superiority vis-à-vis other Christian nations, particularly Catholic ones whose hostility to Jews was seen as hindering Jewish conversion to the true faith. The conversion of Jews in England via benevolent toleration was a crucial step for converting other heathens and the salvation of the world. Jews in England and their emancipation, Cesarani observes, 'served as a foil for Christian triumphalism', attesting to the superiority of Christianity.[64]

Jewish difference, however, was seen as more than just a religious difference to be managed in light of England's relationship with Christianity. It was a difference that ran perhaps even deeper. During the parliamentary debate about the repeal of the Jew Bill, the Duke of Bedford stated that the difference of Jews was even more profound than that of colonial slaves. While it would be possible to naturalise colonial slaves if they married a White person and professed to be Christians, the Duke explained, Jews 'will continue to be, and will consider themselves as a people quite distinct and separate from the ancient people of this island'.[65]

In the face of the public protest that blamed Jews for all kinds of ills, the law was indeed soon repealed again. Historians disagree on how to interpret the Jew Bill debate.[66] For some, it was about party

61 See Andrew Crome, 'The 1753 "Jew Bill" Controversy: Jewish Restoration to Palestine, Biblical Prophecy, and English National Identity', *English Historical Review* 130, no. 547 (2015): 1449–78.

62 Cesarani, 'British Jews'; Michael Ragussis, *Figures of Conversion. 'The Jewish Question' & English National Identity* (Durham; London: Duke University Press, 1995).

63 Cesarani, 'British Jews', p. 42.

64 Cesarani, 'British Jews', p. 40.

65 Shapiro, *Shakespeare and the Jews*, p. 208.

66 For a critical analysis of this debate between historians, see Shapiro, *Shakespeare and the Jews*, pp. 197–99.

politics that only used Jews to attack opponents but had little to do with the actual Jewish presence in England. For others, the episode is evidence of English antisemitism. The debate struck to the heart of a long-standing debate about immigration, naturalisation, toleration, and the association of English identity with Anglican faith. Although antisemitism in England never gained the same political currency as in Germany and the anti-Jewish sentiment stirred up by the Jew Bill did not translate into legal restrictions, there remained an ambivalence towards Jews that expected them to conform to 'homogenous Britishness' and to shed their cultural differences in 'the name of liberal tolerance'.[67] Jews in England certainly did not face the same adversity as Jews in part of continental Europe, but 'the Jew' remained one of the central figures and foils in constructions of English national identity, making references to Jews politically salient and powerful. These references could only be effective by playing to pre-existing ambivalences about the place of Jews. The Jew Bill offered a site at which some of these ambivalences surfaced by revealing a 'deep-seated hostility to Jews and fear of what their enhanced status might signify'[68] and, related to that, an anxiety about what it meant to be English 'if even a Jew could be English'.[69] Whereas the Jew Bill was repealed, the *Plantation Act* was not, reflecting the importance of Jewish merchants for the development of the colonies, which trumped fears of religious differences and Jewish wealth, issues that still mattered at home in England. Jews in England continued to face legal disabilities, including the right to hold office, which required the swearing of the requisite oath.

As England gradually dismantled the confessional state, it also removed disabilities, first from dissenting Protestants in 1828, and from Catholics in 1829. Although opponents of Jewish emancipation continued to invoke the necessity to protect the legislature of a Christian state,[70] civil disabilities for Jews were gradually from 1830 until in 1858, the *Jewish Relief Act* removed the requirement for 'any of Her Majesty's Subjects Professing the Jewish religion' to take an oath referring to Christianity as the true faith when entering Parliament.[71]

[67] Cheyette and Valman, 'Liberalism and Antisemitism', p. 4.
[68] Glick, *Marked in Your Flesh*, p. 107.
[69] Shapiro, *Shakespeare and the Jews*, p. 199.
[70] 'British Jews', p. 43.
[71] *Jewish Relief Act* (23 July 1858) in: Mendes-Flohr and Reinharz, *The Jew in the Modern World*, pp. 152–153. See also Sorkin (2019), pp. 210–12.

However, ambivalences about the place of Jews did not simply disappear and the ethos of utilitarianism continued to privilege Christian interests and accentuated Jewish difference, such as when the Factory Acts introduced Sunday closing laws during the 1860s.[72]

In the Jew Bill debate, circumcision had been a powerful trope for whipping up fears about Jewish influence. Yet, soon, the horror of masturbation and emerging theories of the origins of disease and other afflictions would lead the English as well as Americans to seek a solution in the previously shunned practice that had previously marked the Jewish male as both hypersexual and sexually deficient.[73] Victorian physicians and doctors in the United States began to promote the procedure for its alleged hygienic and moral benefits, for its curative effects for a number of diseases, and as a means to hamper masturbation, a dreaded moral crime of the time. During this period preoccupied with morals, masturbation was not only seen as a moral ailment but as a disease in itself and as the cause of a number of other diseases.[74]

In the late eighteenth century, physicians like the Swiss neurologist Samuel-Auguste Tissot had already argued that the loss of semen led to the waste of bodily energy, which was responsible for general debility, disturbance of the nerves, and deterioration of eyesight.[75] A cure was suggested: Circumcision. The obsessive concern about masturbation did not only target the foreskin as a source of moral evil. Some doctors, albeit controversially, promoted clitoridectomy as a means to tame female masturbation. But while this procedure was as quickly discredited as it had appeared, this did not end the popularity of male circumcision. The 'reflex theory' was discarded, but the newly embraced germ theory provided another justification for the cutting of the foreskin, which was perceived as a breeding ground for infection. Soon, circumcision also became the measure of choice to treat cancer and venereal diseases.[76] Physicians focused their efforts in

72 'British Jews', p. 45.

73 On the contradictory associations of Jewish masculinity and circumcision with hypersexuality and asexuality, see Noelle Gallagher, 'The Jew's Penis: Circumcision and Sexual Pathology in Eighteenth-Century England', *Medical Humanities* 49 (2023): 70–82.

74 Gollaher, 'From Ritual to Science', p. 8.

75 Ornella Moscucci, 'Clitoridectomy, Circumcision, and the Politics of Sexual Pleasure in Mid-Victorian Britain', in *Sexualities in Victorian Britain*, ed. Andrew H. Miller and James Eli Adams (Bloomington; Indianapolis: Indiana University Press, 1996), 60–78, p. 63.

76 Laura M. Carpenter, 'On Remedicalisation: Male Circumcision in the United States and Great Britain', *Sociology of Health & Illness* 32, no. 4 (2010): 613–30, p. 618.

particular on young boys. Since adult men were less likely to undergo the procedure, doctors opted instead for infant circumcision.[77]

The growing enthusiasm for circumcision also raised interest in the Jewish tradition of brit milah because Jews constituted the only consistently circumcised group who could provide evidence for the procedure's benefits. Reports stated lower rates of syphilis and penile cancer as well as less frequent masturbation among Jewish men and boys.[78] This difference was attributed to the absence of the foreskin. Soon circumcision was promoted as a prophylactic surgery, often with praising reference to the 'Hebrews'.[79] Norman Chapman, a neurologist in the United States, recommended the procedure to treat 'nervous affections' which he believed were caused by neglected congenital phimosis. Commending the Jews, he wrote in 1882: 'Moses was a good sanitarian, and if circumcision was more generally practised at the present day, I believe that we would hear far less of the pollutions and indiscretions of youth…'.[80] American physicians in particular praised the virtues of circumcision, a practice that, in their view, Jews had wisely installed as a divine command and that Christians, regrettably, had not adopted, perhaps to not scare away converts.[81] Yet, physicians in the English-speaking world, Jewish and non-Jewish alike, were nonetheless eager to distinguish their own practice of circumcision from brit milah, which they regarded as 'primitive, unsanitary, and potentially dangerous'.[82] They rejected in particular the practice of *metzitzah b'peh*, the oral sucking of the wound. Traditionally, Jewish male circumcision involves three steps: The cut of the foreskin (*milah*) is followed by *periah* (Hebrew for opening), the tearing of the underlying mucous membrane. Then the circumciser sucks the wound (*metzitzah b'peh*) and bandages it. Despite their enthusiasm for the practice, British and American doctors perceived this aspect of Jewish circumcision as repulsive and the source of infections.

Class was another factor for the rise of circumcision, since personal hygiene, robust health, and sexual restraint – the apparent benefits

[77] Robert Darby, 'Targeting Patients Who Cannot Object? Re-examining the Case for Non-therapeutic Infant Circumcision', *SAGE Open* 6, no. 2 (2016): 1–16, p. 2.

[78] Robert Darby, *A Surgical Temptation: The Demonization of the Foreskin and the Rise of Circumcision in Britain* (Chicago: University of Chicago Press, 2013), p. 7.

[79] Glick, *Marked in Your Flesh*, pp. 154–55.

[80] Gollaher, 'From Ritual to Science', p. 10.

[81] Glick, *Marked in Your Flesh*, p. 187.

[82] Gollaher, 'From Ritual to Science', p. 16.

of circumcision – were associated with the privileged class.[83] By the 1930s, at least two thirds of boys in English public schools were circumcised, while only one tenth of working-class boys had undergone the procedure.[84] British imperialism played another role in the upper-class endorsement of circumcision. Since many British men stationed in India contracted venereal diseases in the tropical climate of the colony, colonial physicians advocated for the removal of the foreskin, believing that such infections were growing beneath the foreskin. Circumcision was seen as helping to raise healthy and fit members for the future ruling elite in the colonies overseas.[85]

In the United States, the procedure also took on the function of a mark of social and racial distinction, separating native-born Whites from others. Through the medical shunning of the foreskin, this part of the body became associated with poverty, ignorance, and neglect: 'As white middle class-gentiles adopted circumcision, those left behind were mainly recent immigrants, African Americans, the poor, and others at the margins of society', David Gollaher observes.[86] Circumcision, despite its rearticulation in medical terms, retained its function as a means to draw social boundaries onto the body, though this time Jews did find themselves on the same side as Christians. The strong medical endorsement of the procedure helped to turn it into a widely supported social custom among White Christians in the United States, making the practice almost as routine for newborn care as the cutting of the umbilical cord. At the same time, the shared practice of circumcision began to eradicate the bodily differences between White Jews and White Christians in the United States, a difference which for so long had been seen as marking an unsurmountable theological and racial divide. The medicalisation of male circumcision allowed fair-skinned Jews to further blend into America's privileged racial status.

Soon circumcision also spread to other British settler societies, such as Australia, Canada, and New Zealand and after 1945, to South Korea following the American military occupation.[87] But apart from the United States and, to some extent, Canada, most of the countries

[83] Glick, *Marked in Your Flesh*, p. 150.
[84] Moscucci, 'Clitoridectomy', p. 61.
[85] Glick, *Marked in Your Flesh*, p. 157.
[86] Gollaher, 'From Ritual to Science', p. 24.
[87] Richard A. Shweder, 'Shouting at the Hebrews: Imperial Liberalism V Liberal Pluralism and the Practice of Male Circumcision', *Law, Culture and the Humanities* 5, no. 2 (2009): 247–65, p. 256.

lost their enthusiasm for circumcision soon after the Second World War II. In Britain, the introduction of the National Health Service (NHS) in 1948, which offered universal medical coverage, led to a steep decline in circumcision rates. Given the growing disagreement among British medical professionals about circumcision's benefits, the NHS dropped the procedure from its coverage and parents were less inclined to pay for the surgery themselves.[88] Rates have also fallen significantly in Australia after states withdrew Medicare support for the procedure.[89] The situation has remained different in the United States where a system of private insurance continued to cover the procedure based on the local medical consensus about circumcision's medical benefits, making circumcision one of the most frequently performed surgeries in the United States since the early twentieth century.[90]

The assimilation of circumcision into the cultural mainstream eradicated a crucial difference between Jews and non-Jews and thereby protected it to some extent from scrutiny as a 'foreign' practice. Yet, this assimilation of circumcision into a mainstream and secular practice nonetheless created a different threat to traditional Jewish practices of circumcision, rendering some expressions of Jewish difference more acceptable than others. American Jewish leaders worried that more and more Jewish parents would opt for a hospital circumcision instead of a traditional bris performed by a mohel, turning it into a mere secular surgery. Indeed, during the 1950s and 1960s, at the same time when Jews became 'White folks',[91] circumcision rates soared, and babies were routinely circumcised the day after delivery and thus before the prescribed time under Jewish law. The tendency to discharge new mothers earlier after the birth of their child further incentivised young parents to opt for a hospital circumcision. Jewish leaders responded by emphasising the eight-day rule and advised that any child circumcised prior might have to undergo another round of blood drawing to satisfy religious standards.[92] Medicalisation both

[88] Gollaher, 'From Ritual to Science', p. 25.

[89] Angelika F. Na, Sharman P. T. Tanny, and John M. Hutson, 'Circumcision: Is It Worth It for 21st-Century Australian Boys?', *Journal of Paediatrics and Child Health* 51, no. 6 (2015): 580–83.

[90] Gollaher, 'From Ritual to Science', p. 5.

[91] Brodkin, *How Jews Became White Folks*.

[92] Elizabeth Reis, 'Medicalization and the Mainstreaming of Circumcision in Mid-twentieth-century America', *American Jewish History* 105, no. 3 (2021): 321–42.

'legitimized and threatened' Jewish practice,[93] assimilating a Jewish practice, but in the process, rearticulating and transforming it – in not necessarily Jewish terms.

SIGN OF UNASSIMILABILITY IN THE GERMAN LANDS

While Britain and the United States enthusiastically began to embrace circumcision during the nineteenth century, the procedure remained associated with Jewish Otherness in continental Europe, including in the German-speaking lands. In fact, one of the first circumcision debate of modern times arose during the 1840s in what is now Germany and here too the rite served as a site to consider larger questions of citizenship and the authority of the state. What brought the debate about were two interrelated events. After several boys contracted infections and died following their circumcision, German authorities ordered the medical supervision of the procedure, raising questions about the state's interference in religious affairs in the name of public health. However, a ban was never considered. This proposition came instead from within Judaism. Soon after the deadly complications, a number of Jewish fathers refused to have their sons circumcised, while still insisting on registering their children as Jews in the community. Yet, many rabbis required circumcision as a prerequisite for registration, which brought those fathers into difficulties given that German authorities insisted on the registration of all children with a religious community to maintain a registry of the population.[94] A refusal of circumcision thereby threatened not only Jewish tradition but also the modern German state's secular project of rendering its population more legible with the help of its religious communities.

Whereas some fathers had justified their decision with health concerns, others explained their decision by reference to the position of the religious Reform movement. Reform Judaism was born out of the attempt to reconcile Judaism with secular modernity, which required the reformulation of traditional notions of Jewishness – and circumcision provided one of the sites for this reformulation to take place. The *Reformfreunde* (Friends of Reform), a radical group formed in 1843 within the new movement, had published a manifesto against

[93] Reis, 'Medicalization', p. 342.

[94] Robin Judd, *Contested Rituals: Circumcision, Kosher Butchering, and Jewish Political Life in Germany, 1843–1933* (Ithaca: Cornell University Press, 2007), p. 24.

the rite calling for its abolition. Criticising the tradition as exclusionary and barbaric, they worried that the bodily mark would separate Jews from non-Jews and thereby hinder Jewish integration into the emerging German nation state.[95] Circumcision clashed with how some post-Enlightenment Jews wanted to see themselves, undermining their attempts to assimilate into the national German body politic:

> Since Christians in nineteenth century Germany rarely had their children circumcised, Jewish insistence on doing so had the necessary effect of setting Jewish men apart from non-Jewish men at the very time when Jews wanted to emphasize their similarities rather than differences – how a common Judeo-Christian tradition made all Germans practically the same.[96]

Not all German Jews strove to eliminate their differences. Others feared the dissolution of Jewish distinctiveness through widespread assimilation. These traditionalists quickly condemned the radical Reformers' manifesto and underscored the importance of circumcision. The 'war over circumcision' formed part of a larger struggle between the Orthodox and Reform streams against the background of Jewish emancipation, which had brought Jews out of their closed communities and raised the question of Jewish difference with new urgency. Circumcision, the physical mark of Jewishness, embodied these tensions more than any other Jewish practice. The practice and its future soon turned into a hotly debated topic among rabbis, scholars, and medical professionals, offering both Jews and non-Jews yet another forum to consider crucial questions of their time about the requirements of citizenship, the relation between state and religion, and the nature of Jewishness in the modern secular state: How should Judaism respond to the promises and demands of emancipation? Should the state interfere in religious affairs? Is circumcision mandatory in order to be a Jew? Does it prevent Jews from integrating as equal and loyal citizens into society?

The latter question in particular alluded to the entrenched symbolic meaning of circumcision as a boundary between Jews and non-Jews, a question over which participants in the debate disagreed deeply. Those

[95] Robin Judd, 'Circumcision and Modern Jewish Life. A German Case Study, 1843–1914', in *The Covenant of Circumcision. New Perspectives on an Ancient Jewish Rite*, ed. Elizabeth Wyner Mark (Hanover; London: Brandeis University Press, 2003), 142–56, p. 144.

[96] Hoffman, *Covenant of Blood*, p. 5.

who embraced emancipation's demands and had become acculturated to German majority culture were sceptical of the rites and traditions that marked them as particularistic. Jewish and non-Jewish opponents contended that circumcision's exclusionary character would hamper integration, as it maintained a bodily sign of difference between Jews and Gentiles. In non-Jewish German eyes, circumcision still marked Jews as different despite their emancipation:

> If many German Jews now supposed that they had become truly German, that was not the way most other Germans thought. They saw Jews – specifically male Jews – as categorically different breed, regardless of any amount of behavioural modification. For in the final analysis the distinction was physical. The 'Jew' ... was a peculiar kind of male – one whose body had been irreversibly disfigured by circumcision.[97]

Many Germans who were sceptical of Jewish emancipation indeed shared this view. In 1831, Christian theologian Heinrich E. G. Paulus argued that circumcision represented a *Nationalabsonderungszeichen*, a symbol of national segregation, and therefore a sign of the political aspirations of Judaism, rendering Jews unable to claim equal rights as citizens. Paulus claimed that 'who believes that he has to stay in national segregation, cannot complain that the other nation protects him, but not as what he is not, not as one of our nation'.[98]

Samuel Holdheim, one of the most radical members of the Jewish Reform movement, took a similar view of circumcision as a sign of Judaism's national character. In 1848, he declared himself as 'opposed to circumcision on principle'.[99] For him, religious norms and obligations that were relevant for the idea of an exclusively Jewish state were no longer meaningful under the conditions of diaspora, where Jews were governed by 'the laws of the state and church'.[100] He agreed that circumcision was necessary for membership in a Jewish state, but in his view, it was not a prerequisite for being a Jew by religion – and being a Jew by religion and not by nationality was precisely what citizenship in

97 Glick, *Marked in Your Flesh*, p. 118.

98 Heinrich E. G. Paulus, *Die Jüdische Nationalabsonderung Nach Ursprung, Folgen und Besserungsmitteln* (Heidelberg: Universitätsbuchhandlung Winter, 1831), 66. In German: '... wer in einer Nationalabsonderung zu müssen glaubt, nicht einmal sich beklagen darf, wenn die andere Nation ihn zwar schützt, aber doch nicht als das, was er ist, nicht als einen ihrer Nation behandeln kann und will' (My translation).

99 Quoted in Glick, *Marked in Your Flesh*, p. 123.

100 Judd, *Contested Rituals*, p. 43.

the nation state required. The fear was that circumcision would reinforce the political character of Judaism and thereby threaten Jewish emancipation, which was premised on Judaism being a religion in the sense of a private faith.[101] The discussion of circumcision therefore offered another site for the emancipation debate about the nature of Jewishness and the conditions of Jewish access to equal rights.

Medical professionals also weighed into the debate and offered a very different view from their British and American counterparts. Sixty-six physicians from Vienna issued a statement in 1866 arguing that the procedure weakened Jewish men, made them prone to 'Jewish diseases', and shortened their life as compared to Christians.[102] Many doctors also objected to the practices carried out by *mohalim*, traditional circumcisers, such as *metzitzah b'peh*, the oral sucking of the wound, as dangerous and repulsive. Assimilated Jews agreed and worried that such practices would attract suspicion from non-Jews, thereby endangering their own precarious acceptance.[103] Proponents of circumcision, on the other hand, took a different view of circumcision's medical benefits. Several physicians contended that circumcision created healthier citizens as it prevented phimosis and lowered infant mortality rates. They shared the opinion of their Victorian counterparts that sexual restraint and cleanliness were the markers of bourgeois life.[104] Others emphasised circumcision's moral dimension and civic worthiness. Being circumcised would firmly ground Jews in the moral and ethical foundations of Judaism, helping them to better integrate as moral and ethical citizens into the nation state.[105]

Although their interventions stirred significant controversy among German Jews, Jewish circumcision opponents always remained a minority. Despite the challenges from inside and outside the Jewish community, calls for the abolishment of the rite never succeeded. Even among the Reform movement, most Jews shared the view of Leopold Zunz, the founder of academic Jewish studies (who was not affiliated with Jewish Reform), who declared that an abolition of brit milah would amount to Jewish suicide.[106] Reform rabbis too were reluctant to touch upon the issue. During a number of meetings

[101] Judd, *Contested Rituals*, p. 35.
[102] Cohen, *Why Aren't Jewish Women Circumcised?*, p. 209.
[103] Judd, *Contested Rituals*, p. 35.
[104] Judd, 'Circumcision and Modern Jewish Life', p. 150.
[105] Judd, *Contested Rituals*, p. 32.
[106] Wyner Mark, 'Crossing the Gender Divide', p. xx.

between 1844 and 1846, the liberal German rabbis decided not to discuss brit milah in order to avoid the charged and emotional character of the topic. As Lawrence Hoffman observes, the reformist fervour may have changed wedding customs and mourning rites, declared the Talmud no longer binding, and discarded Hebrew as the liturgical language, yet when it came to circumcision, the Reform rabbis remained 'adamantly tied to their past'.[107] Two other Jewish Reform synods, held in Leipzig in 1869 and in 1871 in Augsburg, similarly declared the 'supreme importance' of the rite for Judaism, although the participating rabbis were willing to accept an uncircumcised boy born to a Jewish mother as a Jew.[108] But they added a caveat. At the age of thirteen, the boy would have to decide whether to undergo circumcision or not. If not, the community was no longer obliged to welcome him in its institutions.[109] The nineteenth-century German circumcision debates ended with the reaffirmation of male circumcision as central to Jewish collective identity. Although law and society exerted a powerful pressure on Jews to assimilate as part of the emancipatory bargain, this pressure did not succeed in eradicating a central mark of Jewish difference.

Racial antisemitism and its focus on biological differences also grappled with this bodily sign. As the only remaining outward marker of Jewishness, circumcision came to be seen as evidence for the racial Otherness of Jews. Sander Gilman argues that Jewish acculturation which had made Jews indistinguishable from other Europeans in how they dressed, spoke, and lived contributed to an ongoing obsession with the circumcised penis as a hidden, yet persistent sign of the Jew's difference.[110] This view was not only held by Germans. Italian physician-anthropologist Paolo Mantegazza, whose books were widely read at the time, described circumcision in 1885 as a 'mark of racial distinction'.[111] Much like the German theologian Paulus, Mantegazza saw in circumcision a deliberate Jewish refusal to assimilate and called upon Jews to

[107] Hoffman, *Covenant of Blood*, p. 9.

[108] Cohen, *Why Aren't Jewish Women Circumcised?*, p. 22.

[109] Judd, 'Circumcision and Modern Jewish Life', p. 147.

[110] Sander L. Gilman, *Freud, Race, and Gender* (Princeton: Princeton University Press, 1993), ch. 2.

[111] Paolo Mantegazza, *The Sexual Relations of Mankind*. Translated by Samuel Putnam (Honolulu: University Press of the Pacific, 1935; repr., 2001), 98. I owe the reference to Mantegazza's work to Sander Gilman, who discusses Mantegazza's work in Gilman, *The Jew's Body*, pp. 88–95.

> [c]ease mutilating yourselves: cease imprinting upon your flesh an odious brand to distinguish you from other me; until you do this you cannot pretend to be our equal. As it is, you, of your own accord, with the branding iron, from the first days of your lives, proceed to proclaim yourselves a race apart, one that cannot, and does not care to, mix with ours.[112]

In the racial imagination, circumcision revealed the Jewish male body as effeminate, damaged, and dangerous. But how could an acquired bodily mark signify the immutable racial difference of the Jew? If it were only a religious practice, a social rite, it could be abandoned, and the traces of Jewishness could be erased from the body via assimilation. This conclusion, however, would have contradicted the idea of the Jew as innately different for which circumcision provided an alleged proof. Circumcision constituted a puzzle for racial theory.[113] Congenital circumcision, that is, the absence of the prepuce by birth, offered one scientific explanation for this conundrum. Studies, albeit not uncontested, argued for the inheritability of acquired traits, such as circumcision, and pointed to supposedly higher incidences of congenital circumcision among Jews. The fact that the Jew could be born circumcised exposed the immutable difference of the Jewish male.[114] Even if Jews would cease to circumcise, their biological difference would eventually show on their bodies and bring the truth about the innate Otherness of Jews to light, rendering the possibility of assimilation an illusion.

CHILDREN'S RIGHTS, GENDER, AND RELIGIOUS DIFFERENCE

No matter how much Christians grappled with circumcision and found it repulsive, backward, or threatening, or viewed it as a sign of Jewish particularity, unassimilability, and therefore as yet another reason to argue against legal reforms that would grant Jews equality, the practice itself was rarely the target of direct legal intervention. Today, however, discontent with the practice, when performed for non-medical reasons, has re-emerged as a matter of human rights, in particular children's rights, with critics calling for a ban on circumcision. A core concern of critics is the impact of male circumcision on

112 Mantegazza, *Sexual Relations of Mankind*, p. 99.
113 Gilman, *Freud, Race, and Gender*, p. 52.
114 Gilman, *Freud, Race, and Gender*, p. 53.

the child's right to an open future, as the irreversible removal of the foreskin precludes the child from taking the decision about circumcision himself.[115] The principle of a child's right to an open future was first suggested by legal philosopher Joel Feinberg.[116] Feinberg argued that children have rights-in-trust, which are anticipatory autonomy rights held prematurely by children before they can exercise them themselves. Since the cutting of the foreskin is irreversible, critics conclude that it deprives the child of the future choice of whether to undergo the procedure or not later in life when he can make an informed decision himself – and I will return to the implications of this concept of the child in Chapter 4. Given that the practice involves the removal of healthy tissue and carries certain risks, the practice is also seen to infringe upon the child's right to bodily integrity. Debra DeLaet, for example, argues that the practice is a 'clear assault on bodily integrity' as it causes pain and involves a number of health risks that should not be neglected.[117] Children's rights activist Stephen Svoboda takes a more drastic stance by arguing that male circumcision amounts to 'medical violence' that infringes on the right to life as enshrined, inter alia, in Article 6 of the *Convention of the Rights of the Child* (CRC).[118] Citing Article 37(a) of the CRC that forbids states from permitting any child to be subjected to torture or other cruel, inhuman, or degrading treatment or punishment, Svoboda further suggests that the deliberate infliction of pain through a circumcision meets the definition of torture.[119]

The lack of medical consensus on both the potential harms and benefits of the procedure further complicates the debate. Supporters of circumcision compare the procedure to vaccination[120] or the

[115] See, for example, Robert Darby, 'The Child's Right to an Open Future: Is the Principle Applicable to Non-Therapeutic Circumcision?', *Journal of Medical Ethics* 39, no. 7 (2013): 463–68; Debra L. DeLaet, 'Framing Male Circumcision as a Human Rights Issue? Contributions to the Debate over the Universality of Human Rights', *Journal of Human Rights* 8, no. 4 (2009): 405–26.

[116] Joel Feinberg, ed. 'The Child's Right to an Open Future', in *Freedom and Fulfillment: Philosophical Essays* (Princeton University Press, 1994), 76–97.

[117] DeLaet, 'Framing Male Circumcision as a Human Rights Issue?', p. 412.

[118] J. Steven Svoboda, 'Circumcision of Male Infants as a Human Rights Violation', *Journal of Medical Ethics* 39, no. 7 (2013): 469–74, pp. 470 and 73.

[119] Svoboda, 'Circumcision of Male Infants', p. 472.

[120] David A. Cooper, Alex D. Wodak, and Brian J. Morris, 'The Case for Boosting Infant Male Circumcision in the Face of Rising Heterosexual Transmission of HIV', *Medical Journal of Australia* 193, no. 6 (2010): 318–19.

piercing of earlobes,[121] and stress its medical benefits, such as lower rates of urinary tract infections during the first year of life, a lower risk of penile cancer, a potential lowering effect on cervical cancer rates among female partners of circumcised men, and a reduced rate of HIV infections in men. UNAids reports that male circumcision can be an effective measure to reduce the risk of HIV transmission by up to 60 per cent.[122] But the target of this recommendation are adult men and not children. As with any surgical procedure, circumcision carries the risk of complications such as bleeding or infection. More serious complications are rare, especially among infants.[123] Data quality and quantity on the impact of circumcision remain limited.[124] Overall, the medical literature seems to suggest that circumcision should be considered as a safe practice if performed by a trained and experienced person under sterile conditions.[125]

Associations of medical professionals reach different conclusions from the data, perhaps also reflecting the degree to which the practice is normalised in certain societies. While a number of European medical associations, such as in the Netherlands, Denmark, and Germany, question the medical benefits of the practice and do not recommend it, the American Association of Pediatrics, on the other hand, reiterated its support in 2012, albeit more hesitantly than was previously the case: 'The health benefits of newborn male circumcision outweigh the risks, but the benefits are not great enough to recommend universal newborn circumcision … the final decision should still be left to parents to make in the context of their religious, ethical and cultural beliefs'.[126]

[121] Allan J. Jacobs and Kavita Shah Arora, 'Ritual Male Infant Circumcision and Human Rights', *American Journal of Bioethics* 15, no. 2 (2015): 30–39, p. 35.

[122] UNAIDS, 'Male Circumcision and HIV: The Here and Now' (Part 2), 26 February 2007, www.unaids.org/en/resources/presscentre/featurestories/2007/february/20070228mcpt2.

[123] Charbel El Bcheraoui et al., 'Rates of Adverse Events Associated with Male Circumcision in US Medical Settings, 2001 to 2010', *JAMA Pediatrics* 168, no. 7 (2014): 625–34.

[124] Jennifer A. Bossio, Caroline F. Pukall, and Stephen Steele, 'A Review of the Current State of the Male Circumcision Literature', *Journal of Sexual Medicine* 11, no. 12 (2014): 2847–64.

[125] Helen A. Weiss et al., 'Complications of Circumcision in Male Neonates, Infants and Children: A Systematic Review', *BMC Urology* 10, 2 (2010).

[126] American Academy of Pediatrics, 'Circumcision Policy Statement' (1 September 2012), https://publications.aap.org/pediatrics/article/130/3/585/30235/Circumcision-Policy-Statement.

Alongside concerns about medical benefits and bodily integrity, critics of infant male circumcision frame their objections increasingly in terms of gender equality and draw attention to the disparate legal and political responses to the alteration of male versus female genitalia, such as via the various forms of female genital cutting (FGC). Whereas many proponents of male circumcision refuse any similarities between the two practices and are eager to distance themselves from FGC,[127] critics argue that the divergent approaches of national and international law to male circumcision as compared to FGC are hard to justify.[128] To refuse any similarities between the two practices, Brian Earp notes, ignores the fact that FGC refers in fact to a variety of practices of different severity.[129] The World Health Organisation (WHO) indeed classifies female genital modifications into four different types, according to their level of severity.[130] Male circumcision is comparable with one of the least severe forms where the clitoral hood is either cut or removed. Critics consequently question if male circumcision and this type of FGC are sufficiently dissimilar in order to justify such different legal approaches.[131] The exclusive legal and political focus on women and girls as 'victims of culture', they argue, neglects the harms inflicted on boys who are being circumcised.[132] A shift in language signals this critical position: The deliberate use of the term 'male genital mutilation' parallel to the value-laden term 'female genital mutilation' is meant to 'extend a sense of the horror of FGM to male circumcision'.[133]

[127] Elissa Strauss, 'How Female Circumcision Is Different from a Brit Milah', *Forward*, 15 July 2014.

[128] For example, s 45 of the Crimes Act 1900 (NSW) makes 'female genital mutilation' an offence. See also the Female *Genital Mutilation Act 2003* (UK). No corresponding legislation exists for male circumcision.

[129] Brian D. Earp, 'Female Genital Mutilation and Male Circumcision: Toward an Autonomy-Based Ethical Framework', *Medicolegal and Bioethics* 5 (2015): 89–104.

[130] World Health Organization, 'Fact Sheet: Female Genital Mutilation', (21 January 2022), www.who.int/mediacentre/factsheets/fs241/en/.

[131] See, for example, Sirkku K. Hellsten, 'Rationalising Circumcision: From Tradition to Fashion, from Public Health to Individual Freedom – Critical Notes on Cultural Persistence of the Practice of Genital Mutilation', *Journal of Medical Ethics* 30, no. 3 (2004): 248–53.

[132] R. Charli Carpenter, 'Some Other Conceptual Problems', *International Feminist Journal of Politics* 6, no. 2 (2004): 308–13.

[133] Robert Darby and J. Steven Svoboda, 'A Rose by Any Other Name? Rethinking the Similarities and Differences between Male and Female Genital Cutting', *Medical Anthropology Quarterly* 21, no. 3 (2007): 301–23, at 302.

Commentators, particularly those in the English-speaking world with its – albeit in the longer context short – history of routine circumcision, therefore, see criticism of the practice as a welcome turn that subjects a *Western* practice to a human rights critique. As John Tobin correctly observes in the context of international law, there is the 'tendency to condemn non-Western cultural practices and condone or overlook the deeply embedded traditional practices within Western cultures that may also be harmful to the health of children'.[134] Despite a growing movement against circumcision, international institutions and national legislators indeed still approach infant male circumcision with leniency, which stands in stark contrast to how the international community has reacted to the practices of FGC.

This is particularly apparent in the United Nations' approach to the two practices. The United Nations CRC calls upon state parties to 'take all effective and appropriate measures with a view to abolishing traditional practices prejudicial to the health of children'.[135] 'Female genital mutilation' is explicitly listed as a harmful practice in a joint statement by the Committee on the Elimination of Discrimination against Women and the Committee on the Rights of the Child.[136] Though the statement acknowledges 'boys as victims of violence, harmful practices and bias', it remains silent on male circumcision. Instead, the United Nations sees male circumcision for religious reasons as a legitimate expression of religious freedom and parental rights. In his 2015 report to the General Assembly of the United Nations, the Special Rapporteur on Freedom of Religion or Belief, for example, noted that male circumcision, if performed under safe and adequate conditions, falls under the right of parents to manifest their religion, which encompasses the initiation of children into religious life.[137] As in the scholarly literature, the deliberate choice of the term 'female

[134] John Tobin, 'The International Obligation to Abolish Traditional Practices Harmful to Children's Health: What Does It Mean and Require of States?', *Human Rights Law Review* 9, no. 3 (2009): 373–96, p. 381.

[135] Article 24(3), UN Convention of the Rights of the Child, adopted 20 November 1989, Entry in Force 2 September 1990.

[136] Joint General Recommendation No. 31 of the Committee on the Elimination of Discrimination against Women/General Comment No. 18 of the Committee on the Rights of the Child on Harmful Practices, UN Doc. CEDAW/C/GC/31-CRC/C/GC/18 (14 November 2014).

[137] Heiner Bielefeldt, Nazila Ghanea, and Michael Wiener, *Freedom of Religion or Belief: An International Law Commentary* (Oxford: Oxford University Press, 2016), 435.

genital mutilation' by several United Nations bodies emphasises the perceived fundamental differences between the practices.

Scholars critical of circumcision advocate for an interrogation of the inherent cultural biases in what is designated as a harmful practice in international and national human rights law and what is constructed as the normal and desirable body that reflects Anglo-Western values and preferences. Marie Fox and Michael Thomson, for example, argue that infant male circumcision in the West is a gendering technology that inscribes ideals of masculinity and manages male sexuality in ways similar to FGC.[138] Fox and Thomson lament the lack of feminist attention to the ways patriarchy operates through the normalisation of circumcision that renders the foreskin as 'feminised flesh'[139] and has helped producing White middle-class identity in the United States and Britain. However, despite their careful attention to the ways in which circumcision has been implicated in entrenching differences of sex, gender, and race through bodily inscription in Anglo-Western societies, their analysis does not consider the different and sometimes contradictory ways in which religion, race, gender, and sex intersect in the matter of circumcision, not only outside but even within the Anglo-West. Or, put differently, how there are different practices of circumcision.

As Suhraiya Jivraj and Didi Herman have shown, in English judicial decisions, male circumcision as performed by non-White and/or non-Christians has been constructed as a premodern practice of unreason and pain of non-Christian cultures and therefore in terms that highlight its Otherness and foreignness to Western cultures.[140] Thus, alongside the normalisation of circumcision that has rendered the foreskin 'redundant, polluted or feminine' in certain Western cultures,[141] there remains a pervasive parallel discourse of the circumcised body as damaged, effeminate, foreign, and scarred, even in contemporary anti-circumcision discourse that replicates elements of Christian ambivalence towards Jews. Indeed, Fox and Thomson quote Carol Delaney's feminist critique of the story of Abraham's circumcision, 'with its interrelated narratives of circumcision and child sacrifice', as one of 'the most patriarchal of stories', which as a 'religious myth' has become 'woven into the moral fabric of our

138 Marie Fox and Michael Thomson, 'Foreskin Is a Feminist Issue', *Australian Feminist Studies* 24, no. 60 (2009): 195–210.

139 Fox and Thomson, 'Foreskin Is a Feminist Issue', p. 203.

140 Jivraj and Herman, 'It is Difficult'.

141 Fox and Thomson, 'Foreskin Is a Feminist Issue', p. 196.

societies'.[142] There is of course nothing wrong with criticising the patriarchal assumptions of religious texts, including Jewish texts. However, in singling out, even if unconsciously, the Jewish story of Abraham's circumcision as a key 'religious myth' for what is identified as a problematic patriarchal practice in Western society not only disregards the variety of Jewish understandings of circumcision but also taps into an older narrative of the Jewish roots of patriarchy. In this narrative, Jewish patriarchy has spoiled – or Judaised – the egalitarian Christian attempt to restore gender equality.[143]

Taking note of these discourses is important in a context where the popularity of circumcision, even in Anglo-Western societies, is declining. In this context, there is, as Kate Green and Hilary Lim warn, the risk 'for male circumcision to shift from the realm of the "normal" and the "culture-free" to being constituted as a fixed and barbaric practice of the west's local others'.[144] Concerns about the rights of a vulnerable group, such as children, can easily converge with anxieties about migration, multiculturalism, and religious pluralism. This dynamic is already apparent in the case in the ongoing discussion about the relationship between Muslim practices of veiling and the rights and equality of another vulnerable group – women, which frequently invokes older colonial phantasies of uncivilised Muslim men and imperilled Muslim women and positions the West as the locus of liberal rights.[145] It does not seem unlikely that children as another vulnerable group and their rights could constitute another site for such an exclusionary agenda. Certainly, banning a harmful practice is not per se problematic, but minority practices make easy targets.[146]

[142] Fox and Thomson, 'Foreskin Is a Feminist Issue', p. 200.

[143] On the association of Judaism with patriarchy and of Christianity with gender equality in Christian feminist discourse, see Susannah Heschel, 'Anti-Judaism in Christian Feminist Theology', *Tikkun* 5, no. 3 (1990): 25–28.

[144] Kate Green and Hilary Lim, 'What Is This Thing about Female Circumcision? Legal Education and Human Rights', *Social & Legal Studies* 7, no. 3 (1998): 365–87, p. 382.

[145] See, for example, Mancin, 'Patriarchy as the Exclusive Domain of the Other'. See also Sara R. Farris, *In the Name of Women's Rights. The Rise of Femonationalism* (Durham: Duke University Press, 2017).

[146] I discuss religious slaughter bans in Riedel, 'They are from Mars'. Iddo Porat has made a moral argument for taking seriously majority–minority relations in the legal regulation of cultural and religious practices: Iddo Porat, 'The Starting at Home Principle: On Ritual Animal Slaughter, Male Circumcision and Proportionality', *Oxford Journal of Legal Studies* 41, no. 1 (2021): 30–58.

A ban of the practice would also have different material effects for different groups despite its apparent neutrality. Banning circumcision may be an inconvenience for non-Jewish and non-Muslim parents used to it, yet for Jews and Muslims, it would constitute a restriction of their rights as minority groups, including to religious freedom and to decide on the education and cultural upbringing of their children. Banning circumcision also has conversionary effects on those groups by setting the uncircumcised body as the norm, a body that, despite normalisation in some English-speaking countries, remains associated with the Christian body, as I will discuss in Chapter 4. It is also noteworthy that to date the majority of political, judicial, and legislative attempts have occurred in countries where circumcision has never entered the societal mainstream. In Sweden, Germany, Iceland, Denmark, and Norway, circumcision never underwent a normalisation, as in the United States, but has remained within the exclusive domain of the Jewish and Muslim communities.

However, even in the United States, intactivism has not been free from anti-minority sentiment. In 2011, the group *MGMBill* that was behind the San Francisco initiative published a comic book called *Foreskin Man* in which the superhero, a fair-skinned and blond 'Foreskin Man', comes to the rescue of a baby and his fair-skinned mother, who are threatened by 'Monster Mohel', a bearded man in a black hat and with a greedy face, a story line that clearly echoes old antisemitic tropes of the forced circumcision of innocent Christians. When accused of antisemitism, the editor of the comic book and *MGMBill's* head stated: 'A lot of people have said that, but we're not trying to be anti-Semitic. We're trying to be pro-human rights'.[147]

[147] For the statement and images from the comic book, see www.huffingtonpost.com/lisa-derrick/foreskin-man-comicbook-at_b_871262.html. The initiative and its comic book project have also tapped into racist stereotypes, depicting the white-skinned and blue-eyed 'Foreskin Man' fighting against African men in tribal gear.

CHAPTER FOUR

THE BODY OF THE OTHER

A German Controversy over Circumcision

Unfortunately, on this point there is also no other way to proceed, other than to say that, from the standpoint of an enlightened and informed third party, there is – apart from a medical indication – absolutely no rational motive for the circumcision of boys.[1]

In 2012, a German district court in the city of Cologne decided that male circumcision for non-therapeutical reasons amounted to criminal assault that could not be justified by parental consent.[2] Although the *Bundestag*, the German parliament, hastily drafted an amendment to the Civil Code to affirm the procedure's legality,[3] it could not undo the social damage. Over a period of several months, between the decision and the drafting of the amending legislation, the German public and academy became embroiled in a remarkably heated and emotional debate about the future of the practice during which a troubling amount of anti-Jewish resentment came to the surface. But

[1] Tonio Walter, 'Der Gesetzentwurf zur Beschneidung – Kritik und Strafrechtliche Alternative', *Juristenzeitung* 67, no. 22 (2012): 1110–17, at 1114. In German: 'Es führt leider auch an dieser Stelle kein Weg daran vorbei, dass es vom Standpunkt eines aufgeklärten und sachkundigen Dritten aus – und abgesehen von einer medizinischen Indikation – überhaupt kein vernünftiges Motiv für die Beschneidung der Jungen gibt'.

[2] District Court of Cologne (Landgericht Köln), 7 May 2012, Case 151 Ns 169/11. An unofficial translation of the decision is available on the website of Durham University: www.dur.ac.uk/ilm/news/?itemno=14984.

[3] § 1631d Circumcision of the Male Child. Section Added Through the Amendment Concerning the Scope of Parental Care with Regard to the Circumcision of the Male Child, German Civil Code, 20 December 2012, Federal Law Gazette I, 28 December 2012.

this time, the resentment did not just appear in the notorious online world but became woven into medical and legal arguments against circumcision. Even though critics of circumcision were eager to stress that their concerns were children's rights alone, the Cologne debate sent a signal to Germany's Jews that the law could easily turn them into strangers again.

Taking Germany as an example, this chapter examines how contemporary secular legal responses to religious infant male circumcision rely on and reproduce Christian ambivalence towards Jews.[4] Unlike in the United States and other Anglo-descent countries, Germany has never endorsed routine male circumcision. It is estimated that only about 11 per cent of German men are circumcised today, many of whom belong to the country's significant Muslim community.[5] In German society, the practice has remained almost exclusively within the domain of religious minorities, such as Jews and Muslims. Any discussion of male circumcision can therefore not be disentangled from sentiments towards these minorities and the procedure's cultural baggage as a sign of racial and religious difference in the continental European–Christian imagination.

Today, debates about integration and belonging in Germany circle mainly around Muslims. The arrival of a high number of migrants and refugees from Muslim countries over the last decades has triggered renewed discussions about the country's so-called *Leitkultur* (leading culture), which some fear is threatened by Islam. For certain politicians, this *Leitkultur* is to be found in the 'Judeo-Christian tradition of the Occident'.[6] As elsewhere in Europe, German law has proved a potent site to defend 'Western values' against the alleged 'threat' of Islam. So far, Jewish practices had appeared to be less of an issue for those concerned about protecting this *Leitkultur*. After the end of the Second World War, there had been little debate about Judaism's compatibility with contemporary German law and culture as Germans tried to repair their relations with Jews, often through an ostensive philosemitism. British Chief Rabbi Jonathan Sacks thus wondered whether the growing opposition to male circumcision was in fact

[4] This chapter is a revised version of 'An Uneasy Encounter: Male Circumcision, Jewish Difference, and German Law' in *Studies of Law, Politics and Society* 79 (2019): 55–84.

[5] Jeremy Laurance, 'Circumcision: A Necessary Cut or Bodily Harm', *Independent*, 7 May 2014.

[6] Andreas Scheuer, 'Es Gibt Keine Alternative', *Cicero*, 7 May 2017.

motivated by suspicion towards Muslims and concerns about their integration, a climate in which Jews become 'collateral damage'.[7] As the numerous headscarf disputes, including in Germany, testify, Muslim immigration has indeed led to a heightened awareness of religious difference. Given that Jews and Muslims share many practices, such as infant male circumcision and slaughter practices without the prior stunning of animals, any discussion of these practices inevitably draws attention to Jews as well. The German debate offers an example of how the Jewish and Muslim questions remain intertwined and shape each other. Explaining attacks on Jewish practices as mere collateral damage would, however, miss the persistence of references to Jews. Given that the initial court decision concerned the circumcision of a Muslim boy, it was remarkable how quickly the discussion shifted to the Jewish act of circumcision.

One reason might be that Jewish commentators were much more vocal in the debate than Muslims and the still delicate relations between Jews and Germans made the issue even more contentious. The whole debate touched upon the question of how to make sense of the German past, making this case distinct from other cases where circumcision has become a legal issue. The Holocaust loomed heavily above the debate. While some wondered whether the 'convalescence period'[8] (*Schonzeit*) from the Shoa was now over, participants in the debate insisted on their right to criticise Jewish traditions when they violate children's rights – even if that meant touching upon a 'taboo'. An open letter signed by hundreds of mostly medical professionals urged lawmakers to take the rights of the child seriously. After all, the signatories asked, did the Enlightenment not teach respect for the dignity of all human life, including that of children?

> It is about the protection of Jewish and Muslim life within the boundaries of the German legal order. As children of the Enlightenment, we have to finally open our eyes: We must not hurt children![9]

[7] Jonathan Sacks, 'The Europeans' Skewed View of Circumcision', *Jerusalem Post*, 5 July 2012.

[8] Vanessa Rau, 'Vehementer Säkularismus Als Antisemitismus?', *Aus Politik und Zeitgeschichte* 28–30 (2014): 31–38, p. 37.

[9] In German: 'Als Kinder der Aufklärung müssen wir endlich die Augen aufmachen: Man tut Kindern nicht weh!' The open letter of 21 July 2012 addressed the German government and parliament and was published on several news websites online, such as www.faz.net/aktuell/politik/inland/offener-brief-zur-beschneidung-religionsfreiheit-kann-kein-freibrief-fuer-gewalt-sein-11827590.html.

CIRCUMCISION IN COURT

The Cologne decision marked a turning point not only for Jewish integration in Germany but also for German legal doctrine on the matter of circumcision. Before the decision, German public authorities had shown little interest in the practice. Only a small number of court decisions had considered the tradition, with the issue, as in other countries, either being the validity of parental consent or violations of medical standards during the procedure. In none of the German cases had courts questioned the general permissibility of a circumcision for non-medical reasons. In fact, an administrative court in the state of Lower Saxony affirmed twice that a Muslim family had the right to receive financial welfare support for the circumcision of their child and the Court compared the practice's importance to a Christian baptism.[10] Similarly, legal commentary, which in Germany's civil law tradition plays an important role in the development of doctrine, had little to say about the rite. Most scholars had no doubt that parents had the right to circumcise their sons. Despite this, a group of criminal law scholars had begun to vigorously write against male circumcision in legal and medical journals. It was this body of opinion to which the court in Cologne referred in its fateful decision, providing a remarkable example of legal agenda-setting driven by the efforts of a group of law school professors.

The case itself began in the medical practice of a Muslim physician. In November 2010, he circumcised *lege artis* a four-year-old Muslim boy on the request of his Tunisian-born mother. Shortly after, the boy suffered from bleeding and the mother took him to the hospital. Hospital staff tried to find out what had happened but had trouble to communicate with the mother, who had only poor German skills and was also visually impaired.[11] A couple of misunderstandings led them to inform the police. The doctor who had circumcised the boy was subsequently charged with causing bodily harm to another person by using a dangerous instrument. The Cologne Local Court (*Amtsgericht Köln*) acquitted the defendant in

[10] Higher Administrative Court Lüneburg (Oberverwaltungsgericht Lüneburg), 23 July 2002, Case 4 ME 336/02; Higher Administrative Court Lüneburg (Oberverwaltungsgericht Lüneburg), 9 February 1993, Case 4 L 5670/92.

[11] For a detailed account of the events leading to the case before the court, see Georg Bönisch et al., 'Circumcision Debate Has Berlin Searching for Answers', *Der Spiegel*, 25 July 2012.

its judgement of 21 September 2011.[12] The Prosecution, however, appealed this decision to the Cologne Regional Court (*Landgericht Köln*), which delivered its fateful decision on 7 May 2012.[13]

In principle, German criminal law doctrine understands any medical operation as an offence of criminal assault, an assault that can be justified by the consent of the patient or a legal guardian via proxy consent. The question of whether consent was valid in the case of a religiously motivated circumcision became the pivotal point of the decision. In this case, the Court found that the circumcision was unlawful because it was not justified by the consent of the boy's parents, since the Court considered the consent given to be invalid. Normally, parents have the right to consent to medical operations, which stems from their parental rights as enshrined in the German constitution and in statutory law.[14] In the case of male circumcision, however, the Court claimed that these parental rights were themselves limited by the constitutional rights of the child, specifically the right to bodily integrity and the right to self-determination,[15] familiar arguments shared by the transnational intactivist movement. Balancing the rights of the child with the rights of the parents, the Court argued that

> the circumcision changes the child's body permanently and irreparably. This change runs contrary to the interests of the child in deciding his religious affiliation independently later in life. On the other hand, the parental right of education is not unacceptably diminished by requiring them to wait until their son is able to make the decision himself whether to have a circumcision as a visible sign of his affiliation to Islam.[16]

The Court declared the child's ability to choose his own religion later in life to be his paramount interest. While the Court acknowledged *en passant* the religious interests and rights of the parents, it

[12] Local Court of Cologne (Amtsgericht Köln), 21 September 2011, Case 528 Ds 30/11.

[13] District Court of Cologne (Landgericht Köln), 7 May 2012, Case 151 Ns 169/11.

[14] See Article 6(2) Basic Law and § 1631 Civil Code.

[15] Article 2(2) Basic Law.

[16] District Court of Cologne (Landgericht Köln), 7 May 2012, Case 151 Ns 169/11, at 15. In German: 'Zudem wird der Körper des Kindes durch die Beschneidung dauerhaft und irreparabel verändert. Diese Veränderung läuft dem Interesse des Kindes später selbst über seine Religionszugehörigkeit entscheiden zu können zuwider. Umgekehrt wird das Erziehungsrecht der Eltern nicht unzumutbar beeinträchtigt, wenn sie gehalten sind abzuwarten, ob sich der Knabe später, wenn er mündig ist, selbst für die Beschneidung als sichtbares Zeichen der Zugehörigkeit zum Islam entscheidet'.

weighed in favour of the individual rights of the child to bodily integrity and religious self-determination. In the Court's reasoning, the right to freedom *from* religion in particular formed the core of the child's interest, with the consequence that parental rights did not encompass the right to circumcise their child if there is no medical necessity. Given the significance of male circumcision in both Islam and Judaism, it is surprising that the decision lacks any substantial discussion of the tradition's religious meaning. It is simply assumed that postponing the circumcision is not only necessary from the standpoint of German law but also easily possible for both Islamic and Jewish religious doctrine. The decision also does not discuss how being circumcised prevents a change of religion later in life, as if the mark itself fixes the religious identity of a person indefinitely and ties him to a community without avenues of escape. Circumcision is constructed as a mark of unfreedom and lost possibilities that calls for the intervention of liberal law.

Despite the unlawfulness of the performed circumcision, the Court found that the doctor acted 'without guilt' because he could invoke the rare defence of non-awareness or mistake of law. Since the legality of circumcision had so far been unclear and not answered unambiguously, the doctor found himself in an unavoidable mistake of law and was therefore acquitted. This acquittal meant that the doctor could not appeal the decision further, which would have allowed a higher court to address the problem in more depth.

To understand the Court's reasoning as well as the subsequent debate, it is important to consider how German legal culture and the country's constitutional tradition shaped the discussion. Fundamental rights, as the German Constitution, the *Grundgesetz* (Basic Law), calls the human and citizens' rights that it protects, are 'omnipresent in the legal order and in the political and social life',[17] and shape public debates in a language of rights. The country's notion of freedom as well as the relationship between citizen and state, which couples rights with duties, is crucial for understanding the Court's reasoning and the legal debate. This conception of freedom and the relation between citizen and state in the German legal order, as Andrew Hammel notes,

[17] Dieter Grimm, 'The Role of Fundamental Rights after Sixty-Five Years of Constitutional Jurisprudence in Germany', *International Journal of Constitutional Law* 13, no. 1 (2015): 9–29, p. 28. The German Constitution, the Basic Law (*Grundgesetz*), speaks of *Grundrechte*, which is usually translated as fundamental rights.

enables the state to make claims on its citizens which would seem controversial in other places, such as the United States.[18]

This particular conception of freedom and the citizen–state relationship also shapes constitutional relations between the state, parents, and children. Article 6(2) of the German Constitution provides that the 'care and upbringing of children is the natural right of parents and a duty primarily incumbent upon them. The state shall watch over them in the performance of this duty'. In practice, this means that the state may interfere with parental decisions if these are deemed harmful for the child or their social integration, thereby interfering with parental rights in ways that may seem foreign to jurisdictions, such as the United States, that grant greater autonomy to parents. German authorities, for example, may refuse a name chosen by parents for their child on a number of grounds, such as that the name might make the child subject to ridicule or because it is known as a surname. Germany also does not permit exclusive homeschooling, instead enforcing compulsory school attendance from which there are only limited exceptions. The coupling of rights and duties in the German legal tradition means that

> Germans face more subtle pressure to conform to the majority social norms, but in return enjoy benefits by that majority itself. This ideology of 'duties rooted deeply in the culture and community' may have influenced the German court's reasoning. Instead of simply endorsing parental autonomy tout court, the judges asked whether the parents' choice would bind their child closer to the majority 'culture and community' in Germany.[19]

COLOGNE'S REPERCUSSIONS

The decision of Cologne took an unlikely trajectory into the public realm. In Germany's civil law tradition, the doctrine of precedent does not apply in the same way as in common law countries and decisions of appeals courts are only persuasive but not binding on other courts. However, when the decision became public, it triggered an emotional and heated debate, partly because it was misrepresented as a 'ban' by international media.[20] What the decision indeed did do

[18] Andrew Hammel, 'Why the Circumcision Judgment Looks So Weird to American Eyes', *UK Constitutional Law Association Blog*, 4 October 2012.

[19] Hammel, 'Why the Circumcision Judgment Looks So Weird'.

[20] See, for example, ABC News, 'German Court Bans Circumcision of Young Boys', *ABC*, 28 June 2012.

was create a situation of legal insecurity, as other courts could have followed the arguments of the case if they considered them persuasive. Several hospitals, including the Jewish hospital in Berlin, temporarily halted the procedure since they could not be sure that public authorities would not prosecute them. Even beyond German borders, in Austria and Switzerland, the repercussions could be felt when several hospitals followed suit.[21] Since a ban on male circumcision would have touched upon a central tenet of Jewish identity, the matter turned quickly into a Jewish issue, with some fearing the end of Jewish life in Germany. 'Do you still want us here in Germany', asked Charlotte Knobloch, the former president of the peak political body of Jews in Germany.[22] Pinchas Goldschmidt from the Conference of European Rabbis called the ruling the 'worst attack on Jewish life since the Holocaust'.[23]

Calls for legal security grew louder, with many asking the parliament to clarify the issue through amending legislation. Chancellor Angela Merkel urged parliamentarians to consider the implications of a ban, which would turn the country into a 'laughingstock'.[24] National and international media fervently debated the future of the ritual, while angry letters reached the offices of politicians and newspapers calling for an end to what they considered to be a primitive ritual. Muslims, although far outnumbering Jews in Germany, remained remarkably quiet in comparison to Jewish voices, perhaps because they perceived the debate to be yet another episode in an ongoing Islamophobic discussion about their integration into German society, which had been repeatedly questioned.[25] Many Jewish commentators, on the other hand, appeared shocked by the amount of hostility stirred up and the sudden attention to their traditions, as Jewish Studies scholar Alfred Bodenheimer writes:

[21] Alfred Bodenheimer, *Haut Ab! Die Juden in Der Beschneidungsdebatte* (Göttingen: Wallstein Verlag, 2012), p. 20.

[22] Charlotte Knobloch, 'Wollt Ihr Uns Juden Noch?', *Süddeutsche Zeitung Online*, 25 September 2012.

[23] Quoted in Ines Burckhardt, 'Circumcision Ruling Riles Muslims and Jews', *Financial Times Online*, 13 August 2012.

[24] Quoted in Gareth Jones, 'Circumcision Ban Makes Germany "Laughing Stock" – Merkel', *Reuters*, 18 July 2012.

[25] Between 2009 and 2010, politician Thilo Sarrazin, back then a member of the Social Democratic Party, had stirred a public debate with his comments and subsequent book on Germany's immigration and integration policy in which he attacked Muslims as exploiting the country's social welfare system.

> The Jews in Germany were used to being treated by the public either with a certain respect or, in their particular role as victims of the Holocaust, being viewed with a certain suspicion, or at most to have to deal with criticism of Israel, which either directly or indirectly affected them. Religion however was always the 'soft' element of Jewishness, which was more accepted among the majority population. The Jews were certainly not used to being included together with the 'non-included', that is to say with those who require integration – but in the minds of many are not capable of integrating – the Muslims.[26]

Ultimately, the *Bundestag*, the German parliament, drafted a bill confirming that parents have the right to consent to the circumcision of their male child.[27] The new provision also permits the circumcision of boys under six months by non-medical professionals. This 'mohel clause' is obviously tailored to the needs of the Jewish community in Germany, where it is more common that mohalim, traditional circumcisers, circumcise newborn boys on the eighth day after their birth. Although the new provision was put into force, unease remained. It seemed, as the magazine *Der Spiegel* concluded, that the debate 'had only brought the truth of people's real differences to light'.[28]

THE SECULAR BODY

As in the international human rights debate on circumcision, the concept of the 'child's best interests' became a central legal battleground for the German debate. The education and upbringing of children have always been a *locus classicus* for the negotiation of cultural and religious differences. The upbringing and education of children provide parents,

[26] Bodenheimer, *Haut ab*, p. 26. (My translation.)

[27] § 1631d Circumcision of the Male Child. Section Added Through the Amendment Concerning the Scope of Parental Care with Regard to the Circumcision of the Male Child, German Civil Code, 20 December 2012, Federal Law Gazette I, 28 December 2012. §1631d reads: Circumcision of the male child (1) The care for the person of the child includes the right to give consent to the medically unnecessary circumcision of a male child who is not capable of reasoning and forming a judgment, if this is to be carried out in accordance with the rules of medical practice. This does not apply if the circumcision, even considering its purpose, jeopardises the best interests of the child. (2) In the first six months after the child is born, circumcision may also be performed pursuant to subsection (1) by persons designated by a religious group to perform this procedure if these persons are specially trained to do so and, without being physicians, are comparably qualified to perform circumcisions.

[28] Matthias Bartsch et al., '"Great Anxiety": Jews Question Their Future in Germany', *Der Spiegel*, 10 September 2012.

communities, and societies with the unique opportunity to expose future generations to the values and norms that they consider most important, linking childhood to processes of nation-building and the formation of collective identities. Sometimes, however, those visions conflict when parents and society do not share the same preferences, as, for example, in *Wisconsin v. Yoder*, in which the United States Supreme Court had to address the different education values of the Amish and the state.[29] Cases such as *Yoder*, male circumcision but also the debate around FGC show how children, including their bodies, can turn into contested subjects of regulation. Far from being a neutral and universal concept, the child's best interests may turn into a vehicle for majoritarian expectations and preferences, demanding the assimilation of minorities to the norms of majorities.

In the German case, critics of circumcision took a position based on the discourse of children's rights with similar arguments as in the international debate: The practice would not be in the best interests of the child because it violates a child's right to bodily integrity by inflicting an irreversible mark on his penis. Since this mark is irreversible, it also violates the child's right to an open future. In particular, it would hinder the child abandoning religion or changing his religion later in life. In response to these claims, the Central Council of Jews in Germany rightly pointed out that Jesus had not only been circumcised but also became the founder of a new religion.[30] Nonetheless, for critics, supposed religious benefits, such as communal belonging, did not warrant the violation of these rights of the child: Either because they rejected religious benefits as something that could not be measured by rational science, or because they understood the child as a hyper-autonomous individual without religious identity. Although critics claimed to argue from the neutral position of secular law in their assessment of the best interest, their assumptions about the body and about religion remained entangled with the predominantly Christian majoritarian culture, reproducing Christian ambivalence through secular legal reasoning and arguments, interwoven with the racialisation of Jewish difference.

The way in which ideas about the body become enmeshed with majority norms, which are rooted in the Christian tradition, becomes

[29] *Wisconsin v. Yoder*, 406 U.S. 205 (1972).

[30] Zentralrat der Juden in Deutschland, *Why Do Jews Circumcise Their Children? Dossier of the Central Council of Jews in Germany on the Issue of Circumcision* (10 July 2012), www.hagalil.com/judentum/2012/beschneidung.pdf.

clearer when we approach the idea of the 'unmarked secular body' from a Jewish perspective. During the German debate, critics insisted that they did not wish to ban circumcision completely, but rather suggested implementing a law that would mean that only those who could legally consent would be able to undergo circumcision. One proposal was that the boy should decide for himself when he is eighteen or fourteen, the age of religious maturity (*Religionsmündigkeit*), when, according to German law, children can decide for themselves which religion, if any at all, they wish to adopt.[31] According to this line of thought, the unmarked body is understood as the secular and neutral state of being that enables all future choices. The uncircumcised body is set as the universal norm, the locus of rationality and humanity.[32]

What many commentators failed to see is that postponing or even the complete omission of circumcision is not a neutral act either but reflects a Christian understanding of religion for two reasons. First, it treats the child as not having any religion at all. Instead, in this understanding, religion is something that is acquired through an individual autonomous act of choice. However, Jewishness is not a chosen identity but an identity that is transmitted through birth to a Jewish mother.[33] Thus, a child is Jewish by birth, and circumcision is an expression of that identity. Requiring a child to decide for himself to undergo circumcision later in life is an attempt to turn Judaism into a religion in the Christian sense, a religion that values autonomy and choice over kinship and genealogical descent.[34]

Second, from the Jewish (and Muslim) perspective, being uncircumcised is not simply the characteristic of the secular and neutral body but rather it 'coincides with the Christian understanding of the physical body'.[35] Leaving the body uncircumcised does not necessarily mean leaving the body open to all possible choices later in life, but it can also

[31] § 5 Law Regarding the Religious Upbringing of Children.

[32] Hannah Tzuberi and Sultan Doughan, 'Säkularismus als Praxis und Herrschaft: Zur Kategorisierung von Juden und Muslimen im Kontext Säkularer Wissensproduktion', in *Der Inspizierte Muslim. Zur Politisierung der Islamforschung in Europa*, ed. Schirin Amir-Moazami (Bielefeld: Transcript, 2018), 269–308, at 296.

[33] Conversion is another pathway for becoming Jewish. Some liberal Jewish denominations also acknowledge Jews born to Jewish fathers.

[34] On genealogy and kinship in Judaism, see Jonathan Boyarin, 'Circumscribing Constitutional Identities in Kiryas Joel', *Yale Law Journal* 106 (1997): 1537–70, p. 1547.

[35] Reut Yael Paz, 'The Cologne Circumcision Judgment: A Blow against Liberal Legal Pluralism', *Verfassungsblog*, 24 July 2012.

mean 'orient[ing] a child towards the majority Christian culture',[36] as a way of subtly converting a child and rearing him within the bodily norms and values of a non-Jewish culture. Being uncircumcised has to be considered as much as a particularistic choice rooted in a particular culture and religion as being circumcised. Yet, as Richard Amesbury remarks, 'by positioning "the body" outside 'culture – as "*intact before the law*"' – law occludes its own culture'.[37]

Christianity of course also has a long history of bodily practices, such as Christian asceticism, as Alexandra Kemmerer has pointed out,[38] but the mark of circumcision has never belonged to the dominant canon of Christianity in the West even if it became assimilated into some Western societies, such as the United States. On the contrary, as discussed in Chapter 3, in the early days of Christendom, the sign of the Jewish covenant played an important role in marking the division between the two religions, as evident in the writings of Paul – that make a reappearance in scholarly commentary. A commentary by a scholar of constitutional law makes the point that male circumcision is alien to German secular law and presents a story of human progress that replicates the Christian narrative of Judaism's supersession by Christianity. In this account (and that of many Christian and secularist thinkers before), 'circumcision replaced human sacrifice' just as on the 'next evolutionary step' the early Christian community replaced the carnal ritual of circumcision with baptism, a 'gender comprehensive' practice through which circumcision endured as the 'circumcision of the heart'. Regrettably, the 'secular state' could not enforce the sublimation process in religions such as Judaism, the comment concluded.[39]

[36] Herman, *An Unfortunate Coincidence*, p. 83.

[37] Richard Amesbury, 'Is the Body Secular? Circumcision, Religious Freedom, and Bodily Integrity', *Journal of the British Association for the Study of Religions* 18 (2016): 1–10, p. 8. Emphasis in original.

[38] Alexandra Kemmerer, 'Naked Law, Lost Traditions. A Comment on Reut Paz and Legal Pluralism', *Verfassungsblog*, 18 August 2012.

[39] Josef Isensee, 'Grundrechtliche Konsequenz Wider Geheiligte Tradition', *JuristenZeitung* 68, no. 7 (2013): 317–27, at 322. In German: 'Man mag die Beschneidung als Ablöse eines solchen furchtbaren Rituals [Menschenopfer] deuten, wie auf der nächsten Entwicklungsstufe die christliche Urgemeinde die fleischliche Komponente der Beschneidung ablöste durch die Taufe, in der das jüdische Initiationsritual in spiritualisierter Form, nunmehr geschlechtsübergreifend als "Beschneidung des Herzens dem Geiste, nicht dem Buchstaben nach" fortlebt. Der säkulare Staat aber kann dem Sublimierungsprozeß nicht nachhelfen und von sich aus vorschreiben, wie man Jude oder Muslim wird'.

Two things are notable in this argument: The progressive narrative from Christianity to the modern secular state, both committed to progressive liberal values such as gender equality, and the implicit invocation of a Christian text within a supposedly secular constitutional law commentary. The Christian roots of the secular state, often muted through references to universalism and religious neutrality, are here made explicit through a supersessionary logic. Christianity becomes, like the secular state, associated with gender equality through its gender-neutral ritual of baptism. Again, this idea is not new and echoes, perhaps unconsciously, what Paul had to say about circumcision in contrast to baptism. For Paul, as Shaye Cohen explains, 'circumcision discriminates, baptism does not'.[40] However, the gender-neutral rite of baptism has in fact done little to alleviate the historically weak position of women in Christianity.

Moreover, the comment reproduces the equation of secularisation with human advancement in which Judaism holds the role of the backward that is stuck in the past and has been superseded by Christianity and the secular state. As Ari Joskowicz and Ethan Katz argue, in discourses about the secular, Jews play a similar role to those they had in Christian theology: As the Other in need of reform and conversion.[41] The obvious reference to Paul makes this link to the historical divide between Judaism and Christianity explicit, where the New Testament opens a world of Christian spirituality, as opposed to the world of Judaic carnality in the Old Testament. Boyarin argues that the true cultural issue that divided Christians from Jews by the second century was the relevance of bodily belonging.[42] At this time, Jews and Christians perceived of circumcision in fundamentally different ways. For Jews, this hidden marker manifested the divine election of the Jewish people, while Christians saw it as 'a stigma, a sign of rejection, punishment, and humiliation, a "mark of Cain"'.[43]

The German circumcision debate with its Pauline echoes could be read as a return to an earlier theological discourse about circumcision as the sign of Judaism's inferiority that now reappears in the language

[40] Cohen, *Why Aren't Jewish Women Circumcised?*, p. 71. The passage in Galatians 3:28 is: 'There is neither Jew nor Greek, there is neither slave nor free, there is neither male nor female; for you are all one in Christ Jesus'.

[41] Ari Joskowicz and Ethan B. Katz, 'Introduction: Rethinking Jews and Secularism', in *Secularism in Question. Jews and Judaism in Modern Times*, ed. Ari Joskowicz and Ethan B. Katz (Philadelphia: University of Pennsylvania Press, 2015), 1–22, p. 2.

[42] Boyarin, *A Radical Jew*, p. 36.

[43] Cohen, *Why Aren't Jewish Women Circumcised?*, p. 11.

of secular knowledge, of law and medicine. However, reading this case only as an expression of Christian *religious* ambivalence would conceal the 'secularist-racializing knot'[44] that weaves through the debate. This knot has become particularly salient in political and legal responses to Muslim practices, where religious symbols and signs, such as the headscarf, have become inscribed with essentialised racialised meanings of foreignness, fundamentalism, and the oppression of women. As Sherene Razack argues, the secular/religious divide that is enacted in contestations of Sharia law functions as a colour line that marks 'the difference between the white, modern, enlightened West, and people of colour, and in particular, Muslims'.[45] A similar racialisation of Jews and Muslims can be observed in the German debate that established a binary between an enlightened, secular, modern, and rational 'us' and a pre-modern, illiberal, religious, violent 'them', positioning both Jews and Muslims as racialised Others with bloodthirsty and degenerate rituals. Circumcision signifies a difference that is constituted as incompatible with the majoritarian culture.

Several public and legal commentators linked male circumcision to violence or even abuse, sometimes expressed through racialised imagery. A German NGO for children called *Kinderhilfe* (Aid for Children) argued that a law allowing circumcision would give a *carte blanche* to 'religiously motivated child abuse',[46] a claim that placed Jews and Muslims in the same category as paedophiles and child abusers. A cartoon in the Swedish newspaper Dagbladet also established this link visually, depicting a Jew and a Muslim standing alongside a deranged-looking paedophile man.[47] The insistence to circumcise is rendered a pathological feature. In a similar vein, another German legal commentary described parents as 'perpetrators' and children as 'victims'.[48]

[44] Vincent W. Lloyd, 'Introduction: Managing Race, Managing Religion', in *Race and Secularism in America*, ed. Jonathan S. Kahn and Vincent W. Lloyd (New York: Columbia University Press, 2016), 1–22, p. 7.

[45] Sherene H. Razack, 'The "Sharia Law Debate" in Ontario: The Modernity/Premodernity Distinction in Legal Efforts to Protect Women from Culture', *Feminist Legal Studies* 15 (2007): 3–32, p. 6.

[46] Quoted in Deutsche Presseagentur, 'Kinderhilfe Warnt Vor 'Blankocheck Für Kindesmisshandlung', *Die Zeit*, 14 July 2012.

[47] Available from: www.haaretz.com/world-news/europe/norwegian-papers-cartoon-suggests-circumcision-akin-to-pedophilia-1.5473430.

[48] Isensee, 'Grundrechtliche Konsequenz', p. 319. In German: 'Die Grundrechte in ihrer Abwehrfunktion auf der einen Seite und die in der Schutzfunktion auf der anderen ergeben das Dreieck Staat – Eltern (Täter) – Kind (Opfer)'.

Circumcising parents are placed in the position of criminals, who need to be civilised and disciplined by German law. Presenting Jewish parents as perpetrators alludes to the old stereotypes of forced circumcisions of innocent Christians, while also echoing medieval accusations of Jews as ritual murderers of both Christians and their own children. Newspaper cartoons echoed this stance by showing Jews and Muslims as hook-nosed and bearded figures, armed with bloody knives and scissors, revealing the true nature of 'the Jew' and 'the Muslim' to their readership.[49]

In his leading commentary on criminal law, its author labelled male circumcision as a form of 'genital mutilation'[50] thereby drawing on the same language that dominates much Western discourse on practices of female genital cutting (FGC), in which the term 'female genital mutilation' already emphasises a particular position: That the practice is absolutely unjustifiable. This naming establishes both the semantic and legal links between male circumcision and FGC, as advocated by the international anti-circumcision discourse. Another comment described circumcision as 'stigmatisation that touches upon human dignity'[51] – a severe accusation given that the German constitution declares human dignity to be inviolable and a bitter irony given that the constitutional emphasis on human dignity was also an attempt to learn from the country's atrocious past with its absolute disregard for those it deemed Other. The same commentary also equates being circumcised with a 'brand mark'.[52] Such comparisons evoke the horror of branding animals to mark their breed or burning signs into objects to assign ownership. It implies that Jewish and Muslim parents do something to their children that one only does

[49] Copies of the cartoons are available from https://blog.zeit.de/joerglau/2012/07/17/islamophobie-und-antisemitismus-vereint-gegen-beschneidungen_5642 as well as in www.giordano-bruno-stiftung.de/meldung/bundestag-will-kinderrechte-beschneiden.

[50] Thomas Fischer, *Strafgesetzbuch Mit Nebengesetzen*, 62nd ed. (München: C.H. Beck, 2015), section 223, p. 43. In German: 'Rechtfertigung von Beschneidungen (Genitalverstümmelungen)'.

[51] Günter Jerouschek, 'Beschneidung und das Deutsche Recht. Historische, Medizinische, Psychologische Und Juristische Aspekte', *Neue Zeitschrift für Strafrecht* 6 (2008): 313–19, p. 319. In German: 'Insoweit tangiert sie [*die Beschneidung*] als Stigmatisierung auch die Menschenwürde des Kindes aus Art. 1I GG'.

[52] Jerouschek, 'Beschneidung', p. 319. In German: 'Die so im Kindesalter erzwungene Beschneidung stellt, vergleichbar einer "Brandmarkung", eine lebenslange sinnfällige Zuordnung zur jeweiligen Religionsgemeinschaft dar, auch wenn die Zugehörigkeit nicht zwingend daraus folgt'.

to non-humans, which, in turn, suggests that those who circumcise dehumanise their children, thereby proving themselves to be inhumane. Dehumanisation as a semantic strategy plays an important role in processes of racialisation. In the critique of circumcision, it enables the construction of subjects that do not value human life and treat their children like cattle. If someone has been dehumanised, there is little normative ground left to claim a human right, such as freedom of religion or the right to educate one's child.

Framing male circumcision through a paradigm of violence and cruelty establishes hierarchies of power through a clash of values – the progressive secular German commitment to non-violence versus the Other's alleged stubbornly backward insistence on cruel practices. The practice undergoes a process of semantic re-interpretation according to majoritarian cultural norms. But the choice of words is not simply a matter of linguistic style. Labelling an act as a 'mutilation', as 'cruel' or 'inhumane' not only constructs this act within a particular paradigm but also provides the justification for intervention. As Juliet Rogers cautions: 'The call of mutilation is the call of law'.[53] In the case of male circumcision, comparing the practice with violence allows to draw an analogy to the legal ban on all forms of violent education in Germany.[54] German law defines violence as physical punishment, psychological injuries, and other degrading measures. Although Jewish and Muslim voices insisted that none of these terms could describe the intentions behind circumcision, which were quite the contrary, the framing pushed the discussion into a particular paradigm that limited the possible ways of speaking about the practice.

The language of cruelty and violence resembles the Western discourse on practices of FGC. By drawing semantic and legal parallels to FGC, opposition to circumcision thereby relied on intactivist efforts to discuss the practice in similar terms as FGC, terms that are highly problematic. While not defensive of the practice per se, scholars criticise how the Western discourse on FGC frequently relies on binaries of modernity/barbarism, of us/them, in which the roles are already clearly assigned – the West as the place of normality, law,

[53] Juliet Rogers, *Law's Cut on the Body of Human Rights: Female Circumcision, Torture and Sacred Flesh* (Abingdon, Oxon; New York: Routledge, 2013), p. 3.

[54] §1631(2) German Civil Code: 'Children have a right to non-violent upbringing. Physical punishments, psychological injuries and other degrading measures are inadmissible'.

and reason and 'their' place as one of dark culture and tradition.[55] Western advocacy against FGC, as Norma Moruzzi points out, tends to perpetuate 'an Orientalist paradigm that still frames the issue as a problem of barbarism and rescue'.[56] This essentialising paradigm underpinning many campaigns against FGC also contrasts with the experiences of some adult women who have undergone the procedure, yet whose voices are mostly silenced. Some women do not necessarily describe their bodies as mutilated, but may experience their altered anatomy as normal, desirable, and beautiful, as Leonore Manderson in her study of women migrants from North Africa and the Middle East in Australia has shown.[57] Associating FGC merely with mutilation, loss, and oppression not only marginalises the voices of these women but also risks imposing Western understandings of the human being, including notions of the normal/natural body. Although highly emotive, such framing can create opposite effects by alienating women and thwarting the efforts of local activists when their advocacy is seen as reproducing earlier colonial interventions.[58] The point here is not to defend practices of FGC and their harms but to acknowledge culturally constructed notions of beauty and desirable anatomy as well as the historically embedded power relations involved in such constructions.

Engaging with cultural and religious difference always involves the question of who speaks, what can be said, and whose voice is silenced. In the German case, an uncircumcised majority and a small minority of circumcised men who expressed regrets about their circumcision dominated the debate. While it is important to consider those voices, their selective reception creates a distorted image of the multiple experiences of circumcision among Jews and Muslims alike. Quite similar to FGC or the headscarf, the sign of circumcision becomes essentialised through a reductive reading as a mark of illiberalism and oppressive culture. An article from 2012 in the

55 See, for example, Green and Lim, 'What Is This Thing'.

56 Norma Claire Moruzzi, 'Cutting through Culture: The Feminist Discourse on Female Circumcision', *Critique: Critical Middle Eastern Studies* 14, no. 2 (2005): 203–20, p. 205.

57 Lenore Manderson, 'Local Rites and Body Politics. Tensions between Cultural Diversity and Human Rights', *International Feminist Journal of Politics* 6, no. 2 (2004): 285–307.

58 See, for example, Anna Winterbottom, Jonneke Koomen, and Gemma Burford, 'Female Genital Cutting: Cultural Rights and Rites of Defiance in Northern Tanzania', *African Studies Review* 52, no. 1 (2009): 47–71.

left-leaning Israeli newspaper *Haaretz* entitled 'Even in Israel, More and More Parents Choose Not to Circumcise Their Sons' became another popular source among critics to support their argument that even Jews had growing doubts about the procedure.[59] The reference to supposedly 'more enlightened' Jews who do not circumcise constructs an ambivalent bifurcation of 'good Jews' who are capable and willing of reform to practice 'good religion' and 'bad Jews' who insist on their tradition and therefore 'bad religion'. Critics however hardly ever mentioned that the article described how this phenomenon called brit shalom concerns not only a tiny portion of the country's Jewish population but also how it occurs within the context of a Jewish majority society where Jewish identity is more secure, less threatened with assimilation through the dominance of Christianity. In such a cultural context, alternative expressions of Jewish identity carry much less of an assimilatory connotation but can be read as counter-hegemonic practices that seek to challenge dominant views of Judaism. Power-relations of the Jewish Diaspora shape Jewish perceptions of the procedure in different ways, as author Philip Roth knew quite well. In his 1986 novel *The Counterlife*, the protagonist Nathan Zuckerman ponders about his own mark of Jewish identity in different societal contexts:

> Only a few hours ago, I went so far as to tell Shuki Elchanan that the custom of circumcision was probably irrelevant to my 'I'. Well, it turns out to be easier to take that line on Dizengoff Street than sitting here beside the Thames.... Here it turns out, by my emotional logic, to be the number one priority.[60]

Critics of circumcision engaged with Jewish sources often selectively and emphasised negative traits without considering their wider context. References focused extensively on Maimonides' account of circumcision as a way to discourage masturbation or on rabbinical quotes that depict the uncircumcised as imperfect.[61] The selective

[59] Netta Ahituv, 'Even in Israel, More and More Parents Choose Not to Circumcise Their Sons', *Ha'aretz*, 14 June 2012. For a reference to the article, see, for example, Walter, 'Gesetzentwurf zur Beschneidung', p. 1114.

[60] Philip Roth, *The Counterlife* (New York: Farrar Straus Giroux, 1986), 324.

[61] See, for example, Andreas Manok, *Die Medizinisch Nicht Indizierte Beschneidung des Männlichen Kindes: Rechtslage vor und nach Inkrafttreten des § 1631d BGB Unter Besonderer Berücksichtigung der Grundrechte* (Berlin: Duncker & Humblot, 2015), pp. 21–23.

quoting of biblical and Talmudic passages purports to be a serious engagement with Jewish sources but ultimately excludes the multiplicity of Jewish voices on the topic. Such hermeneutical ignorance also fails once more to consider the power-relations of the Diaspora, in which the rabbinical interpretation of the foreskin as an imperfection, a blemish, emerged. As Jonathan and Daniel Boyarin argue, this interpretation also has to be understood as a defensive reaction to the charge that Jews mutilate their own children in a context where Jews were a minority and experienced the constant pressure to assimilate to non-Jewish norms. Experiences of anti-Jewish resentments and cultural pressure to assimilate to the dominant norms of the society inevitably shape 'ideas of bodily perfection and imperfection, of what is counted mutilation and what is adornment'.[62] Attitudes of the non-circumcising majority populations, often derogatory or hostile, thereby contributed psychologically to an even stronger commitment to brit milah as essential for Jewish identity. 'One defense against feelings of insecurity and inadequacy that may accompany a condition of difference devalorised by society is to invest in that difference with strong positive valuation', notes Elizabeth Wyner-Mark.[63]

HIERARCHIES OF KNOWLEDGE: THE RATIONAL RELIGION

In the German debate, both medicine and health became dominant frames for the definition of the child's best interest. The turn to health shifts the practice from the realm of religion to the realm of science and medicine, which thereby become the sole determinants of the procedure's legal acceptability. Circumcision is rearticulated from a religious ritual to a health risk, reflecting the general shift of Western societies since the Enlightenment from a culture of religious belief to a culture of medical and scientific knowledge. A framing in mostly medical terms enables a move from considerations about religious identity and community to a cost–benefit analysis in terms of health, reiterating certain forms of knowledge as modern and secular, while discarding others as premodern, irrational, and therefore irrelevant.

62 Jonathan Boyarin and Daniel Boyarin, 'Self-Exposure as Theory: The Double Mark of the Male Jew', in *Rhetorics of Self-Making*, ed. Debbora Battaglia (Berkeley; Los Angeles; London: University of California Press, 1995), 16–42, p. 26.

63 Wyner Mark, 'Crossing the Gender Divide', p. xxiv.

In turn, it requires Jewish organisations to follow this framing and to focus extensively on the health and hygiene benefits of the practice, even though these considerations only play a minor role in the Jewish understanding of the practice as a marker of communal identity. Public statements of Jewish organisations explained in detail the health benefits[64] and the Central Council of Jews in Germany even announced the introduction of a medical and hygienic training course for mohalim, seemingly to alleviate concerns about a lack of regulation – although it is estimated that there are only four to six such traditional circumcisers in Germany and no complications have ever been reported.[65] Yet, even scientific knowledge or the conclusions drawn from scientific data are, to some extent, culturally contingent. The disagreement between various paediatric bodies across the West on whether harms outweigh benefits or vice versa remains tied to the socio-cultural context, as the diverging opinions of medical associations in the United States on the one hand and continental European countries, such as Germany, on the other show.

The whole debate thereby hints at the wider relation between knowledge and power. Among critics, there was the tendency to privilege medical knowledge as legitimate and authoritative, while religious knowledge was discarded as irrelevant and illegitimate. In the German debate, religion and science became juxtaposed as being mutually exclusive, thereby enabling a struggle over how to legally define the benefits of the procedure: By taking into account the 'irrational' benefit of Jewish communal belonging or through a 'rational' utilitarian health assessment? A striking example of such an attitude is given by Markus Löning, the then federal commissioner for human rights, who wrote on his Facebook page with reference to the ongoing debate: 'Too stupid to understand science? Try religion!'[66] The pull towards health as a dominant frame enabled critics to marginalise the actual significance of brit milah as a marker of Jewish identity by labelling such concerns as 'irrational' – an argument of high importance for the legal question of whether the integration into a religious community has any benefits for the child that could warrant the violation of his physical integrity.

[64] Zentralrat der Juden in Deutschland (2012). See also American Jewish Committee Berlin, *Facts & Myths in the Circumcision Debate* (Berlin, 2012).

[65] Heide Sobotka, 'Josef Schuster Über Die Weiterbildung Von Mohalim', *Jüdische Allgemeine*, 15 October 2013.

[66] Quoted in Mariam Lau, 'Die Debatte Über Die Beschneidung Kennt Viele Verlierer', *Die Zeit*, 11 October 2012.

Among critics, there was the tendency to reject any such religious or social benefit with religion understood to be a mere 'metaphysical assertion',[67] which would need to be proved in order to be considered legitimate. Elgar Saraljic for example argued:

> The question about the existence of such an entity is a matter of personal persuasion, the mere presumption can hardly warrant authorizing invasive intervention into the body of another human being, even if in cases of parents and their children. Without a definite proof that such an intervention would bring metaphysical benefits (provided these are defined more precisely) to the child, circumcision cannot be justified.[68]

One of the most outspoken critics of circumcision in Germany, Holm Putzke, took a similar approach, arguing that religious practices have to be rationally justifiable and their benefits empirically measurable.[69] On the surface, such an anti-religious approach may simply be the sign of an increasingly disenchanted society, where secularist distance and incomprehension have replaced empathy for religion. However, the consequences of this approach are far-reaching. Subjecting religious practice to a rational calculus renders the entire concept of freedom of religion obsolete. Furthermore, the dictate of rationalisation particularly targets certain religious groups, such as Jews and Muslims, for whom religion is not just a matter of inner belief, but rather a practice that is necessarily to some extent public, and therefore more prone to the scrutiny of public reason.

The tension in this account then also arises from the notion of religion as first and foremost a matter of inner belief, voluntary and not compulsory – a notion with which Judaism has never easily fit.

[67] Rolf-Dietrich Herzberg, 'Der Abwägungsgedanke und der "Evidenzbasierte Blick" in der Beschneidungsdebatte', *Zeitschrift für Internationale Strafrechtsdogmatik* 9 (2014): 56–65, p. 59. In German: 'Ich bleibe dabei, dass in unserem Streit eine solche metaphysische Behauptung – als Argument pro Einwilligungsrecht wegen Kindeswohlförderung – null und nichtig ist […]'.

[68] Eldar Sarajlic, 'Can Culture Justify Infant Circumcision?', *Res Publica* 20, no. 4 (2014): 327–43, p. 334.

[69] Holm Putzke, 'Die Strafrechtliche Relevanz Der Beschneidung Von Knaben. Zugleich Ein Beitrag Über Die Grenzen Der Einwilligung in Fällen Der Personensorge', in *Strafrecht Zwischen System Und Telos: Festschrift Für Rolf Dietrich Herzberg Zum Siebzigsten Geburtstag*, ed. Holm Putzke et al. (Tübingen: Mohr Siebeck, 2008), 669–709. For reference, see page 19 in the English translation of the chapter, available from www.holmputzke.de/images/stories/pdf/2008_putzke%20fs%20herzberg%20essay%20on% 20circumcision.pdf.

Historically, Judaism has been a religion of law and practice and therefore in many ways necessarily public. The idea that Judaism is a religion in the sense of inner, private belief is in fact rather new, and emerged, as explored in Chapter 2, during the nineteenth century as a prerequisite for Jewish access to citizenship. But the notional transformation of Judaism into a religion in this sense did never completely resolve the tensions around Judaism's public aspects, such as the practice of circumcision, and despite pressures to assimilate, Jewish commitment to the practice has remained overwhelming. This tension now plays out in the debate about male circumcision, in which Jews again face the demand to privatise their difference into a matter of belief in order to fully belong as modern and liberal citizens. These tensions are of course not unique to Judaism but affect all religions that do not fit such a privatised model of religion – a model that is, in fact, not even necessarily supported by German constitutional doctrine on freedom of religion.[70]

Given the difficulty with legal definitions of religion, German lawmakers were probably wise to avoid any reference to religion as a requirement for the validity of parental consent when they drafted the new provision on the legality of male circumcision. The amendment immediately attracted a new criticism: That it would pave the way for 'all kinds of shoddy or outright wicked motives on the parents' side'.[71] Some scholars argued for a restriction on purely religiously motivated circumcisions and suggested that parents should be asked to provide reasons for why male circumcision forms an integral part of their 'educational concept', which would require a religious self-understanding that needs to be demonstrated.[72] But restricting the law to only allow for religious circumcision would face serious practical difficulties. How is religion to be defined? And how would parents prove their religiosity? Is it the frequency of synagogue attendance? Or keeping kosher? What would Jewish mean in this context?

[70] Hans Michael Heinig and Martin Morlok, 'Von Schafen und Kopftüchern: Das Grundrecht auf Religionsfreiheit in Deutschland vor den Herausforderungen Religiöser Pluralisierung', *JuristenZeitung* 15/16, no. 58 (2003): 777–85.

[71] Reinhard Merkel and Holm Putzke, 'After Cologne: Male Circumcision and the Law. Parental Right, Religious Liberty or Criminal Assault?', *Journal of Medical Ethics* 39, no. 7 (2013): 444–49, p. 448.

[72] Tatjana Hörnle, 'Strafrecht: Kultur, Religion, Strafrecht – Neue Herausforderungen in einer Pluralistischen Gesellschaft', in *70. Deutscher Juristentag. Thesen der Gutachter und Referenten* (Hanover: Deutscher Juristentag, 2014), 22–30, p. 23.

The idea of such a religious observance test is, again, informed by a Christian understanding of religion, in which someone is understood to be religious who participates in the observance of religious practice. But this understanding does not sit easily with the way that Judaism defines the Jewishness of a person. Despite the internal pluralism of Judaism, almost all Jewish denominations agree that a person is Jewish either by birth or by conversion, although they differ on the exact criteria. This emphasis on decent, on shared communality and genealogy appears foreign in a world 'dominated by liberalism and cultural Christianity',[73] where religious identity is frequently perceived to be a matter of individual choice.

The way that Western secular courts have grappled with the definition of Jewishness is evident in the 2009 UK Supreme Court case *R v. Governing Body of JFS*.[74] In this decision, the UK Supreme Court found that a state-funded Jewish school's admission policy discriminated on grounds of ethnic origin. In brief, the school had refused admission to a boy because it did not consider him Jewish under the Orthodox Jewish criteria it applied. According to Orthodox Judaism, someone is Jewish if born to a Jewish mother or followed a conversion to Judaism according to Orthodox criteria. Since the mother had converted within the less strict conservative Masorti movement, the school did not acknowledge her conversion, and hence she was not considered to be Jewish and neither was her son for Orthodox purposes. Not only did the Court reach the problematic conclusion that the school had racially discriminated because of this matrilineal test, but the decision also required the school to adopt a new admission policy, which effectively resulted in the 'Christianisation'[75] of the Jewish school. The new admission policy is based on a 'Certificate of Religious Observance' that replaces the genealogical story of Jewishness with Jewishness as belonging through belief and its expression.[76] In practice, the religious observance requirement thereby creates a less diverse body of students by excluding those who are Jewish by birth but non-observant. By requiring the school to abandon the Jewish understanding of Jewishness and to define Jewishness as a

[73] Mancini, 'To Be or Not to Be', p. 490.

[74] *R v. The Governing Body of JFS* (2009 UKSC 15).

[75] Herman, *An Unfortunate Coincidence*, p. 168.

[76] The requirements of the religious observance test, including frequency of synagogue attendance, can be found at: https://jfs.brent.sch.uk/wp-content/uploads/2018/09/11-CRP-2019.pdf.

matter of religious observance, the decision replicates the Christian narrative that it had overcome Judaism's exclusionary view of religious membership by defining membership as a matter of belief. The decision further enforces the idea of Jewishness as a religious identity, despite the multiple dimensions of Jewish identity beyond voluntary faith. As Josef Weiler notes, the UK Supreme Court's decision is

> shaped by the fundamental Christian idea of the New Covenant in which the 'old' covenantal boundaries of Israelite peoplehood were dissolved, and a universal salvific message was extended to all *individuals* regardless of the people to whom they belonged.[77]

If Christianity is the benchmark for what constitutes a legally protected religious identity, the reduction of Judaism to a religion in this sense will be unable to contain the complex and multi-faceted nature of Jewish identity that cuts across modern notions of ethnicity, religion, culture, and nationality. Requiring evidence of 'religious observance test' or a 'religious education concept' would have just been another attempt to Christianise 'the Jew'. By not mentioning religion at all in the new provision that affirmed the legality of male circumcision, the German Parliament avoided the murky waters of such definitions, probably trusting that the large majority of parents have motives other than 'shoddy or wicked' ones.

SHADOWS OF THE PAST: SAVING JEWISH CHILDREN

Although the Cologne decision had not introduced a ban on male circumcision, calls for such restrictions reverberated through the media and academic forums. A public opinion poll found in 2012 that 56 per cent of Germans supported such a ban on male circumcision.[78] Yet, even for some of the most outspoken critics, the criminalisation of religious male circumcision, the effective consequence if a ban had been implemented, caused some uneasiness. The main reason for this was the Holocaust. German-Jewish history played an ambivalent role throughout the debate and added a distinct note to the entire discussion.

[77] Joseph H. H. Weiler, 'Discrimination and Identity in London: The Jewish Free School Case', *Jewish Review of Books*, Spring (2010). Emphasis in original.

[78] According to the opinion poll, which was conducted by the polling institute Emnid, 56 per cent of Germans found the Cologne decision to be right, 35 per cent disagreed, and 10 per cent had no opinion on the matter. See Alexandra Hudson, 'Germany Resumes Ritual Circumcision after Bitter Dispute', *Reuters*, 2 October 2012.

Lawyers in particular were eager to stress that the Holocaust should not prevent a discussion or even regulation of male circumcision; however, they affirmed the 'special obligation' of the German state towards Jewish life.[79] Historical guilt obligated the German state to create special laws for Jews and treat Jewish communities especially carefully, even if this would run counter to the constitutional order. For others, the Third Reich and its carelessness for human life required an absolute protection of human life and bodily integrity under the German constitution, even to the extent that the state had to put an end to the religious practices of those who suffered most under Nazi rule.

Marlene Rupprecht, at the time spokesperson for children's rights in the Social Democratic Party (SPD), argued that she did not wish Germany to become known for being the country that legalised the violation of bodies of vulnerable children because of 'random biblical sources and ancient traditions' and continued that 'The respect for human life – this is our lesson from the Nazi era!'[80] The lesson to be drawn from the atrocities of the Holocaust was the absolute protection of human rights – even if this meant the protection of Jewish babies from their Jewish parents. Or, as another legal comment put it, 'the high moral duty of the state to take into account Jewish matters does not exempt it from protecting the concerned children'.[81] In this legal comment, the 'genital integrity' of 'Jewish children' was a 'legal concern of extraordinary weight',[82] whereby a certain understanding

[79] See, for example, Sven Großmann, '§ 1631d Abs. 2 BGB. Gelungener Ausgleich Zwischen Grundrechten Und Staatsräson?', *HRRS* 14 (2013): 515–25, at 518. In German: 'Als unmittelbare Folge der unmenschlichen Verbrechen des Holocausts ergibt sich die historisch einzigartige politische und gesellschaftliche Pflicht der BRD, den Wiederaufbau des jüdischen Lebens in Deutschland in besonderem Maße zu schützen und zu fördern'.

[80] Quoted in Lau (11 October 2012). In German: 'Ich möchte nicht, dass Deutschland in die Geschichte eingeht als das Land, das Körperverletzung an wehrlosen Kindern legalisiert wegen irgendwelcher Bibelstellen und Tausende von Jahren alten Traditionen. Der Respekt vor dem Leben – das ist doch unsere Lektion aus der Nazizeit!'

[81] Jörg Scheinfeldt, 'Erläuterungen Zum Neuen § 1631d BGB – Beschneidung Des Männlichen Kindes', *HRRS* 14 (2013): 268–83, p. 273.

[82] Scheinfeldt, 'Erläuterungen', p. 273. In German: 'Die aus der Historie abgeleitete moralische Pflicht der deutschen Staatsorgane, auf alle jüdischen Belange von Gewicht besonders Rücksicht zu nehmen, dispensiert den Gesetzgeber nicht von seiner Schutzpflicht gegenüber den betroffenen Kindern! Gerade auch gegenüber den jüdischen Kindern mutet die These paradox an. Ihre Unversehrtheit im Intimbereich ist ein Belang von außerordentlichem Gewicht (Art. 2 I GG mit Art. 1 I GG)'.

of human rights and morals becomes universalised, while at the same time revealing its particularistic historical roots in the German past. Ultimately, this reasoning exposes a Christo-centric and paternalistic view of the German state's responsibility for its Jewish citizens, whereby the state has to eradicate their differences in order to protect them from themselves.

Some framed the question as one of 'whether Jews should have special rights because of the Holocaust'.[83] A member of the German Ethics Council declared the circumcision controversy a 'legal and political state of emergency' that forced Germany to create a special law just for Jews and Muslims. The rule of law, he stated, had to 'commit a sin'.[84] On this account, the globally unique obligation of Germany because of its past required the German legislator to be extraordinarily sensitive to Jewish matters and therefore to tolerate the intolerable and justify the unjustifiable by legalising male circumcision. From this perspective, the new regulation carries the flaw of the illegitimate, as a mere concession to the Jews because of historical guilt. History forces German society to reluctantly integrate 'foreign' or 'alien bodies', as the German-Jewish writer Esther Dischereit once observed about Jewish integration after the Second World War.[85] In German legal doctrine, with its emphasis on human dignity and human life, the new provision constituted for some a 'hardly compatible alien element' for the 'organism of our legal order'.[86] While in earlier racial discourse, Jewish bodies constituted the alien element,

[83] Walter, 'Gesetzentwurf zur Beschneidung', p. 1111. In German: 'Wir streiten um die Befugnisse der Eltern gegenüber ihren Kindern, darum, ob Juden aufgrund des Holocaust Sonderrechte haben dürfen oder müssen, darüber, wie weit die Bundesrepublik gehen soll, um Muslime zu integrieren, und schließlich darüber, wieviel Gleichberechtigung unsere Gesellschaft braucht'.

[84] Reinhard Merkel, in Deutscher Ethikrat, *Vorträge und Diskussion zum Thema 'Religiöse Beschneidung' (Plenarsitzung)* (Berlin, 2012). In German: 'Und damit erweist sich das Dilemma als eine Art rechtspolitischer Notstand für die Politik. [...] Es ist im Kern der Sache nach ein jüdisch-muslimisches Sonderrecht. Das ist eigentlich ein Sündenfall des Rechtsstaates, aber dahinter steht dieses Problem und das ist ein extrem gewichtiges Problem, das ich eben versucht habe zu skizzieren'.

[85] Quoted in Sander L. Gilman and Karen Remmler, 'Introduction', in *Reemerging Jewish Culture in Germany: Life and Literature since 1989*, ed. Sander L. Gilman and Karen Remmler (New York: New York University Press, 1994), 1–12, p. 3.

[86] Herzberg, 'Abwägungsgedanke', p. 60. In German: 'Ihm [dem Gesetzgeber] war gewiss klar, dass er, politischem Druck nachgebend, mit § 1631d Abs. 1 S. 1 BGB dem Organismus unserer Rechtsordnung einen kaum verträglichen Fremdkörper eingefügt hat'.

now a law allowing alien practices is seen as polluting the body of German legal values, echoing earlier fears of the contamination of Christian Europe through the presence of Jews. The feelings of guilt after the Second World War led Germany to a sacralisation of fundamental rights. Yet, the same feelings of guilt collapsed this construct in the face of male circumcision. The lessons of the past did not lead to a respect for difference and the rights and values of others but continued to mask the claim of German superiority behind the alleged universalism of fundamental rights.

For several legal commentators, the reason why the German state refrained from criminalising male circumcision was because of extra-constitutional reasons (German guilt) or because of some free-floating constitutional 'taboo clause'; and not necessarily because of respect for parental rights and the right to freedom of religion, the inherent parameters of the German constitutional nomos.[87] This argument is worrisome as it emphasises once more the Otherness of Jews by labelling the new provision that affirms the legality of male circumcision as a *Sonderrecht*, a special law, which stands outside of, or even in opposition to, the German legal order and its commitment to the protection of fundamental rights. It is an argument that continues to enforce dichotomies between 'our law' and 'their traditions' and the idea of a nomos to which 'we' belong but 'they' do not. In treating the legal permission to circumcise as Jewish special law, the legal discussion reveals what Zygmunt Bauman termed allosemitism, the profound ambivalence towards Jewish difference that singles out Jews as Others who need special treatment in the form of special laws.[88] The question of Jewish belonging becomes one of belonging to the German Constitution. In this line of thought, the 'foreign' law permitting circumcision places Jews outside this community, exposing them as constitutional strangers.

The status as a *Sonderrecht* also puts the Sword of Damocles over the new provision and makes it subject to strict scrutiny and revocation at the discretion of the majority. Although permitting circumcision, a more or less subtle pressure of assimilation is put onto Jews

[87] See, for example, Isensee, 'Grundrechtliche Konsequenz', p. 94; Christian Fahl, 'Wird Das Beschneidungsverbot Kommen? Zur "Sozialadäquanz" Von Beschneidungen', in *Ein Menschengerechtes Strafrecht Als Lebensaufgabe. Festschrift Für Werner Beulke*, ed. Christian Fahl et al. (Heidelberg: C.F. Müller, 2015), 81–94.

[88] Bauman, 'Allosemitism'.

and Muslims, who are given time to civilise themselves. In a criminal law comment, one scholar contemplated a temporal restriction on the validity of the provision in order to enable Jews and Muslims to reform their practices.[89] The argument relies on a vision of successful integration as eliminating difference and as a matter of assimilation to the norms of the dominant culture.

German society indeed remains 'torn between the postulate of assimilation on the one hand and on unconditioned acceptance of otherness on the other hand', Dieter Grimm remarks about the country's struggle to formulate a coherent answer to the realities of an increasingly diverse society.[90] The demand to assimilate is, however, still framed as the necessary and therefore legitimate modernising and civilising of minority groups in need of reform. The new provision stating the legality of male circumcision, on the other hand, is cast as a temporary act of virtue and benevolence, as an act of tolerance, which expects, ultimately, compliance with the dominant norm. The discourse of tolerance that underpins the reading of the legalisation of circumcision as an act of benevolence speaks to how notions of accommodation and tolerance can serve as 'vestiges of the empire that conceptually anchor a hierarchy of privilege that works to maintain a boundary of *otherness*'.[91] The tolerance paradigm through which several circumcision critics in Germany encountered Jewish and Muslim differences is the tolerance that Wendy Brown described as a modern form of power that carries an antagonism to alterity within it, a condition of disapproval while simultaneously affording the tolerating of an air of virtue and benevolence.

> Tolerance is necessitated by something one would prefer did not exist. It involves managing the presence of the undesirable, the tasteless, the faulty – even the revolting, repugnant, or vile. In this activity of management, tolerance does not offer resolution or transcendence, but

[89] Walter (2012), p. 1116. In German: 'Nach Ablauf der fünf Jahre wäre es natürlich möglich, die Geltung zu verlängern, und dies wäre wahrscheinlich auch nötig. Aber der Gesetzgeber hätte deutlich gemacht, dass er die Diskussion in den Glaubensgemeinschaften der Muslime und der Juden zur Kenntnis nimmt und offen dafür bleibt, einem Wandel ihrer religiösen Anschauungen Rechnung zu tragen'.

[90] Dieter Grimm, 'Conflicts between General Laws and Religious Norms', in *Constitutional Secularism in an Age of Religious Revival*, ed. Susanna Mancini and Michel Rosenfeld (Oxford: Oxford University Press, 2014), 3–13, p. 4.

[91] Lori G. Beaman, 'Tolerance and Accommodation as Vestiges of the Empire', in *Secular States and Religious Diversity*, ed. Bruce J. Berman, Rajeev Bhargava, and André Laliberté (Vancouver; Toronto: University of British Columbia Press, 2013), 120–35, at 120–21.

> only a strategy for coping. There is no Aufhebung in the operation of tolerance, no purity and no redemption. As compensation, tolerance anoints the bearer with virtue, with standing for a principled act of permitting one's tastes to be violated. It offers a robe of modest superiority in exchange for yielding.[92]

STILL 'FOREIGN AND ALIEN'

Taking a closer look at the hidden assumptions behind the 'normal' body or the truly 'modern' religion shows how these ideals remain coupled with a secularised and naturalised Christianity and the racialisation of Jewish and Muslim bodies. To be clear, the voices analysed here do not represent the entire debate, but they represent an important line of argument and reveal how secular legal reasoning and discourse can reproduce Christian ambivalence that seeks to remake Jews while affirming the superiority of the majoritarian culture. The supersessionary logic that underpinned parts of the debate analysed here revealed the fragile acceptance of Jewish particularity, which is still expected to dissolve into sameness with the Christian majority culture in the name of constitutional rights.

At the same time, racialisation subtly enacts a deep suspicion towards Jewish and Muslim ability to achieve this assimilation and uses circumcision as a site to affirm legal and cultural superiority but also cultural incompatibility. More muted than in the past, this racialisation draws on a paradigm that resurrects old antisemitic (and Islamophobic) stereotypes of Jews and Muslims as bloodthirsty, violent, and barbaric as evidenced by their persistent insistence on outdated bodily practices. The racialisation of Jewish difference takes a peculiar legal tone when the provision permitting circumcision is rendered a 'foreign and alien element' to the German nomos that is imagined as an organism, threatened by legal pollution.

The German case on infant male circumcision illustrates how secular law can be mobilised for a civilising mission that seeks to remake Jews and Muslims in the name of secular rights, while elevating the majoritarian German religion as the benchmark for the truly modern and civilised religion that is associated with gender equality, autonomy, and reason. My point here is neither to accuse individual commentators of antisemitism, Islamophobia, or racism nor to downplay the real concerns about children's rights, but to highlight how a particular

[92] Brown, *Regulating Aversion*, p. 25.

cultural repertoire undergirds ideas about 'proper religion' and the 'normal' body that perpetuate Christian normativity, while rendering Jews and Muslims as Others in need of reform – if necessary, by force of criminal law. One could argue that the German case is unique in light of the country's history. However, politicians in other countries, such as Iceland and Denmark, have called for a ban on the practice too, often with similar arguments.[93] In Germany and across the border in Switzerland, some continue to question the compatibility of circumcision with modern secular law, thereby signalling to Jews and Muslims that their rights may come once again under scrutiny.[94]

[93] Christina Caron, 'Bill Banning Circumcision in Iceland Alarms Religious Groups', *New York Times*, 28 February 2018; Press (3 June 2018).

[94] Fahl, 'Wird das Beschneidungsverbot kommen?'. See, for example, the campaign to ban circumcision in Switzerland by the children's rights group *Pro Kinderrechte* www.pro-kinderrechte.ch and the statement by the German Academy for Pediatric and Adolescent Medicine: www.dakj.de/pressemitteilungen/5-jahre-beschneidungsgesetz-rechtsfrieden-zu-lasten-von-kinder-und-menschenrechten/.

CHAPTER FIVE

DIVIDING LINES

The Eruv, Urban Space, and Public Religiosity

During a visit to Warsaw in 1911, Franz Kafka, the Bohemian novelist and writer of short stories, noted in his diary a peculiar structure installed above the streets of the Polish capital:

> As a result of bribery the telephone and telegraph wires around Warsaw were put up in a complete circle, which in the sense of the Talmud makes the city a bounded area a courtyard, as it were, so that on Saturday it is possible even for the most pious person to move about, carry trifles (like handkerchiefs) on his person, within this circle.[1]

What Kafka describes in his diary is an eruv, a rabbinical device that enables observant Jews to transfer 'trifles' in public on Shabbat, an activity otherwise forbidden during the Jewish day of rest. By virtually extending the domestic sphere into the public space of the city, the eruv creates the fiction of a shared home for one day of the week, allowing observant Jews to move freely through the public space enclosed by the eruv. The walls of this imagined home are demarcated by existing boundary structures, and the remaining gaps are closed by poles and wires. Finally, the space is 'rented' for a notional sum from a city authority, a transaction which perhaps led Kafka to describe this agreement as 'bribery'. While the Warsaw eruv does not exist anymore, cities such as New York, Los Angeles, Montreal, Vienna, Melbourne, Antwerp, and London are home to these structures. Although eruvin may seem an innocent Talmudic fiction, the establishment of these imagined religious spaces can be fraught with immense difficulties.

[1] Franz Kafka, *The Basic Kafka* (New York: Pocket Books, 1979), p. 236.

The eruv is the only Jewish practice that requires Jews to interact with non-Jews and this is often where the trouble begins. From Outremont to Johannesburg, from Palo Alto to Sydney, neighbours have had heated disputes with each other over what looks like an ordinary piece of string. The minimalist architecture of the eruv contrasts with the fierce opposition that some neighbours voice against proposals to set up such a device, often investing significant resources and time to prevent the eruv from being established. The eruv makes visible the difference of the Jewish neighbour – a difference which some residents do not wish to confront.

That the eruv can be a lightning rod for conflict should not come as a surprise. Public space has long been a central site for the management and contestation of difference given its association with the nation, the power of the state, and the public sphere. Legal geographers have drawn attention to the intimate nexus between law and space, describing space as one of the 'enabling technologies'[2] through which the law has produced and sustained social hierarchies and reproduced exclusion and domination. In the realm of religion, the dress of Muslim women, the erection of crosses, the building of mosques, and the wearing of religious gear, such as the kirpan, the ceremonial dagger worn by baptised Sikhs, have been at the centre of public and legal controversy. While arguments about the necessity of keeping public space a secular blank canvas and about preventing the intrusion of religious particularity loom large, these conflicts also reveal some of the deeper anxieties of established majoritarian cultures who wrestle with the public presence of minorities that challenge their dominance over access to and governance of public space.

This chapter is the first of two in which I examine the legal encounter with Jewishness in public space through the Orthodox practice of the eruv. Other than circumcision, the eruv is a distinctly Orthodox practice and fault lines here do not run simply between Jews and non-Jews but also between different Jews. In the modern secular legal arena, questions of non-establishment and the boundaries of religious freedom serve as the dominant legal frames, turning the eruv into a matter of excessive religiosity to be contained by law. Yet underneath the lofty language of constitutional separation often lurk concerns about national and local identity as well as sovereignty and ownership that are enacted, protected, and contested locally. Moreover,

[2] David Delaney, 'The Space That Race Makes', *The Professional Geographer* 54, no. 1 (2002): 6–14, p. 7.

while circumcision has often galvanised Jews of different denominations, including those identifying as secular, the eruv exposes internal Jewish rifts about the proper Jewish relationship to secular modernity and about authentic Jewishness. Indeed, some Jews themselves have not shied away from mobilising the authority of secular law to enforce their vision of what they consider the acceptable boundaries of Jewishness in the modern secular state. Hence, the eruv also offers a prism into how the demands of assimilation can work to divide Jews living in modern secular societies, and how the language and authority of secular law are mobilised by Jews and non-Jews to contain a perceived 'excess' of Jewishness that the eruv comes to represent.

SHABBAT SPACES

On Shabbat, the Jewish day of rest, all kinds of labour are prohibited, including the transfer of objects both from the private domain to the public and within the public space. This means that Shabbat-observant Jews are not allowed to carry, push, or pull objects in or into the public space during the day of rest. In everyday life, this restriction can lead to very mundane problems. Keys, prayer books, and food may not be carried. The rule also affects families with small children who cannot walk yet and need to be carried or pushed in a pram, as the halakha, the Jewish law, makes no distinction between carrying a child and other items. Elderly people or people with disabilities who need a wheelchair cannot move as freely as they wish. While a walking stick can be used since it is considered to be an extension of the arm, a wheelchair may not be pushed. The prohibition has a significant impact on the enjoyment of Shabbat for already vulnerable community members who find themselves tied to their homes, unable to attend synagogue service or dinner with friends and family. The ability of all community members to attend service is especially relevant in very small communities with ageing members. In order to conduct a prayer service, a minimum quorum of ten adult males, called *minyan*, has to be reached. If some community members cannot attend because of the lack of an eruv, this may impact on the ability of the entire community to hold a service. Although not used by all Jews, an eruv can constitute a significant community asset among Jews with a stricter level of observance.[3]

[3] At the time of writing, there has been a proposal to set up an eruv in Basel, the home of Switzerland's oldest Jewish community, to attract Orthodox Jews and counter

The point of departure for the establishment of an eruv is the intricate spatial logic of the Shabbat laws, which is distinct from the order of ordinary weekdays and relies on the distinction between domestic and non-domestic space. Through the eruv, non-domestic space in the halakhic sense is virtually transformed into halakhic domestic space. Once the location of an eruv has been determined, it has to be encircled by boundaries to mimic an enclosed space. Cliff faces, water fronts, creeks, walls, fences, railway tracks, and utility poles can all turn into the walls of an eruv. The Sydney eruv, located in the suburb of Bondi, for example, claims to be the only eruv in the world whose boundaries are mostly formed by using existing solid infrastructure.[4] In most cases, remaining gaps need to be closed by additional infrastructure, for which a method called *tzuras hapesach* is used, which literally means 'the form of a doorway'[5] where poles and wires mimic doorposts (*lechi*) and lintel. Either a new pole is erected or the lechi is attached to a utility pole usually by using plastic conduit that stands for the doorpost (Figure 1).

In addition to demarcating the eruv space, the Jewish community has to symbolically rent the eruv territory from local authorities in order to turn it into a domestic Jewish space, a transaction which may have led Kafka to believe that Jewish bribes had been involved. Usually, the rent does not amount to more than a dollar or a little more for the lease period.[6] The purpose of the lease is to obtain permission from all the residents who live within the confines of the eruv. In practice, obtaining consent from all residents is difficult, but rabbinical reasoning holds that permission from local authorities such as the police or the mayor is sufficient.[7] Hence, the involvement of secular authorities is a crucial step in creating this religious space. A third step to make the fiction of the eruv complete involves the connecting of the eruv community itself to create the fiction of a shared household, which is achieved through a deposit of bread. Over time it

migration away from the city: Patrick Künzle, 'Ein Eruv Soll Die Abwanderung Stoppen', *SRF*, 18 April 2018.

4 These solid eruv walls are called *mechitzot*, see www.sydneyeruv.org.au/index.htm.

5 Yosef Gavriel Bechhofer, *The Contemporary Eruv: Eruvin in Modern Metropolitan Areas* (Jerusalem; New York: Feldheim Publishers, 2002), 3.

6 See, for example, the Boston eruv lease agreement: www.bostoneruv.org/kinyan_kesef.htm.

7 The Melbourne eruv relies on this logic, see Peter M. Kloot, 'History of Melbourne Eruv', 21 April 2010, www.cosv.org.au/index.php?article=485.

Figure 1 Eruv Installations in Montreal (a barely visible wire between the buildings) and in Coogee, Sydney (photos by author)

Figure 2 Box of matza bread symbolising the eruv community in a rabbi's office (photo by author)

has become practice to use a box of *matzah*, an unleavened bread for the holiday of *Pessah* (Passover), that often sits in some inconspicuous corner of the rabbi's office and is replaced every year with a fresh box just before Passover (Figure 2). The shared food, the matzah, symbolises the community that is unified through the eruv. As Margaret Olin writes, 'for twenty-four hours a week the deposit of bread conceptually turns one of the homes into a pantry, and a courtyard of homes into a single courtyard home'.[8] The eruv's purpose is practical, but there is also a symbolic dimension to this partly real, partly imagined space. Through the shared ritual experience of space, the eruv enables Jewish communities to create a sense of spatial belonging by transforming the urban space notionally into 'a city within a city: a Jewish one within the Christian one'.[9] As a form of 'diaspora cartography',[10] the eruv has provided a subtle spatial means for Jewish communities to maintain a sense of ownership and belonging in largely non-Jewish environments. Work in Jewish Studies therefore describes the eruv as an alternative form of sovereignty over and relationship to space, a

[8] Margaret Olin, 'Introduction. The Poetics of the Eruv', *Images* 5 (2011): 3–13, p. 3.

[9] Micha J. Perry, 'Imaginary Space Meets Actual Space in Thirteenth-Century Cologne: Eliezer Ben Joel and the Eruv', *Images* 5, no. 1 (2011): 26–36, p. 27.

[10] Charlotte Elisheva Fonrobert, 'Diaspora Cartography: On the Rabbinic Background of Contemporary Ritual Eruv Practice', *Images* 5 (2011): 14–25.

non-exclusive form of territoriality that allows for multidimensional readings of space.[11] However, in eruv controversies, this subtlety is often lost when the eruv is assessed through a Western framework of sovereignty that rests on exclusive authority over and ownership of land, in which the eruv is interpreted as a dangerous Jewish political affront, a covert grab to power.

FROM THE GHETTO INTO THE ENLIGHTENED CITY

Long before ideas about the secularity of public space entered the legal and political lexicon, Christians were already worried about the 'polluting' and 'disruptive' presence of Jews in their streets and neighbourhoods. The European Christian encounter with Jews, as discussed in Chapter 2, often dwelled on how to manage the physical presence of Jewish bodies in Christian spaces. Different to Muslims who mainly constituted Christian Europe's 'external enemy', perceived as threatening its borders from outside, Jews as strangers within resided alongside Christians, often interacting and mingling with Christians in everyday life. Jewish residency depended on the tolerance and permission of secular local rulers, which could be revoked at any time, forcing Jews to migrate elsewhere, such as when England expelled its Jewish inhabitants in 1290 and Spain in 1492.

Even if Jews were allowed to reside, Christian societies often tightly regulated the presence of Jews on their territory, such as in England during the thirteenth century where Jews were only allowed to reside and transact in certain cities and towns and required official permission to change their residence.[12] Jewish residential segregation was not simply the result of disdain for Jews but also resulted from the need of local authorities to protect Jews as well as the preferences of Jews to live close to one another.[13] However, the spatiolegal governance of Jewish difference also reflected the ambivalent status of Jews in Christian economy and theology: Christians depended on Jews for economic reasons and as witnesses to the Christian truth, but also reviled them as usurers, and as killers of Christ. Christian ambivalence therefore at times translated into spatial arrangements that were meant to keep Jews at once at bay and under control but also close enough to benefit from their presence.

[11] See also Charlotte Elisheva Fonrobert, 'The Political Symbolism of the Eruv', *Jewish Social Studies* 11, no. 3 (2005): 9–35.

[12] Heng, *Invention of Race*, p. 29.

[13] See Boyarin, *The Unconverted Self*, p. 59.

One of these spatial arrangements was the Venetian Ghetto. While it forms one of the best-known examples of Jewish spatiolegal containment, it did by no means constitute the norm for Jewish living conditions during medieval and early modern times in Europe. Periods of co-habitation alternated and intersected with periods of segregation and, in extreme cases, expulsion. However, here, I focus on the Ghetto for two of reasons: First, because this episode not only provides insights into how Christian ambivalence translated into a particular spatiolegal configuration of 'inclusive exclusion'[14] that became increasingly racialised. Second, contemporary eruv opposition frequently refers to the eruv as a re-enactment of the ghetto, while also echoing earlier narratives about public Jewish religiosity as potentially 'polluting' and 'dangerous'. Nowadays, tearing down symbolic walls by force of law has become the preferred way of managing the alleged threat of Jewish 'contamination'. However, dissolving into the city space also requires the dissolving of any visible attachments to Jewishness.

In the merchant city of Venice, the Ghetto was established in 1516. After the city's defeat in the battle of Agnadello in 1510, Venice began a restructuring and rebranding of itself as New Jerusalem, which also involved the relegations of Jews to the city's geographical margins.[15]. Large part of Venice's Jews had to settle in the so-called Ghetto Nuovo (the New Ghetto), a derelict foundry district, enclosed by waterways and accessible only by drawbridges that were closed at night. Its outward-facing balconies were removed, and its windows were shut to seal off the Jewish quarter from the rest of Venice. In 1541 and 1633, Venetian authorities expanded the Jewish quarters to include the Ghetto Vecchio (Old Ghetto) and the Ghetto Nuovissimo (Newest Ghetto). Many Jewish merchants who had found a home in the Ottoman Empire after their expulsion from Spain were required to live in the Ghetto Vecchio while conducting their business in the city. This Ghetto also housed conversos fleeing from Spain and the Venetian government required that they revert back to Judaism as a condition of their residence.[16] Although one of the

[14] Piero Zanini cited in: Shaul Bassi, 'The Venetian Ghetto and Modern Jewish Identity', *Judaism* 51, no. 4 (2002): 469–80, p. 471.

[15] Bassi, 'Venetian Ghetto', pp. 470–71.

[16] Benjamin Ravid, 'The Legal Status of the Jewish Merchants of Venice, 1541–1638', *The Journal of Economic History* 35, no. 1 (1975): 274–79.

best-known examples, Venice was not the first to confine its Jewish population to special areas. In 1179, the Catholic Church's Third Council of the Lateran had decreed that Christians should no longer live among Jews. Jewish quarters appeared in cities across Europe, such as in Frankfurt, Prague, Siena, and Florence, segregating Jews from Christians in urban space and the Counter-Reformation led to even more ghettos being established during the eighteenth century.[17] In 1412, John I of Castile required that Jews and Muslim had to live in enclosed quarters. In 1555, Pope Paul IV required all Jews in Rome to live in one single street, and Pope Sixtus V later ordered that Jewish men attend Christian sermons for a minimum of six times a year.[18] In Venice, Muslims lived separately too. Turks had to apply to have their own designated area, which the city granted in 1621.[19]

It was in Venice though, Bruce Haynes argues, that the forced segregation of Jews took on a distinctly racial character.[20] As discussed in Chapter 2, Jewish bodies had already become increasingly racialised as diseased and polluted during the late Middle Ages, shifting the theological discourse of Jewish difference into a racially inflected paradigm. The Jewish body, however, was not only seen as essentially different from the Christian body; its presence in the streets was also perceived as inherently dangerous and impure. By confining Jews into segregated quarters, Richard Sennett suggests, Venetians believed to contain a disease that had befallen the Christian community: 'Christians were afraid of touching Jews: Jewish bodies were thought to carry venereal diseases as well as contain more mysterious polluting powers. The Jewish body was unclean'.[21] The forced segregation appeared as a reaction to the perceived threat of the Jewish body, but it also further entrenched the racialising process, as Bruce Haynes and Ray Hutchinson describe:

> Racialization begins with the forced relocation of a group of persons distinguished as morally different and identified by a particular ethnic feature – their religion – to a physical space that is isolated from other

[17] Sorkin, *Jewish Emancipation*, p. 102.

[18] Robert Bernasconi, 'The Ghetto and Race', in A *Companion to Racial and Ethnic Studies*, ed. John Solomos and David Theo Goldberg (Williston: Blackwell, 2001), 340–47, p. 342.

[19] Bernasconi, 'Ghetto and Race', p. 341.

[20] Bruce D. Haynes, *The Soul of Judaism. Jews of African Descent in America* (New York: New York University Press, 2018), p. 33.

[21] Richard Sennett, *Flesh and Stone. The Body and the City in Western Civilization* (New York; London: W.W. Norton, 1994), p. 215.

> areas of the city. The very space of the city becomes identified with the stigmatized; persons living outside of the Ghetto view the behavior and beliefs of those inside the Ghetto with suspicion and their bodies as dangerous.[22]

Even though Jews were forced to reside in the Ghetto, their economic activity, often as doctors and moneylenders, required them to mingle with Venetian Christians on a daily basis.[23]. Once outside the Ghetto walls, the Jewish body was a threat, diseased and hence contagious but also Oriental and therefore seductive.[24] In order to manage the threat of Jewish-Christian interaction outside of the Ghetto walls, Jewish men were made to wear the yellow badge to be recognised by Christians and soon this requirement was also extended to Jewish women to prevent relations with Christian men.[25] The colour yellow was the same as worn by prostitutes, marking out those kinds of bodies deemed impure.[26] As the badge proved not conspicuous enough, Jews were eventually forced to wear a yellow hat, a practice introduced also elsewhere in Europe, such as in Germany and Bohemia.

The Ghetto and the badge enabled Christian Venetians to safely reap the economic benefits of Jews whose loans supported trade and helped the poor, while their taxes were a source of income to the city. The Ghetto, Robert Bernasconi writes, 'was a way of incorporating those who would nevertheless continue to be treated as outsiders'.[27] When the Papacy complained about the Venetian policy to allow conversos to return to Judaism, Venetian authorities asserted their power in the face of the Church and argued that this policy prevented these Jews to migrate to the Ottoman Empire and instead allowed Jews to benefit Christian Europe with their wealth.[28] This episode demonstrates once more that if Jews were useful to secular authorities, such as in Venice, they were willing to go against the desires of the Church.

When the Venetian republic fell in 1797, the new revolutionary municipal government, fuelled by the spirit of the Enlightenment and

[22] Bruce Haynes and Ray Hutchison, 'The Ghetto: Origins, History, Discourse', *City & Community* 7, no. 4 (2008): 353–57, p. 348.

[23] Sennett, *Flesh and Stone*, p. 222.

[24] Sennett, *Flesh and Stone*, p. 216.

[25] Ravid, 'Legal Status of the Jewish Merchants', p. 278.

[26] Sennett, *Flesh and Stone*, p. 240.

[27] Bernasconi, 'The Ghetto and Race', p. 341.

[28] Ravid, 'Legal Status of the Jewish Merchants'.

by Napoléon's arrival in Italy, pushed for the end of Jewish segregation and called for the demolition of the old wooden gates that had locked the Ghetto. Soon they were chopped down in order to 'remove the mark of separation between the Jewish Citizens and the other Citizens, where no such mark should exist',[29] although it took until 1818 for Jews to be granted full civil rights.[30] While many Jews celebrated the opening of their quarters, there was also unease. Though residential segregation enforced Jewish Otherness, the Ghetto had also allowed Jews to maintain a degree of autonomy and self-determination within its walls. Spatial separation enabled a level of legal and religious autonomy. Encircled by the waters of Venice, the Ghetto had been a space where Jewish law and culture could flourish, protected to some extent by the Christian rulers of the city albeit occasionally threatened with expulsion. Within the Ghetto, Venetian Jews had established synagogues and built communal organisations, shielded from the threat of conversion that lurked outside the Ghetto walls. The Ghetto provided a 'refuge in a sea of Christians'.[31] With the gates open, the walls of the Ghetto as well as those of Jewish quarters elsewhere proved less powerful against the pressure of assimilation.

The period of Jewish emancipation instigated a fundamental shift in the spatiolegal governance of not only Venetian Jews but also of Jews all over Europe. Physical segregation and marking through attire became slowly replaced with policies aiming to integrate Jews not only legally but also spatially. While this spatial integration may seem like a benign and welcoming strategy in comparison to segregation, it continued to treat the spatial presence of Jewish difference as a problem to be managed. While residential segregation or expulsion rested on a logic of dissimilation and differentiation that had required Jews to remain apart, the Enlightenment project of spatial integration expected Jews to hide public elements of their identity – to not enter the public space as Jews. Although the freeing of Jews out of their ghettos was part of the larger sociolegal project of turning them into equal citizens, spatial integration remained fraught with difficulties. Venetian Jews, for example, still

[29] Quoted in Robert C. Davis, 'Introduction', in *The Jews of Early Modern Venice*, ed. Robert C. Davis and Benjamin Ravid (Baltimore: Johns Hopkins University Press, 2001), vii-xix, at vii. Capitalisations in original.

[30] Bassi, 'Venetian Ghetto', p. 473.

[31] Davis, 'Introduction', p. vii.

faced obstacles to buy land outside of the Ghetto walls and integration into the urban space often still occurred on the terms of the dominant Christian society.

It will come as no surprise that the eruv as a manifestation of Jewish identity and community in the space of the modern city would sometimes clash with such demands. Living in walled quarters had the advantage that these walls could often serve as the boundaries of an eruv, requiring little further manipulation of the urban space. But as Jews left those walls, the geography of integration posed new challenges for observant community members. Now eruvin had to encircle a much more dispersed community and required additional structures to create a continuous line for Shabbat, often traversing and criss-crossing streets shared with Christians and sometimes becoming the source of conflict about the place of religion on public land, such as in the case of the Bromberg eruv.

On 7 December 1822, the Municipality of Bromberg (now Bydgoszcz in Poland), in the northeast of Prussia in the Province of Posen, a territory that Prussia seized after the partitions of Poland, wrote to the Prussian Minister of the Interior regarding the 'string walls' of the Jews in the town.[32] The Municipality wanted to know whether it could let its police forces dismantle these 'symbolic walls'. The strings and poles of the eruv, the Municipality claimed, would add further clutter to the streets, which would disfigure the already unsightly cityscape. Moreover, the structure of the eruv would serve a religious purpose and Jews did not have the right to practice their religion in public. Prussia had left the legal status of Jews in the territories it seized from Poland initially unresolved. The Prussian government considered Posen's Jews inferior to Jews in its other regions and not worthy of the rights granted by the 1812 edict. The Poznan Diet had decided against adopting the statute.[33] The Municipality therefore

[32] My discussion draws on the excellent documentation of the Bromberg eruv in Joachim Schlör, *Das Ich Der Stadt: Debatten Über Judentum Und Urbanität 1822–1938* (Göttingen: Vandenhoeck & Ruprecht, 2005). Translations from German to English are mine. See also the discussion of eruvin in Peter Freimark, 'Eruw/"Judentore". Zur Geschichte Einer Rituellen Institution Im Hamburger Raum (Und Anderswo)'. in *Judentore, Kuggel, Steuerkonten. Untersuchungen Zur Geschichte Der Deutschen Juden, Vornehmlich Im Hamburger Raum*, ed. Peter Freimark, Ina Lorenz, and Günter Marwedel (Hamburg: Hans Christians Verlag, 1983), 10–55.

[33] Sorkin, *Jewish Emancipation*, p. 152.

invoked provisions of the General State Laws for the Prussian States (*Allgemeines Landrecht for die Preußischen Staaten (1794)*), arguing that tolerated religious communities such as the Jews were only allowed to practise their traditions within the confines of designated buildings, such as synagogues, or in the private apartments of members of that community.[34] Even if the practice of the eruv had a long tradition, the Municipality reasoned, Prussian law did not allow the Jews to use the public roads for these purposes. Given these considerations, the Municipality deemed it reasonable to forbid the practice and thereby to also eliminate an object that would only foster the segregation of the 'Mosaic fellow believer'.[35]

The Municipality had to wait patiently for a response from the Prussian officials. After two years, a letter arrived from the authorities in Berlin stating the view that it would be left to the Municipality to intervene according to police laws if the strings constituted a significant grievance. This response initiated a lively exchange of letters between Prussian authorities, rabbinical scholars, and the Municipality of Bromberg. In a letter to the Prussian ministry, Bromberg's Rabbi Abraham Weschnau asked to tolerate the 'Shabbat strings' which had been, he argued, a common feature in Prussian towns for ages. The Ministry, however, replied that it would not be able to override the ordinance of the Bromberg Municipality that had the right to ban the eruv based on Section 25 of the Prussian General State Laws that does not allow tolerated religious communities to 'use bells, or engage in public ceremonies outside the walls of their congregation building'. The regional Chief Rabbi countered that the Ministry had an exaggerated idea of the visual appearance of the strings which he considered to be a quiet religious practice in which neither prayers nor any assembly or religious festival would take place.[36] In other correspondence, Prussian authorities claimed that 'these traditions are not appropriate to our contemporary culture'. In 1835, the Ministry finally issued an ordinance by the Prussian King, which granted permission to establish an eruv if no additional poles were erected and the strings were unobtrusive and high enough to not disturb traffic and pedestrians.[37]

[34] The relevant provisions are to be found in Part Two of the *General State Laws for the Prussian States* (1794), Eleventh Title, Sections 20, 23, 25

[35] Quoted in Schlör, *Das Ich der Stadt*, pp. 11–12.

[36] Schlör, *Das Ich der Stadt*, p. 13.

[37] Schlör, *Das Ich der Stadt*, p. 13.

The Prussian opponents of the Jewish 'Shabbat borders' interpreted the eruv within a framework of secularisation and emancipation. The practice of the eruv clashed with the reformist project of the times that aimed to slowly turn the subjects of the monarch into citizens of a nation. The spatial dimension of this transformative project required the opening of the city and hence the liberation of Jews from their separate quarters to which they had been – sometimes voluntarily, sometimes involuntarily – confined.[38] The insistence on these ritual boundaries marked Jewish communities in the eyes of those who pushed for this transformation as not willing or capable of reform and modernisation.[39] Prussian authorities believed that the segregation of Jews into separate quarters was not only in contravention of the law of their times. Segregation also stood in the way of Jewish regeneration. Preventing particularistic spatial practices such as the eruv would 'foster the spiritual and moral culture of the Jews' by 'working against the natural tendency of Jews to segregate themselves' and by 'urging them to amalgamate with Christians as much as possible'.[40] The 'liberation' of Jews from their traditional modes of living proved complex on the ground because of the ways that entrenched boundaries, both physical and social, continued to contain the presence of Jews in the Christian towns of Prussia. Official Prussian policies sometimes clashed with municipal practices and local expectations by both Jews and non-Jews that still aimed to preserve the spatial segregation of Jews.

JEWISH SPACES IN THE CONTEMPORARY CITY

More than a century later, arguments expressed in Bromberg still resonate with contemporary disputes over eruvin even though the local nature often adds a vernacular twist to eruv opposition.[41] Not all of these

[38] Schlör, *Das Ich der Stadt*, pp. 13–14.
[39] Schlör, *Das Ich der Stadt*, p. 23.
[40] Schlör, *Das Ich der Stadt*, p. 14.
[41] Eruv conflicts reflect local concerns, such as in Johannesburg where residents worried that an eruv would increase criminal behaviour in the streets: Steve Lipman, 'Letter From South Africa', Winter 2011, www.jewishaction.com/jewish-world/travel/letter_from_south_africa. In Los Angeles, residents feared the eruv would endanger local wildlife: Jerusalem Post Staff, 'LA Jews Meet Resistance to Eruv Wall', *Jerusalem Post*, 24 October 2006.

cases have entered the courtroom, instead remaining on the level of the local, fought out in council halls, community meetings, and local newspapers. The majority of eruv litigation has taken place in the United States, perhaps reflecting the size of the Jewish-American population of whom almost a tenth identifies as Orthodox.[42] Once the eruv enters the formal realm of litigation, legal questions of constitutional separation, the secularity of public space, and the boundaries of public religiosity often take centre stage, such as in the case of the eruv in Tenafly in the US state of New Jersey. The trouble began in 1999, when the Tenafly Eruv Association approached the Mayor of Tenafly to obtain permission from the Borough to erect an eruv in the town. While the Mayor was initially supportive of the project, other Council members were less inclined.[43] In response to the proposal to attach lechis to poles, the Borough eventually invoked an ordinance which states that

> No person shall place any sign or advertisement, or other matter upon any pole, tree, curbstone, sidewalk or elsewhere, in any public street or public place, excepting such as may be authorized by this or any other ordinance of the Borough.[44]

Although the Borough based its refusal of the eruv on the application of the ordinance, it had in fact granted many exemptions to it. Residents had used the utility poles to attach house numbers or lost pet signs. Local churches had pinned their directional signs with crosses to the poles, and for a while, supporters of a local high school had installed orange ribbons to express their view on school regionalisation – actions the Council so far had condoned. But things were different with the eruv. When the Council voted against the eruv, the lechis had already been attached to the power poles, which belonged to the local cable company. The Borough thus ordered the cable company to take the eruv down, an order against which the Eruv Association filed a complaint in the District Court. The District Court ruled in favour of the town[45] but the Eruv Association

[42] Michelle Boorstein, 'New Poll: Young U.S. Jews Becoming More Orthodox as American Judaism Splits between Devout and Secular', *Washington Post*, 11 May 2021.

[43] For a detailed account of the events in Tenafly, see Susan H. Lees, 'Jewish Space in Suburbia: Interpreting the Eruv Conflict in Tenafly, New Jersey', *Contemporary Jewry* 27, no. 1 (2007): 42–79, pp. 53–62.

[44] Quoted in *Tenafly Eruv Association, Inc. v. Borough of Tenafly*, 309 F.3d 144 (3d Cir. 2002), at 151 ('*Tenafly Eruv Association v. Borough of Tenafly*').

[45] *Tenafly Eruv Association v. Borough of Tenafly*, 155 F. Supp. 2d (D.N.J. 2001).

immediately appealed this decision to the US Court of Appeals of the Third Circuit.[46] The plaintiffs based their appeal on both a free speech claim, which the Court dismissed, as it did not consider the eruv to be a form of speech, and on a free exercise of religion claim based on the First Amendment of the US Constitution, which the Court addressed in detail.

The Free Exercise Clause of the Constitution of the United States provides that 'Congress shall make no law respecting the establishment of religion, or prohibiting the free exercise thereof …' – a clause to which the Borough is bound through the Fourteenth Amendment.[47] A law that is neutral and generally applicable, and therefore burdens religious conduct only incidentally, does not violate the Free Exercise Clause. If the law is, however, not neutral (because it discriminates, for example, against religiously motivated conduct), or it is not generally applicable (because it forbids, for example, certain conduct only when religiously motivated), the Free Exercise clause is violated unless the public authority has the law narrowly tailored in order to advance a compelling government interest.[48] The Borough had insisted that enforcing its ordinance was of such compelling interest. But the Court immediately dismissed this argument as the Borough had tolerated all sorts of permanent signs on the utility poles in violation of the ordinance. The Mayor had tried to downplay this signage by calling the church signs 'directional' and the lights and garlands during Christmas 'temporary holiday displays'.[49] The Borough was convinced that the eruv was different and sent a religious message, which made its ban a compelling interest in order to prevent 'an Establishment controversy'. Because of the lechis' religious nature, allowing them onto public poles would amount to an unconstitutional endorsement of Orthodox Judaism, the Borough contended.[50]

[46] *Tenafly Eruv Association, Inc. v. Borough of Tenafly*, 309 F.3d 144 (3d Cir. 2002). For a discussion of the background history of the Tenafly case, see Zachary Heiden, 'Fences and Neighbors', *Law and Literature* 17, no. 2 (2005): 225–48.

[47] *Tenafly Eruv Association. v. Borough of Tenafly*, at 151.

[48] *Tenafly Eruv Association, Inc. v. Borough of Tenafly*, at 165.

[49] Quoted in Matthew Purdy, 'A Wire-Thin Line Sharply Divides a Suburb's Jews', *New York Times*, 25 March 2011.

[50] While Courts have focused on the visibility of the lechis as sending a message of endorsement, legal scholars have argued that the endorsement problem may actually lie in the lease agreement whereby the public authority rents out a portion of the public space to the eruv community, see, for example, Alexandra Lang Susman, 'Strings Attached: An Analysis of the Eruv under the Religion Clauses

At this point, the case became a matter of defining the symbolic message of the eruv, revealing how the law ultimately evaded dealing with the deeper and ambiguous symbolism of the eruv. The Court relied on the 'Endorsement test'[51] in order to ascertain if the action constituted a forbidden establishment of religion.[52] The Endorsement test asks whether a government action is sending 'a message to non-adherents that they are outsiders, not full members of the political community, and an accompanying message to adherents that they are insiders, favored members of the political community'.[53] Residents who opposed the eruv had indeed feared that the wires and poles would turn them into outsiders in their town. For those residents, as Susan Lees argues, the Tenafly eruv expressed 'an inherent exclusion of others – not so much in the creation of boundaries, but in the expression of communality through the shared (but exclusive) observance of communal "walls" that are essential to an eruv'.[54] Indeed, one resident, who identified himself as Jewish, saw the eruv as threatening Jewish belonging to the wider urban community and argued that the eruv was the 'antithesis of inclusion' which would create 'a separation in Tenafly, us from them, the tribe from the rest of the community'.[55]

The Court, however, did not concern itself with the symbolic message that residents wished to have acknowledged by law. Instead, the Court considered what 'a reasonable observer' would think about the permission itself to attach the lechis.[56] The Court concluded that such a reasonable observer, who knew of the Borough's obligation to treat the eruv's lechis like other postings, would not believe that the

of the First Amendment and the Religious Land Use and Institutionalized Persons Act', *University of Maryland Law Journal of Race, Religion, Gender & Class* 9 (2009): 93–134, pp. 114–18.

[51] On the Endorsement test, see, for example, Jesse H. Choper, 'The Endorsement Test: Its Status and Desirability', *Journal of Law & Politics* 18, no. 2 (2002): 499–536.

[52] In fact, three other courts have held that allowing an eruv is constitutional, see the discussion of the Westhampton Beach in this chapter as well as *East End Eruv Association v. Town of Southampton*, No. 14-21124 (Sup. Ct. Suffolk Co. June 30, 2015); *ACLU of N.J. v. City of Long Branch*, 670 F. Supp. 1293, 1295–97 (D.N.J. 1987); *Smith v. Community Board No. 14*, 128 Misc. 2d 944 (Sup. Ct. Queens Co. Special Term 1985), affirmed, 133 A.D.2d 79 (2d Dept. 1987).

[53] *Lynch v. Donnelly*, 465 U.S. 668 (1984), p. 688.

[54] Lees, 'Jewish Space', p. 68.

[55] Quoted in George James, 'Drawing a Line in Tenafly', *The New York Times*, 31 December 2000.

[56] *Tenafly Eruv Association, Inc. v. Borough of Tenafly* (2002), at 176–177.

Borough would promote Orthodox Judaism or attribute the decision of attaching lechis to the State. Moreover, the Court dismissed the idea of the eruv's symbolic communication and stated that it did not see any evidence that 'the unobtrusive lechis are intended to send a religious message to anyone',[57] thereby treating the eruv's materiality as an almost mundane piece of street furniture. Even if an observer would mistake the eruv as an establishment, the Court reasoned, there was a greater risk that an observer could perceive the removal of the eruv as a hostility towards Orthodox Jews.[58] Thus, while the Court dismissed the opponents' fear of the eruv's ambiguous symbolism, it was well aware of another symbolism that a ban on the eruv would send – the unequal treatment of the Orthodox Jewish lechis as compared to other signage. The town appealed the decision to the US Supreme Court, which declined to hear the case. In 2006, the Borough agreed with the Eruv Association to reimburse the group for the court costs, which had amounted to $325,000.[59]

Similar questions underpinned a 2001 dispute in the Canadian city of Outremont in which Orthodox Jews claimed protection for the eruv as a matter of religious freedom and challenged the neutrality of the city authority in matters of religion. Outremont is today an arrondissement of Montréal and is still home to unlikely neighbours. It is a preferred location for wealthier francophone Quebecois and at the same time home to a large Jewish population. Almost a quarter of Outremont's population is Hasidic, making it one of the largest Hasidic communities outside Israel.[60] Trendy cafés and traditional Orthodox Jewish garb both form part of the arrondissement's street scenery. Tensions arose between Outremont's residents when

[57] *Tenafly Eruv Association. v. Borough of Tenafly*, at 177.

[58] *Tenafly Eruv Association. v. Borough of Tenafly*, at 177.

[59] Tina Kelley, 'Town Votes for Marker Used by Jews', *The New York Times*, 25 January 2006.

[60] Hasidic Judaism is a form of strictly Orthodox Judaism, originating in the eighteenth century in Eastern Europe as a movement of religious revival. Hasidism is in fact a collective term for a variety of groups, who live in tight-knit communities, centred around a dynastic leader who is known as the Rebbe. The names of these groups often derive from the names of the East European towns from where the dynastic leaders originated, such as the Lubavitch from Lubovicze in the Polish-Lithuanian Commonwealth (today in Russia) or the Bobov from Bobova in Polish Galicia. Today, large Hasidic groups can be found, for example, in Israel, in New York, and in Melbourne. It is important to note that the eruv conflict in Outremont did not break down neatly along Jewish-non-Jewish lines. Many non-Jewish

an application to erect an eruv reached the City Council. The City Council rejected the proposal on the grounds that it would disturb the city's efforts to remain secular[61] and further argued that the eruv contravened the idea that public property belongs to everybody.[62] The Jewish community obtained a temporary court injunction against the Council's decision, which made it possible to set up an eruv just before the holiday of Passover in 2000. But following complaints by local residents, the City began to cut down the wires of the eruv soon after. Jewish residents appealed against this action to the Quebec Superior Court. They argued that the dismantling of the eruv constituted a violation of the exercise of their right to religion and sought an accommodation under Section 3 of the *Quebec Charter of Human Rights and Freedoms*, which provides that 'every person is the possessor of fundamental freedoms, including ... freedom of religion ...' and Section 2(b) of the *Canadian Charter of Rights and Freedoms*, which enshrines the freedom of belief as a fundamental freedom. Moreover, the claimants questioned the neutrality of the Council's action as Christmas decorations had been allowed to be attached onto public property for years.[63] As in Tenafly, the Jewish community held that their right to religious freedom included the erection of an eruv and that the principle of religious equality warranted their right to access and use public space as did Christianity.

The City of Outremont argued that its hands were tied given that it did not have 'jurisdiction to permit anything to be done on religious grounds because of [its] secular vocation'.[64] The dismantling of the eruv, the City argued, would not violate the right to religious freedom of Shabbat-observant Jews as the place in which freedom of religion is practiced was not a component part of said right, allowing the City to legally control the use of the air space over its streets.[65]

French-Canadians voiced their support for the eruv, while some Hasidim opposed the eruv. For a detailed analysis of the case, see Valerie Stoker, 'Drawing the Line: Hasidic Jews, Eruvim, and the Public Space of Outremont, Quebec', *History of Religions* 43, no. 1 (2003): 18–49.

61 Bram Eisenthal, 'Canadian Court Rules for Jews in Shabbat Case', *Jewish Telegraphic Agency*, 25 June 2011.

62 Ingrid Peritz, 'Chi-Chi Quebec Enclave Clashes with Hasidim', *The Globe and Mail*, 18 October 2000.

63 *Rosenberg v. Outremont (City)*, [2001] R.J.Q. 1556 (S.C.), at 12 ('*Rosenberg v. Outremont*')

64 *Rosenberg v. Outremont*, at 12.

65 *Rosenberg v. Outremont*, at 14.

Moreover, the City stated that, even if the dismantling of the eruv violated the religious freedom of the applicants, this violation was justified by competing rights, which in this case was the City's 'duty to maintain the public domain accessible to all residents on the same basis and without distinction'.[66] The City had also argued before that allowing Christmas decorations did not contradict its secular stance, as these were 'primarily a commercial prop put up at the request of shopkeepers'.[67] Whereas the eruv was clearly a religious structure, Christian symbols had acquired a commercialised meaning, detaching them, in the opinion of the City, from their religious meanings and roots.

The City received vocal support from a local secularist group, the 'Mouvement Laïque Québécois', which claimed that the eruv violated its freedom *from* religion. The group argued that the eruv would transform the area into 'an officially recognized religious territory' which, other than a synagogue or a church, they would not be able to avoid.[68] The group opposed the eruv because it saw the eruv as a type of zoning for religious neighbourhoods to the effect that religious principles would prevail over the civil laws of Quebec.[69] The eruv, it argued, would violate the right to freedom from religion as it imposed itself onto all residents.[70] Instead of seeking accommodation from the City, the group contended that Orthodox Jews should seek relief from their own Orthodox Jewish authorities, which constituted the actual source of the problem by upholding restrictive Shabbat laws.[71]

In its decision, the Quebec Superior Court addressed all these concerns but found none of them convincing. The Court noted that the Canadian Constitution does not itself contain an Establishment clause as in the United States, but it acknowledged that there may be a conflict between the state's duty to accommodate religion and the obligation of neutrality.[72] First, the Court determined whether

66 *Rosenberg v. Outremont*, at 14.

67 Peritz, 'Chi-Chi Quebec Enclave'.

68 *Rosenberg v. Outremont*, at 18.

69 Annick Germain and Julie Elizabeth Gagnon, 'Minority Places of Worship and Zoning Dilemmas in Montréal', *Planning Theory & Practice* 4, no. 3 (2003): 295–318, p. 312.

70 *Rosenberg v. Outremont*, at 19.

71 *Rosenberg v. Outremont*, at 20.

72 *Rosenberg v. Outremont*, at 29.

the eruv was protected by the right to freedom of religion and, if so, whether the claimants were entitled to an accommodation including the 'use of air space over City streets'.[73] On the first question, the Court had no doubt that the eruv did fall under the right to religious freedom, interpreting the eruv as 'essential for the attendance of Orthodox Jews at Sabbath services, and their participation in related activities upon completion'.[74] The Court then refuted the idea that Orthodox Jews should seek an accommodation from their own authorities, as the eruv already constituted such an accommodation to facilitate the observance of Shabbat laws.[75] It also rejected the City's argument of religious neutrality, noting that Canadian and Quebec law were themselves not absolutely neutral, given, for example, the official observance of Christian religious holidays in the Quebecois calendar.[76]

The accommodation of the eruv, the Court continued, would not constitute any inconvenience or hardship to other residents considering the absence of any demonstrated harm. Indeed, complaining residents had refused to provide evidence for the hardship they had claimed the eruv would impose on them. Thus, the Court held, the actual impact of the eruv had to be proven by showing how the eruv would alter the quality of life of those living within its boundary. Mere symbolic impact or impact that is comparable to the ringing of church bells was not sufficient to warrant the restriction of the Orthodox Jews' religious freedom, the Court explained.[77] Moreover, the Court rejected the idea that the eruv would create a religious zone, pointing out that the eruv only affected the practitioners of Orthodox Judaism.[78] As Valerie Stoker observes, the decision thereby endorsed a multivalent view of public space by refusing to accept that the eruv would cast a 'religious shadow' onto all residents.[79] Ultimately, the Court concluded that the City had a constitutional duty to accommodate the eruv as a religious practice which did not impose undue hardship on other residents of Outremont.[80]

[73] *Rosenberg v. Outremont*, at 30.
[74] *Rosenberg v. Outremont*, at 36.
[75] *Rosenberg v. Outremont*, at 38.
[76] *Rosenberg v. Outremont*, at 42.
[77] *Rosenberg v. Outremont*, at 25.
[78] *Rosenberg v. Outremont*, at 44.
[79] Stoker, 'Drawing the Line', p. 43.
[80] *Rosenberg v. Outremont*, at 46.

DEFENDING THE NAKED PUBLIC SPACE: JEWISH OPPOSITION TO ERUVIN

Whereas opposition to circumcision has been largely driven by non-Jews, the eruv has also been a source of discontent between different groups of Jews, pitting more secular and liberal-leaning Jews against their Orthodox Jewish neighbour. That secular and liberal Jews belong to the most vocal opponents of an eruv is in fact not rare.[81] In Tenafly, several Jewish residents joined their non-Jewish neighbours, creating 'oddly ecumenical effects'[82] in their union against the eruv. Historically, such cases were argued only within the realm of Jewish law and concerned the ifs and hows of an eruv. Today, opposing Jews do not shy away from appealing to secular law in order to intervene in what could pass as an internal Jewish matter if read as a claim about the authenticity of Jewish practice.

One such case is the dispute over the Westhampton Beach eruv where the people who objected to the eruv most vehemently were themselves Jewish. The group called *Jewish People for the Betterment of Westhampton Beach* (also known as JPOE – Jewish People Opposed to the Eruv) consisted of a number of liberal and secular leaning Jews who had organised themselves in order to protest an eruv, which had been put forward by the Modern Orthodox Synagogue of Westhampton Beach in 2008. Fearing that the eruv would 'create another ghetto', one of JPOE's leaders complained that 'As a reform Jew, I find it extremely offensive to create a distinction that this is a Jewish area'.[83] The events in the affluent Hamptons even made it into national television. A short segment in *The Daily Show* introduced the Jewish eruv to the wider public and mocked both proponents and opponents alike by suggesting a 'portable eruv hat' as an easy solution to what seemed to some to be a bizarre quarrel.[84]

In 2011, JPOE took the Village of Westhampton Beach and the local power provider to court, arguing that the attachment of the eruv's

[81] In Barnet, London, secular and liberal Jews also objected to an eruv, see the excellent analysis by Davina Cooper, 'Talmudic Territory? Space, Law, and Modernist Discourse', *Journal of Law and Society* 23, no. 4 (1996): 529–48, p. 538.

[82] Myer Siemiatycki, 'Contesting Sacred Urban Space: The Case of the Eruv', *Journal of International Migration and Integration/Revue de l'integration et de la migration internationale* 6, no. 2 (2005): 255–70, p. 262.

[83] Quoted in Matt A. V. Chaban, 'Hamptons Town Nears a Deal on a Jewish Ritual Boundary', *The New York Times*, 29 May 2016.

[84] The video is available online via www.jewishhumorcentral.com/2011/03/daily-show-pokes-fun-at-eruv-battle-in.html.

lechis on public utility poles constituted an unconstitutional establishment of religion – arguments similar to those of the residents in Tenafly. The members of JPOE rejected the claim that the eruv would be inconspicuous and complained that:

> The eruv, of course, will not go unnoticed; rather it will be a constant and ever-present symbol, message and reminder to the community at large, that the secular public spaces of the Village have been transformed for religious use and identity; to the non-Jewish residents, that the Village and LIPA [the local power provider] have given preferred status to the Jewish religion as the only faith permitted to permanently affix religious symbols to utility poles within the Village or to physically demarcate certain public spaces with particular religious significance; and to large portions of the Jewish community within the Village, that one particular form of Judaism has been preferred and endorsed by the Village over another.[85]

In order to refute any allegations of antisemitism, the plaintiffs were eager to stress that they too were 'proud and observant Jews' – albeit belonging to denominations that would take a critical stance towards the eruv as a valid interpretation of Jewish law. Citing the official position of the Central Conference of American Rabbis (an umbrella organisation of Reform Judaism) in their complaint to the Court, JPOE attacked the eruv for elevating 'such legalistic constructs over the true spiritual values of Judaism'.[86] What JPOE presents, then, is a version of Judaism that emphasises internal belief over the more public nature of Orthodoxy.

The US Court of Appeals for the Second Circuit ultimately rejected JPOE's complaint in 2015 after applying the Lemon test.[87] In US constitutional jurisprudence on religious freedom, the Lemon test has been used next to the Endorsement test to assess whether an action violates the Establishment clause of the US Constitution. According to the Lemon test, a government action or a law complies with the requirements of the Establishment Clause if the law has a legitimate secular purpose, if it does not have a primary effect of either advancing

[85] *Complaint: Jewish People for the Betterment of Westhampton Beach v. Village of Westhampton Beach*, No. CV-123760, 30 July 2012, p. 1 ('*Complaint*') Available from https://westhamptonbeach.org/wp-content/uploads/2012/10/complaint-JPOE-against-village.pdf. Emphasis in original.

[86] *Complaint*, p. 2.

[87] *Jewish People for the Betterment of Westhampton Beach v. Village of Westhampton Beach*, 778 F.3d 390 (2d Cir. 2015) ('*JPOE v. Westhampton Beach*')

or inhibiting religion, and if it does not result in an excessive entanglement of government and religion.[88] Although the plaintiffs had argued that the establishment of an eruv served no secular purpose, the Court found that the mere action of allowing lechis to be attached to public power poles did indeed have a secular purpose. 'Neutral accommodation of religious practice', the Court reasoned, 'qualifies as a secular purpose under Lemon'.[89] Hence, simply accommodating religion did not give an action itself a religious purpose. In a second step, the Court asked, as in the case of Tenafly, whether a reasonable observer would perceive the lechis as a message of government endorsement or sponsorship of a religion and quickly dismissed this possibility by stating that no reasonable observer would draw the conclusion that a state actor was endorsing religion by allowing simple plastic strips to be attached to poles.[90] Finally, the fact that the maintenance and financing lay solely in the hands of the Modern Orthodox community, there was also no risk of excessive government entanglement with religion.[91] The Court thus decided in favour of the eruv and in line with other courts in the US, which have so far been overwhelmingly sympathetic to eruvin.[92]

Jewish opposition to eruvin is driven by a complex amalgam of concerns. Sophie Watson has suggested that more liberal Jews perceive the public display of Jewish Orthodoxy as 'a source of discomfort of being publicly exposed as Jewish'.[93] In this interpretation, the spatial manifestation of Jewish difference represents a threat to a precarious sense of belonging and acculturation to the Christian majority. Indeed, the eruv, to some extent, brings to the surface the complex work of assimilation. While assimilation, Zygmunt Bauman observed, is an essentially individual task, its success is assessed at the level of the community that faces the consequences of individual members' failure to assimilate. Being assimilated only confers privileges if achieved by everyone because assimilation is assessed 'like the carrying capacity of a bridge' with the focus on the

88 *Lemon v. Kurtzman*, 403 U.S. 602 (1971), at 612–613.
89 *JPOE v. Westhampton Beach* (2015), at 395.
90 *JPOE v. Westhampton Beach*, at 396.
91 *JPOE v. Westhampton Beach*, at 396.
92 In addition to the cases discussed here, see also, for example, *American Civil Liberties Union v. City of Long Branch*, 670 F. Supp. 1293 (D.N.J. 1987).
93 Sophie Watson, 'Symbolic Spaces of Difference: Contesting the Eruv in Barnet, London and Tenafly, New Jersey', *Environment and Planning D: Society and Space* 23, no. 4 (2005): 597–613, at 610. See also Cooper, 'Talmudic Territory', at 530.

weakest part.[94] Hence, the excess of Orthodox Jewish religiosity is seen as undermining the successful assimilation and therefore the acceptance of *all Jews*. In this reading, mobilising the law of the state and its core values, such as constitutional separation, constitutes an attempt of disciplining of 'bad Jews' by 'good Jews'. The demands of assimilation thus work even without the direct involvement of members of the dominant culture and instead play out through an internal process of policing and control by the subjects of assimilation who are willing to mobilise the law of the state to enforce compliance.

However, it would be reductive to read these conflicts through the prism of assimilation alone and imply that liberal and Reform Jews suffer from 'false consciousness', acting only as agents of assimilation, and thereby wrongly present Orthodox Judaism as the more authentic form of Jewishness. Disputes over eruvin also bring to the fore concerns about internal Jewish pluralism that some see under threat by Orthodox Judaism's growing assertiveness and claim to authenticity at the expense of other forms of Jewishness. Indeed, David Schraub ponders whether the ongoing trend towards a more robust legal protection of religious freedom in the United States coupled with a resurging conservative Christian nationalism will make it more difficult for liberal Jews to secure legal protection for their vision of Jewishness.[95] At the same time, Schraub observes, Orthodox Jews benefit from aligning with more conservative Christians, thereby assimilating into an equally powerful norm of 'devout religiosity' that resonates with American society.[96]

Hence, the call upon the authority of state law by eruv-opposing Jews can be read not only as defence of a precarious assimilation but also equally as an attempt to safeguard Jewish pluralism against a perceived Orthodox pursuit of dominance. As one opponent in Westhampton Beach stressed: 'All Jews are not lumped together. They come in many forms'.[97] This is an ongoing struggle within American Jewry over internal Jewish pluralism that Samuel Freedman describes in his book *Jew vs. Jew*:

> One is unity and the other is pluralism, and both are innocuous euphemisms for more controversial agendas. As invoked by America's Orthodox Jews, 'unity' means unity if all Jews act and think as we do,

94 Bauman, *Modernity and Ambivalence*, p. 142.
95 Schraub, 'Liberal Jews'.
96 Schraub, 'Liberal Jews', pp. 35–36.
97 Quoted in Kelly Carroll, 'Westhampton's Anti-Eruv Group Claims 85 Percent of Village Opposed to Religious Designation', *Hamptons.com*, 11 September 2008.

> accepting the inerrancy of Torah and the yoke of all 613 commandments, the mitzvoth. As invoked by America's non-Orthodox Jews, 'pluralism' means that any variation of Judaism must be accepted by everyone, no obligation required and no questions asked.[98]

An eruv therefore reflects not only the perils of assimilation as a regulatory regime but also reveals internal Jewish struggles over power and authenticity, pluralism, and unity. For some of Westhampton Beach's Reform and secular Jews, the eruv seemed to have undermined the co-existence of competing visions of Jewish identity, as its wires anchored Orthodoxy in the public sphere. By invoking the constitutional provision against establishment, JPOE tried to push back against the symbolic overreach of their Orthodox neighbours and to safeguard their vision of public space, where no Jewish denomination was to predominate. Moreover, the public accommodation of only one form of Jewishness may have been seen as a potentially slippery slope to Israeli conditions where Orthodox Jews have repeatedly sought to impose their interpretation of Jewish law onto Israeli society as a whole.

For JPOE in Westhampton Beach, the protection of a naked public space devoid of religion appeared to be the most suitable legal strategy for protecting Jewish identity and pluralism. Historically, American Jews have been strong supporters of constitutional separation of state and church, constituting, as Pierre Birnbaum describes, the 'last Habermassians, the only remaining lovers of reason seeking the benefits of a public space under the protection of an enlightened law'.[99] American Jewish support for strict separation meant pushing back against the entrenched dominance of Protestantism, which would have relegated Jews to second-class citizenship. Only during the 1960s, Naomi Cohen describes, some American Jews found the confidence to litigate in favour of the inclusion of Jewish practices alongside Christian symbols under the free exercise clause.[100] The Westhampton Beach eruv conflict speaks to the unresolved question of what constitutes the best legal pathway for achieving equality for Jews and other non-Christians in a still predominantly Christian nation – either via strict separation or via equal accommodation. In Westhampton, either

98 Samuel G. Freedman, *Jew vs. Jew: The Struggle for the Soul of American Jewry* (New York: Simon & Schuster, 2000), 26.

99 Pierre Birnbaum, 'On the Secularization of the Public Square: Jews in France and in the United States', *Cardozo Law Review* 30, no. 6 (2009): 2431–43, p. 2433.

100 Cohen, *Jews in Christian America*, pp. 6–7.

pathway appeared to give preference to a certain notion of Jewishness as the one most suited to American church-state relationships.

The dispute over the Westhampton Beach eruv is an important reminder that eruvin are not merely matters of contention between Jews and non-Jews, but frequently involve other Jews. At times, opposition to an eruv comes even from strictly observant Jews, who see their values and understandings of law and space threatened by the appearance of an eruv. This type of eruv controversy is distinct, not only because it usually remains within the realms of Jewish religious law but also because it sheds a different light on the internal pluralism of answers that Jews have found to the pressure of assimilation and the challenges of secular modernity. In 2016, in Crown Heights in Brooklyn, New York, an eruv became the subject of a dispute between a local modern Orthodox and a strictly Orthodox community who lived in close proximity neighbourhood space, but did not share the same vision of Jewish law and life.[101]

Crown Heights is home to a significant African American population, but it is also known as the location of the headquarters of Chabad Lubavitch, a Hasidic movement originating from Lithuania.[102] Several thousand Lubavitch Jews call this part of Brooklyn their home. Hasidism was founded by Israel Ba'al Shem Tov in what is today Western Ukraine in the eighteenth century. Like other strictly Orthodox Jewish groups, the Lubavitch Jews pursue a lifestyle of strict Torah observance and strive to limit their contact with the non-Hasidic world.[103] However, as Jan Feldman notes, while seeking to preserve their thousands of years old traditions, they are 'anything but isolated from the secular, liberal world', often engaging in a pragmatic fashion with the surrounding world.[104]

101 For an account of the events, see Sam Kestenbaum, 'Controversial Brooklyn Eruv for Modern Orthodox Vandalized Amid Dispute with Chabad', *Forward*, July 12, 2016, http://forward.com/news/344767/controversial-brooklyn-eruv-for-modern-orthodox-vandalized-amid-dispute-wit/?attribution=articles-article-related-1-headline.

102 On relations between Hasidic Jews and African Americans in the Crown Heights, see Henry Goldschmidt, *Race and Religion among the Chosen People of Crown Heights* (New Brunswick: Rutgers University Press, 2006).

103 Chabad Lubavitch Jews differ from other strictly Orthodox (Haredi) Jewish groups in their attitude towards non-Haredi Jews, with whom they seek contact in order to encourage them to adopt a more stringent religious observance, a practice termed *kiruv*, which means 'bringing close', see www.chabad.org/library/article_cdo/aid/676588/jewish/What-is-Kiruv.htm.

104 Jan Feldman, *Lubavitchers as Citizens. A Paradox of Liberal Democracy* (Ithaca; London: Cornell University Press, 2003), p. 13.

Over the years, the neighbourhood had seen a growing number of non-Hasidic Modern Orthodox Jews moving to the area seeking affordable housing. Modern Orthodoxy is the most liberal stream within Orthodox Judaism that, among other things, allows for greater participation of women. The Modern Orthodox congregation *Kol Israel* began planning an eruv which encompassed significant parts of the traditional settlement area of the Lubavitch Jews. As soon as the Greater Crown Heights eruv, which complements two other eruvin in the area, was set up, the Hasidic rabbinical court (*Beit Din*) immediately opposed the structure. The Beit Din reminded the community that Rabbi Menachem Schneerson himself, the late Lubavitcher leader, had forbidden the building of an eruv in Crown Heights. Since Schneerson had not appointed a successor, his edicts remain guiding for many of his followers. In June 2014, the Beit Din issued an edict deeming the new eruv to be not kosher because of its inclusion of unsuitable areas.[105] Rabbi Shlomo Yehuda Segal, a member of the Hasidic Beit Din, feared that the religious boundary would lead to 'the devastation of the Shabbat in our honourable neighbourhood'.[106] Another rabbi called the eruv the same as Reform Judaism[107] – an allegation which questioned the authenticity of their Modern Orthodox neighbours.

Although opposition to the Crown Heights eruv was articulated in technical-halakhic terms, the argument appeared to be not just about the exact interpretation of halakha but to concern an entire way of life that seemed to be threatened by the influx of Modern Orthodox Jews and their appropriation of neighbourhood space through the eruv. The fear seemed that some Lubavitchers could start using the Modern Orthodox eruv, undermining the authority of Lubavitch rabbinical authorities. From the perspective of the Hasidic Jews, the eruv appeared to have the potential to erode their distinct culture built on a strict observance of Jewish law by watering down Shabbat rules and ultimately the general standards of observance in the neighbourhood.[108]

105 JTA, 'Lubavitch Rabbis Issue Edict against Modern Orthodox Eruv in Crown Heights', 24 June 2016.

106 Kestenbaum, 'Controversial Brooklyn Eruv for Modern Orthodox Vandalized Amid Dispute with Chabad'.

107 See 'Rabbi Heller: Crown Heights Eruv Is Reform Judaism', *Crown Heights Info*, 24 June 2016, https://crownheights.info/communal-matters/537984/rabbi-heller-eruv-is-reform-judaism/.

108 Amy Sara Clark, 'Fight over New Eruv Erupts in Crown Heights', *Jewish Week*, 22 June 2016.

The wires of the new eruv thus posed a threat to the existing spatiolegal order of the Lubavitch society, rooted in the shared belief that no eruv was permissible in the area and that no Jew should carry in the public space of Crown Heights during the Shabbat. 'For many orthodox leaders', Oliver Valins explains, 'the institutionalisation of space provides a mechanism to maintain the social order (and a visible symbol of orthodox space), and thus any weakness to this must be countered'.[109] Quite differently from other controversies, in which opponents interpreted the eruv as a pre-modern and archaic practice, for the Lubavitch Jews, the Crown Heights eruv was precisely the opposite: The spatial manifestation of modernity's threat to their insular way of life. The eruv appeared as part and parcel of the growing gentrification and change of their neighbourhood driven by Modern Orthodox Jews. By introducing alternative readings of Jewish law and its spatiotemporal order into the streets of Brooklyn, the eruv brought the perceived dangers of the more secularised world closer to Hasidic doorsteps, threatening assimilation by undermining the primacy of Jewish law.

For Lubavitch Jews, resisting the eruv was a way to defend their way of life. The women of the community also weighed in. One of them refuted the gender equality argument of the Modern Orthodox community which presented the eruv in the classic way as a means to liberate young mothers from being trapped in the house during Shabbat: 'Do they think that they're trying to save me from myself, as a young mother? Do they think I'm sitting crying, trapped in my house on Shabbos and, now, they made me an eruv and I'm a liberated woman? That's offensive'.[110] In modern times, gender equality and the inclusion of the elderly and community members with a disability have become a core argument to sell eruvin to a liberal-minded public that will be less convinced by religious rationales alone. Some attribute the proliferation of eruvin in the United States during the twentieth century to the changing role of women in Jewish Orthodoxy. As women are often still the primary care givers, the prohibition on carrying often affects them disproportionately. Blu Greenberg, an Orthodox feminist scholar and activist, suggests that 'although no eruv has come out of a women's protest group, I think the increase in eruvin has something

[109] Oliver Valins, 'Institutionalised Religion: Sacred Texts and Jewish Spatial Practice', *Geoforum* 31, no. 4 (2000): 575–86, pp. 583–84.

[110] Quoted in Rachel Holliday Smith, 'Newly Built Eruv Repeatedly Vandalized Amid Uproar in Crown Heights', *DNA Info*, 25 July 2016.

to do with the new perception women have of themselves, their needs and their place in community life'.[111] But as this Hasidic woman's comment makes clear, the gender equality argument can be perceived as disrespectful and patronising, thereby reflecting the broader problem of advocating for women's rights in a way that remains attentive to cultural differences and the plurality of experiences of what it means to be a woman. Writing from a Lubavitch perspective, Jan Feldman points out that for Lubavitcher Jews, liberalism embodies 'the secular masculine ethos of individualism, aggressiveness, ambition, and self-gratification' whereas Judaism exemplifies the 'feminine ethos of collectivity, caring, and responsibility'.[112]

Differently to the secular-liberal Jews in Westhampton Beach, the Hasidic Jews of Crown Heights made no establishment claim in secular courts in order to prevent the eruv. Instead, they took matters in their own hands.[113] Only days after the Hasidic authorities published their verdict, the wire was cut.[114] Eventually the conflict spilled over to the neighbouring Park Slope eruv, which was damaged too. Two Hasidic men were arrested and charged with hate crime – a charge the police eventually dropped.[115] The Lubavitch leaders distanced themselves from the actions. Some community members took a more peaceful strategy to question the eruv and published a Dr Seuss-style poem on Facebook calling for peaceful co-existence while warning of the subversive dangers of the wires brought in by their Modern Orthodox neighbours:

> I would not carry in the street/But not because YOU'RE not elite/It's cause the Rebbe made concrete/
>
> A Crown Heights Eruv no matter how neat/Will only confuse – and breed deceit.[116]

111 Blu Greenberg, *How to Run a Traditional Jewish Household* (New York; London; Toronto; Sydney: Simon & Schuster, 1983), 49. See also Lees, 'Jewish Space', p. 44.

112 Feldman, *Lubavitchers as Citizens*, p. 8.

113 Strictly Orthodox Jews in the United States have frequently and successfully mobilised secular law and used secular courts to protect the homogeneity and insularity of their community. See Stolzenberg and Myers, *American Shtetl*.

114 Holliday Smith, 'Newly Built Eruv'.

115 'Two Arrested in Connection with Eruv Vandalism', *Crown Heights Info*, 27 October 2016, https://crownheights.info/crime/552088/two-arrested-in-connection-with-eruv-vandalism/.

116 'Crown Heights Eruv Feud Gets Its Dr. Seuss Moment', *Crown Heights Info*, 23 July 2016, https://crownheights.info/crown-heights-news/541777/crown-heights-eruv-feud-gets-its-dr-seuss-moment/.

In Crown Heights, the religious eruv morphed into a signifier of the encroaching outside secular world anchoring a more liberal interpretation of Jewish law in the Hasidic space. For the Lubavitch Jews, the eruv was not only a violation of their interpretation of Jewish law. Instead, the eruv appeared as a covert agent of secular modernity and a naked public space a way to maintain the religious integrity of the Lubavitch neighbourhood.

JEWISH DIFFERENCE AND THE POLITICS OF PUBLIC SPACE

The eruv cases discussed here illustrate the elusive, contextual, and ambiguous nature of religious symbols and of the category of 'religion' that defy essentialising and singular readings. Yet, they also illustrate that identities and relationships are locally enacted, creating a plurality of secular landscapes with the help of law. The eruv also acts like a prism that allows us to view the shifting relationships between Jews and Christians as they have manifested in and through both law and space. As space came to be less defined as Christian and instead as secular, the legal strategies to manage the spatial presence of Jews changed too. Jews were no longer to be separated but to be integrated. However, while this change in strategy was profound and reflected opportunities for greater rights and equality for Jews, it would be too simplistic to read it as ending domination. The ideology of integration, as David Delaney observes, is 'often bound up with a vision whereby propinquity breeds familiarity'.[117] Jews were to integrate on Christian terms, practising their religion in a particular way that confined Jewishness to the home in a non-territorial way. While in medieval and early modern times, Jews had to remind Christian neighbours of their Jewishness by wearing badges that warned of the religio-racial difference of 'the Jew', beginning with the Enlightenment, secularised Christians demanded that Jews blend in, allowing Christians to ignore their difference. Tolerance became dependent on invisibility, at least in theory and sometimes in law, but not necessarily in practice. The eruv then can be seen for some as a symbol of resistance to the expectation of invisibility, while for others constituting an excess of Jewishness to be contained. Even today, to contain this excess of Jewishness, residents in Canada, England, the United States, and

[117] Delaney, 'The Space That Race Makes', p. 7.

Australia have mobilised the separation of state and church, a hallmark of the normative vocabulary of secular legality. This fight is not merely one that pits Jews against non-Jews. Eruv litigation shows that while there is no singular and unified Jewish position on what it means to be Jewish, there is also no agreement on the most suitable legal strategy through which to achieve Jewish equality and protect Jewish interests in a society still dominated by Christianity that ultimately sets the norm for 'religion', thereby potentially privileging one form of Jewishness over others to the extent that it fits prevailing norms of religiosity.[118]

So far, no secular court has enforced a ban on an eruv on the grounds that it violates norms of secular legality. Eruv litigation could be read as a win for pluralist secularism, the liberating potential of law, and the rights of (Orthodox) Jews – an interpretation to which I will return in Chapter 7. Here, I would like to emphasise the importance of considering some of the deep-seated anxieties that brought these cases to the fore in the first place. While the official legal system channels the eruv into a framework of legal secularism that considers the eruv mainly as an issue of public religiosity, what made the eruv contentious prior to its entry into the courtroom draws on a more complex mélange of fears and suspicions towards the presence of Orthodox Jews in public space. In Tenafly, for example, a member of the eruv association recalled comments by opponents that resonate with earlier racial depictions of Jewish bodies as polluting the space they share with others: 'Someone at a public meeting said, "I don't want them in my town. I don't want to see them when I walk outside. I don't want to breathe the same air they breathe"'.[119] For others, the Tenafly eruv contradicted American identity: 'Why should they have the right to put a wire around a property that I own? It's something that is not very American to a lot of us'.[120] Glossing over the fact that the modern American nation has been built on dispossession and violence, the Jewish eruv is constituted as a territorial threat

118 These questions are of course also relevant in Israel's Jewish majority society, where eruvin have been at the heart of tensions over the growing influence of strictly Orthodox Judaism. See, for example, the report on the eruv in the Jerusalem neighbourhood of Kiryat Yovel: Yair Ettinger, 'Rift Has Roots in Eruv Dispute', *Haaretz*, 22 February 2010.

119 Quoted in Deena Yellin, 'Eruv Lawsuit in Tenafly Provides a Cautionary Tale', *NorthJersey.Com*, 20 July 2017.

120 Quoted in Yellin, 'Eruv Lawsuit'.

to American regimes of property law that are built around rightful ownership and exclusion. The legal language of non-establishment distracts from these racialised claims of ownership over American space, instead channelling the conflict into the language of religious freedom and constitutional separation, thereby foregrounding religion as the primary concern.

Similarly, opponents of the eruv in Outremont took offence at its alleged dangerous territoriality: 'It's never been done before, that on public property a religion, whatever it is, Muslim, Catholic, whatever, that they could make a territory out of it'.[121] Another resident complained: 'They're letting fundamentalists take over a territory.... It's something Catholics never did'.[122] Again, the fact that Quebec and the modern state of Canada are like the United States founded on the dispossession of native populations by Catholics and other Christians disappears in a narrative that presents Christian settlers in Quebec as peaceful and rightous. What appears superficially as a strange local conflict over Jews, religion, and secularism in Quebec and elsewhere feeds into and off an ongoing settler-colonial narrative that affirms the sovereignty and rightful ownership over land as vested in White settlers. 'The national mythologies of white settler societies', Sherene Razack observes, 'are deeply spatialized stories. Although the spatial story that is told varies from one time to another, at each stage the story installs Europeans as entitled to the land, a claim that is codified in law'.[123] Of course, such claims are not unique to settler societies even though this is where they take on a particular salience. As Davina Cooper has shown insightfully, concerns about the political affront of the eruv on hierarchical and singular notions of English sovereignty also underpinned the Barnet eruv controversy in London.[124] The eruv, then, casts light on the ambivalent position of different Jews in these spatiolegal stories and in the legal narratives of national belonging and sovereignty, as well as on the contested boundaries of Jewish difference that challenge dominant categories.

121 CBC News, 'Outremont Not to Appeal Eruv Decision', *CBC*, 10 July 2001.

122 Ingrid Peritz, 'Jewish Community Can Build Religious Symbol, Court Rules', *The Globe and Mail*, 22 June 2001.

123 Sherene H. Razack, 'When Place Becomes Race', in *Race, Space, and the Law: Unmapping a White Settler Society*, ed. Sherene H. Razack (Toronto: Between the Lines, 2002), 1–20, p. 3.

124 Cooper, 'Talmudic Territory', pp. 540–41.

CHAPTER SIX

WHEN ORTHODOX JUDAISM GOES PUBLIC

An Eruv Dispute in Australia

In the upper North Shore of Sydney on the edge of the Ku-ring-gai National Park lies St Ives, a verdant and quiet suburb approximately eighteen kilometres from the city's central business district. The atmosphere is sleepy around the detached houses, neat gardens, and tree-lined streets. Strolling through St Ives, one will eventually notice the highly secured grounds of Masada College, the only Jewish high school in Sydney's north. The school shares grounds with the synagogue Kehillat Masada, the largest congregation in St Ives, which describes itself as Orthodox, yet 'embracing all levels of observance'.[1] The synagogue also houses another smaller Torah-observant community called *Ohr Ha Tzafon*. In addition, the Sephardic Modern Orthodox *Ohel Avraham* community has been holding services in St Ives since 2013. Chabad Lubavitch has a presence in St Ives too. In 1989, the Hasidic movement opened the Chabad house in the upper North Shore, which also includes a preschool, a daycare for children, and a *mikveh*, a ritual bath. Today St Ives is home to Sydney's second-largest Jewish population. Whereas the majority of Sydney's Jews have settled in the eastern suburbs such as Dover Heights, Bondi, Rose Bay, and Vaucluse, the upper North Shore (Ku-ring-gai Local Government Area (LGA)), in particular St Ives, has become another preferred location for New South Wales' Jews. In the 2021 census, 8.1 per cent of St Ives' residents identified as Jewish.[2]

[1] From the Masada Synagogue website: www.masada.org.au.

[2] Australian Bureau of Statistics, '2021 Census on Population and Housing, St Ives (NSW) All Persons Quick Stats', available from www.abs.gov.au/census/

In 2002, Jewish communities in the eastern suburbs established their first eruv, which stretches along the Bondi and Tamarama beaches. This eruv has been operating since its erection without interruption except for one week.[3] A second eruv in Sydney's eastern suburbs, the Coogee and Maroubra eruv, which joins the southern border of the Bondi eruv, became functional in late 2017.[4] In Sydney's north, planning for an eruv began in the early 2000s by a group of Shabbat-observant Jews. What looked like an innocent project which did not involve much more than erecting a couple of poles in inconspicuous colours with wire attached to them, most of them on private lands with the consent of the owners, became a several years-long dispute in which the imagined boundary turned into a real one for many residents, which they sought to prevent by recourse to planning law.

This chapter explores how residents and councillors in St Ives mobilised planning law to draw the acceptable boundaries of Jewishness. The case of the St Ives is instructive as it constitutes, to my knowledge, the only case in which a secular court has upheld a ban on an eruv, offering insights into how law can function as a powerful vehicle for excluding Orthodox Jews from public space for almost a decade. By analysing public documents, including a survey on the eruv commissioned by the Local Council as well as Council meeting minutes, media reports, and submissions to local newspapers, I trace the implicit religious and racial boundaries of belonging in this Australian suburb that the eruv rendered visible and I examine how the planning law regime participated in protecting these boundaries, thereby affirming White Christian settlers as rightful inhabitants of this suburban land.[5]

find-census-data/quickstats/2021/SAL13654. For comparison, only 0.5 per cent of all NSW residents identify as Jewish.

3 See www.sydneyeruv.org.au/index.htm. The website does not specify what led to the interruption of the eruv.

4 For a map of the Coogee Maroubra eruv, see www.coogeesynagogue.org/eruv.

5 Survey on file with author. Throughout this chapter, all quotes without a source are drawn from the survey. For all other quotes (including from council documents, media reporting, and letters to the editor), I provide the source in the footnotes. These documents were analysed and coded to identify dominant themes and ideas. I also draw on conversations with local rabbis, council members, and people involved in the eruv group who generously offered insights into the halakhic background of the eruv and the sequence of events. These conversations were recorded and transcribed with participant consent. The Human Research Ethics Committee of The Australian National University approved this research in July 2016 (Protocol 2016/040).

AN ERUV FOR ST IVES

In October 2007, several development applications reached Ku-ring-gai Council. The applications had been submitted by an organisation called *Northern Eruv Incorporated* with the motto 'Linking the Community' for the purpose of installing poles and wires on public and private land in St Ives. The Council rejected the application for failing to provide sufficient information on the project and for not having obtained the consent of the owners of the affected land.[6] In 2008, when another application was lodged, it became clear that not everyone welcomed an eruv in St Ives. At this stage, the Council had received fifteen objections from local residents who raised concerns about the 'impact of poles on views and visual intrusion of poles' and the allegedly preferential treatment of one religious group over others.[7] The eruv group published a promotional video in order to make the eruv palatable to residents by explaining its purpose for families and emphasising that its set-up would not involve the construction of any fencing or walls.[8] The video aimed to assure the community that the eruv would be designed in the most unobtrusive way by using poles that resembled existing poles in similar colours.

Despite these efforts, many residents did not appreciate the unusual proposal. The St Ives Progress Association (SIPA), a local community group founded in 1913 whose aim has been to 'promote, enhance and protect the natural and built amenity of St Ives',[9] was among the most vocal and active opponents and devoted significant energy and time to fight the proposal. In a flyer distributed to residents in 2010, SIPA warned of the eruv as a 'part-symbolic and part-physical wall' which would 'encapsulate most of St Ives' and be 'inconsistent with the visual character' of the suburb.[10] Doubting the eruv's religious purpose, the group's president stated that the eruv's purpose was 'not about following their [Orthodox Jews'] beliefs' but 'about imposing structures on the community'.[11]

6 Ku-ring-gai Planning Panel, 'Agenda', 6 April 2011, at GB.1/8.

7 Jano Gibson, 'Jews Seek Religious Freedom with a Ring around St Ives', *Sydney Morning Herald*, 1 October 2008.

8 'North Shore Eruv', *YouTube*, 25 November 2008, available from www.youtube.com/watch?v=U6Nkr24lxDQ.

9 See SIPA's self-description at sipa.org.au/index.html.

10 Quoted in Josephine Tovey, 'Residents Draw Line over Jewish Boundary', *The Sydney Morning Herald*, 3 July 2010.

11 Quoted in Tovey, 'Residents Draw Line'.

The media had already fuelled the impression of the eruv as a highly intrusive installation. The local newspaper, the *North Shore Times*, called the development application in 2008 'a bizarre proposal … to build a "virtual wall" enclosing part of St Ives for Orthodox Jews'.[12] The TV programme *A Current Affair* reported in 2010 that Jews were trying to turn the suburb into a 'religious enclave'. The segment was later posted on the programme's website and received several hundreds of comments, some of them openly antisemitic. The comments were taken down after a request by the New South Wales Jewish Board of Deputies, a political body representing Jews in New South Wales.[13] Even on Australia's public broadcaster ABC, a reporter misrepresented the project in 2010 as 'a religious zone for ultra-Orthodox Jews'.[14] The choice of language reinforced the idea that the eruv was much more than a simple wire: It was a boundary solid enough to cut right through the neighbourhood to the detriment and exclusion of other residents.

Between 2010 and 2011, the eruv group again submitted development applications for the erection of poles and also sought consent under Section 138 of the *Roads Act 1993* (NSW) in order to connect the poles with non-live wiring within public road reserves.[15] This time the proposed eruv structure relied mainly on existing structures to form the 20-kilometre boundary, but it also required the erection of twenty-seven additional poles on public and private land to close gaps. Soon the Local Council received five petitions from local residents, two in support of the eruv (with a total of 678 signatures) and three opposing the eruv (with a total of 1,423 signatures).[16] The objecting petitions raised concerns about the visual impact of the eruv, the use of public space for private purposes, and community cohesion. In August 2011, the Council rejected the applications after receiving advice from the Council's Director of Operations. While

[12] Katrina Adamski, 'Wall of Opposition', *North Shore Times*, 7 October 2008.

[13] Joshua Levi, 'Nine's Racism Claim', *Australian Jewish News*. Comments included such antisemitic slurs as 'The bosh (Germans) didn't finish their job'. Another said: 'Quick, hide your babies. The Jews are going to drain their blood to bake bread'.

[14] Deborah Cornwall, 'The Eruv', *ABC News*, 12 July 2010.

[15] Summary of applications in Ku-ring-gai Planning Panel, 'Agenda', 6 April 2011, at GB. 1/1.

[16] For the supporting petitions, see Ku-ring-gai Council, 'Late Agenda', Ordinary Council Meeting, 23 August 2011, at PT.4 and PT.5. For the objecting petitions, see Ku-ring-gai Council, 'Agenda', 23 August 2011 and Ku-ring-gai Council, 'Late Agenda', Ordinary Council Meeting, 23 August 2011, at PT.2 and PT.3.

the report recommended the approval of poles on private land, it advised rejecting the poles on public land because, as the Director noted, 'there is no significant community benefit to the council or the community arising from this proposal'.[17] The Deputy Mayor was eager to emphasise that religious intolerance was not the reason for the refusal and that the Council had based its decision entirely on planning considerations:

> The majority of residents objected to the proposed eruv, with many residents concerned with the negative impact the visual clutter from the additional poles and wires would have on the streetscape. This was the major concern and not religious or racial views.[18]

Eruv supporters expressed doubt about the motivations of their objectors. One St Ives resident wrote to the local newspaper voicing disappointment about the decision of the Council:

> As a rational and thoughtful individual, I am willing to accept that one cannot always get what one asks for and am left not bitter or angry but disappointed over the meeting's outcome (…). I am saddened by the intolerance of some of the opposition arguments, which lead me to question if the issue was about the poles or rather about the people it would serve. Having felt blessed to spend my years in St Ives, finishing school this year, I am disappointed that my first taste of the cruel and brutal 'real world' had to be in the place I call home. I am not bitter, nor angry, as mentioned before, but suddenly wary if my neighbourhood is the accepting and warm environment I had always thought it to be.[19]

One of St Ives' rabbis recalled a similar feeling of alienation among members of the Jewish community:

> When the meeting happened at the Council, the Jewish community walked away shuddering, they walked around St Ives thinking that this is a wonderful place to live, and we all get along so well with our non-Jewish neighbours, and all of a sudden, this was all bubbling to the top. So, people were thinking, hold on a second, we have to re-look at our neighbours, who are really deep inside seething with hatred towards us and they've just masked it for so long. The Jewish community took a

[17] Quoted in Fiona Brady, 'Pole Position Key to Success of Eruv', *North Shore Times*, 19 August 2011.

[18] Quoted in Joshua Levi, 'St Ives Eruv Turned Down by Council', *Australian Jewish News*, 25 August 2011.

[19] Supporter 1, 'Letter to the Editor', *North Shore Times*, 31 August 2011, at 21.

> lot of emotional strain, even though 90 per cent of the community has no interest in the eruv one way or the other. They just saw the ugly side of the broader St Ives community.[20]

In the spring of 2012, the eruv group appealed the decision in the New South Wales Court of Environment. The Court, however, ultimately dismissed the appeal in November 2012, stating its lack of jurisdiction with regard to the applications under the *Roads Act 1993* (NSW).[21] The materiality of the eruv played an unfortunate role when the Court assessed its jurisdiction. Differently to a house of worship, the eruv entered the planning realm as a set of individual poles scattered across the suburb, which, given the subdivision of land into individual parcels of public and private land, meant that each required an individual application, either under the *Roads Act* or the *Environmental Planning and Assessment Act 1979* (NSW ('EPA Act'). The Court's power to decide on the application under the *Roads Act* required a nexus with the applications under the *EPA Act*. Since there was no eruv yet that could have connected the poles, the Court found that the nexus between the individual applications was missing. The Court thereby took a strictly material approach to the poles as individual developments, without considering the symbolic meaning of each of the poles and their function as building blocks for the whole of the eruv space.

The Court's decision could have been the end for the St Ives eruv, had not an unlikely actor helped the eruv come into being. The local power provider, Ausgrid, granted permission to use its power poles to attach lechis and complete the eruv boundary. The perimeter had been redesigned in a way that did not require the erection of additional poles. The result was that the eruv now enclosed a much larger part of St Ives than initially planned. The *Australian Jewish News* eventually made the eruv public in April 2015, quoting one of St Ives' rabbis who praised the eruv as 'a fantastic piece of North Shore infrastructure that I think will being [sic] an enormous amount of harmony and unity to the community'.[22]

[20] Conversation with St Ives Rabbi I, Sydney, July 2016.

[21] *The Northern Eruv Incorporated v. Ku-ring-gai Council* [2012] NSWLEC 249 (30 November 2012).

[22] Quoted in Gareth Narunsky, 'St Ives Gets Its Eruv', *The Australian Jewish News*, 28 May 2015.

Local residents soon noticed the sudden appearance of the eruv, and some seemed to disagree with the rabbi's assessment of the eruv as a vehicle for harmony and unity. After it had become functional, the eruv was vandalised several times.[23] One resident attached post-it notes to each lechi to inform the public of the unlawfulness of the structure.[24] Eventually, the issue came back before the Council, which had been approached by residents 'concerned with the amenity of their local area'.[25] After receiving legal advice on the matter, the Council ordered the eruv's dismantling on 4 July 2016, just fourteen months after its installation.[26] The costs for removing the structure from the 571 Ausgrid poles were estimated to amount to $50,000, a sum the Council would have to bear if no one would claim responsibility for erecting the eruv. The state member of parliament for Ku-ring-gai weighed in, criticising the Council for 'wasting ratepayers' money on this non-issue.[27] At some point, the individual members of the eruv group revealed themselves to the Council but remained reluctant to make their identities public after receiving numerous threats.[28]

Before things escalated, the eruv group successfully sought an injunction in the NSW Supreme Court in July 2016. The group based its claim on matters of ownership and the *Electricity Supply Act 1994* (NSW) to prevent the Council from interfering with the poles owned by Ausgrid.[29] The group also offered to lodge a retrospective application under the *Roads Act 1993* (NSW). In August 2016, the group, now called 'Helping Families Unite', submitted this application for retrospective approval of the placement of plastic conduit. On 2 September 2016, the Council sent out a survey to 2,400 residents whose properties were affected by the eruv boundaries asking them for

[23] See Executive Council of Australian Jewry, 'Report on Antisemitism in Australia 2016', 27 November 2016, p. 78, www.ecaj.org.au/wp-content/uploads/2012/08/ECAJ-Antisemitism-Report-2016d-WEB.pdf.

[24] Personal conversation with St Ives Rabbi I, Sydney, July 2016.

[25] Jessica Rapana, 'Ku-Ring-Gai Council Takes on Prominent Jewish Community over St Ives Eruv', 30 June 2016.

[26] David D. Knoll, 'Protecting Religious Freedom and Places of Worship – The Example of the Eruv', *Solidarity: The Journal of Catholic Social Thought and Secular Ethics* 7, no. 1 (2016): 1–18, p. 16.

[27] Quoted in Rapana, 'Ku-Ring-Gai Council Takes on Prominent Jewish Community'.

[28] Jessica Rapana, 'Threats Follow Boundary Action', *North Shore Times*, 15 July 2016, p. 3.

[29] See Knoll, 'Protecting Religious Freedom', p. 16.

their opinion on the eruv (Figure 3).[30] Six hundred responses reached the Council, of which 50 per cent disagreed with the proposal, while 41 per cent agreed.[31] The rest felt neutral about the eruv.[32]

The Council now confirmed that the eruv lechis neither constituted a safety risk to the general public nor did they impede public access.[33] Technically, the Council admitted, there were no reasons for refusing the eruv. However, the Council emphasised that 'due to the number and extent of the plastic conduits', it was important to seek community views and opinions, which 'any approval for the application should consider'.[34] Meanwhile, the dispute took a nasty turn when SIPA distributed an openly antisemitic leaflet in the neighbourhood which claimed that the eruv was an attempt to fundamentally change St Ives' demographics by encouraging 'those of their faith to settle in the area'.[35] Another letter, sent anonymously to residents, made claims about a Jewish conspiracy to take over the suburb.[36] Politicians, councillors, and residents condemned the letters' messages, but the tone had become increasingly harsh.[37] One day a lechi was found with a swastika etched into it, which St Ives community leaders quickly condemned as 'racial hatred at its worst'[38].

Finally, in November 2016, more than 200 residents came to the scheduled Council meeting in which the final fate of the eruv was to be decided. The list of speakers had been limited to ten for and ten against the eruv. St Ives Jewish community was well prepared to argue their cause. In the lead up to the debate, Jewish mothers appeared

[30] Survey in Ku-ring-Gai Council, 'Agenda for Ordinary Meeting', 8 November 2016, Appendix No. 2 (Survey Information Sent to Residents).

[31] Ku-ring-Gai Council, 'Agenda for Ordinary Meeting', 8 November 2016, Appendix No. 3 (Eruv Responses Submissions via Returned Survey Form).

[32] The Council also received a folder containing 462 signatures in support of the eruv and another thirty-one responses which were not submitted via the survey form (with seventeen of them agreeing, thirteen disagreeing, and one neutral). Those submissions were not included in the official survey, which only considered directly affected residents who had responded through the survey form.

[33] Ku-ring-Gai Council, 'Agenda for Ordinary Meeting', 8 November 2016, at GB. 6/295.

[34] Ku-ring-Gai Council, 'Agenda for Ordinary Meeting', 8 November 2016, at GB. 6/295.

[35] SIPA, 'Letter to St Ives Residents', 7 September 2016 (on file with author – see also note 37).

[36] 'Aspects of the Eruv You Should Know About', Anonymous Letter Sent to St Ives Residents, 7 September 2016 (on file with author – see also next note).

[37] Jessica Rapana, 'Anti-Eruv Flyer: "One of the Worst Examples of Anti-Semitism" in Sydney', *North Shore Times*, 15 September 2016. The report also contains photos of the two letters sent to residents.

[38] Jessica Rapana, 'Nazi Sign 'Hatred at Its Worst', *North Shore Times*, 30 September 2016.

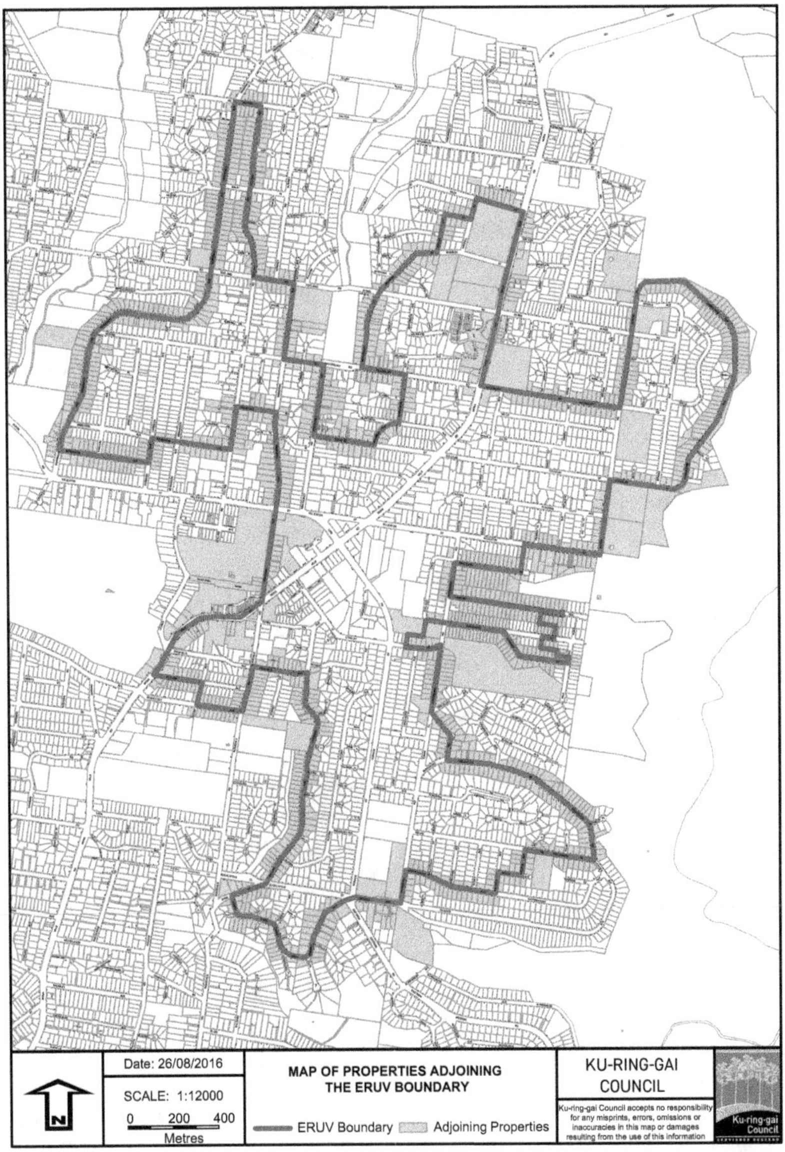

Figure 3 Map of the St Ives Eruv August 2016 (With permission from Ku-Ring-Gai Council).

frequently as respondents in the local newspaper, stressing the positive impact the eruv had in particular on families and mothers. One Jewish woman posted on the website *North Shore Mums*: 'The only notable impact of the Eruv in the past eighteen months has been the sight of happy families walking to and from synagogue and friends on Saturdays'.[39] Even a Jewish Paralympic tennis champion, who relies on a wheelchair, joined the debate to support the eruv and underlined the benefits of an eruv for disabled people: 'For any disabled person who uses any kind of wheelchair or walking device, it's incredibly important that they stay involved in community activity', he said.[40] For him, the eruv presented an opportunity 'to enhance peace and equality in this area'.[41] Other residents also argued in support of the eruv, such as one Christian neighbour, who emphasised: 'Let us be real – these people are our neighbours, our friends – let us not discriminate based on faith'.[42] This time the meeting ended in applause: Councillors approved the eruv by eight votes out of ten. The Mayor expressed her satisfaction with what she saw as an impartial process and stressed that it was the duty of the Council 'to assess the application on its merits and ensure proper process was followed'.[43]

THE ERUV AS A MATTER OF THE BUILT ENVIRONMENT

Reading the legal documents produced throughout the dispute, the case of the St Ives eruv never appeared to be about the grand questions of religious freedom that have framed eruv litigation elsewhere. Instead, the entire legal discussion circled around the optics of poles and the impact of wires on the streetscape. This framing reflects not only the particular ways in which religious diversity is governed on the level of the local, but it also results from the Australian legal context. Australia is still the only Western liberal democracy without a full bill of rights. The country's Constitution only mentions a handful of rights, which traditionally the Australian High Court has interpreted in a rather narrow fashion.[44] Among these few provisions is Section

[39] Megan Rosettenstein, 'The St Ives Eruv: One Community Member's View', *North Shore Mums*, 20 September 2016.

[40] Quoted in Jessica Rapana, 'Ku-Ring-Gai Council Has Approved the Jewish Eruv in St Ives in a Landmark Decision', *North Shore Times*, 7 November 2016.

[41] Supporter 2, quoted in Shane Desiatnek, 'Eruv Decision a Win for the Community', *The Australian Jewish News*, 10 November 2016.

[42] Supporter 3, quoted in Desiatnek, 'Eruv Decision a Win'.

[43] Quoted in Rapana, 'Ku-Ring-Gai Council Has Approved the Jewish Eruv'.

[44] George Williams, *Human Rights under the Australian Constitution* (Oxford: Oxford University Press, 2002).

116 concerning religion, which is modelled on the First Amendment of the Constitution of the United States but drafted in narrower terms:

> The Commonwealth shall not make any law for establishing any religion, or for imposing any religious observance, or for prohibiting the free exercise of any religion, and no religious test shall be required as a qualification for any office or public trust under the Commonwealth.

The words make it clear that the section only applies to the Commonwealth government but not to the states nor to local councils. On the state and territory level, Victoria, the Australian Capital Territory, and Queensland have introduced their own human rights legislation. The Tasmanian *Constitution Act 1934* protects the 'freedom of conscience and the free profession and practice of religion'. New South Wales, where the eruv was to be built, lacks such a protection. Australia's reluctance towards enshrining human rights is the result of a number of different factors, among them the 'utilitarian confidence' in governmental structures.[45] Protecting a human right such as religious freedom has been largely left to political and democratic processes,[46] which do not always succeed in securing the rights of minority groups, as the quarrel over the St Ives eruv shows.

Even though Australia and the state of New South Wales lack comprehensive protection of human rights, the national Australian multicultural policy from 2011, the relevant policy document at the time of the eruv's planning, asserted the right of all citizens to practice and maintain their heritage and culture.[47] Moreover, the *Multicultural NSW Act 2000* obligates institutions to, inter alia, 'respect and

[45] There were formal attempts to introduce a more comprehensive protection of rights into the Constitution, in 1944 and 1988, both unsuccessful. As Hilary Charlesworth explains: 'The Australian suspicion of constitutionally entrenched rights has been enduring. It has been supported by arguments that constitutional rights could both politicize the judiciary and legalize public policy, thus undermining our legal culture. The suspicion also rests on regional instincts of preserving states' rights. At a more fundamental level, reservations about rights are linked to a utilitarian confidence in our existing governmental structure'. See Hilary Charlesworth, 'The Australian Reluctance about Rights', *Osgoode Hall Law Journal* 31 (1993): 195–232, p. 201.

[46] Carolyn Evans, 'Religion as Politics Not Law: The Religion Clauses in the Australian Constitution', *Religion, State & Society* 36, no. 3 (2008): 283–302, p. 284.

[47] Australian Government, 'The People of Australia – Australia's Multicultural Policy', 16 February 2011. In March 2017, Australia's latest multicultural statement at the time of writing – *Multicultural Australia – United, Strong, Successful* – merely states 'support for freedom of religion'.

make provisions for the … religion of others'.[48] In the local politics of diversity, however, these policies and laws prove often toothless. Despite government direction and statutory efforts, matters of religious diversity and multiculturalism more broadly remain only poorly implemented at the level of local planning and government.[49] As David Knoll observes, in the daily planning business, many councils avoid dealing with politically sensitive issues of religious diversity and instead pass the ball to the Land and Environment Court of NSW after refusing a proposal in order to not be held accountable by their constituency, as also happened in St Ives.[50] This strategy leads to little protection for minority communities as the *Multicultural NSW Act* also stipulates in its Section 22 that the multicultural principles do not 'give rise to, or can be taken into account, in any civil cause of action'. Hence, in its appeal decision on the matter of the St Ives eruv, there was no need for the Land and Environment Court to consider the multicultural dimension of the Council's decision to refuse development consent for the eruv.[51]

In light of this legal context, when one of the Ku-ring-gai Councillors called the looming removal of the eruv the 'removal of the human rights of many members of the community',[52] his claim had little legal edge. In turn, the particular legal context made it easy for opponents to dismiss appeals to human rights as a diversion and to refer the dispute back to the realms of planning law with its concerns for amenity and the environment, as one opponent made clear:

> Let's not get side-tracked with statements about democracy or religion. The eruv is about permanent physical infrastructure imposed on public and private land affecting the amenity and environment of the entire community.[53]

[48] *Multicultural NSW Act* 2000 (NSW), s 3(1d). The Act requires authorities to observe these principles in Section 3(4).

[49] Kevin Dunn et al., 'Multicultural Policy within Local Government in Australia', *Urban Studies* 38, no. 13 (2001): 2477–94.

[50] Knoll, 'Protecting Religious Freedom', p. 12.

[51] This does not mean that the Court never considers questions of religion. In *New Century Developments Pty Limited v. Baulkham Hills Shire Council* [2003] NSWLEC 154, the Court upheld an appeal against the refusal of planning consent for a mosque and emphasised the preservation of religious equality and religious freedom as public interest.

[52] Quoted in Rapana, 'Ku-Ring-Gai Council Takes on Prominent Jewish Community'.

[53] Quoted in Fiona Brady, 'Four Years on, Still Eruv Uncertainty', *North Shore Times*, 26 August 2011, at 4.

The categories of planning law tend to channel opposition into a particular, often highly technical vocabulary: The height and size of a building, parking space, proper land use, noise and other emissions, heritage, character, and amenity of the area. Mariana Valverde has called for closer attention to the level of the local and the ways in which local authorities and local laws micro-manage religious and other aspects of diversity on the ground. In her empirical study of local law in action, Valverde shows how the particular mechanisms of local law can work to reinforce dominant and ethnocentric norms through prima facie technical and apolitical categories concerned with buildings, objects, and spaces and seemingly inclusive democratic features, such as planning consultations.[54] In tandem, these features can work to enshrine 'the wishes of civic society's squeaky wheels',[55] the established and well-resourced residents who use the planning regime in a way that perpetuates exclusion and inequality. In order to wield power in the local context, Valverde argues, residents have to learn 'seeing like a city' – that is, to frame their concerns as relevant to the categories of local law, such as planning law.[56] In St Ives, both residents and the local council based their rejection of the eruv on the planning category of amenity. Amenity is one of those multivalent terms that allows local authorities 'to govern people – and relations of class, ethnicity and respectability – without governing through persons'.[57] In its assessment of the eruv application, the Ku-ring-gai Planning Panel described amenity as encompassing considerations that are

> practical and tangible such as traffic generation, noise, and nuisance, appearance and even the way of life of the neighbourhood. Other considerations are more difficult to appreciate such as the standard or class of

[54] See, for example, Mariana Valverde, *Everyday Law on the Street. City Governance in an Age of Diversity* (Chicago; London: University of Chicago Press, 2012); see also Amelia Thorpe, 'Between Rights in the City and the Right to the City: Heritage, Character and Public Participation in Urban Planning', in *Heritage, Culture and Rights. Challenging Legal Discourses*, ed. Andrea Durbach and Lucas Lixinski (Oxford; Portland: Hart, 2017), 121–62.

[55] Valverde, *Everyday Law*, pp. 22 and 211.

[56] Valverde, *Everyday Law*, p. 3. See also my discussion in Mareike Riedel, 'The Difference a Wire Makes: Planning Law, Public Orthodox Judaism and Urban Space in Australia', *International Journal of Law in Context* 16, no. 4 (2020): 403–21.

[57] Mariana Valverde, 'Taking Land Use Seriously: Toward an Ontology of Municipal Law', *Law Text Culture* 9 (2005): 34–59, p. 45.

> a neighbourhood and the reasonable expectations of a neighbourhood. In particular, knowing the use to which a particular site is or may be put by a particular user group may affect one's perception of amenity.[58]

Amenity is not per se an exclusionary term. Yet, the category's lack of a clear statutory definition in NSW planning law means that decision makers are tasked to give meaning to a somewhat elusive and subjective term, making it prone, much like the 'best interests of the child' to becoming a container for all kinds of claims about what constitutes 'the way of life of a neighbourhood' or 'the reasonable expectations of a neighbourhood'. Amenity as a legal category can therefore work to preserve the status quo as favoured by the dominant cultural group who yield their local political power to define these standards.

Residents' statements in development consultations play an important role throughout many Western planning systems that often afford great weight to the claims made by local residents. Although on the surface a laudable democratic feature to make planning more responsive to local residents' needs, the participatory nature of the planning process can skew the process in a way that privileges some views over others. Research demonstrates that residents have been able to successfully manipulate categories such as amenity alongside 'character', 'heritage', but also 'land use' for exclusionary agendas not only in Australia but also in other Western jurisdictions. Applications lodged by religious and cultural minority groups then fail on the grounds that the development would produce excessive noise, have an 'exotic appearance' which is unsuitable to the locality, or create parking issues in the area.[59]

The planning regime, as Amelia Thorpe notes, not only invites residents to frame their objections in terms of significance to the wider public, such as amenity, rewarding discursive strategies that present objections to people in more palatable ways as objections to objects and buildings, it also then often treats them as in fact representing the 'public interest'.[60] 'Public interest', like amenity,

[58] Ku-ring-gai Planning Panel, 'Agenda', 6 April 2011, at GB.1/35.

[59] See, for example, Noel G. Villaroman, '"Not in My Backyard": The Local Planning Process in Australia and Its Impact on Minority Places of Worship', *Religion and Human Rights* 7, no. 3 (2012): 215–39; Laura Beth Bugg, 'Citizenship and Belonging in the Rural Fringe: A Case Study of a Hindu Temple in Sydney, Australia', *Antipode* 45, no. 5 (2013): 1148–66; Leonie Sandercock, 'When Strangers Become Neighbours: Managing Cities of Difference', *Planning Theory & Practice* 1, no. 1 (2000): 13–30.

[60] Thorpe, 'Between Rights', p. 140.

is a key concept in planning regimes that authorities have to consider during their decision-making process, although it is often not defined in legislation and therefore needs to be interpreted.[61] It is this legal interpretation process in which objections raised by residents can become conflated with the public interest.

Indeed, in St Ives, residents' objections were interpreted as representing the public interest. In 2011, Ku-ring-Gai's Director of Operations noted in his report to the Council that twenty-five objections had been received from residents that opposed the eruv proposal. The Director concluded that the proposal should not be supported: 'Given that the majority of the residents surrounding the proposals are objecting to the installation of the poles and wires, it is considered that there is no significant benefit to Council and the community arising from this proposal'.[62] The Council followed this recommendation when it denied development consent to the eruv:

> While the decision will be disappointing to many people in Ku-ring-gai's Jewish community, we needed to take into account the wider public interest. The majority of residents objected to the proposal, with many concerned about the negative impact of visual clutter the additional structures would have on the streetscape. This was the major concern and not a religious or racial view.[63]

As one Councillor who was generally supportive of the eruv further explained:

> You can't just make a logical decision based on your own personal perspective when part of the process is to engage the local community who are impacted by it, no matter what the impact is. The overwhelming response from residents was that they didn't want it.... [As] a Councillor, I feel that if you have latitude to make a decision and the community isn't with you for whatever reason, it's much better to not go ahead and take the status quo as your basis for your decision and retain the status quo unless there is a shift in the thinking of your population.[64]

[61] See Chris Wheeler, 'The Public Interest We Know It's Important, but Do We Know What It Means', *AIAL Forum*, no. 48 (2006): 12–25.

[62] Ku-ring-gai Council, 'Agenda of Ordinary Meeting of Council', 23 August 2011, item GB.1/70.

[63] Quoted in Joshua Levi, 'Eruv Now Only One Pole Away', *Australian Jewish News*, 22 March 2012.

[64] Personal conversation with Councillor, Sydney, December 2016.

This understanding of participation in local planning as, in effect, majority rule makes minority populations vulnerable. It creates a dynamic in local planning processes in which majorities seek to assert their hegemony over the public space against the 'intrusion' of groups that are depicted as newcomers with fewer rights to shape the architecture of the locality. In what follows, I take a closer look at how objecting residents conceptualised the amenity of their neighbourhood and presented the public interest. In so doing, I unpack the cultural, religious, and racialising assumptions underpinning their claims and what these assumptions tell us about the place of Jewish difference in this Australian suburb as well as the rights of Jewish residents. As we will see, residents' objections to the eruv echo some persistent anxieties around Jewish difference in multicultural Australia and reveal how planning law became mobilised to contain a perceived excess of Jewishness that was deemed to be threatening.

POROUS WALLS OF SEPARATION

Despite the absence of constitutional and statutory provisions that entrench secularism and religious freedom in a comprehensive way in the Australian legal system, participants in the debate frequently appealed to them as powerful ideals. One key theme of opposition to the eruv was the vision of St Ives as a secular space in which religion had to remain in the private sphere – a common claim in many eruv controversies. Opponents took this stance for two reasons: As a matter of principle regarding the secularity of public space, and in order to prevent the eruv from violating the rights of other residents. In survey responses sent to the Council, residents argued that 'streets should not be for religious purposes' and stated that they were 'against religious matters on public land'. Opponents advanced a vision of St Ives as a well-ordered space in which religion had its clearly assigned place behind walls in order to prevent it from leaking into the public streets in a secular society:

> There is no place for religious symbols on public crown land. Religion in a secular state, such as we are fortunate to enjoy in Australia, is foremost for the homes and then for those places zoned by government, including councils for that purpose.[65]

[65] Opponent 18, 'Letters', *Sydney Morning Herald*, 26 August 2011, p. 10.

Another explained that

> [p]eople come to this suburb because it is still a residential area with peaceful green areas, the houses do not have religious symbols outside advertising to which religion they belong. People go to their places of worship where these symbols belong.[66]

These arguments, echoing the earlier concerns of Bromberg's Prussian authorities, produce a specific politics of visibility in which the practice of religion is tightly controlled through architecture and zoning. While opponents acknowledged that religion is not a purely private exercise for the home, to them the only legitimate public expression is in designated and circumscribed spaces such as the synagogue, whose walls mimic the walls of the house and therefore do not confront outsiders with the religiosity and therefore difference which is contained inside. By attaching lechis to poles, the eruv spilled religion into the street, turning the halakhic fiction of privatised public space into an affront to the secular order of St Ives' public space.

For some, the eruv also violated their rights, in particular their right to freedom *from* religion, the flip side of the right to freedom of religion. Opponents worried that the eruv would be 'imposing religious beliefs' and 'assert[ing] religious authority' over non-Jews. Another resident feared that 'the whole area within the eruv becomes a place of worship'.[67] Underlying this claim was a view of the eruv as imposing itself on all residents, regardless of whether they are Orthodox Jews or not, thereby exerting undue religious coercion. Objecting residents refused the idea that symbolism can exist only for some. In their view, the eruv 'stained'[68] space, affecting everyone regardless of their membership in the Jewish community or not. In order to prevent the eruv from encroaching on the 'civil rights' of 'tolerant' Australians,[69] Jewish difference had to remain private. This was seen as a matter of religious equality before Australian law. As one resident argued, 'in Australia all religions are equal and should respect and accept the rule of law in Australia'.[70] In this understanding, the rule of Australian law did not allow for exclusive access to public space for any religion.

66 Opponent 17, 'Letters to the Editor', *North Shore Times*, 25 June 2010, p. 36.
67 Opponent 19, 'Opinion', *North Shore Times*, 18 March 2011, p. 36.
68 Cooper, 'Talmudic Territory', p. 534.
69 Opponent 20, 'Opinion/Letters', *North Shore Times*, 9 March 2011, p. 21.
70 Opponent 7, 'Letters', *North Shore Times*, 16 September 2011, p. 36.

Accusing the eruv of transgressing the public-private distinction glosses over the incoherent policing of such transgressions. The tendency of Western secular law to conceive of religion as a private matter is certainly part of the problem by disadvantaging religions that do not fit easily within the confines of private faith. Yet another tension arises from the instability or porosity of the boundary between private religion and the public itself. Anxieties around religious difference and demographic change, as Silvio Ferrari observes, have led to

> a constant oscillation between the impulse to confine religion more strictly to the private sphere, excluding it from the process of building the national identity, and the desire to strengthen national identity through the revitalization (and therefore re-publicization) of the majority religion(s) only.[71]

The result is an inconsistent enforcement of the public–private distinction that often serves to maintain the privileged status of the majority religion, enabling nativity creches, crucifixes, and crosses to pass as natural and supposedly shared secular background culture.[72] Non-Christian symbols, on the other hand, are more often scrutinised and interpreted as overreaching into a public sphere imagined to be otherwise devoid of religious symbols. This reasoning is particularly evident if we contrast responses to the headscarf with responses to Christian symbols in Western secular jurisdictions. In *Dahlab v. Switzerland*, the European Court of Human Rights (ECtHR), for example, sanctioned in 2001 a ban on headscarves for teachers in public schools by noting that

> [t]he Court accepts that it is very difficult to assess the impact that a powerful external symbol such as the wearing of a headscarf may have on the freedom of conscience and religion of very young children.... It cannot be denied that the wearing a headscarf might have some kind of proselytising effect...[73]

[71] Silvio Ferrari, 'Religion in the European Public Spaces: A Legal Overview', in *Religion in Public Spaces. A European Perspective*, ed. Silvio Ferrari and Sabrina Pastorelli (London; New York: Routledge, 2012), 139–56, p. 145.

[72] See, for example, the decision of the US Supreme Court on a cross-shaped memorial: *American Legion v. American Humanist Association*, 139 S. Ct. 2067 [2019] as well as the French Conseil d'Etat, decision of 9 November 2016, no. 395122 on a creche. See also the analysis by Lori G. Beaman, 'Battles over Symbols: The "Religion" of the Minority Versus the "Culture" of the Majority', *Journal of Law and Religion* 28, no. 1 (2013): 67–104.

[73] *Dahlab v. Switzerland*, European Court of Human Rights, 15 February 2001, Appl. No 42393/98, p. 13.

While the headscarf is seen as an active and powerful symbol, the Court acknowledged at the same time that 'the principle of proportionality has led the cantonal government to allow teachers to wear discreet religious symbols at schools, such as small pieces of jewellery'. In short, the discreet Christian crucifix is tolerated, but the 'powerful external' headscarf is not; an approach not limited to the ECtHR.[74] The same Court again showed a lenient attitude towards Christian symbols in its *Lautsi* decision in 2011 concerning the permissibility of the display of a crucifix in an Italian school. Here, the Court deemed the crucifix to be an 'essentially passive symbol'[75] and, *de facto*, followed the reasoning of Italian courts which had presented the crucifix as a 'symbol of our history and our culture … and also of the principle of secularism'.[76] Some symbols, Lorenza Zucca notes, are apparently 'more neutral than others'.[77] Whereas one religious symbol is allowed into the public as either a watered-down and naturalised cultural symbol or as a negligible passive accessory, the other is prohibited as an active and dangerous agent, proving that the wall of secular separation can crumble at any time – feeding into the suspicion that, at times, 'secularization is just Christianity by another name'.[78]

A similar dynamic was at play in St Ives. Although eruv opponents stressed their commitment to religious equality, they did not take offence at the various Christian symbols in their suburb's public space. This inconsistency did not go unnoticed among eruv supporters. One asked:

[74] See, for example, the German state laws and the case law on the wearing of the headscarf by Muslim school teachers as discussed in Susanna Mancini, 'The Tempting of Europe, the Political Seduction of the Cross: A Schmittian Reading of Christianity and Islam in European Constitutionalism', in *Constitutional Secularism in an Age of Religious Revival*, ed. Susanna Mancini and Michel Rosenfeld (Oxford; New York: Oxford University Press, 2014), 111–35.

[75] *Lautsi and Others v. Italy*, European Court of Human Rights (Grand Chamber), 18 March 2011, Appl. no. 30814/06, at 72.

[76] Quoted in Mancini, 'The Tempting of Europe', p. 123. Mancini notes that some Catholics do not agree with the appropriation of the crucific by the state as it waters down the religious significance, see Mancini, 'The Power of Symbols', p. 2635.

[77] Lorenzo Zucca, 'Lautsi: A Commentary on a Decision by the ECtHR Grand Chamber', *International Journal of Constitutional Law* 11, no. 1 (2013): 218–29, at 221.

[78] Gil Anidjar in Nermeen Shaikh, 'The Jew, the Arab: An Interview with Gil Anidjar'.

> Have any of them objected to Christmas decorations in the street and flashing lights installed on many homes during Christmas? Why pick on Jews when the impact is far, far less noticeable?[79]

Indeed, a Christmas tree is placed every year in front of the chambers of Ku-ring-gai Council and the Council has given significant annual subsidies to sponsor the Christian event *Carols in the Park*, which takes place in the public Bicentennial Park.[80] While this financial and logistical support does not involve the setting up of permanent structures, it affords Christianity a much more prominent and visible forum as compared to the eruv – a structure that is barely noticeable. Moreover, no public subsidy or state endorsement is given to the eruv, as it is maintained by the Jewish community alone.

The fact that eruv opponents remained oblivious to Christian symbols in their public space speaks to the mundane operation of Christian privilege that makes Christianity seem normal, natural, ordinary, and invisible. Australian society is often described as highly secular or even 'post-religious'.[81] The 2021 census noted that almost 40 per cent of Australians reported having no religion, while 43.9 per cent identified with Christianity.[82] Yet, what the census categories do not tell us is to which extent these non-religious Australians remain 'culturally' Christian even if they do not identify with Christianity on a census form. While organised Christianity may be in decline, residual Christianity, its traditions, ways of thinking, preferences, sensibilities, and expectations, still holds significant cultural and political power.

Moreover, despite the constitutional barrier against the establishment of religion, Christianity continues to enjoy a privileged position in Australian society and public institutions. The practice of parliamentary prayers, for example, reinforces Christian symbolism in an

[79] Supporter 5, 'Your Say – Letters to the Editor', *North Shore Times*, 12 August 2016, p. 30.

[80] Julie Huffer, 'Song and Dance over Carols', *North Shore Times*, 22 October 2010, p. 5. The article quotes a Ku-ring-gai Councillor who criticised the Council for its support of a Church event: 'It's not fair for one group to get $15,000 for one event that will not be attended by all residents. What if the Jewish community said we have an eruv approved by Ku-ring-gai Planning Panel you have given support to churches, why can't you support us to the same extent?'

[81] This is often more assumed than 'carefully worked out', argue Stephen Chavura and Ian Tregenza, 'Introduction: Rethinking Secularism in Australia (and Beyond)', *Journal of Religious History* 38, no. 3 (2014): 299–306, at 301.

[82] Australian Bureau of Statistics, 'Religious Affiliation in Australia', 4 July 2022, www.abs.gov.au/articles/religious-affiliation-australia

official public setting. Attempts to change this practice in order to reflect the religiously plural make-up of society have been, to date, unsuccessful.[83] The National School Chaplaincy Programme, introduced in 2006 by the conservative Howard government, provides funding to religious chaplains in state schools. Despite several legal challenges to the programme, the policy has so far remained in place, confirming the government's sympathetic approach to religion and Christianity in particular.[84] Conservative Christian groups continue to push with support from members of the Liberal Party for legal exemptions to sack and exclude LGBTQI+ teachers and students from religious schools in order to defend Christian values allegedly under siege from secularists. Moreover, Australia has one of the highest numbers of religious schools among Western countries: Around one third of Australian schools are affiliated with a religion.[85] Almost all religious schools are private schools that cater to around 35 per cent of students.[86] Given the strong hold that Christianity maintains on Australian society, Stuart Piggin observes that 'historically Australia is a country as "Christianised" as secular, and, in terms of its values possibly more Christianised than secular'.[87]

As an ideal and a powerful legal and cultural myth, however, the impartial 'wall of separation' still influences the discourse over the place of religion in the public realm, providing powerful and seemingly neutral arguments which in fact camouflage the special place of majoritarian, hence Christian, values and sentiments and the way they seep into everyday culture and perceptions. In Australia and elsewhere in the world, the appeal to secularism and religious equality has functioned as a selective filter that distributes access to public space unevenly and is deployed in a flexible manner to either grant privileged access to public space to established majority religions or deny access to minority religions.

83 Margaret Davies, 'The Future of Secularism: A Critique', in *Law and Religion in Public Life. The Contemporary Debate*, ed. Nadirsyah Hosen and Richard Mohr (London and New York: Routledge, 2011), 52–66, p. 60.

84 Emma Rowe, 'Religion in Australian Schools: An Historical and Contemporary Debate', *The Conversation*, 23 August 2017.

85 Rowe, 'Religion in Australian Schools'.

86 Australian Bureau of Statistics, 'Schools', 23 February 2022, www.abs.gov.au/statistics/people/education/schools/latest-release

87 Stuart Piggin, 'Power and Religion in a Modern State: Desecularisation in Australian History', *Journal of Religious History* 38, no. 3 (2014): 320–40, p. 322.

The argumentative move that underpins cases such as the eruv, the headscarf, and *Lautsi* draws on the different significance that secular law attaches to 'religion' as opposed to 'culture'. Culture can be subsumed under secular national identity, as heritage and tradition that all citizens are expected to share. This argumentative move allows to withdraw religious symbols turned culture from secular law's strict scrutiny. 'Religion', on the other hand, especially when it is public, is to be scrutinised in light of secular law's authority to set the boundaries of what constitutes appropriate religion.[88] This legal reasoning translates into law how the separation between religion and the secular has historically functioned to maintain the dominance of Christianity, while covering its traces. As Gil Anidjar summarises, secularism is a discourse of power in which 'secularism is a name Christianity gave itself when it invented religion, when it named its other or others as religions'.[89]

Consequently, the different argumentative moves are not available in the same way to minority non-Christian religions as they are to majority religions. In St Ives, the Jewish community's attempt to represent the eruv as a symbol of Australia as a multicultural nation did not gain much traction. Mayanthi Fernando argues that under secular configurations of space, any public expression of religion 'must take place under the sign of sharable culture'.[90] The religion of the majority becomes the benchmark culture, defining not only what constitutes proper religion but also what can be rendered as culture under law. Not sharable practices, such as the headscarf in Fernando's example, or in St Ives, the eruv, become defined as 'excess of religion',[91] associated with religious fundamentalism and political claims, such as the fear of the Jewish takeover of St Ives. Secular law is called upon to contain this excess and to protect the majority religion's prerogative to shape public space as a common, shared, and therefore universal culture.[92] As Gil Anidjar observes, '[l]ike that unmarked race, which, in the related discourse of racism, became invisible or white, Christianity invented the distinction between religious and

[88] On the transformation of majority religion into culture, see also Lori G. Beaman, *The Transition of Religion*.

[89] Anidjar, 'Secularism', p. 62.

[90] Fernando, *The Republic Unsettled*, p. 139.

[91] Fernando, *The Republic Unsettled*, p. 139.

[92] Holly Randell-Moon analyses how Australian secularism functions to negate Indigenous sovereignty, see Holly Randell-Moon, 'The Secular Contract: Sovereignty, Secularism and Law in Australia', *Social Semiotics* 23, no. 3 (2013): 352–67.

secular and thus *made* religion. It made religion the problem – rather than itself'.[93] Christian normativity therefore operates in law and society in similar ways to Whiteness, naturalising and privileging certain identities, while marking others as different and suspect and therefore in need of regulation and containment. At the same time, this regulation reinforces a specific mode of 'religion' that reproduces Christianity as the invisible norm.

WHOSE VISUAL AMENITY? TEMPORALITIES OF SOVEREIGNTY

Claims about the destructive aesthetic effects of an eruv have been the bread and butter of eruv opponents around the world. In St Ives, objecting petitions warned that the eruv would be an 'eyesore', 'ugly and intrusive to the landscape' and that the 'streetscape and trees would be destroyed'.[94] In survey responses, forty-one residents stated that they were concerned about the 'visual and environmental impact the boundary structures would have on residential amenity'. While objectors expressed their concerns in terms of visual amenity, these claims nonetheless contained assumptions about who can rightfully claim and shape urban space, establishing hierarchies of belonging in the suburb:

> The environment and the general public have more than enough to deal with due mandatory signage, light poles and wires without adding 27 more poles with wiring to assist a small group who embrace a way of life which is very restrictive in modern society.[95]

For objectors, the clutter of the eruv was an undue burden on the majority, and they made clear that in 'not representing the views of the majority of the St Ives community, the applications are contrary to public interest and should be rejected', a claim the Council followed. The pseudo-inclusive paradigm that underpins this reasoning is that public space has to be a space for all, and changes or developments have to cater to the needs of all, or at least most, residents. Opponents in St Ives explained this need by differentiating between the useful purpose of electricity poles and telecommunication cables

93 Anidjar, 'Secularism', p. 62.
94 In Ku-ring-gai Council, 'Minutes of Ordinary Meeting of Council', 23 August 2011, items 272 and 273.
95 Opponent 13, 'Opinion/Letters', *North Shore Times*, 9 July 2010, p. 23.

as a basic necessity, and the eruv as a private luxury for a limited few in the neighbourhood. Installations that would negatively affect the visual amenity would only be acceptable when they bring an advantage to a majority of residents, a benefit which is equated with the public interest. It is an understanding that corresponds with the assumption that 'the right to difference disappears once the majority has spoken'.[96]

One St Ives resident, a Jewish Holocaust survivor who had been very outspoken against the eruv also called upon Orthodox Jews to keep their differences to themselves in order to not burden the majority:

> If it is an inconvenience for a minority of orthodox Jews not to be able to push a pram on the Sabbath, they should accept it and not make it a problem for the Australian people.[97]

The call for assimilation is understandable in light of Jewish history that is a testament to the perils of being visibly Jewish and thereby also speaks to an ongoing sense of precarity among some Jews for whom invisibility may still be the best strategy for Jewish safety. As noted previously, it is not uncommon that other Jews object to an eruv. In fact, in opposing the eruv, this St Ives resident was not the only one who identified as Jewish. One of the objecting petitions noted that the signatories represented both Jews and non-Jews,[98] but later statements made no reference to this background and opposition to the eruv in St Ives never presented itself as Jewish, as in the case of the Westhampton Beach eruv. Compared to other eruv controversies though, Jewish voices constituted only a minority among eruv opponents. Instead, most opposition appeared to come from the non-Jewish-identifying population of St Ives, who refuted Orthodox Jews' wish to mark their presence onto the urban space as illegitimate and rude. Insisting on an eruv became a matter of local manners and etiquette, a way of behaving that is sensitive to the needs and expectations of long-time residents and aware of one's own status as a newcomer. Several opponents presented the eruv proposal as an unheard-of demand of newly arrived people which not only contravened the suburb's amenity, but also disrupted locally expected appropriate behaviour and sensibilities. As one resident argued:

96 Sandercock, 'When Strangers', p. 15.

97 Opponent 14, quoted in Karen Michelmore, 'Court to Decide on Religious Structure', *ABC Sydney*, 19 March 2012.

98 Petition (3) (see note 16).

> I've been here 50 years and it's been a very congenial, harmonious atmosphere. But these Orthodox people seem to have a different set of values and they're aggressively insensitive to what people feel about them moving in with their poles and wires.[99]

Another resident stated:

> I'm utterly amazed at what I've been reading about miles of mystical wire and the destruction of many trees, which I strongly object to. I've lived here for more than 40 years and we like it the way it is. Keep your views and religion to yourselves please.[100]

These statements overlook the fact that Jews have lived in the North Shore for several decades – the North Shore Synagogue opened its doors in 1947 – and picture Jews within an assimilatory framework as new immigrants who have to acculturate to the longstanding standards of the locality. One opponent, emphasising that she had lived in the suburb since 1977, complained about the *chutzpah* of the Orthodox Jews:

> How is that a minority group of Orthodox Jews who have recently come to live in St Ives, in the name of their religion, have the right to request alteration to the whole environment of this suburb against the opinion of the majority of residents, newcomers and those who have been in this area for many years. What is proposed would further deface St Ives nearly as badly as the new high-rise.[101]

The status quo, seen as natural and rightful, is contrasted with the alleged novelty of the eruv and the people it serves. Such an argument normalises the presence of a certain segment of the population, while rendering Orthodox Jews as strangers who do not fully belong and who are expected to keep a low profile. In opposing the eruv, objectors expressed a nostalgia for the ideal of assimilationism as the appropriate pathway to belonging in Australia,[102] an ideal that the planning regime honoured through its protection of the status quo. Appealing to planning terms such as amenity, heritage, or local character is a powerful tool to preserve entrenched power relations.

[99] Opponent 15, quoted in Cornwall, 'The Eruv'.
[100] Opponent 16, 'Letters', *North Shore Times*, 16 July 2010, p. 34.
[101] Opponent 17, 'Letters to the Editor', *North Shore Times*, 25 June 2010, p. 36.
[102] Kevin Dunn, 'Repetitive and Troubling Discourses of Nationalism in the Local Politics of Mosque Development in Sydney, Australia', *Environment and Planning D* 23 (2005): 29–50.

Yet, it also helps to reproduce a crucial temporality that underpins claims to sovereignty in settler societies. Sherene Razack describes this temporality in which White settlers figure as the cultivators and therefore rightful owners of uncultivated land. Non-White migrants, on the other hand, are seen as late-comers to this process of pioneering cultivation and regardless of the actual time of their arrival, their work on the land and their contributions to building the settler society are seen as later and therefore less significant. Their designation as forever newcomers means that non-White migrants cannot claim a privileged relationship to the settled land. Crucially, in this temporality, Indigenous peoples are relegated to an uncultivated past. Thereby, any of their claims to the land and to sovereignty are erased. As Razack summarises with reference to North America: 'If Aboriginal peoples are consigned forever to an earlier space and time, people of colour are scripted as late arrivals, coming to the shores of North America long after much of the development has occurred'.[103] By disrupting this racialised temporality and its religious underpinnings, the St Ives eruv became not only a threat to the civilisational narrative that has underpinned the colonisation of Australia and continues to underpin the sovereignty of the modern Australian nation state,[104] but it also raised questions about the Whiteness of observant Jews.

THE THREAT OF A GHETTO

In reading the St Ives eruv conflict, it is easy to focus on religious difference and questions of amenity as the primary concern. Yet, much like the bodily mark of male circumcision, the eruv enters the public sphere as a racialising agent that brings to the surface a lingering suspicion about the 'essence' of 'the Jew' whose body carries the threat of subversion. Some objectors tapped into openly antisemitic stereotypes, such as the anonymous letter sent to residents in 2016 that spread rumours about rabbinical plans to seize control over the suburb:

[103] Razack, 'When Place Becomes Race', p. 3.

[104] In 1992, the Australian High Court overturned the doctrine of Terra Nullius that had held that Australia had been uncultivated and therefore uninhabited in its decision *Mabo v Queensland (No. 2)* (1992) 175 CLR 1. However, the decision did not challenge that the Crown acquired sovereignty.

> The motivation to build an Eruv has very little to do with the stated purpose of enabling carrying on the Sabbath or mothers pushing a pram, as it is so often stated. It has much more to do with establishing a modern version of the ghetto under Rabbinical control.[105]

The eruv appears as a sneaky Trojan horse that masquerades as an innocent device for families, while preparing for the conquest of St Ives. Claiming scholarly support for their argument, the leaflet authors referred to the work of two Israeli sociologists to bolster their claims about the real 'desires and intent of the Orthodox':

> This has been true of every city of the world where an Eruv has been erected. The downstream long term consequence of an Eruv establishment is the division of the community and eventual expulsion of secular people who live within the Eruv and who want nothing to do with it.[106]

Friedman and Heilman, the two sociologists to whom the leaflet attributes this claim, describe a particular group of strictly Orthodox Jews, the Haredim in Israel.[107] Haredi Jews follow an insular lifestyle in which the separation from and distance to the secular society is central – different from modern Orthodox Judaism which does not reject integration into the secular world. Regardless of the significance of this distinction, the leaflet agitates against the rights of St Ives' observant Jewish inhabitants by welding together old antisemitic tropes and present anxieties about Haredi territorialism in Israel that allegedly displaces secular citizens. The fear seemed to be that St Ives would turn into Mea She'arim or Beit Shemesh, Haredi neighbourhoods in Israel, where residents block streets and throw stones at cars if they dare to enter the area on Shabbat.[108]

105 'Aspects of the Eruv You Should Know About', Anonymous Letter Sent to St Ives Residents, 7 September 2016 (see note 37).

106 'Aspects of the Eruv You Should Know About', Anonymous Letter Sent to St Ives Residents, 7 September 2016 (see note 37).

107 Haredi Judaism (Haredim meaning the 'trembling') describes a broad spectrum of strictly Orthodox Jews, often also called ultra-Orthodox, characterised by their rejection of secular culture. Hasidic Jews, such as the Lubavitch Jews in Crown Heights (see Chapter 5) constitute a subgroup of Haredi Jews. Hasidic Jews place great emphasis on the joy of performing the commandments of the Torah, see the entry in the Jewish Virtual Library on Orthodox Judaism: Hasidim and Mitnagdim: www.jewishvirtuallibrary.org/hasidim-and-mitnagdim.

108 Disputes between secular and Haredi Jews in Israel are often fought over space and the regulation of Shabbat, see Gillad Rosen and Anne B. Shlay, 'Whose Right to Jerusalem?', *International Journal of Urban and Regional Research* 38, no. 3 (2014): 935–50.

Media reports fuelled the impression that Haredi Jews were planning the eruv. The misleading *A Current Affair* report, for example, illustrated its feature with a picture of strictly Orthodox Jewish men in traditional black garb, creating the impression of St Ives' Jews as Hasidic.[109] As one of St Ives' Rabbis notes about the fears of eruv opponents, 'They thought they would have lots of black hats and frocks and they didn't want that'.[110]

It is no secret that Haredi Jews in Israel, the case to which Friedman's and Heilman's article refers, have used spatial strategies, including the creation of eruvin, to try to enforce their lifestyle onto neighbourhoods, such as in Jerusalem, which has led to conflict with other Jews. However, in representing themselves as beleaguered and threatened, the leaflet authors turn the local suburban power relations in Australia on their heads to present themselves as a minoritised group in need of legal protection. Accommodating the eruv today, the leaflet warned, would lead to the tyranny of fundamentalist religion tomorrow. Planning law becomes the tool to contain the threatening political aspirations of Jews. Jews are essentialised as fundamentalist and subversive, creating a climate of fear around the presence of the Jewish neighbour – a narrative that echoes the hysterical representations of Muslims as extremists in Western public discourse in which public religiosity is seen as a premodern and backward mixing of religion and politics.

Another line of racialising discourse hid behind the seemingly inclusive language of multiculturalism. Several objecting residents compared the eruv to a ghetto. One petition warned of the 'propensity which an eruv would have in the longer term to develop into a religious enclave',[111] while one survey response argued that the eruv would 'perpetuate societal division and reduce integration into the municipality'. Another resident urged 'We need to integrate them rather than segregate communities'.[112] Consequently, like their Prussian predecessors in Bromberg, eruv opponents saw the prevention of an eruv as a necessity to liberate Jews from their self-imposed segregation and to enable their integration into the suburb by freeing them out of their 'ghetto' and stripping them of their Jewish particularities.

109 Available from https://ajnwatch.blogspot.com/2010/07/current-affair-report-on-st-ives-eruv.html.
110 Personal conversation with St Ives Rabbi 1, Sydney, July 2016.
111 Petition (1) (see note 16).
112 Opponent 10, quoted in Katrina Adamski, 'Siege over Imaginary Wall', *North Shore Times*, 19 September 2008.

The construal of Jewish practices as practices of separation has a long history in Western thought. Not only Christian thinkers but also modern Western anthropological and sociological writing have tended to interpret Jewish obligations, such as the laws of kashrut but also the laws of Shabbat, as primarily means of social separation.[113] However, scholars have challenged such limited interpretations by emphasising that Jewish practices such as the eruv but also the laws of kashrut have enabled and even required the interaction between Jews and non-Jews and that separation is not necessarily the prime concern of these laws. Elisheva Fonrobert, for example, emphasises the role of neighbourly interactions for the eruv. In the diaspora, the eruv relies on persuading and negotiating with neighbours and jurisdictions. Thus, while the eruv certainly 'mingles' Jews into one community, it does so by 'negotiating the status of the community as an accepted, affirmed and supported minority community within the larger body-politic'.[114] Fonrobert describes the genius of the diaspora eruv as allowing for a multidimensionality of urban space as the eruv does not lay claim to sovereignty given that its non-exclusionary territoriality that allows anyone and anything to be part of it, whether Jewish or not.[115] The contemporary tendency to interpret Jewish laws primarily through the lens of social boundaries and Jewish separationism, Shai Lavi argues, reflects the legacy of Christianity and Protestant theology in particular to understand Jewish practices through the idea of Jewish particularistic separation.[116] There is no doubt that shared practices such as the eruv, circumcision, or shechita enforce communal bonds and therefore create boundaries, but from the perspective of Jewish law or of observant Jews, this may not necessarily be their only purpose.

[113] See the discussion in Shai Lavi, 'Our Food Is Our Bond: A History of Jewish and Muslim Animal Slaughter and Post-Christian Social Science', *History of the Present: A Journal of Critical History* 8, no. 1 (2018): 29–56.

[114] Fonrobert, 'Diaspora Cartography', p. 20.

[115] Fonrobert, 'Diaspora Cartography', p. 25. See also Charlotte Elisheva Fonrobert, 'Installations of Jewish Law in Public Urban Space: An American Eruv Controversy', *Chicago-Kent Law Review* 90 (2015): 63–77.

[116] Lavi, 'Our Food Is Our Bond', p. 39. Lavi shows how Jews and non-Jews forged relations when non-Jews bought meat from Jewish butchers. Moreover, the laws of kashrut make no distinction between who consumes the meat and therefore do not exempt a Jewish butcher from the rules when supplying meat to a non-Jew. For Lavi, the main aim of the laws lies in regulating the animal-human-divine relationship that only incidentally affects social relationships (p. 51).

Supporters of the St Ives eruv took the opposite view of the eruv as a space of inclusion. As one Councillor, who supported the eruv, emphasised: 'The eruv has been a part of the Jewish population for over 2000 years – it is an instrument of integration'.[117] Similarly, for one of St Ives' rabbis, far from being a separatist device, the eruv instead fostered the integration of Orthodox Jews into St Ives public spaces. After the eruv had been set up with Ausgrid's help, the community's rabbi praised the integrating effect of the eruv:

> [I]t allows us to build community between Jewish and non-Jewish people because people could move on Shabbat. It created no boundaries in the community, it opened up our lives, and caused inclusion.[118]

Indeed, in a seemingly contradictory way, by drawing a boundary, the eruv enables observant Jews to integrate into the public space and take part in social life more fully, including potentially interacting with non-Jews. The religious structure allows Orthodox Jews 'to come out as "ordinary" citizens'.[119] For the Chief Executive Officer of the New South Wales Jewish Board of Deputies, this made the eruv quintessentially Australian:

> This is not about forming enclosures or separating people from each other. The reverse, in fact. It's about enabling people to get out and mix while respecting their distinctive cultures and faiths. Isn't that what Australia is so proudly, and rightly, all about?[120]

For some eruv opponents, however, the walls of the eruv were real and their purpose was separation. They argued that the eruv would foster spatial segregation and societal disintegration, which would undermine the vision of Australia as a multicultural space:

> There is no benefit for St Ives and/or Ku-ring-gai residents who are not eruv supporters. Australia is about multiculturalism and the benefits it brings to everyone; it is not about creating ghettos for the promotion of religious minorities.[121]

The desire to build an eruv is seen as un-Australian and therefore as contradicting national character. In her analysis on judicial representations

[117] Councillor, quoted in Desiatnek, 'Eruv Decision a Win'.
[118] Personal conversation with St Ives Rabbi 2, December 2016, Sydney.
[119] Cooper, 'Talmudic Territory', p. 537.
[120] Vic Alhadeff, 'Poles but No Polarisation to Support Needs of Faith', *North Shore Times*, 11 April 2011.
[121] Opponent 11, 'Letters', *North Shore Times*, 30 June 2010, p. 19.

of Jews and Judaism in English law, Didi Herman shows how Jewishness is articulated in seemingly raceless terms but nonetheless in ways that constitute it as foreign to Englishness, especially after the experience of the Holocaust that has somewhat muted the explicit statement of racial superiority in law and society. Englishness is produced as a set of national characteristics and qualities that Jews do not possess, no matter their citizenship. Herman's analysis reveals how judges depict Jews as behaving 'strangely', as disregarding the English rule of law, and as exhibiting 'un-English behaviours', thereby perpetuating racialised exclusions without explicit racial references.[122] Herman concludes that 'the Jew', no matter how assimilated, 'remains the not quite/not yet/not ever "Englishman"'.[123] Similarly, in St Ives, using an eruv is seen as not in line with Australian behaviour and the ideal of multiculturalism as a defining feature of national character. Building an eruv is 'out of character'. What precisely constitutes the core of Australian multiculturalism remains, however, contested. The resistance to the St Ives eruv echoes the broader conservative backlash against Australian multiculturalism in which the accommodation of minority cultures is seen as marginalising 'mainstream' Australians at the expense of non-mainstream, that is, non-Anglo-Christian groups.[124] Allowing Orthodox Jewishness into the public space is seen as carrying the risk of turning the dominant culture of St Ives into the new 'dispossessed' and 'oppressed'.[125]

The type of multiculturalism that lurks behind eruv opponents' language is what Ghassan Hage describes as 'white multiculturalism'. While clouded in a language of tolerance, 'white multiculturalism' works towards 'containing the increasingly active role of non-White Australians in the process of governing Australia'.[126] Opposition

122 Herman, *An Unfortunate Coincidence*. See also the analysis in Cooper and Herman, 'Jews and Other Uncertainties'.

123 Didi Herman, '"An Unfortunate Coincidence": Jews and Jewishness in Twentieth-Century English Judicial Discourse', *Journal of Law and Society* 33, no. 2 (2006): 277–301, p. 300.

124 James Forrest and Kevin Dunn, '"Core" Culture Hegemony and Multiculturalism. Perceptions of the Privileged Position of Australians with British Backgrounds', *Ethnicities* 6, no. 2 (2006): 203–30, at 208; see also Justine Dandy and Rogelia Pe-Pua, 'Attitudes to Multiculturalism, Immigration and Cultural Diversity: Comparison of Dominant and Non-Dominant Groups in Three Australian States', *International Journal of Intercultural Relations* 34 (2010): 34–46.

125 Cooper, 'Talmudic Territory', p. 535.

126 Ghassan Hage, *White Nation. Fantasies of White Supremacy in a Multicultural Society* (New York; London: Routledge, 2000), p. 19.

to the eruv revealed the precarious and conditional Whiteness of Orthodox Jews in St Ives. As discussed in Chapter 2, Jews, especially those from a Western European background, had been able to be accepted as White in the early days of the Australian colonies, despite some ambiguities. The extension of Whiteness to Jews, however, relied on a logic of assimilationism that required the abandonment of cultural particularities to protect the hegemony of Australia's British heritage – a pathway that Australian Jews had been able to navigate relatively successfully. In St Ives, the sense of Whiteness that many Jews had of themselves was further entrenched by the fact that many community members in the suburb had migrated from South Africa, where apartheid had rendered Jews White.[127] As one of St Ives' Rabbis explained:

> … that's why the Jewish community got such a big shock, because they consider themselves part of the White mainstream, especially the South Africans. The South Africans grew up under apartheid, where we were not part of the blacks, we were part of the Whites, and coming here, all of a sudden they are the Other, and being the Other is very frightening because we've only heard about that from our grandparents, we've never experienced that as a people in Australia, at least not in any major way.[128]

The vehement opposition to the eruv thereby revealed not only Orthodox Jews' precarious Whiteness but also the cultural and religious contours of Whiteness in Australia. Jon Stratton has argued that, historically, Australian constructions of Whiteness linked 'looking White' with cultural homogeneity. 'If one looked physically different one was likely to be culturally different. Conversely, if one was culturally different, if one's culture made one visible within the dominant culture, then one could be identified as looking different. "Looking different" was the key marker of racial Difference'.[129] For Jews, this meant keeping a low profile in order to not 'look different'. As the St Ives dispute shows, despite official endorsements of multiculturalism, these associations still resonate. By making their difference visible, Orthodox Jews in St Ives troubled St Ives 'White look' that required them to not look or behave too Jewish.

127 Australia, in particular Sydney, had been a preferred destination for Jews migrating from South Africa. On the role of South African migrants in Jewish Australia, see Rutland, 'Reflections'.

128 Personal conversation with Rabbi 1, Sydney, July 2016.

129 Stratton, *Coming Out Jewish*, p. 222. Spelling with capital letter in the original.

Looking White also requires looking and behaving culturally Christian. An intimate link remains between Australian notions of Whiteness and Christianity, whereby non-Christianity has been associated with non-Whiteness.[130] Historically, the idea of Australia as a White British nation incorporated Christianity. Different to England, Australia never instituted a state church. Nonetheless, the Anglican church and its values sailed along British settlers to Australian shores and constituted the 'de facto, of not *de jure*, established church of the new colony'.[131] Although Christianity and religion more broadly never played such a prominent and overt role as they did for example in the United States, Christianity was still seen as a central source of British morals that rendered British civilisation and British settlers superior.[132] The perceived lack of religion among Indigenous Australians, for example, provided further justification for their dispossession alongside their failure to cultivate the land. English missionaries in Australia understood the spread of Christianity to Indigenous Australians as a way of leading them to the 'first step of civilisation'[133] even though conversion did not grant them any more rights. For a long time, Anglican officials supported the White Australia Policy as it favoured British migrants and therefore membership in the Anglican Church.[134]

The Christian dimension of Australian national identity eventually became more expansive, including Catholics and Orthodox Christians alongside Anglicans. Nonetheless, as Jon Stratton has argued: 'In the core-periphery structure of Australian multiculturalism where Anglos and Celts make up the core and Italians, Greek, Maltese, and other "white" groups make up the ethnic periphery, with the exception of most Irish, the core is Anglican and Protestant while the periphery is Catholic and Orthodox'.[135] The St Ives eruv controversy suggests that Judaism, especially in its more public variants,

130 Stratton, 'Whiteness, Morality and Christianity in Australia', p. 30.

131 Renae Barker, *State and Religion. The Australian Story* (Abingdon, Oxon: Routledge, 2018), p. 326.

132 Brian Fletcher, 'Anglicanism and Nationalism in Australia, 1901–1962', *The Journal of Religious History* 23, no. 215–133 (1999).

133 Stratton, 'Whiteness, Morality and Christianity in Australia', p. 21.

134 Fletcher, 'Anglicanism and Nationalism', pp. 225–56. Of course, many Anglicans also opposed the White Australia Policy, finding it incompatible with their idea of universal humanity.

135 Stratton, 'Whiteness, Morality and Christianity in Australia', p. 24.

occupies an ambivalent space in this structure. While the former conservative Prime Minister John Howard frequently invoked 'Judeo-Christian' in his speeches, mainly to exclude Islam on the one hand and Indigenous spirituality and its connection to sovereignty on the other, the Judeo-Christianity of St Ives required a privatised and largely invisible form of 'Judeo' that understands its position vis-à-vis Christianity as subjugated and non-equal.

CONTAINING EXCESS JEWISHNESS

The St Ives eruv dispute could be seen as an unfortunate exception to the general success of Jews in Australian society – a momentary exclusionary lapse. While it is true that Jewish belonging in Australia has been less fraught or contested than elsewhere due to the particularities of the settler-colonial context, anxieties over Jewish difference have never been fully absent.[136] The eruv's materiality made it an easy target for expressing resentment and ambivalence in a realm of law concerned with objects, spaces, and things instead of people and their rights. 'A fear of difference is projected onto objects and spaces comprising the home or locality which can be polluted by the presence of non-conforming people, activities or artefacts', David Sibley once observed.[137] At the same time, the envisaged democratisation of planning law through its process of public participation enables the manipulation and exploitation of its processes and its malleable legal categories by influential and powerful groups in neighbourhoods.

However, this is not just a problem of suburban NIMBYism. The local has long been a potent site for managing religious and racial difference against the backdrop of broader national anxieties. Sherene Razack observes that 'all systems of domination operate at the local level' working through 'legal and social practices that reproduce racial hierarchies'.[138] Conflict over land in a settler society, including in suburbia, is embedded in broader narratives of colonial sovereignty

[136] See, for example, the Executive Council of Australian Jewry's Report on Antisemitism in Australia 2019, www.sydney.edu.au/content/dam/corporate/documents/sydney-law-school/research/centres-institutes/antisemitism-report-2019.pdf.

[137] David Sibley, *Geographies of Exclusion. Society and Difference in the West* (London; New York: Routledge, 1995), p. 91.

[138] Razack, 'When Place Becomes Race', pp. 16–17.

and rightful ownership marked by race and its intersections with religion. Kim Huynh and Siobhan Neyland observe that

> Australian whiteness is distinctively proprietorial. It manifests itself in a perceived need to exert mastery over Australia's territory and the people of colour who occupy or seek to enter it; that is, it is about spatial and racial control. This whiteness operates in a horizontally racist manner that stirs fears of invasion, and in a vertically racist fashion that privileges white agency at the expense of all others.[139]

Property law but also laws governing the use of land have been central in maintaining racial regimes of ownership and of access to and use of public space.[140] While on the surface, religiously and racially blind categories, such as amenity and public interest, constitute mechanisms through which planning law can reproduce a colonial vision of space that privileges the spatial imaginaries of settlers while suppressing Indigenous relationships to land and devaluing the place of non-White inhabitants.

Many Australian Jews have long enjoyed the privileges of Whiteness and the access to land and space it has granted as they bolstered the number of White settlers, allowing them to participate in and benefit from the process of colonial dispossession. Yet, the eruv reveals that their Whiteness is conditional and policed. In St Ives, the planning dispute split Jews into 'good Jews' who keep their difference private and to themselves and into 'bad Jews' who challenged Christian superiority, which remains entangled with Australian notions of Whiteness. Those 'bad Jews' found themselves pushed to the periphery of Whiteness. Although not concerned with the lofty values of religious freedom, planning law thereby operated as a conduit for disciplining observant Jews whose public religiosity and claim to space overstepped the notion of privatised and contained faith that does not challenge the Christian dominance in and sovereignty over public spaces.

[139] Kim Huynh and Siobhan Neyland, 'Australian Whiteness and Refugee Politics', *Australian Journal of Politics and History* 66, no. 1 (2020): 111–29, p. 113.

[140] See, for example, Brenna Bhandar, *Colonial Lives of Property: Law, Land, and Racial Regimes of Ownership* (Durham: Duke University Press, 2018).

CHAPTER SEVEN

PERSISTENT AMBIVALENCE

Concluding Thoughts

While I was writing this book, secular law was once again mobilised for drawing the boundaries of acceptable Jewish *and* Muslim difference. In 2017, the Belgian regions of Wallonia and Flanders had joined other European jurisdictions, such as Sweden, Switzerland, and Denmark, by changing legislation that had granted an exemption for religious slaughter from mandatory pre-slaughter stunning under EU law. The legislation now required reversible stunning for religious slaughter that does not result in the death of the animal. Under Jewish and Islamic law, animals must be in perfect health when slaughtered and pre-stunning would violate this requirement though some schools of Islamic legal thought permit prior-stunning. The practices of shechita and dhabihah have long been the target of animal welfare activists who perceive of the practices as cruel, and backward. The director of the Belgian group *Global Action in the Interest of Animals* accused Jews and Muslims of being stuck in the past: 'They want to keep living in the Middle Ages and continue to slaughter without stunning – as the technique didn't yet exist back then – without having to answer to the law. Well, I'm sorry, in Belgium the law is above religion and that will stay like that'.[1] For another Belgian activist, the Orthodox Jewish practice of shechita placed Jews not only out of time but also out of place, rendering them somewhat non-human aliens: 'With Kashrut [the laws governing food in Judaism, my addition], you have scholars who are fundamentalists, a

[1] Milan Scheuer, 'Belgium Bans Religious Slaughtering Practices, Drawing Praise and Protest', *New York Times*, 5 January 2019.

total unwillingness to evolve. That's a problem in a secular society…. It is like we are from two different planets, we are from Earth and they are from Mars or Jupiter'.[2]

Jewish and Muslim communities challenged the Flemish decree in domestic courts in the name of religious freedom. The Belgian Constitutional Court (Grondwettelijk Hof) referred the question to the European Court of Justice, seeking a preliminary ruling on whether European law precludes member states from introducing a requirement of reversible stunning in the practice of religious slaughter. Against the legal opinion of the Advocate General Gerard Hogan, who had found the ban to violate the right to religious freedom in his non-binding opinion,[3] the Grand Chamber of the Court of Justice found the ban on religious slaughter justified, noting that member states may adopt more stringent rules aimed at the protection of animals than required by EU regulation. The Court argued that the ban did not completely outlaw religious slaughter, but only regulated that animals had to be stunned prior to slaughter, thereby striking a fair balance between animal welfare and religious freedom.[4] The Flemish minister for animal welfare, Ben Weyts from the right-wing party *Vlaams Belang* celebrated the decision by stating that Flanders was 'writing history'.[5]

I conclude with the Flemish case because it offers another illustration of some of the themes analysed in this book.[6] The argument I have advanced is that we cannot understand contemporary responses to Jewish difference in secular law separately from the long history of Christian ambivalence towards Jews. I have suggested that secular law and legal reasoning still participate in reproducing a Christian supersessionary logic that relies on notions of temporality and progress that relegate Jews and other non-Christians to an overcome time, while affirming implicitly the superiority of a secularised Christian culture. This dynamic can also be seen at play in the Flemish case,

[2] Eddy Wax, 'Belgium Tests EU Rules on Halal and Kosher Slaughter', *Politico*, 19 August 2019.

[3] Advocate General's Opinion in Case C-336/19 *Centraal Israëlitisch Consistorie van België and others* (10 September 2020).

[4] Court of Justice of the European Union (Grand Chamber), Case C-336 *Centraal Israëlitisch Consistorie van België and others* (17 December 2020).

[5] 'EU Court Backs Ban on Animal Slaughter without Stunning', *BBC News*, 17 December 2020.

[6] I discuss the history of religious slaughter bans in more detail in Riedel, 'They are from Mars'.

where Christian ambivalence and the logic of supersession again reared its head in the calls for secular law to intervene in order to civilise Jews and Muslims. Certainly, the treatment of animals is an important and often severely neglected legal and moral issue, and animal rights activists do not spare majoritarian practices from criticism in an equally drastic tone. Yet, such language resonates even more strongly when it can mobilise an entrenched supersessionary logic that reproduces a set of binaries that condemns Jewish and Muslim carnality, literalism, and barbarism and locates 'them' in an earlier time, deficient and inferior, providing 'us' with the comfort of being in the superior here and now. Law is called upon to modernise and properly secularise observant Muslims and Jews. Flemish and EU law participate in the remaking of both observant Jews and Muslims by constituting private faith as the most appropriate site for religion and distracting from the continued suffering of animals at the hands of the majority culture.

Moreover, as I have argued, once religion has been made the problem, race is never far, casting doubt on the assimilability of those deemed different by rendering their difference insurmountable and incurable as if 'they are from planet Mars or Jupiter'. Much more muted than in the past, the racialisation of Jewish difference in legal debates today manifests in subtler ways, often expressed as matters of national character, of civilisational hierarchy, or by more or less vaguely gesturing to old antisemitic tropes, such as Jewish bloodthirstiness and violent tendencies. Despite the popular narrative of the West as 'Judeo-Christian', this cultural racism perhaps also reflects deeper anxieties about Jewish equality and religious pluralism more broadly that threaten lingering self-narratives of the Christian majority's cultural superiority. Law here becomes a crucial tool for re-asserting this hierarchical relationship by controlling and circumscribing Jewish identity, and marking Jewish culture and tradition as suspect and dangerous. My point is not to suggest a structural relationship between Christian ambivalence and race. This would require further research.[7] Yet, this process of differentiation, although seemingly contradictory to assimilation, contributes to maintaining the superiority of the dominant Christian identity by explaining the persistence of Jewish difference and their stubborn refusal to adhere to majoritarian values as

[7] Daniel Boyarin, A *Radical Jew* ponders the link between Pauline universalism, coercive sameness, and racism (at 233).

rooted in a supposedly innate inability to modernise. These ambivalent struggles around the accommodation of Jewish difference reveal a persistent desire to anchor the identity of 'the West' in an exclusionary vision in Christianity and Whiteness, while simultaneously maintaining an inclusive vision of 'the West' as the locus of liberalism, secularism, as well as religious and racial equality.

The case of religious slaughter also gestures to three further questions that arise from my analysis and, which, by way of conclusion, I will briefly attempt to address here. These questions relate to the relationship between Christian ambivalence and legal progress, the role of Jewish engagements with secular law, and the entanglement of Jewish and Muslim questions in the contemporary politics of religious difference.

CHRISTIAN AMBIVALENCE AND LEGAL PROGRESS

One of the arguments I have advanced in this book concerns the role of law in circumscribing what I termed the acceptable boundaries of Jewish difference. I suggested that in the case of circumcision and in the case of the eruv, Jewish difference appears most acceptable when it fits within a notion of private faith. The same can be said about the Flemish law that curtailed the public elements of Orthodox Jewish identity alongside of course Muslim identity. However, while in the Flemish context, the law indeed participated directly in the regulation of Jewish difference by removing the exemption of religious slaughter from the pre-stunning requirement (although kosher meat remains available via import), in the cases of the eruv and circumcision, the law did not directly enforce this notion of Jewish difference. The eruv in Sydney, as in other parts of the world where an eruv has been challenged in secular courts, received legal approval eventually, whereas in Germany, the Parliament amended the Civil Code to protect the rights of Jews and Muslims to circumcise their male children. In fact, no country has so far followed through with a ban on circumcision. What do these dynamics tell us about the relationship between secular law and Christian ambivalence? Is the significance of Christian ambivalence limited to the social realm, while secular law acts as the protector of religious pluralism? While my argument has not been that there is a determinative relationship between Christian ambivalence and certain legal outcomes, have I nonetheless overstated the significance of the law's role in any lingering assimilationism that seeks to remake Jews?

First, it is important to note that even though the law may have protected Jews in the cases of eruvin and circumcision, the path to this outcome has often been long and socially and financially costly.[8] Eruvin cases have often dragged on for many years, delaying the rights of observant Jews. In St Ives, the eruv came into being not thanks to the law but in spite of it. By creating facts on the ground and leveraging their networks, Jews were able to resist. In the case of circumcision, the legal turmoil was much shorter, but ongoing initiatives across European countries to outlaw the practice signal to Jews and Muslims that their right to maintain their practices remains up for debate. Moreover, legal conflict as a site of discursive struggle over values and meanings has a symbolic dimension that communicates to society what is desirable and what is not without requiring the full force of the law's authority. In analysing the discourse of tolerance in modern liberal states, Wendy Brown argues that tolerance operates as a form of governmentality, that is, 'a consortium of para-legal and para-statist practices in modern constitutional liberalism – practices that are associated with the liberal state and liberal legalism but are not precisely codified by it'.[9] Even absent any formal legal command, tolerance works to produce subjects, as well as meanings of identity, and marks bodies when lengthy legal processes, such as protracted planning deliberations or parliamentary debates about the legality of circumcision, convey messages about what is desirable and what is not, and remind the tolerated of their conditional inclusion by the majoritarian culture.[10]

One might argue that the assimilationist pressures of contemporary Christian ambivalence are benign compared to the past when conversion was the only option to escape violence or death or when assimilation was the only pathway to equal citizenship. In his critique of Stephen Feldman's analysis of the role of US law in perpetuating antisemitism, Mark Graber emphasises the need to distinguish between 'the oppressive inequalities of the past and the insensitive

[8] See also Joshi, *White Christian Privilege*, p. 154.

[9] Brown, *Regulating Aversion*, p. 4.

[10] See, for example, the 2018 survey of Jewish perceptions of antisemitism in Europe that included questions about potential bans of Jewish practices: European Union Agency for Fundamental Rights, *Experiences and Perceptions of Antisemitism. Second Survey on Discrimination and Hate Crime against Jews in the Eu*, Publications Office of the European Union (Luxembourg, 2018), https://fra.europa.eu/sites/default/files/fra_uploads/fra-2018-experiences-and-perceptions-of-antisemitism-survey_en.pdf.

inconveniences of the present'.[11] Legal progress has been made without doubt, but it should neither prevent us from seeing how socio-legal pressure to assimilate can still circumscribe the boundaries of acceptable Jewish difference nor to downplay this pressure as merely insensitive and inconvenient. In his critical reading of the evolution of the rights of gay and lesbian people, Kenji Yoshino proposes a more fine-grained framework for understanding and critiquing the complex operation of assimilationism. Drawing on Erwin Goffman's work on stigma, Yoshino distinguishes different forms of assimilationist demands:

> Conversion means the underlying identity is altered. Conversion occurs when a lesbian changes her orientation to straight. Passing means the underlying identity is not altered, but hidden. Passing occurs when a lesbian presents herself to the world as straight. Covering means the underlying identity is neither altered nor hidden, but is downplayed. Covering occurs when a lesbian both says she is lesbian, but otherwise makes it easy for others to disattend her orientation.[12]

Yoshino understands his intervention as a corrective to an unqualified narrative of progress in rights that trivialises the persistence of assimilationist demands that sexual minorities face. Instead, Yoshino shows how these various assimilationist demands – conversion, passing, and covering – have not simply replaced each other over time but in fact continue to operate simultaneously, thereby confronting gay and lesbian people with a multiplicity of assimilationist demands. Conversion and passing demands still persist, even if in less pronounced ways, and, as Yoshino warns, progress is always fragile.[13] Moreover, Yoshino argues against marginalising covering demands as benign, showing how covering still denies essential parts of a person's identity, impacts on their dignity and status, and can ultimately mask how societal perceptions that underpin conversion demands have been merely re-articulated as covering.[14]

[11] Mark A. Graber, 'Jewish Voices and Religious Freedom. A Jewish Critique of Critical Jewish Thinking', in *Law and Religion: A Critical Anthology*, ed. Stephen M. Feldman (New York: New York University Press, 2000), 278–95, p. 284.

[12] Yoshino, 'Covering', p. 772.

[13] Yoshino, 'Covering', p. 777. I first developed this argument in my article 'Law and the Construction of Jewish Difference', *Journal of Law and Society* 48, no. 2 (2021): 158–178. My thanks to one of the reviewers for drawing my attention to Yoshino's work.

[14] Yoshino, 'Covering', part II.

Yoshino's framework offers a useful starting point for considering the legal progress made by Jews in Western societies alongside the conditions that continue to regulate and circumscribe Jewish identity. What emerges in relation to both practices is that Jewish difference appears most acceptable when it is not too visible, not too Jewish, making it easy, to use Yoshino's word, to 'disattend' or cover Jewish difference. Calling for a ban on circumcision, as I have argued, reflects a conversionist attitude that seeks to alter Jewish identity, so it resembles a Christian notion of religion. Seeking to prevent an eruv could be read as an attempt to enforce passing through the enforced hiding of the public spatial presence of Orthodox Jews. These attempts may not have succeeded legally, and how Jews in those communities experience and express their identities in light of this assimilationist pressure is an empirical question beyond the scope of this book. However, both circumcision and the eruv point to a persistent ambivalence about the presence and place of Jews in Western societies that communicates ideas about appropriate behaviour and identity and about what the law ought to protect and what not.

Second, as I have argued in this book, Christian ambivalence does not necessarily imply the exclusion of Jewishness but involves seemingly contradictory processes of both differentiation and inclusion – even though inclusion is often only provisional and premised on assimilation. Moreover, historically, as I have explored in Chapter 2 in particular, the toleration of Jews often depended on their utility for theological, political, and economic projects and not necessarily on benevolent ideas about the equality of Jews. Later, Jewish emancipation was not only necessary for Jews but also from the perspective of the state, including for consolidating state power and sovereignty, for ensuring a level of homogeneity in the modern nation state, and for the economic benefits these new citizens would bring. The Whitening of Jews in settler societies, such as the United States and Australia, on the other hand, supported the colonising enterprise, served economic and political rationales, and helped bolstering a White identity at the expense of those racialised as non-White – even though the inclusion of fair-skinned Jews has often remained ambiguous and Jews of Colour have remained marginalised.[15] Today, it seems that Jewish inclusion provides a certain cultural currency,

[15] On how Jews became White in the US, see Brodkin, *How Jews Became White Folks*. On Jews of Colour, see Haynes, *Soul of Judaism*.

as a symbol of religious pluralism that allows to gloss over persistent exclusions and inequalities along religious and racial lines, encapsulated in the narrative of Judeo-Christianity that signals diversity while excluding Muslims and other non-Christian faiths. Moreover, by presenting (some) Jews as equal members and therefore themselves as pluralist and tolerant, Western societies attempt to 'redeem' and 'heal' themselves from their past atrocities – be it the Holocaust or racial injustice.[16]

The dynamic in which legal change is not animated by genuine concerns about the rights and equality of minorities but by the self-interests of majoritarian groups is reminiscent of what critical race theorist Derrick Bell described as interest convergence in the context of the United States. Sceptical of the motives behind progress in racial justice, Bell argued that African Americans only gained rights and justice when and to the extent in which their interests aligned with those of the (elite) White population.[17] For Bell, the Supreme Court's landmark decision in *Brown v. Board of Education* on the end of school segregation was not the result of morality and altruism but of an attempt to increase the United States' political capital in Cold War competition for allies, to reassure returning Black veterans, and to help domestic efforts to industrialise the South.[18]

In his analysis of the US Supreme Court's treatment of non-Christian claims for accommodation, Stephen Feldman has made an argument similar to Bell in that non-Christian gains in equality happen to a significant extent only when they align with the interest of Christians.[19] Moreover, for Feldman, progress for religious minorities, such as Jews, is incidental and often imposes costs on these groups, such as the implicit requirement to present claims in a way that resembles majoritarian understandings of religion in order to succeed, thereby perpetuating both Christian cultural dominance and the Christianisation of non-Christians.[20] For example, in Germany, as I discussed in Chapter 4, Jewish organisations had to follow the dominant discursive script by appealing to the medical

16 Gil Hochberg and Shir Alon, 'Decolonizing Judaism: Barbarism and the Return to Nativism', *boundary 2* 44, no. 4 (2017): 179–94, p. 184.

17 Derrick A. Bell, 'Brown v. Board of Education and the Interest-Convergence Dilemma', *Harvard Law Review* 93, no. 3 (1980): 518–33.

18 Bell, 'Interest-Convergence Dilemma', p. 525.

19 Feldman, *Please Don't Wish Me a Merry Christmas*, pp. 273–74.

20 Feldman, *Please Don't Wish Me a Merry Christmas*, pp. 280–81.

benefits of circumcision to render the practice legible to an audience for whom embodied religion was unintelligible. The prevalent bifurcation of the right to freedom of religion, including in Germany's constitutional order, as well as the resulting need to define 'religion' set structural limits to the kinds of claims that can be made. In St Ives, due to the absence of a proper rights framework, the eruv group had to present the eruv as a vehicle of liberal accommodation and within a regime of property rights to advance their interests (Chapter 6) within the utilitarian planning framework and land use regime.

In Germany, commentators also questioned whether the new provision that enshrines the rights of parents to consent to the circumcision of their male child for non-therapeutical reasons – and therefore protected a non-privatised notion of Jewishness – was motivated by an acknowledgement of the equality of Jews and Muslims or by the utility of Jewish inclusion. They raised the question of whether the legal intervention was the result of concerns about Germany's international image, in which good relations with its Jewish community remain a paramount political concern and a yardstick of the country's democratic credentials.[21] This interpretation makes sense given how 'the Jew' remains essential to the country's self-definition and the way that the provision that confirms the rights of parents to a religious circumcision was couched by many participants in the debate as an act of toleration that still labels the tolerated as outside 'our' normative universe as otherwise there would be no need for toleration.

Similarly, when Denmark discussed a ban on circumcision, Danish Prime Minister Mette Fredriksen explained the decision against proceeding with a ban by affirming Jewish, yet not Muslim belonging in Denmark: 'Many Jews don't find it compatible to live in a country where circumcision is banned, and I simply don't think we can make a decision with which we don't live up to our promise – that the Jews will remain part of Denmark'.[22] However, concerns about Jewish belonging did not prevent the country from banning religious slaughter in 2014. In fact, religious slaughter has been the Jewish practice that has faced the most legal restrictions so far, particularly in Europe.

[21] See, for example, Tzuberi and Doughan, 'Säkularismus als Praxis'; Salaymeh and Lavi, 'Religion Is Secularised Tradition'.

[22] Christian Wenande, 'Denmark Refuses to Ban the Ritual Circumcision of Boys', *CPH Post*, 11 September 2020, https://cphpost.dk/?p=118305.

Given that following the laws of kashrut is not universal among Jews, banning religious slaughter excludes only some forms of Jewish difference, allowing Western societies to still proclaim their 'Judeo-Christian' credentials, while creating distinctions between 'good Jews' and 'bad Jews'. Circumcision, on the other hand, is almost universally practiced, so a ban would affect and alienate all Jews, thereby severely undermining the credibility of the narrative of 'Judeo-Christian pluralism', even though if it means tolerating the intolerable. Of course, discerning what leads to a certain legal outcome is a complex question and there will often not be one singular motivation given that law is always the result of reconciling a multitude of competing and sometimes contradictory concerns and motivations.[23]

While in St Ives, reputational damage and 'facts on the ground' made it too costly for the Council to proceed with its opposition, the success of eruv litigation in North America, at least in the context of the United States, could appear, at first sight, to contradict the idea of interest convergence. However, the eruv's minimal nature may have helped as the challenge to Christian dominance is barely visible, and therefore is perhaps seen as less threatening. Moreover, the accommodation of the eruv could be seen as part of a larger trend in the United States to allow 'cracks' in the wall of separation,[24] a trend which benefits not only Shabbat-observant Jews but ultimately also helps to entrench and cement the historical public dominance of Christianity. David Schraub suggests that the trend towards greater accommodation for conservative religious rights in US Supreme Court jurisprudence could also shift the norm for what constitutes the most acceptable form of Jewishness in the United States from liberal Jews who fit the Protestant notion of private faith to more conservative Orthodox Jews. Previously often seen as 'too Jewish' due to their 'excess' of Jewishness, conservative Orthodox Jews could now benefit from being able to present their religiosity in terms more palatable to conservative Christians who value a more devout form of religion. Yet, as Schraub notes, this shift does not necessarily mean a more inclusive protection of Jewishness as it simply adjusts what constitutes the most acceptable form of Jewishness according to

[23] Mary L. Dudziak's archival work ultimately confirmed Bell's interest convergence thesis in relation to the landmark Supreme Court decision *Brown v. Board of Education* Mary L. Dudziak, *Cold War Civil Rights. Race and the Image of American Democracy* (Princeton; Oxford: Princeton University Press, 2000).

[24] See Stolzenberg and Myers, *American Shtetl*, p. 7.

prevailing Christian interests.[25] This renders what I termed the 'acceptable boundaries of Jewish difference' in the context of the West malleable, dynamic, and contingent, whereas the only feature that remains unchanged is the role of the dominant, however secularised, Christian culture in setting the norm for what kind of 'Judeo' is included in the 'Judeo-Christian subject'. Thinking about how the interests of the majority align with particular Jewish interests in a given context therefore invites us to consider how and to which extent legal progress for Jews remains tied to prevailing majoritarian interests.

JEWISH ENGAGEMENTS WITH WESTERN SECULAR LAW

While it is important to take note of how majoritarian interests limit and circumscribe legal progress, it is equally important to acknowledge the agency and contributions of Jewish individuals and institutions as well as Jewish thought to legal reform and legal change to avoid perpetuating a narrative of Western secular law as the sole product and harbinger of Christian cultural dominance. Painting Jews as powerless in the face of a dominant Christian culture would ultimately mean that little has changed about the 'oldest hatred' and retell a history of Europe/the West and its law in purely binary terms, in which Jews had nothing to contribute aside from offering a foil for Western anxieties. While the pervasiveness of Christian normativity circumscribes without doubt the kinds of legal arguments, claims, and gains Jews and other non-Christian can make, it would be too simplistic to treat secular legal reasoning and legal progress as shaped by Christian ambivalence difference alone. In fact, Christian ambivalence itself has been influenced by encounters and exchanges between Christians and Jews, even though such encounters and exchanges Jews could challenge entrenched images of the 'hermeneutical Jew'. Moreover, Christian ambivalence developed and was tempered and modified within a complex web of everyday professional, social, and cultural interactions of Jews and Christians living alongside each other, even though unequal power relationships cannot be ignored.[26]

[25] Schraub, 'Liberal Jews', p. 36.

[26] On Jewish and Christian mutuality, see Heschel, 'Jews and Christianity'. On interactions and mutual influence between Jews, Muslims, and Christians, see also David Nirenberg, *Neighbouring Faiths. Christianity, Islam, and Judaism in the Middle Ages and Today* (Chicago; London: University of Chicago Press, 2014).

While not the main focus of my analysis, the cases and events in this book show that the assimilatory urges of Western societies have not never fully succeeded in remaking Jewish identity. The persistence of Jewish particularity – from the Orthodox Jewish eruv to the more mainstream Jewish practice of brit milah – is both a reminder of the limits to law's power to enforce sameness and conformity and also of its potential to protect difference and particularity. Jews, individually and collectively, have been active participants in debates about their legal rights, contesting, negotiating, and adapting the discourses of law but also of religion and race to pursue their own interests and visions in myriad ways. The diversity of Jewish identifications means that what could be seen as prioritising a Christian normativity in fact aligns with a certain Jewish normativity too, such as when other Reform and secular Jewish groups oppose an eruv for their own reasons (Chapter 5). These are reasons that are no less authentically Jewish than the reasons that Orthodox Jews have for their use of an eruv unless we believe that we can assume that there is one form of Jewishness that is more authentic than another, which is doubtful. Similarly, some Jewish commentators, such as Jonathan Romain, a Reform Rabbi, welcomed the UK Supreme Court's JFS case, which I discussed in Chapter 4, as a necessary push-back against what he perceived as exclusionary tendencies among Orthodox Jews against other non-Orthodox Jews.[27] However, Romain nonetheless worried that the Court imposed a Christian notion of religion onto Jews and that a better solution would have been an intra-Jewish solution by which the School accepted the student without endorsing his Jewishness and therefore without the secular state seeking to answer the question of 'who is a Jew'.[28]

Law, Sally Merry has pointed out, is a double-edged sword. It serves not only as a tool for oppression and domination but also as a site and a resource for struggle, contestation, and resistance: 'Law as an ideological weapon has two edges: it is a source of domination and, at the same time, contains the possibilities of a challenge to that domination'.[29] In her study of the legal consciousness of working-class Americans, Merry describes the law as ambiguous, inconsistent, and contradictory, which

[27] Jonathan Romain, 'The JFS Ruling is a Victory for Jews', *The Guardian*, 17 December 2009.

[28] Jonathan Romain, 'JFS Puts Faith Schools in the Dock', *The Guardian*, 28 October 2009.

[29] Sally Engle Merry, *Getting Justice and Getting Even: Legal Consciousness among Working-Class Americans* (Chicago: University of Chicago Press, 1990), p. 8.

opens it up for contestation and interpretation.[30] These interpretations are not completely autonomous and open-ended, but they nonetheless provide an opportunity to challenge and resist cultural and legal domination. Similarly, countering entirely pessimistic readings of liberal law's liberating potential for Black Americans, Kimberlé Crenshaw argues that law and its dominant ideology contain both communal and liberating visions alongside hegemonic visions.[31] While engaging liberal law has the potential of entrenching a harmful ideology that legitimises and obscures racial inequality, Crenshaw notes that it is also a pragmatic and powerful move. Mobilising this liberating potential can provide an avenue for resistance for subjugated groups, for example, by manoeuvring, transforming, expanding, and manipulating the dominant legal vision and its exclusionary and subjugating agenda.[32] In engaging with the law, marginalised actors are not only able to mobilise its liberating potential, but, in the process, they also alter and modify its meanings and scope to create a 'counter-hegemony'.

Therefore, while my focus in this book has been on one particular discourse and the cultural and legal labour it performs, it is important to emphasise that this discourse has intersected with other discourses, such as when Jews and their supporters in both Germany and Australia advanced a more pluralist vision of secular law. Understanding law as plural means acknowledging that it reflects a complex mélange of ideas and values, a mélange in which Christian ambivalence, the self-interest of the dominant culture, state pursuits of sovereignty, but also more pluralist interests intersect and converge even if they stand in tension with one another. The permission of eruvin and the legal protection of circumcision are therefore not only reflective of the self-interest of the dominant culture but can also be read as reflections of the liberating and pluralising potential of secular law (however limited by persistent power imbalances and the structural constraints of law) and as a testament to the advocacy and influence of minority groups, such as Jews, who leave their imprint on the law.

There is indeed a growing body of work within the historiography of international law that explores the engagement of Jewish institutions and individuals with the modern global legal system. This work

30 Merry, *Getting Justice*, p. 9.

31 Kimberlé Crenshaw, 'Race, Reform, and Retrenchment: Transformation and Legitimation in Antidiscrimination Law', *Harvard Law Review* (1988): 1331–87, p. 1387.

32 Crenshaw, 'Race, Reform, and Retrenchment', p. 1386.

documents how during the nineteenth and twentieth centuries Jews turned to international law for answers to their Jewish questions and in the process engaged and shaped international legal regimes of minority protections, human rights law, and crucial elements of international law, such as the law on crimes against humanity. Much of this work takes a biographical approach to examine the contributions of individual Jewish lawyers to the development of international law but also considers the work of transnational networks, such as the Alliance Israélite Universelle.[33] James Loeffler, for example, has explored the crucial origins of modern international human rights law in the Jewish pursuit of minority rights in Eastern Europe during the interwar period, when Jewish activists sought to reconcile the universalist language of the human rights idea with the local politics of Jewish communal survival.[34] Reut Yael Paz examines how Jewish lawyers, in their engagement with international law, also responded to their relationship with a field dominated and shaped by Christian influence and its ambivalence towards Jews.[35] While what is decidedly Jewish about these contributions remains subject to debate given the diversity of Jewish identifications and Jewish thought, these histories reflect the complex relationship between Jewishness and Western secular legality that cannot be reduced to a question of domination.[36]

Similarly, domestic secular legal approaches to difference have not been solely shaped by Christian thought and power over Jews and Others but also by centuries of Jewish advocacy for equal rights. Emancipation legislation that granted Jews rights did not simply elevate a passive and voiceless group of marginalised people to equal citizenship. Jews, such as Moses Mendelsohn and Samuel Holdheim, actively engaged in these debates and provided their own vision of the place of Jews in predominantly Christian societies, while trying to navigate the preservation of Jewish culture and the expectations

[33] See, for example, Paz, A *Gateway*; Loeffler, *Rooted Cosmpolitans*'; James Loeffler and Moria Paz, *The Law of Strangers. Jewish Lawyers and International Law in the Twentieth Century* (Cambridge: Cambridge University Press, 2019). On the Alliance Israélite Universelle, see Moria Paz, 'A Non-Territorial Ethnic Network and the Making of Human Rights Law: The Case of the Alliance Israélite Universelle', *Interdisciplinary Journal of Human Rights Law* 4 (2009): 1–24.

[34] Loeffler, *Rooted Cosmopolitans*.

[35] Pazm. See also Reut Yael Paz, 'Religion, Secularism, and International Law', in *The Oxford Handbook of the Theory of International Law*, ed. Anne Orford and Florian Hoffmann (Oxford: Oxford University Press, 2016), 923–938.

[36] See, for example, Loeffler and Paz, *Law of Strangers*.

of the Christian majority culture. In post-emancipatory times, Jews have remained heavily involved in the struggle against Christian dominance in law. In France, Pierre Birnbaum notes, Jews together with Protestants were at the forefront of supporting *laïcité* to push back against Catholic dominance through the 1905 law enshrining the French approach to the separation between state and church.[37] In the United States, American Jews have challenged Protestant hegemony through litigation and appeals to legislatures, while carefully navigating Christian political and social power.

For a long time, US Jews pursued a strategy of separationism grounded in the belief that 'public religion in the United States could never be truly neutral, for it always connoted an advantage to Christianity'.[38] Only beginning in the 1960s, Jewish organisations felt confident enough to mobilise the free exercise clause to defend Jewish practices. By engaging with the law, Naomi Cohen argues, Jews successfully worked towards pushing back against the dominance of Christianity. Alongside other religious minorities, Jews 'helped expand the liberties of all Americans and worked to transform the United States from a Protestant nation into one that acknowledged the needs of different religions'.[39]

Although there is not necessarily a consensus among Jews on how to best protect Jewish culture and identity, as the eruv cases discussed in Chapter 5 remind us, and different Jews will find different answers in different legal contexts, these histories serve as an important reminder to remain attentive to secular law's both liberating and dominating potentials. The crucial question remains, however, whether Western secular law as a vehicle for 'Christianism'[40] will always privilege a particular form of Jewishness over others that in

[37] Birnbaum, 'Secularization of the Public Square'.

[38] Cohen, *Jews in Christian America*, p. 5.

[39] Cohen, *Jews in Christian America*, p. 10. Nomi Stolzenberg and David Myers have analysed the conundrum of how the strictly Orthodox community of Kiryas Yoel has successfully mobilised American secular legal norms to create a hospitable legal environment for their separatist aspirations, now often aligning with the views of the Christian Right about religious liberty, see Stolzenberg and Myers, *American Shtetl*.

[40] Jewish activist and writer Melanie Kaye/Kantrowitz once argued for a term that describes; the system that normalizes and honours Christianity, just as racism names the system that normalizes and honours whiteness.... We sorely need a term such as Christianism to name the system of Christian domination'. Melanie Kaye/Kantrowitz, *The Colors of Jews. Racial Politics and Radical Diasporism* (Bloomington; Indianapolis: Indiana University Press, 2007), p. 30.

one way or another aligns with the prevailing interests of the majority Christian culture. Or whether secular law in such a context can be truly inclusive of all forms of Jewish and other differences and live up to the liberal promise without assimilating difference into sameness or rejecting it as inherently unable to ever be truly liberal and secular.

THE POLITICS OF SEMITIC DIFFERENCE

Although my focus in this book has been on Jewish difference, this does not mean that the events I have analysed play out in isolation from other questions of difference. The Flemish ban on religious slaughter, similar to the controversies over infant male circumcision, highlights the entanglement of Jewish and Muslim questions in secular law. Evidently, current anxieties about religious difference circle mainly around Muslims and the place of Islam in the societies of the West. Commentators, such as the former British Chief Rabbi Jonathan Sacks, have sometimes interpreted attempts to ban or restrict these practices – whether successful or not – as primarily aimed at Muslims, making Jews accidental victims.[41] There is a good reason for this conclusion, given the role of Islamophobic parties such as *Vlaams Belang* in supporting bans on religious slaughter or infant male circumcision.[42]

However, it would be too quick to dismiss the significance of ambivalence towards Jews in these events. The surfacing of supersessionary arguments in legal debates about circumcision or religious slaughter reflects how Christian ambivalence towards Jews has influenced secular legal thinking about religious difference in Western societies. However, as I have argued in this book, there also remains a persistent concern over Jewishness independently of Muslim practices even when the practice is shared with Muslims, as I have explored in this book in relation to circumcision. Moreover, Jewish practices have been scrutinised on their own, such as in the various conflicts involving eruvin or in the UK Supreme Court's JFS case to which I referred in Chapter 4. Finally, even if Muslims form the primary target of certain legal interventions, in accepting Jews as 'collateral damage', Western societies signal that they are willing to throw the rights of Jews under the wheels

41 See Sacks, 'Europeans' Skewed View'.

42 On the philosemitic politics of populist parties, see my discussion in Riedel, 'They are from Mars'.

of Islamophobic politics as long as it does not threaten too much the partial inclusion of Jews as evidence for pluralist credentials.

The intersection of Jewish and Muslim questions in contemporary secular law, I would suggest, gestures to the long and interrelated history of Jews and Muslims in the 'Christo-secular imagination',[43] a history that has been veiled by the tensions in the Middle East and the discourse of Judeo-Christianity. This history is not simply one of analogy. Ethan Katz speaks of an historical entanglement of antisemitism and Islamophobia that perceived of Jews and Muslims in close and suspicious proximity as 'Semites' that colonial powers strategically divided for their own agendas.[44] There is much to learn from historical studies on how colonial laws were instrumental in entrenching boundaries and divisions between Jews and Muslims in the colonies that remain significant today not only in the colonies but also in the metropoles. In her study of Jewish-Muslim legal interactions in Morocco, for example, Jessica Marglin demonstrates how French colonial law created an understanding of Muslims and Jews in Morocco as legally and administratively different.[45] French colonial law erected more rigid boundaries between the two communities and their religious legal systems, even though Jews and Muslims had previously interacted through a complex web of legal pluralism. Eventually, through these legal reforms but also via the involvement of the Alliance Israélite Universelle, Jews were able to access low-level positions in the French colonial government and to succeed in the economy dominated by Europeans, which undermined their relationships with Muslims.[46] Being wedged into the position of intermediaries afforded Jews certain privileges as compared to Muslims, yet this position also served the interests of colonial rule, not only in countries ruled by France.

Imperial Britain advocated freedom and citizenship for Jews in the Middle East during the nineteenth century, while domestically, the

[43] Yolande Jansen and Nasar Meer, 'Genealogies of 'Jews' and 'Muslims': Social Imagineries in the Race-Religion Nexus', *Patterns of Prejudice* 54, no. 1–2 (2020): 1–14.

[44] Ethan B. Katz, 'An Imperial Entanglement: Anti-Semitism, Islamophobia, and Colonialism', *American Historical Review* 123, no. 4 (2018): 1190–209, p. 1208.

[45] Jessica M. Marglin, *Across Legal Lines. Jews and Muslims in Modern Morocco* (New Haven; London: Yale University Press, 2016). On Jews in colonialism, see also Katz, Leff, and Mandel, *Colonialism and the Jews*.

[46] Marglin, *Across Legal Lines*, p. 199. On the Alliance Israélite Universelle, see also Paz, 'A Non-Territorial Ethnic Network'.

country still remained reluctant to fully include Jews. Protecting and defending the rights of Jews abroad, Abigail Green argues, served British imperial interests that relied on Jews as key intermediaries, particularly where there was no competition from native Christians.[47] Support for the Jewish cause overseas helped legitimising British Empire and civilisation.[48] As David Cesarani has argued, the English also ranked other nations based on their treatment of Jews. However, this was not because of genuine care about Jews in those nations but about the usefulness of Jews in a narrative of the superiority of English Protestant Christianity and its capacity to convince Jews of the Christian truth, which required a benevolent toleration of Jews in the first place.[49] The question arises then how dynamics of using Jews as cultural and political 'intermediaries' and 'benchmarks' for pluralist credentials play out today and what these dynamics mean for the politics of religious difference and freedom. As Alana Lentin notes:

> Far from Jews and Christians being in natural alliance, in reality both Jews and Muslims are racialized as the intrinsic Other within; as inimical to the West and to Christian culture ... this is despite the fact that contemporary antisemitism often takes a 'philosemitic' tone that, while pitting 'good' Jews 'against' bad Muslims, can only do so while racializing and essentializing Jewish people.[50]

Taking seriously the interconnections between the legal marginalisation of Jews and of Muslims today is not meant to suggest that Jews face the same amount of prejudice as Muslims in law and society. Compared to Jews, Muslims have borne the brunt of contemporary legal and political attempts to ban or restrict their religious practices, alongside their racialised surveillance in the name of national security and anti-terrorism measures. Jews, in comparison, have often been treated with more leniency in law, a situation which was challenged with the rise of suspicion towards Muslims.

A philosemitic concern seems to have played not only a role in thwarting attempts to ban circumcision. States have also at times regulated practices shared by both Jews and Muslims differently. As I discussed in Chapter 4, in the case of infant male circumcision, a legal concession

[47] Abigail Green, 'The British Empire and the Jews: An Imperialism of Human Rights', *Past & Present*, no. 199 (2008): 175–205.

[48] Green, 'British Empire and the Jews', p. 192.

[49] Cesarani, 'British Jews', p. 42.

[50] Alana Lentin, *Why Race Still Matters* (Cambridge: Polity Press, 2020), pp. 190–91.

was granted to German Jews allowing traditional mohels to carry out the circumcision within six months after the child's birth, whereas no such concession is granted to Muslims who circumcise their male children later in life. The German legal solution is here similar to the Swedish regulation that also requires a medical professional to carry out the surgery unless the child is under the age of two months.[51] Apart from the contested justification that newborn children experience less pain and that the practice involves fewer risks if carried out earlier, the six-month limitation remains arbitrary as it does neither align with the Jewish eight-day rule nor with medical research and it disadvantages Muslims for whom the age of circumcision is more flexible with the upper limit usually at the onset of puberty.

The issue I want to point out here is not whether a medical professional is indeed better suited to perform a circumcision, but rather to whom an exception is granted and to whom not even though the concession appears neutral in not explicitly catering to the Jewish rules around the timing of circumcision. Although the explanatory comment that accompanied the Bill suggests that the majority of Muslims in Germany have their sons circumcised by a physician, no medical rationale is provided for this particular distinction.[52] The law thereby creates hierarchies of Semitic difference through differentiated rights protections. Lena Salaymeh and Shai Lavi suggest that the 'mohel clause' also reflects a perception of Jewish law as binding, whereas Muslim law is seen as custom and therefore as less worthy of protection.[53] Secular states and secular law, they argue, often consider and assess Muslim practices in relation to Jewish practices, thereby adopting 'a Christian historical perspective that categorises traditions in a linear, chronological hierarchy, such that Judaism, the "older" tradition, is elevated above Islam, the "younger" tradition'.[54] Treating Jewish and Muslim difference in tandem as 'Semitic questions'[55]

[51] See Johanna Schiratzki, 'Banning God's Law in the Name of the Holy Body: The Nordic Position on Ritual Male Circumcision', *The Family in Law* 5 (2011): 35–53.

[52] Gesetzesentwurf der Bundesregierung, Entwurf eines Gesetzes über den Umfang der Personensorge bei einer Beschneidung des männlichen Kindes, 5 November 2011, BT Drucksache 17/11295, at 9.

[53] Salaymeh and Lavi, 'Religion Is Secularised Tradition', p. 448.

[54] Salaymeh and Lavi, 'Religion Is Secularised Tradition', p. 434.

[55] I use the term 'Semitic' to gesture to the racialised category invoked by Christian Europeans during the eighteenth and nineteenth centuries to initially group Jews and Muslims/Arabs as a religio-racial group, before the term antisemitism was

therefore provides not only an important opportunity to critically examine the Christian biases of law. It is also a reminder to take seriously the role of law in playing Jews and Muslims off against one another as yet another strategy for rendering the dominance of Christianity invisible, for undermining Jewish-Muslim solidarity, and for obscuring the persistent othering of Jews behind the assimilatory pluralism of Judeo-Christianity.

EPILOGUE

Banning an eruv or regulating circumcision are certainly not the most serious challenges that Jews face today. In the twenty-first century, antisemitism remains alive and well and still has deadly consequences. However, focusing only on the most extreme and overt manifestations of antisemitism risk perpetuating a view of antisemitism as the problem of societal fringes and prevents us from acknowledging the ambivalent place of 'the Jew' at the heart of Western secular societies. It also prevents us to grapple with how Christianity's struggles with its Jewish origins have influenced and shaped meanings and knowledge, values and sensibilities in secular law and legal reasoning. While sociolegal and critical legal scholarship has been highly attentive to the role of law in reproducing hierarchies and inequalities based on race, gender, and sexuality, fewer studies have attended to Christian privilege, to the myriad of legal technologies through which it is sustained, and to how ideas about Christian superiority and the Christian tradition's universalising but also exclusionary ambitions have shaped secular legal regimes. One reason might be the still prevalent perception of religion as external to secular liberal law or perhaps of religion as less important in the structures and practices of domination in secular legality. However, as Abigail Green and Simon Levis Sullam point out, 'if … the liberal political tradition was founded not only on universalizing, democratic ideals, but also on a series of important exclusions,

coined in relation to Jews alone. See my brief discussion in Chapter 2 as well as Anya Topolski, 'Rejecting Judeo-Christian Privilege: The First Step towards Semitic Solidarity', *Jewish Studies Quarterly* 27, no. 3 (2020): 298–318. In the literature to date, there has been a tendency to either treat Jewish questions as historical predecessor of contemporary Muslim questions and their legal manifestations or to discuss the usefulness of comparing antisemitism and Islamophobia. For a critical review of this literature, see Lavi and Salaymeh, 'Secularism'.

subjugations and deferrals related to gender, race and class, then thinking about Jews reminds us that religion (Christianity) was part of this exclusionary matrix'.[56]

Daniel Boyarin has argued that the unresolved tensions between sameness and difference that still plague Western liberal societies today find some of their ideological foundations in the writings of Paul about Jews.[57] In Paul's writing, Boyarin locates a fateful 'impulse towards universalism' in contrast to Jews' alleged particularism, an impulse that became part of the Christian tradition and, as I have tried to show in this book, has seeped into secular legal thinking. There are echoes of this Paulinian Christian universalism in the contemporary assimilationist strategies in secular law that often equate equality with sameness, thereby denying those designed as Other the right to be different and to maintain their identity. My conclusion here is not – and neither is it that of Boyarin – to suggest that all tensions between universalism and particularism in Western secular law or in liberalism more broadly can trace their roots via a straight line to Paul and Christianity's struggle with Jewish difference. It has also not been my aim to offer a grand and complete account of Western secular law. This is only a tentative investigation of certain argumentative patterns and legal dynamics. However, as populist politics across the West tap once again into exclusionary narratives of the Christian roots of Western civilisation, taking seriously the cultural-legal history of Christian ambivalence and the entrenched 'Christianism' in our secular laws and legal assumptions offers an opportunity to critically reflect on how elements of our past shape and limit the possibilities of our secular legal imagination in the present.

[56] Abigail Green and Simon Levis Sullam, 'Introduction: Jews, Liberalism, Antisemitism: Towards a Twenty-First Century History', in *Jews, Liberalism, Antisemitism. A Global History*, ed. Abigail Green and Simon Levis Sullam (Cham: Palgrave Macmillan, 2020), 1–20, at 3.

[57] Boyarin, *A Radical Jew*, pp. 8–9 and 233.

BIBLIOGRAPHY

ABC News. 'German Court Bans Circumcision of Young Boys'. *ABC*, 28 June 2012. www.abc.net.au/news/2012-06-28/german-court-bans-circumcision-of-young-boys/4096998.

Abulafia, Anna Sapir. 'Response to "The Gifts and the Calling of God Are Irrevocable"'. *European Judaism* 50, no. 1 (2017): 92–98.

Abusch, Ra'anan. 'Circumcision and Castration under Roman Law in the Early Empire'. In *The Covenant of Circumcision: New Perspectives on an Ancient Jewish Rite*, edited by Elizabeth Wyner Mark, 75–86. Hanover; London: Brandeis University Press, 2003.

Adamski, Katrina. 'Siege over Imaginary Wall'. *North Shore Times*, 19 September 2008.

Adamski, Katrina. 'Wall of Opposition'. *North Shore Times*, 7 October 2008.

Ahituv, Netta. 'Even in Israel, More and More Parents Choose Not to Circumcise Their Sons'. *Ha'aretz*, 14 June 2012. www.haaretz.com/israel-news/even-in-israel-more-and-more-parents-choose-not-to-circumcise-their-sons-1.436421.

Akbari, Suzanne Conklin. *Idols in the East: European Representations of Islam and the Orient 1100–1450*. Ithaca; London: Cornell University Press, 2009.

Akbari, Suzanne Conklin. 'Placing the Jews in Late Medieval English Literature'. In *Orientalism and the Jews*, edited by Ivan Davidson Kalmar and Derek Jonathan Penslar, 32–50. Hanover; London: Brandeis University Press, 2005.

Alhadeff, Vic. 'Poles but No Polarisation to Support Needs of Faith'. *North Shore Times*, 11 April 2011.

Altmann, Alexander. 'Introduction'. In *Jerusalem: Or on Religious Power and Judaism*, edited by Moses Mendelssohn. Waltham: Brandeis University Press, 1983.

American Jewish Committee Berlin. *Facts & Myths in the Circumcision Debate*. Berlin: American Jewish Committee Berlin, 2012.

Amesbury, Richard. 'Is the Body Secular? Circumcision, Religious Freedom, and Bodily Integrity'. *Journal of the British Association for the Study of Religions* 18 (2016): 1–10.

Anidjar, Gil. *Blood: A Critique of Christianity*. New York: Columbia University Press, 2014.

Anidjar, Gil. 'Secularism'. *Critical Inquiry* 33, no. 1 (2006): 52–77.

Anidjar, Gil. *Semites: Race, Religion, Literature*. Stanford: Stanford University Press, 2008.

Anidjar, Gil. *The Jew, the Arab: A History of the Enemy*. Stanford: Stanford University Press, 2003.

Appiah, Kwame Anthony. 'The Case for Capitalizing the B in Black'. *The Atlantic*, 20 June 2020. www.theatlantic.com/ideas/archive/2020/06/time-to-capitalize-blackand-white/613159/.

Asad, Talal. *Formations of the Secular: Christianity, Islam, Modernity*. Stanford: Stanford University Press, 2003.

Asad, Talal. *Genealogies of Religion: Discipline and Reasons of Power in Christianity and Islam*. Baltimore; London: Johns Hopkins University Press, 2009.

Asad, Talal. 'Thinking about the Secular Body, Pain, and Liberal Politics'. In *Living and Dying in the Contemporary World: A Compendium*, edited by Veena Das and Clara Han, 337–53. Oakland: University of California Press, 2015.

Associated Press. 'Danish Parliament to Consider Becoming First Country to Ban Circumcision of Boys'. *Independent*, 3 June 2018. www.independent.co.uk/news/world/europe/denmark-boyhood-circumcision-petition-danish-parliament-debate-a8381366.html.

Axinn, Sidney. 'Kant on Judaism'. *The Jewish Quarterly Review* 59, no. 1 (1968): 9–23.

Barker, Renae. *State and Religion: The Australian Story*. Abingdon: Routledge, 2018.

Barkey, Karen, and Ira Katznelson. 'States, Regimes, and Decisions: Why Jews Were Expelled from Medieval England and France'. *Theory and Society* 40, no. 2 (2011): 475–503.

Baron, Salo W. 'Newer Approaches to Emancipation'. *Diogenes* 8, no. 29 (1960): 56–81.

Bartsch, Matthias, Patrick Kremers, Juliane von Mittelstaedt, Conny Neumann, and Peter Wensierski. '"Great Anxiety": Jews Question Their Future in Germany'. *Der Spiegel*, 10 September 2012. www.spiegel.de/international/germany/amid-circumcision-debate-jews-question-their-future-in-germany-a-854863.html.

Bassi, Shaul. 'The Venetian Ghetto and Modern Jewish Identity'. *Judaism* 51, no. 4 (2002): 469–80.

Batnitzky, Leora. 'Between Ancestry and Belief: "Judaism" and "Hinduism" in the Nineteenth Century'. *Modern Judaism – A Journal of Jewish Ideas and Experience* 41, no. 2 (2021): 194–219.

Batnitzky, Leora. *How Judaism Became a Religion: An Introduction to Modern Jewish Thought*. Princeton: Princeton University Press, 2011.

Bauman, Zygmunt. 'Allosemitism: Premodern, Modern, Postmodern'. In *Modernity, Culture, and 'The Jew'*, edited by Bryan Cheyette and Laura Marcus, 143–56. Cambridge: Polity Press, 1998.

Bauman, Zygmunt. 'Modernity and Ambivalence'. *Theory, Culture & Society* 7, no. 2 (1990): 143–69.

Bauman, Zygmunt. *Modernity and Ambivalence*. Ithaca: Cornell University Press, 1991.

BBC. 'EU Court Backs Ban on Animal Slaughter without Stunning'. *BBC News*, 17 December 2020. www.bbc.com/news/world-europe-55344971.

Beaman, Lori G. 'Battles over Symbols: The "Religion" of the Minority Versus the "Culture" of the Majority'. *Journal of Law and Religion* 28, no. 1 (2013): 67–104.

Beaman, Lori G. 'Tolerance and Accommodation as Vestiges of the Empire'. In *Secular States and Religious Diversity*, edited by Bruce J. Berman, Rajeev Bhargava and André Laliberté, 120–35. Vancouver; Toronto: University of British Columbia Press, 2013.

Beaman, Lori G. *The Transition of Religion to Culture in Law and Public Discourse*. London: Routledge, 2020.

Bechhofer, Yosef Gavriel. *The Contemporary Eruv: Eruvin in Modern Metropolitan Areas*. Jerusalem; New York: Feldheim Publishers, 2002.

Bell, Derrick A. 'Brown v. Board of Education and the Interest-Convergence Dilemma'. *Harvard Law Review* 93, no. 3 (1980): 518–33.

Benbassa, Esther. *The Jews of France. A History from Antiquity to the Present*. Translated by M. B. DeBevoise. Princeton: Princeton University Press, 1999.

Bernasconi, Robert. 'The Ghetto and Race'. In *A Companion to Racial and Ethnic Studies*, edited by John Solomos and David Theo Goldberg, 340–47. Williston: Blackwell, 2001.

Beydoun, Khaled A. 'Faith in Whiteness: Free Exercise of Religion as Racial Expression'. *Iowa Law Review* 105, no. 4 (2020): 1475–536.

Bhaba, Homi. 'Of Mimicry and Man. The Ambivalence of Colonial Discourse'. In *Tensions of Empire*, edited by Laura Ann Stoler and Frederick Cooper, 152–60. Berkeley: University of California Press, 1997.

Bhandar, Brenna. *Colonial Lives of Property: Law, Land, and Racial Regimes of Ownership*. Durham: Duke University Press, 2018.

Bielefeldt, Heiner, Nazila Ghanea, and Michael Wiener. *Freedom of Religion or Belief: An International Law Commentary*. Oxford: Oxford University Press, 2016.

Birnbaum, Pierre. 'On the Secularization of the Public Square: Jews in France and in the United States'. *Cardozo Law Review* 30, no. 6 (2009): 2431–43.

Bodenheimer, Alfred. *Haut Ab! Die Juden in Der Beschneidungsdebatte*. Göttingen: Wallstein Verlag, 2012.

Bonilla Maldonado, Daniel. 'The Cultural Analysis of Law: Questions and Answers with Paul Kahn'. *German Law Journal* 21 (2020): 284–98.

Bönisch, Georg, Özlem Gezer, Marc Hujer, Souad Mekhennet, Ralf Neukirch, René Pfister, and Christoph Scheuermann. 'Circumcision Debate Has

Berlin Searching for Answers'. *Der Spiegel*, 25 July 2012. www.spiegel.de/international/germany/circumcision-debate-has-german-government-scrambling-for-a-law-a-846144.html.

Boorstein, Michelle. 'New Poll: Young U.S. Jews Becoming More Orthodox as American Judaism Splits between Devout and Secular'. *Washington Post*, 11 May 2021. www.washingtonpost.com/religion/2021/05/11/orthodox-jews-poll-secular-trump-republican.

Bossio, Jennifer A., Caroline F. Pukall, and Stephen Steele. 'A Review of the Current State of the Male Circumcision Literature'. *Journal of Sexual Medicine* 11, no. 12 (2014): 2847–64.

Bousenna, Youness. 'Le Judéo-Christianisme, Ou Les Ombres D'une Fausse Evidence'. *Le Monde*, 28 September 2022. www.lemonde.fr/idees/article/2022/09/28/le-judeo-christianisme-ou-les-ombres-d-une-fausse-evidence_6143460_3232.html.

Boyarin, Daniel. *A Radical Jew: Paul and the Politics of Identity*. Berkeley: University of California Press, 1994.

Boyarin, Jonathan. 'Circumscribing Constitutional Identities in Kiryas Joel'. *Yale Law Journal* 106 (1997): 1537–70.

Boyarin, Jonathan. *The Unconverted Self. Jews, Indians, and the Identity of Christian Europe*. Chicago; London: University of Chicago Press, 2009.

Boyarin, Jonathan, and Daniel Boyarin. 'Self-Exposure as Theory: The Double Mark of the Male Jew'. In *Rhetorics of Self-Making*, edited by Debbora Battaglia, 16–42. Berkeley; Los Angeles; London: University of California Press, 1995.

Brady, Fiona. 'Four Years on, Still Eruv Uncertainty'. *North Shore Times*, 26 August 2011.

Brady, Fiona. 'Pole Position Key to Success of Eruv'. *North Shore Times*, 19 August 2011.

Brodkin, Karen. *How Jews Became White Folks and What That Says about Race in America*. New Brunswick: Rutgers University Press, 1998.

Brown, Wendy. 'Civilizational Delusions: Secularism, Tolerance, Equality'. *Theory & Event* 15, no. 2 (2012).

Brown, Wendy. *Regulating Aversion: Tolerance in the Age of Identity and Empire*. Princeton: Princeton University Press, 2006.

Buell, Denise Kimber. *Why This New Race. Ethnic Reasoning in Early Christianity*. New York: Columbia University Press, 2008.

Bugg, Laura Beth. 'Citizenship and Belonging in the Rural Fringe: A Case Study of a Hindu Temple in Sydney, Australia'. *Antipode* 45, no. 5 (2013): 1148–66.

Burckhardt, Ines. 'Circumcision Ruling Riles Muslims and Jews'. *Financial Times Online*, 13 August 2012. www.ft.com/content/d4735d40-e2c7-11e1-a463-00144feab49a?mhq5j=e3.

Caron, Christina. 'Bill Banning Circumcision in Iceland Alarms Religious Groups'. *New York Times*, 28 February 2018. www.nytimes.com/2018/02/28/world/europe/circumcision-ban-iceland.html.

Carpenter, Laura M. 'On Remedicalisation: Male Circumcision in the United States and Great Britain'. *Sociology of Health & Illness* 32, no. 4 (2010): 613–30.

Carpenter, R. Charli. 'Some Other Conceptual Problems'. *International Feminist Journal of Politics* 6, no. 2 (2004): 308–13.

Carroll, Kelly. 'Westhampton's Anti-Eruv Group Claims 85 Percent of Village Opposed to Religious Designation'. *Hamptons.com*, 11 September 2008. www.hamptons.com/Community/Main-Articles/4814/Westhamptons-Anti-Eruv-Group-Claims-85-Percent.html#.WtjEDy9L1TY.

Carter, J. Kameron. *Race: A Theological Account*. Oxford: Oxford University Press, 2008.

CBC News. 'Outremont Not to Appeal Eruv Decision'. *CBC*, 10 July 2001. www.cbc.ca/news/canada/outremont-not-to-appeal-eruv-decision-1.293448.

Cesarani, David. 'British Jews'. In *The Emancipation of Catholics, Jews and Protestants: Minorities and the Nation State in Nineteenth-Century Europe*, edited by Rainer Liedtke and Stephan Wendehorst, 33–55. Manchester: Manchester University Press, 1999.

Chaban, Matt A. V. 'Hamptons Town Nears a Deal on a Jewish Ritual Boundary'. *The New York Times*, 29 May 2016. www.nytimes.com/2016/05/30/nyregion/hamptons-town-nears-a-deal-on-a-jewish-ritual-boundary.html.

Charlesworth, Hilary. 'The Australian Reluctance about Rights'. *Osgoode Hall Law Journal* 31, no. 1 (1993): 195–232.

Chavura, Stephen, and Ian Tregenza. 'Introduction: Rethinking Secularism in Australia (and Beyond)'. *Journal of Religious History* 38, no. 3 (2014): 299–306.

Chazan, Robert. *The Jews of Medieval Western Christendom 1000–1500*. Cambridge: Cambridge University Press, 2006.

Cheyette, Bryan. 'English Anti-Semitism: A Counter-Narrative'. *Textual Practice* 25, no. 1 (2011): 15–32.

Cheyette, Bryan. 'Postcolonialism and the Study of Anti-Semitism'. *American Historical Review* 123, no. 4 (2018): 1234–45.

Cheyette, Bryan, and Nadia Valman. 'Introduction: Liberalism and Anti-semitism'. *Jewish Culture and History* 6, no. 1 (2003): 1–26.

Chon, Margaret, and Donna E. Arzt. 'Walking While Muslim'. *Law and Contemporary Problems* 68, no. 2 (2005): 215–54.

Choper, Jesse H. 'The Endorsement Test: Its Status and Desirability'. *Journal of Law and Politics* 18, no. 2 (2002): 499–536.

Clark, Amy Sara. 'Fight over New Eruv Erupts in Crown Heights'. *Jewish Week*, 22 June 2016. https://jewishweek.timesofisrael.com/fight-over-new-eruv-erupts-in-crown-heights/.

Cockburn, Alexander James Edmund. *Nationality: Or the Law Relating to Subjects and Aliens, Considered with a View to Future Legislation*. London: William Ridgway, 1869.

Cohen, Jeremy. *Living Letters of the Law. Ideas of the Jew in Medieval Christianity*. Berkeley and Los Angeles: University of California Press, 1999.

Cohen, Jeremy. 'Supersessionism, the Epistle to the Romans, Thomas Aquinas, and the Jews of the Eschaton'. *Journal of Ecumenical Studies* 52, no. 4 (2017): 527–53.

Cohen, Naomi W. *Jews in Christian America: The Pursuit of Religious Equality*. Oxford; New York; Toronto: Oxford University Press, 1992.

Cohen, Shaye J. D. *Why Aren't Jewish Women Circumcised? Gender and Covenant in Judaism*. Berkeley; Los Angeles; London: University of California Press, 2005.

Collier, Roger. 'Tasmania Moving toward Circumcision Ban'. *CMAJ: Canadian Medical Association Journal* 184, no. 13 (2012): E690.

Conley, Mikaela. 'Proposed Circumcision Ban Struck from San Francisco Ballot'. *ABC News*, 29 July 2011. www.abcnews.go.com/Health/san-francisco-circumcision-ban-striken/story?id=14179024.

Cooper, David A., Alex D. Wodak, and Brian J. Morris. 'The Case for Boosting Infant Male Circumcision in the Face of Rising Heterosexual Transmission of HIV'. *Medical Journal of Australia* 193, no. 6 (2010): 318–19.

Cooper, Davina. 'Talmudic Territory? Space, Law, and Modernist Discourse'. *Journal of Law and Society* 23, no. 4 (1996): 529–48.

Cooper, Davina, and Didi Herman. 'Jews and Other Uncertainties: Race, Faith and English Law'. *Legal Studies* 19, no. 3 (1999): 339–66.

Corbin, Caroline Mala. 'Justice Scalia, the Establishment Clause, and Christian Privilege'. *First Amendment Law Review* 15, no. 22 (2017): 185–220.

Cornwall, Deborah. 'The Eruv'. *ABC News*, 12 July 2010. www.abc.net.au/news/2010-07-09/the-eruv/899286.

Crenshaw, Kimberlé. 'Race, Reform, and Retrenchment: Transformation and Legitimation in Antidiscrimination Law'. *Harvard Law Review* 133, no. 9 (1988): 1331–87.

Crome, Andrew. 'The 1753 "Jew Bill" Controversy: Jewish Restoration to Palestine, Biblical Prophecy, and English National Identity'. *English Historical Review* 130, no. 547 (2015): 1449–78.

Dandy, Justine, and Rogelia Pe-Pua. 'Attitudes to Multiculturalism, Immigration and Cultural Diversity: Comparison of Dominant and Non-dominant Groups in Three Australian States'. *International Journal of Intercultural Relations* 34, no. 1 (2010): 34–46.

Darby, Robert. *A Surgical Temptation: The Demonization of the Foreskin and the Rise of Circumcision in Britain*. Chicago: University of Chicago Press, 2013.

Darby, Robert. 'Targeting Patients Who Cannot Object? Re-examining the Case for Non-therapeutic Infant Circumcision'. *SAGE Open* 6, no. 2 (2016): 1–16.

Darby, Robert. 'The Child's Right to an Open Future: Is the Principle Applicable to Non-therapeutic Circumcision?'. *Journal of Medical Ethics* 39, no. 7 (2013): 463–68.

Darby, Robert, and J. Steven Svoboda. 'A Rose by Any Other Name? Rethinking the Similarities and Differences between Male and Female Genital Cutting'. *Medical Anthropology Quarterly* 21, no. 3 (2007): 301–23.

Darian-Smith, Eve. *Laws and Societies in Global Contexts: Contemporary Approaches*. Cambridge: Cambridge University Press, 2013.

Darian-Smith, Eve. *Religion, Race, Rights: Landmarks in the History of Modern Anglo-American Law*. Oxford; Portland: Hart Publishing, 2010.

Dave, Sangeeta S., Anne M. Johnson, K. A. Fenton, Catherine H. Mercer, Bob Erens, and Kaye Wellings. 'Male Circumcision in Britain: Findings from a National Probability Sample Survey'. *Sexually Transmitted Infections* 79, no. 6 (2003): 499–500.

Davies, Margaret. 'The Ethos of Pluralism'. *Sydney Law Review* 27, no. 1 (2005): 87–112.

Davies, Margaret. 'The Future of Secularism: A Critique'. In *Law and Religion in Public Life. The Contemporary Debate*, edited by Nadirsyah Hosen and Richard Mohr, 52–66. London; New York: Routledge, 2011.

Davis, Robert C. 'Introduction'. In *The Jews of Early Modern Venice*, edited by Robert C. Davis and Benjamin Ravid, vii–xix. Baltimore: Johns Hopkins University Press, 2001.

DeLaet, Debra L. 'Framing Male Circumcision as a Human Rights Issue? Contributions to the Debate over the Universality of Human Rights'. *Journal of Human Rights* 8, no. 4 (2009): 405–26.

Delaney, David. 'The Space That Race Makes'. *The Professional Geographer* 54, no. 1 (2002): 6–14.

Desiatnek, Shane. 'Eruv Decision a Win for the Community'. *The Australian Jewish News*, 10 November 2016. www.jewishnews.net.au/eruv-decision-win-community/56601.

Deutsche Presseagentur. 'Kinderhilfe Warnt vor 'Blankocheck für Kindesmisshandlung'. *Die Zeit*, 14 July 2012. www.zeit.de/gesellschaft/zeitgeschehen/2012-07/beschneidungen-kinderschutzbund.

Dohm, Christian Wilhelm. *Über die Bürgerliche Verbesserung der Juden*. Berlin; Stettin: Friedrich Nicolai, 1781.

Dresser, Madge. 'Minority Rites: The Strange History of Circumcision in English Thought'. *Jewish Culture and History* 1, no. 1 (1998): 72–87.

Dudziak, Mary L. *Cold War Civil Rights. Race and the Image of American Democracy*. Princeton; Oxford: Princeton University Press, 2000.

Dunn, Kevin. 'Repetitive and Troubling Discourses of Nationalism in the Local Politics of Mosque Development in Sydney, Australia'. *Environment and Planning D* 23, no. 1 (2005): 29–50.

Dunn, Kevin, Susan Thompson, Bronwyn Hanna, Peter Murphy, and Ian Burnley. 'Multicultural Policy within Local Government in Australia'. *Urban Studies* 38, no. 13 (2001): 2477–94.

Earp, Brian D. 'Female Genital Mutilation and Male Circumcision: Toward an Autonomy-Based Ethical Framework'. *Medicolegal and Bioethics* 5, no. 1 (2015): 89–104.

Edwards, John. 'Race and Religion in 15th and 16th Century Spain: The 'Purity of Blood' Laws Revisited'. *Proceedings of the World Congress of Jewish Studies*, Division B, Volume II: The History of the Jewish People (1989): 169–66.

Eisenthal, Bram. 'Canadian Court Rules for Jews in Shabbat Case'. *Jewish Telegraphic Agency*, 25 June 2011. www.jta.org/2001/06/25/life-religion/features/canadian-court-rules-for-jews-in-shabbat-case.

El Bcheraoui, Charbel, Xinjian Zhang, Christopher S. Cooper, Charles E. Rose, Peter H. Kilmarx, and Robert T. Chen. 'Rates of Adverse Events Associated with Male Circumcision in Us Medical Settings, 2001 to 2010'. *JAMA Pediatrics* 168, no. 7 (2014): 625–34.

Endelman, Todd M. 'Assimilation and Assimilationism'. In *The Cambridge History of Judaism. Volume Eight: The Modern World 1815–2000*, edited by Mitchell B. Hart and Tony Michels, 312–36. Cambridge: Cambridge University Press, 2017.

Ettinger, Yair. 'Rift Has Roots in Eruv Dispute'. *Haaretz*, 22 February 2010. www.haaretz.com/2010-02-22/ty-article/rift-has-roots-in-eruv-dispute/0000017f-f88b-d2d5-a9ff-f88f2acc0000.

European Union Agency for Fundamental Rights. *Experiences and Perceptions of Antisemitism. Second Survey on Discrimination and Hate Crime against Jews in the EU*. Luxembourg: Publications Office of the European Union, 2018. https://fra.europa.eu/sites/default/files/fra_uploads/fra-2018-experiences-and-perceptions-of-antisemitism-survey_en.pdf.

Evans, Carolyn. 'Religion as Politics Not Law: The Religion Clauses in the Australian Constitution'. *Religion, State & Society* 36, no. 3 (2008): 283–302.

Fahl, Christian. 'Wird das Beschneidungsverbot Kommen? Zur "Sozialadäquanz" von Beschneidungen'. In *Ein Menschengerechtes Strafrecht als Lebensaufgabe. Festschrift für Werner Beulke*, edited by Christian Fahl, Eckhart Müller, Helmut Satzger and Sabine Swoboda, 81–94. Heidelberg: C.F. Müller, 2015.

Farris, Sara R. 'From the Jewish Question to the Muslim Question. Republican Rigorism, Culturalist Differentialism and Antinomies of Enforced Emancipation'. *Constellations* 21, no. 2 (2014): 296–307.

Farris, Sara R. *In the Name of Women's Rights. The Rise of Femonationalism*. Durham: Duke University Press, 2017.

Feinberg, Joel. 'The Child's Right to an Open Future'. In *Freedom and Fulfillment: Philosophical Essays*, edited by Joel Feinberg, 76–97. Princeton: Princeton University Press, 1994.

Feldman, Jan. *Lubavitchers as Citizens. A Paradox of Liberal Democracy*. Ithaca; London: Cornell University Press, 2003.

Feldman, Stephen M. *Please Don't Wish Me a Merry Christmas: A Critical History of the Separation of Church and State*. New York: New York University Press, 1998.

Fernando, Mayanthi L. *The Republic Unsettled. Muslim French and the Contradictions of Secularism*. Durham; London: Duke University Press, 2014.

Ferrari, Silvio. 'Religion in the European Public Spaces: A Legal Overview'. In *Religion in Public Spaces. A European Perspective*, edited by Silvio Ferrari and Sabrina Pastorelli, 139–56. London; New York: Routledge, 2012.

Fischer, Thomas. *Strafgesetzbuch mit Nebengesetzen*, 62nd ed. München: C.H. Beck, 2015.

Fletcher, Brian. 'Anglicanism and Nationalism in Australia, 1901–1962'. *The Journal of Religious History* 23, no. 2 (1999): 215–33.

Fogle, Lauren. 'Between Christianity and Judaism: The Identity of Converted Jews in Medieval London'. *Essays in Medieval Studies* 22, no. 1 (2005): 107–16.

Fonrobert, Charlotte Elisheva. 'Diaspora Cartography: On the Rabbinic Background of Contemporary Ritual Eruv Practice'. *Images* 5, no. 1 (2011): 14–25.

Fonrobert, Charlotte Elisheva. 'Installations of Jewish Law in Public Urban Space: An American Eruv Controversy'. *Chicago-Kent Law Review* 90, no. 1 (2015): 63–77.

Fonrobert, Charlotte Elisheva. 'The Political Symbolism of the Eruv'. *Jewish Social Studies* 11, no. 3 (2005): 9–35.

Forrest, James, and Kevin Dunn. '"Core" Culture Hegemony and Multiculturalism. Perceptions of the Privileged Position of Australians with British Backgrounds'. *Ethnicities* 6, no. 2 (2006): 203–30.

Fox, Marie, and Michael Thomson. 'Foreskin Is a Feminist Issue'. *Australian Feminist Studies* 24, no. 60 (2009): 195–210.

Freedman, Samuel G. *Jew vs. Jew: The Struggle for the Soul of American Jewry*. New York: Simon & Schuster, 2000.

Freimark, Peter. 'Eruw/"Judentore". Zur Geschichte einer Rituellen Institution im Hamburger Raum (und Anderswo)'. In *Judentore, Kuggel, Steuerkonten. Untersuchungen Zur Geschichte der Deutschen Juden, Vornehmlich im Hamburger Raum*, edited by Peter Freimark, Ina Lorenz and Günter Marwedel, 10–55. Hamburg: Hans Christians Verlag, 1983.

Friedman, Jerome. 'Jewish Conversion, the Spanish Pure Blood Laws and Reformation: A Revisionist View of Racial and Religious Antisemitism'. *Sixteenth Century Journal* 18, no. 1 (1987): 3–30.

Gager, John G. *The Origins of Anti-Semitism. Attitudes toward Judaism in Pagan and Christian Antiquity*. New York; Oxford: Oxford University Press, 1985.

Gallagher, Noelle. 'The Jew's Penis: Circumcision and Sexual Pathology in Eighteenth-Century England'. *Medical Humanities* 49 (2023): 70–82.

Gerber, Jane S. *Jews of Spain. A History of the Sephardic Experience*. New York: The Free Press, 1994.

Germain, Annick, and Julie Elizabeth Gagnon. 'Minority Places of Worship and Zoning Dilemmas in Montréal'. *Planning Theory & Practice* 4, no. 3 (2003): 295–318.

Getzler, Israel. *Neither Toleration nor Favour. The Australian Chapter of Jewish Emancipation*. Melbourne: Melbourne University Press, 1970.

Gibson, Jano. 'Jews Seek Religious Freedom with a Ring around St Ives'. *Sydney Morning Herald*, 1 October 2008.

Gilman, Sander L. *Freud, Race, and Gender*. Princeton: Princeton University Press, 1993.

Gilman, Sander L. *The Jew's Body*. New York; London: Routledge, 1991.

Gilman, Sander L., and Karen Remmler. 'Introduction'. In *Reemerging Jewish Culture in Germany: Life and Literature since 1989*, edited by Sander L. Gilman and Karen Remmler, 1–12. New York: New York University Press, 1994.

Glauz-Todrank, Annalise. *Judging Jewish Identity in the United States*, Lanham: Lexington Books, 2022.

Glenn, Susan A., and Naomi B. Sokoloff. *Boundaries of Jewish Identity*. Seattle: University of Washington Press, 2011.

Glick, Leonard B. *Marked in Your Flesh. Circumcision from Ancient Judea to Modern America*. Oxford; New York: Oxford University Press, 2005.

Goldschmidt, Henry. *Race and Religion among the Chosen People of Crown Heights*. New Brunswick: Rutgers University Press, 2006.

Goldstein, Eric L. *The Price of Whiteness: Jews, Race, and American Identity*. Princeton: Princeton University Press, 2006.

Gollaher, David L. 'From Ritual to Science: The Medical Transformation of Circumcision in America'. *Journal of Social History* 28, no. 1 (1994): 5–36.

Gordon, Lewis R. 'Rarely Kosher: Studying Jews of Color in North America'. *American Jewish History* 100, no. 1 (2016): 105–16.

Gotanda, Neil. 'The Racialization of Islam in American Law'. *Annals of the American Academy* 637, no. 1 (2011): 184–95.

Graber, Mark A. 'Jewish Voices and Religious Freedom. A Jewish Critique of Critical Jewish Thinking'. In *Law and Religion: A Critical Anthology*, edited by Stephen M. Feldman, 278–95. New York: New York University Press, 2000.

Green, Abigail. 'The British Empire and the Jews: An Imperialism of Human Rights'. *Past & Present* 199, no. 1 (2008): 175–205.

Green, Abigail, and Simon Levis Sullam. 'Introduction: Jews, Liberalism, Antisemitism: Towards a Twenty-First Century History'. In *Jews, Liberalism, Antisemitism. A Global History*, edited by Abigail Green and Simon Levis Sullam, 1–20. Cham: Palgrave Macmillan, 2020.

Green, Kate, and Hilary Lim. 'What Is This Thing about Female Circumcision? Legal Education and Human Rights'. *Social & Legal Studies* 7, no. 3 (1998): 365–87.

Greenberg, Blu. *How to Run a Traditional Jewish Household*. New York; London; Toronto; Sydney: Simon & Schuster, 1983.

Greenberg, Udi. 'Is Religious Freedom Protestant? On the History of a Critical Idea'. *Journal of the American Academy of Religion* 88, no. 1 (2020): 74–91.

Grimm, Dieter. 'Conflicts between General Laws and Religious Norms'. In *Constitutional Secularism in an Age of Religious Revival*, edited by Susanna Mancini and Michel Rosenfeld, 3–13. Oxford: Oxford University Press, 2014.

Grimm, Dieter. 'The Role of Fundamental Rights after Sixty-Five Years of Constitutional Jurisprudence in Germany'. *International Journal of Constitutional Law* 13, no. 1 (2015): 9–29.

Großmann, Sven. '§ 1631d Abs. 2 BGB. Gelungener Ausgleich zwischen Grundrechten und Staatsräson?'. *HRRS* 14 (2013): 515–25.

Grzymala-Busse, Anna. 'Once, the "Judeo-Christian Tradition" United Americans. Now It Divides Them'. *The Washington Post*, 17 April 2019. www.washingtonpost.com/politics/2019/04/17/once-judeo-christian-tradition-united-americans-now-it-divides-them/.

Hage, Ghassan. *White Nation. Fantasies of White Supremacy in a Multicultural Society*. New York; London: Routledge, 2000.

Hammel, Andrew. 'Why the Circumcision Judgment Looks So Weird to American Eyes'. *UK Constitutional Law Association Blog*, 4 October 2012. https://ukconstitutionallaw.org/2012/10/04/andrew-hammel-why-the-circumcision-judgment-looks-so-weird-to-american-eyes/.

Harvey, L. P. *Muslims in Spain 1500 to 1614*. Chicago; London: University of Chicago Press, 2005.

Haynes, Bruce D. *The Soul of Judaism. Jews of African Descent in America*. New York: New York University Press, 2018.

Haynes, Bruce D., and Ray Hutchison. 'The Ghetto: Origins, History, Discourse'. *City & Community* 7, no. 4 (2008): 353–57.

Hefner, Robert A. 'Varieties of Religious Freedom and Governance: A Practical Perspective'. In *Politics of Religious Freedom*, edited by Winnifred Fallers Sullivan, Elizabeth Shakman Hurd, Saba Mahmood and Peter G. Danchin, 127–34. Chicago; London: University of Chicago Press, 2015.

Heiden, Zachary. 'Fences and Neighbors'. *Law and Literature* 17, no. 2 (2005): 225–48.

Heinig, Hans Michael, and Martin Morlok. 'Von Schafen und Kopftüchern: Das Grundrecht auf Religionsfreiheit in Deutschland vor den Herausforderungen Religiöser Pluralisierung'. *JuristenZeitung* 15/16, no. 58 (2003): 777–85.

Hellsten, Sirkku K. 'Rationalising Circumcision: From Tradition to Fashion, from Public Health to Individual Freedom – Critical Notes on

Cultural Persistence of the Practice of Genital Mutilation'. *Journal of Medical Ethics* 30, no. 3 (2004): 248–53.

Heng, Geraldine. *The Invention of Race in the European Middle Ages*. Cambridge: Cambridge University Press, 2018.

Henriques, H. S. Q. 'The Jews and the English Law IV'. *Jewish Quarterly Review* 14, no. 4 (1902): 653–97.

Herman, Didi. *An Unfortunate Coincidence: Jews, Jewishness, and English Law*. Oxford: Oxford University Press, 2011.

Herman, Didi. '"An Unfortunate Coincidence": Jews and Jewishness in Twentieth-Century English Judicial Discourse'. *Journal of Law and Society* 33, no. 2 (2006): 277–301.

Herzberg, Rolf-Dietrich. 'Der Abwägungsgedanke und der "Evidenzbasierte Blick" in der Beschneidungsdebatte'. *Zeitschrift für Internationale Strafrechtsdogmatik* 9 (2014): 56–65.

Heschel, Susannah. 'Anti-Judaism in Christian Feminist Theology'. *Tikkun* 5, no. 3 (1990): 25–28.

Heschel, Susannah. 'Jews and Christianity'. In *The Cambridge History of Judaism. Volume Eight: The Modern World 1815–2000*, edited by Mitchell B. Hart and Tony Michels, 1038–62. Cambridge: Cambridge University Press, 2017.

Heschel, Susannah. 'Revolt of the Colonized: Abraham Geiger's Wissenschaft Des Judentums as a Challenge to Christian Hegemony in the Academy'. *New German Critique* 77 (1999): 61–85.

Hess, Jonathan M. *Germans, Jews and the Claims of Modernity*. New Haven; London: Yale University Press, 2002.

Hess, Jonathan M. 'Johann David Michaelis and the Colonial Imaginary: Orientalism and the Emergence of Racial Antisemitism in Eighteenth-century Germany'. *Jewish Social Studies* 6, no. 2 (2000): 56–101.

Hochberg, Gil, and Shir Alon. 'Decolonizing Judaism: Barbarism and the Return to Nativism'. *boundary 2* 44, no. 4 (2017): 179–94.

Hoffman, Lawrence. *Covenant of Blood: Circumcision and Gender in Rabbinic Judaism*. Chicago; London: University of Chicago Press, 1996.

Holliday Smith, Rachel. 'Newly Built Eruv Repeatedly Vandalized Amid Uproar in Crown Heights'. *DNA Info*, 25 July 2016. www.dnainfo.com/new-york/20160725/crown-heights/newly-built-eruv-repeatedly-vandalized-amid-uproar-crown-heights.

Hörnle, Tatjana. 'Strafrecht: Kultur, Religion, Strafrecht – Neue Herausforderungen in Einer Pluralistischen Gesellschaft'. In *70. Deutscher Juristentag. Thesen der Gutachter und Referenten*, 22–30. Hanover: Deutscher Juristentag, 2014.

Hudson, Alexandra. 'Germany Resumes Ritual Circumcision after Bitter Dispute'. *Reuters*, 2 October 2012. www.reuters.com/article/us-germany-circumcision-idUSBRE8900US20121001.

Huffer, Julie. 'Song and Dance over Carols'. *North Shore Times*, 22 October 2010, 5.

Hunt, Lynn. *The French Revolution and Human Rights. A Brief Documentary History*. Boston; New York: Bedford, 1996.

Huynh, Kim, and Siobhan Neyland. 'Australian Whiteness and Refugee Politics'. *Australian Journal of Politics and History* 66, no. 1 (2020): 111–29.

Hyman, Paula E. *The Jews of Modern France*. Berkeley; Los Angeles; London: University of California Press, 1998.

Isensee, Josef. 'Grundrechtliche Konsequenz wider Geheiligte Tradition'. *JuristenZeitung* 68, no. 7 (2013): 317–27.

Jacobs, Allan J., and Kavita Shah Arora. 'Ritual Male Infant Circumcision and Human Rights'. *American Journal of Bioethics* 15, no. 2 (2015): 30–39.

Jacobs, Louis. *The Jewish Religion: A Companion*. Oxford; New York: Oxford University Press, 1995.

Jakobsen, Janet R., and Ann Pellegrini. 'Introduction: Times Like These'. In *Secularisms*, edited by Janet R. Jakobsen and Ann Pellegrini, 1–35. Durham: Duke University Press, 2008.

James, George. 'Drawing a Line in Tenafly'. *The New York Times*, 31 December 2000. www.nytimes.com/2000/12/31/nyregion/church-and-state-drawing-a-line-in-tenafly.html.

Jansen, Yolande. *Secularism, Assimilation and the Crisis of Multiculturalism: French Modernist Legacies*. Amsterdam: Amsterdam University Press, 2013.

Jansen, Yolande, and Nasar Meer. 'Genealogies of "Jews" and "Muslims": Social Imagineries in the Race-Religion Nexus'. *Patterns of Prejudice* 54, no. 1–2 (2020): 1–14.

Jerouschek, Günter. 'Beschneidung und das Deutsche Recht. Historische, Medizinische, Psychologische und Juristische Aspekte'. *Neue Zeitschrift für Strafrecht* 6 (2008): 313–19.

Jerusalem Post. 'LA Jews Meet Resistance to Eruv Wall'. *Jerusalem Post*, 24 October 2006. www.jpost.com/jewish-world/jewish-news/la-jews-meet-resistance-to-eruv-wall.

Jewish Telegraphic Agency (JTA). 'Lubavitch Rabbis Issue Edict against Modern Orthodox Eruv in Crown Heights'. *Jewish Telegraphic Agency*, 24 June 2016.

Jivraj, Suhraiya. 'Interrogating Religion: Christian/Secular Values, Citizenship and Racial Upliftment in Governmental Education Policy'. *International Journal of Law in Context* 9, no. 3 (2013): 318–42.

Jivraj, Suhraiya. *The Religion of Law. Race, Citizenship and Children's Belonging*. Basingstoke: Palgrave Macmillan, 2013.

Jivraj, Suhraiya, and Didi Herman. 'It Is Difficult for a White Judge to Understand: Orientalism, Racialisation, and Christianity in English Child Welfare Cases'. *Child and Family Law Quarterly* 21, no. 3 (2009): 283–308.

Jones, Gareth. 'Circumcision Ban Makes Germany 'Laughing Stock' – Merkel'. *Reuters*, 18 July 2012. www.reuters.com/article/uk-germany-circumcision-idUKBRE86G11D20120717.

Joshi, Khyati Y. *White Christian Privilege: The Illusion of Religious Equality*. New York: New York University Press, 2020.

Joskowicz, Ari, and Ethan B. Katz. 'Introduction: Rethinking Jews and Secularism'. In *Secularism in Question. Jews and Judaism in Modern Times*, edited by Ari Joskowicz and Ethan B. Katz, 1–22. Philadelphia: University of Pennsylvania Press, 2015.

Judaken, Jonathan. 'AHR Roundtable: Rethinking Anti-Semitism. Introduction'. *American Historical Review* 123, no. 4 (2018): 1122–38.

Judd, Robin. 'Circumcision and Modern Jewish Life. A German Case Study, 1843–1914'. In *The Covenant of Circumcision. New Perspectives on an Ancient Jewish Rite*, edited by Elizabeth Wyner Mark, 142–56. Hanover; London: Brandeis University Press, 2003.

Judd, Robin. *Contested Rituals: Circumcision, Kosher Butchering, and Jewish Political Life in Germany, 1843–1933*. Ithaca: Cornell University Press, 2007.

Kafka, Franz. *The Basic Kafka*. New York: Pocket Books, 1979.

Kant, Immanuel. *Religion within the Boundary of Pure Reason*. Translated by J. W. Semple. Edinburgh: Thomas Clark, 1838. (Original Publication: Die Religion Innerhalb der grenzen der Bloßen Vernunft, 1793).

Kaplan, M. Lindsay. *Figuring Racism in Medieval Christianity*. Oxford: Oxford University Press, 2018.

Kapur, Ratna. 'Secularism's Others: The Legal Regulation of Religion and Hierarchy of Citizenship'. In *Constitutions and Religions*, edited by Susanna Mancini, 41–58. Cheltenham: Edward Elgar, 2020.

Katz, Ethan B. 'An Imperial Entanglement: Anti-Semitism, Islamophobia, and Colonialism'. *American Historical Review* 123, no. 4 (2018): 1190–209.

Katz, Ethan B. 'Where Do the Hijab and the Kippah Belong? On Being Publicy Jewish or Muslim in Post-Hebdo France'. *Jewish History* 32, no. 1 (2018): 99–114.

Katz, Ethan B., Lisa Moses Leff, and Maud S. Mandel, eds. *Colonialism and the Jews*. Bloomington; Indianapolis: Indiana University Press, 2017.

Katznelson, Ira. 'Between Separation and Dissappearance: Jews on the Margins of American Liberalism'. In *Paths of Emancipation. Jews, States, and Citizenship*, edited by Pierre Birnbaum and Ira Katznelson, 157–205. Princeton: Princeton University Press, 1995.

Kaye/Kantrowitz, Melanie. *The Colors of Jews. Racial Politics and Radical Diasporas*. Bloomington; Indianapolis: Indiana University Press, 2007.

Keel, Terence. 'Blumenbach's Race Science in the Light of Christian Supersessionism'. In *Johann Friedrich Blumenbach. Race and Natural History, 1750–1850*, edited by Nicolaas Rupke and Gerhard Lauer, 123–41. Abingdon, Oxon: Routledge, 2019.

Keel, Terence. *Divine Variations: How Christian Thought Became Racial Science*. Stanford: Stanford University Press, 2018.

Kelley, Tina. 'Town Votes for Marker Used by Jews'. *The New York Times*, 25 January 2006. www.nytimes.com/2006/01/25/nyregion/town-votes-for-marker-used-by-jews.html.

Kemmerer, Alexandra. 'Naked Law, Lost Traditions. A Comment on Reut Paz and Legal Pluralism'. *Verfassungsblog*, 18 August 2012. https://verfassungsblog.de/naked-law-lost-traditions-comment-reut-paz-legal-pluralism/.

Kennedy, David. 'Images of Religion in International Legal Theory'. In *Religion and International Law*, edited by Mark Janis and Carolyn Evans, 145–53. The Hague: Martinus Nijhoff, 1999.

Kestenbaum, Sam. 'Controversial Brooklyn Eruv for Modern Orthodox Vandalized Amid Dispute with Chabad'. *Forward*, July 12, 2016. https://forward.com/news/344767/controversial-brooklyn-eruv-for-modern-orthodox-vandalized-amid-dispute-wit/?attribution=articles-article-related-1-headline.

Kline, Marlee. 'Child Welfare Law, "Best Interests of the Child" Ideology, and First Nations'. *Osgoode Hall Law Journal* 30, no. 2 (1992): 375–426.

Kline, Marlee. 'The Colour of Law: Ideological Representations of First Nations in Legal Discourse'. *Social & Legal Studies* 3 (1994): 451–76.

Knobloch, Charlotte. 'Wollt Ihr Uns Juden Noch?' *Süddeutsche Zeitung Online*, 25 September 2012. www.sueddeutsche.de/politik/beschneidungen-in-deutschland-wollt-ihr-uns-juden-noch-1.1459038.

Knoll, David D. 'Protecting Religious Freedom and Places of Worship – The Example of the Eruv'. *Solidarity: The Journal of Catholic Social Thought and Secular Ethics* 7, no. 1 (2016): 1–18.

Kovács, Éva, and Júlia Vajda. 'Circumcision in Hungary after the Shoa'. In *The Covenant of Circumcision. New Perspectives on an Ancient Jewish Rite*, edited by Elizabeth Wyner Mark, 177–87. Hanover; London: Brandeis University Press, 2003.

Künzle, Patrick. 'Ein Eruv soll die Abwanderung Stoppen'. *SRF*, 18 April 2018. www.srf.ch/news/schweiz/juden-in-basel-ein-eruv-soll-die-abwanderung-stoppen.

Kushner, Tony. 'Anti-Semitism in Britain: Continuity and the Absence of a Resurgence?'. *Ethnic and Racial Studies* 36, no. 3 (2013): 434–49.

Laborde, Cécile. 'Rescuing Liberalism from Critical Religion'. *Journal of the American Academy of Religion* 88, no. 1 (2020): 58–73.

Lau, Mariam. 'Die Debatte über die Beschneidung Kennt viele Verlierer'. *Die Zeit*, 11 October 2012. www.zeit.de/2012/42/Beschneidung-Gesetz/komplettansicht.

Laurance, Jeremy. 'Circumcision: A Necessary Cut or Bodily Harm'. *Independent*, 7 May 2014. www.independent.co.uk/life-style/health-and-families/features/circumcision-a-necessary-cut-or-bodily-harm-9328250.html.

Lauwers, A. Sophie. 'Religion, Secularity, Culture? Investigating Christian Privilege in Western Europe'. *Ethnicities* 23, no. 3 (2023): 403–25.

Lavi, Shai. 'Our Food Is Our Bond: A History of Jewish and Muslim Animal Slaughter and Post-Christian Social Science'. *History of the Present: A Journal of Critical History* 8, no. 1 (2018): 29–56.

Lavi, Shai, and Lena Salaymeh. 'Secularism'. In *Key Concepts in the Study of Antisemitism*, edited by Sol Goldberg, Scott Ury and Kalman Weiser, 257–72. London: Palgrave, 2021.

Leff, Lisa Moses. 'Jews, Liberals and the Civilizing Mission in Nineteenth-Century France'. In *The Jews of Modern France*, edited by Zvi Jonathan Kaplan and Nadia Malinovich, 129–153. Leiden: Brill, 2016.

Lees, Susan H. 'Jewish Space in Suburbia: Interpreting the Eruv Conflict in Tenafly, New Jersey'. *Contemporary Jewry* 27, no. 1 (2007): 42–79.

Lentin, Alana. *Why Race Still Matters*. Cambridge: Polity Press, 2020.

Levi, Joshua. 'Eruv Now Only One Pole Away'. *Australian Jewish News*, 22 March 2012. www.australianjewishnews.com/eruv-now-only-one-pole-away/.

Levi, Joshua. 'Nine's Racism Claim'. *Australian Jewish News*, 9 July 2010. www.jewishnews.net.au/nines-racism-claim/14285.

Levi, Joshua. 'St Ives Eruv Turned Down by Council'. *Australian Jewish News*, 25 August 2011. www.jewishnews.net.au/st-ives-eruv-turned-down-by-council/22612.

Levine-Rasky, Cynthia. 'White Privilege. Jewish Women's Writing and the Instability of Categories'. *Journal of Modern Jewish Studies* 7, no. 1 (2008): 51–66.

Levitt, Laura. 'Other Moderns, Other Jews: Revisiting Jewish Secularism in America'. In *Secularisms*, edited by Janet R. Jakobsen and Ann Pellegrini, 108–38. Durham: Duke University Press, 2008.

Liphshiz, Cnaan. 'Netherlands Health Ministry Says Jewish Cirucmcisers Are Breaking the Law'. *The Times of Israel*, 31 May 2019. www.timesofisrael.com/netherlands-health-ministry-says-jewish-circumcisers-are-breaking-the-law/.

Lloyd, Vincent W. 'Introduction: Managing Race, Managing Religion'. In *Race and Secularism in America*, edited by Jonathon S. Kahn and Vincent W. Lloyd, 1–22. New York: Columbia University Press, 2016.

Locke, John. *Letters Concerning Toleration*. London: Printed for A (and this is also how it is provided in the footnote reference in chapter 2), 1765. https://babel.hathitrust.org/cgi/pt?id=coo1.ark:/13960/t5r78xn80&seq=9.

Loeffler, James. *Rooted Cosmopolitans. Jews and Human Rights in the Twentieth Century*. New Haven; London: Yale University Press, 2018.

Loeffler, James. 'The Religions of Human Rights'. *Harvard Theological Review* 116, no. 1 (2023): 147–71.

Loeffler, James, and Moria Paz. 'Introduction'. In *The Law of Strangers. Jewish Lawyers and International Law in the Twentieth Century*, edited by

James Loeffler and Moria Paz, 1–20. Cambridge: Cambridge University Press, 2019.

Loeffler, James, and Moria Paz, eds. *The Law of Strangers: Jewish Lawyers and International Law in the Twentieth Century*. Cambridge: Cambridge University Press, 2019.

López, Ian Haney. *White by Law. The Legal Construction of Race*, 10th ed. New York; London: New York University Press, 2006.

Lopez, Julia Costa. 'Beyond Eurocentrism and Orientalism: Revisiting the Othering of Jews and Muslims through Medieval Canon Law'. *Review of International Studies* 42, no. 3 (2016): 450–70.

Mahmood, Saba. 'Secularism, Hermeneutics, and Empire: The Politics of Islamic Reformation'. *Public Culture* 18, no. 2 (2006): 323–47.

Mahmood, Saba, and Peter G. Danchin. 'Immunity or Regulation? Antinomies of Religious Freedom'. *South Atlantic Quarterly* 113, no. 1 (2014): 129–59.

Maimonides, Moses. *The Guide of the Perplexed.* Translated by Shlomo Pines. Chicago: University of Chicago Press, 1963.

Mancini, Susanna. 'Patriarchy as the Exclusive Domain of the Other: The Veil Controversy, False Projection and Cultural Racism'. *International Journal of Constitutional Law* 10, no. 2 (2012): 411–28.

Mancini, Susanna. 'The Power of Symbols and Symbols as Power: Secularism and Religion as Guarantors of Cultural Convergence'. *Cardozo Law Review* 30, no. 6 (2009): 2629–68.

Mancini, Susanna. 'The Tempting of Europe, the Political Seduction of the Cross: A Schmittian Reading of Christianity and Islam in European Constitutionalism'. In *Constitutional Secularism in an Age of Religious Revival*, edited by Susanna Mancini and Michel Rosenfeld, 111–35. Oxford; New York: Oxford University Press, 2014.

Mancini, Susanna. 'To Be or Not to Be Jewish: The UK Supreme Court Answers the Question; Judgement of 16 September 2009, R v Governing Body of JFS UKSC 2015'. *European Constitutional Law Review* 6 (2010): 481–502.

Manderson, Lenore. 'Local Rites and Body Politics. Tensions between Cultural Diversity and Human Rights'. *International Feminist Journal of Politics* 6, no. 2 (2004): 285–307.

Manok, Andreas. *Die Medizinisch Nicht Indizierte Beschneidung des Männlichen Kindes: Rechtslage vor und nach Inkrafttreten des § 1631d BGB unter Besonderer Berücksichtigung der Grundrechte*. Berlin: Duncker & Humblot, 2015.

Mantegazza, Paolo. *The Sexual Relations of Mankind.* Translated by Samuel Putnam. Honolulu: University Press of the Pacific, 1935.

Marglin, Jessica M. *Across Legal Lines. Jews and Muslims in Modern Morocco.* New Haven; London: Yale University Press, 2016.

Markell, Patchen. *Bound by Recognition.* Princeton; Oxford: Princeton University Press, 2003.

Martinez, María Elena. *Genealogical Fictions: Limpieza De Sangre, Religion, and Gender in Colonial Mexico*. Stanford: Stanford University Press, 2008.

Masuzawa, Tomoko. *The Invention of World Religions. Or, How European Universalism Was Preserved in the Language of Pluralism*. Chicago: University of Chicago Press, 2005.

Matar, Nabil I. 'John Locke and the Jews'. *Journal of Ecclestial History* 44, no. 1 (1993): 45–62.

Mehta, Uday. 'Liberal Strategies of Exclusion'. *Politics & Society* 18, no. 4 (1990): 427–54.

Mendes-Flohr, Paul. 'The Emancipation of European Jewry. Why Was It Not Self-Evident?' *Studia Rosenthaliana* 30, no. 1 (1996): 7–20.

Mendes-Flohr, Paul and Jehuda Reinharz, eds., *The Jew in the Modern World. A Documentary History*, 2nd ed. Oxford: Oxford University Press, 1995.

Mensch, Elizabeth. 'Christianity and the Roots of Liberalism'. In *Christian Perspectives on Legal Thought*, edited by Robert F. Cochran, Michael W. McConnell and Angela C. Carmella, 54–72, New Haven: Yale University Press, 2001.

Merkel, Reinhard, and Holm Putzke. 'After Cologne: Male Circumcision and the Law. Parental Right, Religious Liberty or Criminal Assault?' *Journal of Medical Ethics* 39, no. 7 (2013): 444–49.

Merry, Sally Engle. *Getting Justice and Getting Even: Legal Consciousness among Working-Class Americans*. Chicago: University of Chicago Press, 1990.

Michelmore, Karen. 'Court to Decide on Religious Structure'. *ABC Sydney*, 19 March 2012. www.abc.net.au/local/stories/2012/02/07/3424598.htm.

Moruzzi, Norma Claire. 'Cutting through Culture: The Feminist Discourse on Female Circumcision'. *Critique: Critical Middle Eastern Studies* 14, no. 2 (2005): 203–20.

Moscucci, Ornella. 'Clitoridectomy, Circumcision, and the Politics of Sexual Pleasure in Mid-Victorian Britain'. In *Sexualities in Victorian Britain*, edited by Andrew H. Miller and James Eli Adams, 60–78. Bloomington; Indianapolis: Indiana University Press, 1996.

Mosse, Werner E. 'From "Schutzjuden" to "Deutsche Staatsbürger Jüdischen Glaubens": The Long and Bumpy Road of Jewish Emancipation in Germany'. In *Paths of Emancipation: Jews, States, and Citizenship*, edited by Pierre Birnbaum and Ira Katznelson, 59–93. Princeton: Princeton University Press, 1995.

Moyn, Samuel. *Christian Human Rights*. Philadelphia: University of Pennsylvania Press, 2015.

Muldoon, James. *Popes, Lawyers, and Infidels: The Church and the Non-Christian World, 1250–1550*. Philadelphia: University of Pennsylvania Press, 1979.

Na, Angelika F., Sharman P. T. Tanny, and John M. Hutson. 'Circumcision: Is It Worth It for 21st-century Australian Boys?'. *Journal of Paediatrics and Child Health* 51, no. 6 (2015): 580–83.

Narunsky, Gareth. 'St Ives Gets Its Eruv'. *The Australian Jewish News*, 28 May 2015.

Nirenberg, David. *Anti-Judaism: The Western Tradition*. New York; London: WW Norton, 2013.

Nirenberg, David. 'Enmity and Assimilation. Jews, Christians, and Converts in Medieval Spain'. *Common Knowledge* 9, no. 1 (2003): 137–55.

Nirenberg, David. *Neighbouring Faiths. Christianity, Islam, and Judaism in the Middle Ages and Today*. Chicago; London: University of Chicago Press, 2014.

Nirenberg, David. 'Was There Race before Modernity? The Example of "Jewish" Blood in Late Medieval Spain'. In *The Origins of Racism in the West*, edited by Eliav-Benjamin Isaac Feldon and Joseph Ziegler, 232–64. Cambridge: Cambridge University Press, 2013.

Olin, Margaret. 'Introduction. The Poetics of the Eruv'. *Images* 5 (2011): 3–13.

Pang, Myung-Geol, and DaiSik Kim. 'Extraordinarily High Rates of Male Circumcision in South Korea: History and Underlying Causes'. *British Journal of Urology International* 89, no. 1 (2008): 48–54.

Pasto, James. 'Islam's "Strange Secret Sharer": Orientalism, Judaism, and the Jewish Question'. *Comparative Studies in Society and History* 40, no. 3 (1998): 437–74.

Paulus, Heinrich E. G. *Die Jüdische Nationalabsonderung Nach Ursprung, Folgen Und Besserungsmitteln*. Heidelberg: Universitätsbuchhandlung Winter, 1831.

Paz, Moria. 'A Non-Territorial Ethnic Network and the Making of Human Rights Law: The Case of the Alliance Israélite Universelle'. *Interdisciplinary Journal of Human Rights Law* 4, no. 1 (2009): 1–24.

Paz, Reut Yael. *A Gateway between a Distant God and a Cruel World: The Contributions of Jewish German-Speaking Scholars to International Law*. Leiden: Brill, 2012.

Paz, Reut Yael. 'Religion, Secularism, and International Law'. In *The Oxford Handbook of the Theory of International Law*, edited by Anne Orford and Florian Hoffmann, 923–38. Oxford: Oxford University Press, 2016.

Paz, Reut Yael. 'The Cologne Circumcision Judgment: A Blow against Liberal Legal Pluralism'. *Verfassungsblog*, 24 July 2012. https://verfassungsblog.de/cologne-circumcision-judgment-blow-liberal-legal-pluralism/.

Pellegrini, Ann. 'Whiteface Performances: "Race," Gender, and Jewish Bodies'. In *Jews and Other Differences. The New Jewish Cultural Studies*, edited by Daniel Boyarin and Jonathan Boyarin, 108–49. Minneapolis; London: University of Minnesota Press, 1997.

Peritz, Ingrid. 'Chi-Chi Quebec Enclave Clashes with Hasidim'. *The Globe and Mail*, 18 October 2000. www.theglobeandmail.com/news/national/chi-chi-quebec-enclave-clashes-with-hasidim/article25473739/.

Peritz, Ingrid. 'Jewish Community Can Build Religious Symbol, Court Rules'. *The Globe and Mail*, 22 June 2001. www.theglobeandmail.com/news/national/jewish-community-can-build-religious-symbol-court-rules/article18415690.

Perry, Micha J. 'Imaginary Space Meets Actual Space in Thirteenth-century Cologne: Eliezer Ben Joel and the Eruv'. *Images* 5, no. 1 (2011): 26–36.

Piggin, Stuart. 'Power and Religion in a Modern State: Desecularisation in Australian History'. *Journal of Religious History* 38, no. 3 (2014): 320–40.

Porat, Iddo. 'The Starting at Home Principle: On Ritual Animal Slaughter, Male Circumcision and Proportionality'. *Oxford Journal of Legal Studies* 41, no. 1 (2021): 30–58.

Poulos, Elenie. 'Protecting Freedom/Protecting Privilege: Church Responses to Anti-discrimination Law Reform in Australia'. *Australian Journal of Human Rights* 24, no. 1 (2018): 117–33.

Purdy, Matthew. 'A Wire-thin Line Sharply Divides a Suburb's Jews'. *New York Times*, 25 March 2011. www.nytimes.com/2001/03/25/nyregion/our-towns-a-wire-thin-line-sharply-divides-a-suburb-s-jews.html.

Putzke, Holm. 'Die Strafrechtliche Relevanz der Beschneidung von Knaben. Zugleich ein Beitrag über die Grenzen der Einwilligung in Fällen der Personensorge'. In *Strafrecht Zwischen System und Telos: Festschrift für Rolf Dietrich Herzberg zum Siebzigsten Geburtstag*, edited by Holm Putzke, Bernhard Hardtung, Tatjana Hörnle, Reinhard Merkel and Jörg Scheinfeldt, 669–709. Tübingen: Mohr Siebeck, 2008.

Rabello, Alfredo M. 'The Ban on Circumcision as a Cause of Bar Kokhba's Rebellion'. *Israel Law Review* 29, no. 1–2 (1995): 176–214.

Ragussis, Michael. *Figures of Conversion. 'The Jewish Question' & English National Identity*. Durham; London: Duke University Press, 1995.

Rana, Junaid. *Terrifying Muslims. Race and Labor in the South Asian Diaspora*. Durham; London: Duke University Press, 2011.

Randell-Moon, Holly. 'The Secular Contract: Sovereignty, Secularism and Law in Australia'. *Social Semiotics* 23, no. 3 (2013): 352–67.

Rapana, Jessica. 'Anti-Eruv Flyer 'One of the Worst Examples of Anti-Semitism' in Sydney'. *North Shore Times*, 15 September 2016. www.dailytelegraph.com.au/newslocal/north-shore/antieruv-flyer-one-of-worst-examples-of-antisemitism-in-sydney/news-story/da7eeac9e11718449ca9f886c58d6716

Rapana, Jessica. 'Ku-Ring-Gai Council Has Approved the Jewish Eruv in St Ives in a Landmark Decision'. *North Shore Times*, 7 November 2016. www.dailytelegraph.com.au/newslocal/north-shore/kuringgai-council-has-approved-the-jewish-eruv-in-st-ives-in-a-landmark-decision/news-story/a8da5184dac58242eb5c449634046cf3.

Rapana, Jessica. 'Ku-Ring-Gai Council Takes on Prominent Jewish Community over St Ives Eruv'. 30 June 2016. www.dailytelegraph.com.au/newslocal/north-shore/kuringgai-council-takes-on-prominent-jewish-community-over-st-ives-eruv/news-story/c7e0176213109548d295e61cdb01f4e3.

Rapana, Jessica. 'Nazi Sign 'Hatred at Its Worst'. *North Shore Times*, 30 September 2016.

Rapana, Jessica. 'Threats Follow Boundary Action'. *North Shore Times*, 15 July 2016.

Rau, Vanessa. 'Vehementer Säkularismus als Antisemitismus?'. *Aus Politik und Zeitgeschichte* 28–30 (2014): 31–38.

Ravid, Benjamin. 'The Legal Status of the Jewish Merchants of Venice, 1541–1638'. *The Journal of Economic History* 35, no. 1 (1975): 274–79.

Raz-Krakotzkin, Amnon. 'Secularism, the Christian Ambivalence toward the Jews and the Notion of Exile'. In *Secularism in Question*, edited by Ari Joskowicz and Ethan B. Katz, 276–98. Philadelphia: University of Pennsylvania Press, 2015.

Razack, Sherene H. *Casting Out: The Eviction of Muslims from Western Law and Politics*. Toronto: Toronto University Press, 2008.

Razack, Sherene H. 'The "Sharia Law Debate" in Ontario: The Modernity/Premodernity Distinction in Legal Efforts to Protect Women from Culture'. *Feminist Legal Studies* 15, no. 1 (2007): 3–32.

Razack, Sherene H. 'When Place Becomes Race'. In *Race, Space, and the Law: Unmapping a White Settler Society*, edited by Sherene H. Razack, 1–20. Toronto: Between the Lines, 2002.

Reinhard Lupton, Julia. 'Othello Circumcised: Shakespeare and the Pauline Discourse of Nations'. *Representations*, 57 (1997): 73–89.

Reis, Elizabeth. 'Medicalization and the Mainstreaming of Circumcision in Mid-Twentieth-Century America'. *American Jewish History* 105, no. 3 (2021): 321–42.

Resnick, Irven M. *Marks of Distinction. Christian Perceptions of Jews in the High Middle Ages*. Washington, DC: Catholic University of America Press, 2012.

Revesz, Rachel. 'Norwegian Ruling Party Votes to Ban Circumcision for Men under 16 Years'. *Independent*, 8 May 2017. www.independent.co.uk/news/world/europe/norwegian-ruling-progress-party-ban-circumcision-men-under-16-years-old-vote-annual-conference-europe-a7723746.html.

Riedel, Mareike. 'An Uneasy Encounter: Male Circumcision, Jewish Difference, and German Law'. *Studies of Law, Politics and Society* 79 (2019): 55–84.

Riedel, Mareike. 'Law and the Construction of Jewish Difference'. *Journal of Law and Society* 48, no. 2 (2021): 158–78.

Riedel, Mareike. 'Studying While Muslim: Anti-discrimination Law, Countering Violent Extremism, and Suspect Youth'. *Griffith Law Review* 31, no. 2 (2022): 193–216.

Riedel, Mareike. 'The Difference a Wire Makes: Planning Law, Public Orthodox Judaism and Urban Space in Australia'. *International Journal of Law in Context* 16, no. 4 (2020): 403–21.

Riedel, Mareike. '"They Are from Mars": The Othering of Jews and Muslims in European Legal Debates'. In *Religious Othering. Global Dimensions*, edited by Mark Juergensmeyer, Kathleen Moore and Dominic Sachsenmaier, 77–93. Abingdon, Oxon: Routledge, 2022.

Rigg, James Macmullen. *Select Pleas, Starrs, and Other Records from the Rolls of the Exchequer of the Jews: A.D. 1220–1284*. London: Quaritch, 1902.

Roediger, David R. *Working towards Whiteness. How America's Immigrants Became White. The Strange Journey from Ellis Island to the Suburbs*. New York: Basic Books, 2005.

Rogers, Brubakers. 'Between Nationalism and Civilizationism: The European Populist Moment in Comparative Perspective'. *Ethnic and Racial Studies* 40, no. 8 (2017): 1191–226.

Rogers, Juliet. *Law's Cut on the Body of Human Rights: Female Circumcision, Torture and Sacred Flesh*. Abingdon, Oxon; New York: Routledge, 2013.

Romain, Jonathan. 'JFS Puts Faith Schools in the Dock'. *The Guardian*, 28 October 2009. www.theguardian.com/commentisfree/belief/2009/oct/27/jfs-supreme-court-jewish-school.

Romain, Jonathan. 'Postwar Anti-Jewish Refugee Hysteria: A Case of Racial or Religious Bigotry?' *Journal of Australian Studies* 27, no. 77 (2003): 69–79.

Romain, Jonathan. 'Reflections on "Culture Mavens" from an Australian Jewish Perspective'. In *Jews at Home. The Domestication of Identity*, edited by Simon J. Bronner, 307–15. Oxford; Portland: Littman Library of Jewish Civilization, 2010.

Romain, Jonathan. 'The JFS Ruling is a Victory for Jews'. *The Guardian*, 17 December 2009. www.theguardian.com/commentisfree/belief/2009/dec/16/jfs-supreme-court-ruling.

Rönne, Ludwig von, and Heinrich Simon. *Die Früheren und Gegenwärtigen Verhältnisse der Juden in den Sämmtlichen Landestheilen des Preußischen Staates*. Breslau: Aderholz, 1843.

Rosen, Gillad, and Anne B. Shlay. 'Whose Right to Jerusalem?'. *International Journal of Urban and Regional Research* 38, no. 3 (2014): 935–50.

Rosettenstein, Megan. 'The St Ives Eruv: One Community Member's View'. *North Shore Mums*, 20 September 2016. www.northshoremums.com.au/the-st-ives-eruv-one-community-members-view/.

Roth, Philip. *The Counterlife*. New York: Farrar Straus Giroux, 1986.

Rowe, Emma. 'Religion in Australian Schools: An Historical and Contemporary Debate'. *The Conversation*, 23 August 2017. www.theconversation.com/religion-in-australian-schools-an-historical-and-contemporary-debate-82439.

Rürup, Reinhard. 'The Tortuous and Thorny Path to Legal Equality: "Jew Laws" and Emancipatory Legislation in Germany from the Late Eighteenth Cent'. *Leo Baeck Institute Year Book* 31, no. 1 (1986): 3–33.

Rutland, Suzanne D. *Edge of the Diaspora: Two Centuries of Jewish Settlement in Australia*. Rose Bay: Brandl & Schlesinger, 1997.

Sacks, Jonathan. 'The Europeans' Skewed View of Circumcision'. *Jerusalem Post*, 5 July 2012. www.jpost.com/Opinion/Columnists/The-Europeans-skewed-view-of-circumcision.

Said, Edward W. *Orientalism*, 25th ed. New York: Vintage Books, 1994 [1979].

Salaymeh, Lena. 'The Eurocentrism of Secularism'. *West Windows*, 14 September 2020. www.uni-erfurt.de/philosophische-fakultaet/forschung/forschungsgruppen/was-ist-westlich-am-westen/.west-windows/26-the-eurocentrism-of-secularism.

Salaymeh, Lena, and Shai Lavi. 'Religion Is Secularised Tradition: Jewish and Muslim Circumcisions in Germany'. *Oxford Journal of Legal Studies* 41, no. 2 (2021): 431–58.

Samuels, Maurice. *The Right to Difference: French Universalism and the Jews*. Chicago: Chicago University Press, 2016.

Sandercock, Leonie. 'When Strangers Become Neighbours: Managing Cities of Difference'. *Planning Theory & Practice* 1, no. 1 (2000): 13–30.

Sarajlic, Eldar. 'Can Culture Justify Infant Circumcision?' *Res Publica* 20, no. 4 (2014): 327–43.

Sarat, Austin, and Thomas R. Kearns. 'The Cultural Lives of Law'. In *Law in the Domains of Culture*, edited by Austin Sarat and Thomas R. Kearns, 1–20. Ann Arbor: University of Michigan Press, 2009.

Scheinfeldt, Jörg. 'Erläuterungen zum Neuen § 1631d BGB – Beschneidung des Männlichen Kindes'. *HRRS* 14 (2013): 268–83.

Scheuer, Andreas. 'Es Gibt keine Alternative'. *Cicero*, 7 May 2017. www.cicero.de/innenpolitik/debatte-um-leitkultur-Es-gibt-keine-Alternative.

Scheuer, Milan. 'Belgium Bans Religious Slaughtering Practices, Drawing Praise and Protest'. *New York Times*, 5 January 2019. www.nytimes.com/2019/01/05/world/europe/belgium-ban-jewish-muslim-animal-slaughter.html

Schiratzki, Johanna. 'Banning God's Law in the Name of the Holy Body: The Nordic Position on Ritual Male Circumcision'. *The Family in Law* 5 (2011): 35–53.

Schlör, Joachim. *Das Ich der Stadt: Debatten über Judentum und Urbanität 1822–1938*. Göttingen: Vandenhoeck & Ruprecht, 2005.

Schraub, David H. 'Liberal Jews and Religious Liberty'. *New York University Law Review* 98 (2023): 1–72.

Selod, Saher. *Forever Supect: Racialized Surveillance of Muslim Americans in the War on Terror*. New Brunswick: Rutgers University Press, 2018.

Selod, Saher, and David G. Embrick. 'Racialization and Muslims: Situating the Muslim Experience in Race Scholarship'. *Sociology Compass* 7/8 (2013): 644–55.

Sennett, Richard. *Flesh and Stone. The Body and the City in Western Civilization*. New York; London: W.W. Norton, 1994.

Shaikh, Nermeen. 'The Jew, the Arab: An Interview with Gil Anidjar'. https://asiasociety.org/jew-arab-interview-gil-anidjar.

Shapiro, James. *Shakespeare and the Jews*. New York: Columbia University Press, 2016.

Sherwood, Harriett. 'Iceland Law to Outlaw Male Circumcision Sparks Row over Religious Freedom'. *The Guardian*, 18 February 2018. www.theguardian.com/society/2018/feb/18/iceland-ban-male-circumcision-first-european-country.

Shortall, Sarah. 'From the Three Bodies of Christ to the King's Two Bodies: The Theological Origins of Secularization Theory'. *Modern Intellectual History* 20, no. 3 (2022): 1–23. https://doi.org/10.1017/S147924432200035X.

Shweder, Richard A. 'Shouting at the Hebrews: Imperial Liberalism v Liberal Pluralism and the Practice of Male Circumcision'. *Law, Culture and the Humanities* 5, no. 2 (2009): 247–65.

Sibley, David. *Geographies of Exclusion. Society and Difference in the West*. London; New York: Routledge, 1995.

Siemiatycki, Myer. 'Contesting Sacred Urban Space: The Case of the Eruv'. *Journal of International Migration and Integration/Revue de l'integration et de la migration internationale* 6, no. 2 (2005): 255–70.

Sobotka, Heide. 'Josef Schuster über die Weiterbildung von Mohalim'. *Jüdische Allgemeine*, 15 October 2013. www.juedische-allgemeine.de/unsere-woche/fuer-das-wohl-des-kindes/.

Sorkin, David. *Jewish Emancipation. A History across Five Centuries*. Princeton and Oxford: Princeton University Press, 2019.

Spinoza, Benedictus. *The Chief Works of Benedict De Spinoza: Volume I: Introduction, Tractatus Theologico-Politicus, Tractatus Politicus*. Translated by Robert Harvey Monro Elwes. London: George Bell and Sons, 1891.

Stacey, Robert. 'The Conversion of Jews to Christianity in Thirteenth-Century England'. *Speculum* 67, no. 2 (1992): 263–83.

Statt, Daniel. 'The City of London and the Controversy over Immigration, 1660–1722'. *The Historical Journal* 33, no. 1 (1990): 45–61.

Stoler, Laura Ann. 'Racial Histories and Their Regimes of Truth'. *Political Power and Social Theory* 11 (1997): 183–206.

Stoler, Laura Ann and Frederick Cooper. 'Between Metropole and Colony. Rethinking a Research Agenda'. In *Tensions of Empire*, edited by Laura Ann Stoler and Frederick Cooper, 1–56. Berkeley: University of California Press, 1997.

Stoker, Valerie. 'Drawing the Line: Hasidic Jews, Eruvim, and the Public Space of Outremont, Quebec'. *History of Religions* 43, no. 1 (2003): 18–49.

Stolzenberg, Nomi Maya. 'Righting the Relationship between Race and Religion in Law'. *Oxford Journal of Legal Studies* 31, no. 3 (2011): 583–602.

Stolzenberg, Nomi Maya, and David N. Myers. *American Shtetl: The Making of Kiryas Joel, a Hasidic Village in Upstate New York*. Princeton: Princeton University Press, 2022.

Stone, Suzanne Last. 'Religion and State: Models of Separation from within Jewish Law'. *International Journal of Constitutional Law* 6, no. 3–4 (2008): 631–61.

Stratton, Jon. *Coming Out Jewish*. London: Routledge, 2000.

Stratton, Jon. 'Whiteness, Morality and Christianity in Australia'. *Journal of Intercultural Studies* 37, no. 1 (2016): 17–32.

Strauss, Elissa. 'How Female Circumcision Is Different from a Brit Milah'. *Forward*, 15 July 2014. https://forward.com/opinion/201806/how-female-circumcision-is-different-from-a-brit-m/.

Sullivan, Winnifred Fallers. *The Impossibility of Religious Freedom*. New Haven: Princeton University Press, 2005.

Sullivan, Winnifred Fallers, Robert A. Yelle, and Mateo Taussig-Rubbo, eds. *After Secular Law*. Stanford: Stanford University Press, 2011.

Surkis, Judith. *Sex, Law, and Sovereignty in French Algeria, 1830–1930*. Ithaca; London: Cornell University Press, 2019.

Susman, Alexandra Lang. 'Strings Attached: An Analysis of the Eruv under the Religion Clauses of the First Amendment and the Religious Land Use and Institutionalized Persons Act'. *University of Maryland Law Journal of Race, Religion, Gender & Class* 9 (2009): 93–134.

Svoboda, J. Steven. 'Circumcision of Male Infants as a Human Rights Violation'. *Journal of Medical Ethics* 39, no. 7 (2013): 469–74.

Tartakoff, Paola. 'Testing Boundaries: Jewish Conversion and Cultural Fluidity in Medieval Europe, C. 1200–1391'. *Speculum* 90, no. 3 (2015): 728–62.

Teter, Magda. *Christian Supremacy: Reckoning with the Roots of Antisemitism and Racism*. Princeton: Princeton University Press, 2023.

Teter, Magda. 'The Catholic Church'. In *Key Concepts in the Study of Antisemitism*, edited by Sol Goldberg, Scott Ury and Kalman Weiser, 65–78. Cham: Palgrave Macmillan, 2021.

Thomas, James M. 'The Racial Formation of Medieval Jews: A Challenge to the Field'. *Ethnic and Racial Studies* 33, no. 10 (2010): 1737–55.

Thornton, Margaret, and Trish Luker. 'The New Racism in Employment Discrimination: Tales from the Global Economy'. *Sydney Law Review* 32, no. 1 (2010): 1–28.

Thornton, Margaret, and Trish Luker. 'The Spectral Ground: Religious Belief Discrimination'. *Macquarie Law Journal* 9 (2009): 71–91.

Thorpe, Amelia. 'Between Rights in the City and the Right to the City: Heritage, Character and Public Participation in Urban Planning'. In *Heritage, Culture and Rights. Challenging Legal Discourses*, edited by Andrea Durbach and Lucas Lixinski, 121–62. Oxford; Portland: Hart, 2017.

Tobin, John. 'The International Obligation to Abolish Traditional Practices Harmful to Children's Health: What Does It Mean and Require of States?'. *Human Rights Law Review* 9, no. 3 (2009): 373–96.

Topolski, Anya. 'Rejecting Judeo-Christian Privilege: The First Step towards Semitic Solidarity'. *Jewish Studies Quarterly* 27, no. 3 (2020): 298–318.

Tovey, Josephine. 'Residents Draw Line over Jewish Boundary'. *The Sydney Morning Herald*, 3 July 2010.

Tzuberi, Hannah, and Sultan Doughan. 'Säkularismus als Praxis und Herrschaft: Zur Kategorisierung von Juden und Muslimen im Kontext Säkularer Wissensproduktion'. In *Der Inspizierte Muslim. Zur Politisierung der Islamforschung in Europa*, edited by Schirin Amir-Moazami, 269–308. Bielefeld: Transcript, 2018.

Valins, Oliver. 'Institutionalised Religion: Sacred Texts and Jewish Spatial Practice'. *Geoforum* 31, no. 4 (2000): 575–86.

Valverde, Mariana. *Everyday Law on the Street. City Governance in an Age of Diversity*. Chicago; London: University of Chicago Press, 2012.

Valverde, Mariana. 'Taking Land Use Seriously: Toward an Ontology of Municipal Law'. *Law Text Culture* 9 (2005): 34–59.

Villaroman, Noel G. '"Not in My Backyard": The Local Planning Process in Australia and Its Impact on Minority Places of Worship'. *Religion and Human Rights* 7, no. 3 (2012): 215–39.

Vincent, Nicholas. 'Two Papal Letters on the Wearing of the Jewish Badge, 1221 and 1229'. *Jewish Historical Studies* 34 (1994–1996): 209–24.

Walter, Tonio. 'Der Gesetzentwurf zur Beschneidung – Kritik Und Strafrechtliche Alternative'. *Juristenzeitung* 67, no. 22 (2012): 1110–17.

Watson, Sophie. 'Symbolic Spaces of Difference: Contesting the Eruv in Barnet, London and Tenafly, New Jersey'. *Environment and Planning D: Society and Space* 23, no. 4 (2005): 597–613.

Wax, Eddy. 'Belgium Tests EU Rules on Halal and Kosher Slaughter'. *Politico*, 19 August 2019. www.politico.eu/article/belgium-becomes-eu-test-case-on-halal-and-kosher-slaughter-religious-freedoms-animal-welfare/.

Wayno, Jeffrey M. 'Rethinking the Fourth Lateran Council of 1215'. *Speculum* 93, no. 3 (2018): 611–37.

Weiler, Joseph H. H. 'Discrimination and Identity in London: The Jewish Free School Case'. *Jewish Review of Books*, Spring (2010).

Weir, Todd H. 'The Specter of "Godless Jewry": Secularism and the "Jewish Question" in Late Nineteenth-Century Germany'. *Central European History* 46, no. 4 (2014): 815–49.

Weiss, Helen A., Natasha Larke, Daniel Halperin, and Inon Schenker. 'Complications of Circumcision in Male Neonates, Infants and Children: A Systematic Review'. *BMC Urology* 10 (2010): 2.

Wendehorst, Stephen. 'Emancipation as Path to National Integration'. In *The Emancipation of Catholics, Jews and Protestants. Minorities and the Nation State in Nineteenth Century Europe*, edited by Rainer Liedtke and Stephen Wendehorst, 188–206. Manchester; New York: Manchester University Press, 1999.

Wenger, Tisa Joy. *Religious Freedom. The Contested History of an American Ideal*. Chapel Hill: University of North Carolina Press, 2017.

Westerduin, Matthea. 'Questioning Religio/Secular Temporalities: Mediaeval Formations of Nation, Europe and Race'. *Patterns of Prejudice* 54, no. 1 (2020): 136–49.

Wheeler, Chris. 'The Public Interest: We Know It's Important, but Do We Know What It Means'. *AIAL Forum* 48 (2006): 12–25.

Williams, George. *Human Rights under the Australian Constitution*. Oxford: Oxford University Press, 2002.

Winterbottom, Anna, Jonneke Koomen, and Gemma Burford. 'Female Genital Cutting: Cultural Rights and Rites of Defiance in Northern Tanzania'. *African Studies Review* 52, no. 1 (2009): 47–71.

Wistrich, Robert S. *Antisemitism. The Longest Hatred*. London: Thames Methuen, 1991.

Wyner Mark, Elizabeth. 'Crossing the Gender Divide: Public Ceremonies, Private Parts, Mixed Feelings'. In *The Covenant of Circumcision: New Perspectives on an Ancient Jewish Rite*, edited by Elizabeth Wyner Mark, xiii–xxvi. Hanover; London: Brandeis University Press, 2003.

Yelle, Robert A. '"By Fire and Sword": Early English Critiques of Islam and Judaism as "Impostures" or Political and "Unfree" Religions'. *Patterns of Prejudice* 54, no. 1–2 (2020): 91–108.

Yelle, Robert A. 'Imagining the Hebrew Republic: Christian Genealogies of Religious Freedom'. In *Politics of Religious Freedom*, edited by Winnifred Fallers Sullivan, Elizabeth Shakman Hurd, Saba Mahmood and Peter Danchin, 17–28. Chicago: University of Chicago Press, 2015.

Yelle, Robert A. '"Moses' Veil". Secularization as Christian Myth'. In *After Secular Law*, edited by Winnifred Fallers Sullivan, Robert A. Yelle and Mateo Taussig-Rubbo, 24–42. Stanford: Stanford University Press, 2011.

Yelle, Robert A. 'The Hindu Moses: Christian Polemics against Jewish Ritual and the Secularization of Hindu Law under Colonialism'. *History of Religions* 49, no. 2 (2009): 141–71.

Yellin, Deena. 'Eruv Lawsuit in Tenafly Provides a Cautionary Tale'. *NorthJersey.Com*, 20 July 2017. www.northjersey.com/story/news/2017/07/30/tenaflys-eruv-lawsuit-provides-cautionary-tale/507868001.

Yoshino, Kenji. 'Covering'. *Yale Law Journal* 111, no. 4 (2002): 769–940.

Youngster, Ilan, and Ben Z. Katz. 'Tradition… Tradition'. *Journal of the Pediatric Infectious Diseases Society* 4, no. 2 (2014): 132–33.

Zentralrat der Juden in Deutschland. *Why Do Jews Circumcise Their Children? Dossier of the Central Council of Jews in Germany on the Issue of Circumcision* (10 July 2012). www.hagalil.com/judentum/2012/beschneidung.pdf.

Zucca, Lorenzo. 'Lautsi: A Commentary on a Decision by the ECtHR Grand Chamber'. *International Journal of Constitutional Law* 11, no. 1 (2013): 218–29.

INDEX

CAMBRIDGE STUDIES IN LAW AND SOCIETY

Books in the Series

Diseases of the Will: Alcohol and the Dilemmas of Freedom
Mariana Valverde

The Politics of Truth and Reconciliation in South Africa: Legitimizing the Post-Apartheid State
Richard A. Wilson

Modernism and the Grounds of Law
Peter Fitzpatrick

Unemployment and Government: Genealogies of the Social
William Walters

Autonomy and Ethnicity: Negotiating Competing Claims in Multi-Ethnic States
Yash Ghai

Constituting Democracy: Law, Globalism and South Africa's Political Reconstruction
Heinz Klug

The Ritual of Rights in Japan: Law, Society, and Health Policy
Eric A. Feldman

Governing Morals: A Social History of Moral Regulation
Alan Hunt

The Colonies of Law: Colonialism, Zionism and Law in Early Mandate Palestine
Ronen Shamir

Law and Nature
David Delaney

Social Citizenship and Workfare in the United States and Western Europe: The Paradox of Inclusion
Joel F. Handler

Law, Anthropology, and the Constitution of the Social: Making Persons and Things
Edited by Alain Pottage and Martha Mundy

Judicial Review and Bureaucratic Impact: International and Interdisciplinary Perspectives
Edited by Marc Hertogh and Simon Halliday

Immigrants at the Margins: Law, Race, and Exclusion in Southern Europe
Kitty Calavita

Lawyers and Regulation: The Politics of the Administrative Process
Patrick Schmidt

Law and Globalization from Below: Towards a Cosmopolitan Legality
Edited by Boaventura de Sousa Santos and César A. Rodríguez-Garavito

Public Accountability: Designs, Dilemmas and Experiences
Edited by Michael W. Dowdle

Law, Violence and Sovereignty among West Bank Palestinians
Tobias Kelly

Legal Reform and Administrative Detention Powers in China
Sarah Biddulph

The Practice of Human Rights: Tracking Law between the Global and the Local
Edited by Mark Goodale and Sally Engle Merry

Judges beyond Politics in Democracy and Dictatorship: Lessons from Chile
Lisa Hilbink

Paths to International Justice: Social and Legal Perspectives
Edited by Marie-Bénédicte Dembour and Tobias Kelly

Law and Society in Vietnam: The Transition from Socialism in Comparative Perspective
Mark Sidel

Constitutionalizing Economic Globalization: Investment Rules and Democracy's Promise
David Schneiderman

The New World Trade Organization Knowledge Agreements: Second Edition
Christopher Arup

Justice and Reconciliation in Post-Apartheid South Africa
Edited by François du Bois and Antje du Bois-Pedain

Militarization and Violence against Women in Conflict Zones in the Middle East: A Palestinian Case-Study
Nadera Shalhoub-Kevorkian

Child Pornography and Sexual Grooming: Legal and Societal Responses
Suzanne Ost

Darfur and the Crime of Genocide
John Hagan and Wenona Rymond-Richmond

Fictions of Justice: The International Criminal Court and the Challenge of Legal Pluralism in Sub-Saharan Africa
Kamari Maxine Clarke

Conducting Law and Society Research: Reflections on Methods and Practices
Simon Halliday and Patrick Schmidt

Planted Flags: Trees, Land, and Law in Israel/Palestine
Irus Braverman

Culture under Cross-Examination: International Justice and the Special Court for Sierra Leone
Tim Kelsall

Cultures of Legality: Judicialization and Political Activism in Latin America
Javier Couso, Alexandra Huneeus, and Rachel Sieder

Courting Democracy in Bosnia and Herzegovina: The Hague Tribunal's Impact in a Postwar State
Lara J. Nettelfield

The Gacaca Courts, Post-Genocide Justice and Reconciliation in Rwanda: Justice without Lawyers
Phil Clark

Law, Society, and History: Themes in the Legal Sociology and Legal History of Lawrence M. Friedman
Edited by Robert W. Gordon and Morton J. Horwitz

After Abu Ghraib: Exploring Human Rights in America and the Middle East
Shadi Mokhtari

Adjudication in Religious Family Laws: Cultural Accommodation, Legal Pluralism, and Gender Equality in India
Gopika Solanki

Water on Tap: Rights and Regulation in the Transnational Governance of Urban Water Services
Bronwen Morgan

Elements of Moral Cognition: Rawls' Linguistic Analogy and the Cognitive Science of Moral and Legal Judgment
John Mikhail

Mitigation and Aggravation at Sentencing
Edited by Julian V. Roberts

Institutional Inequality and the Mobilization of the Family and Medical Leave Act: Rights on Leave
Catherine R. Albiston

Authoritarian Rule of Law: Legislation, Discourse and Legitimacy in Singapore
Jothie Rajah

Law and Development and the Global Discourses of Legal Transfers
Edited by John Gillespie and Pip Nicholson

Law against the State: Ethnographic Forays into Law's Transformations
Edited by Julia Eckert, Brian Donahoe, Christian Strümpell and Zerrin Özlem Biner

Transnational Legal Ordering and State Change
Edited by Gregory C. Shaffer

Legal Mobilization under Authoritarianism: The Case of Post-Colonial Hong Kong
Waikeung Tam

Complementarity in the Line of Fire: The Catalysing Effect of the International Criminal Court in Uganda and Sudan
Sarah M. H. Nouwen

Political and Legal Transformations of an Indonesian Polity: The Nagari from Colonisation to Decentralisation
Franz von Benda-Beckmann and Keebet von Benda-Beckmann

Pakistan's Experience with Formal Law: An Alien Justice
Osama Siddique

Human Rights under State-Enforced Religious Family Laws in Israel, Egypt, and India
Yüksel Sezgin

Why Prison?
Edited by David Scott

Law's Fragile State: Colonial, Authoritarian, and Humanitarian Legacies in Sudan
Mark Fathi Massoud

Rights for Others: The Slow Home-Coming of Human Rights in the Netherlands
Barbara Oomen

European States and Their Muslim Citizens: The Impact of Institutions on Perceptions and Boundaries
Edited by John R. Bowen, Christophe Bertossi, Jan Willem Duyvendak, and Mona Lena Krook

Environmental Litigation in China: A Study in Political Ambivalence
Rachel E. Stern

Indigeneity and Legal Pluralism in India: Claims, Histories, Meanings
Pooja Parmar

Paper Tiger: Law, Bureaucracy and the Developmental State in Himalayan India
Nayanika Mathur

Religion, Law and Society
Russell Sandberg

The Experiences of Face Veil Wearers in Europe and the Law
Edited by Eva Brems

The Contentious History of the International Bill of Human Rights
Christopher N. J. Roberts

Transnational Legal Orders
Edited by Terence C. Halliday and Gregory Shaffer

Lost in China? Law, Culture and Society in Post-1997 Hong Kong
Carol A. G. Jones

Security Theology, Surveillance and the Politics of Fear
Nadera Shalhoub-Kevorkian

Opposing the Rule of Law: How Myanmar's Courts Make Law and Order
Nick Cheesman

Ironies of Colonial Governance: Law, Custom and Justice in Colonial India
James Jaffe

The Clinic and the Court: Law, Medicine and Anthropology
Edited by Ian Harper, Tobias Kelly, and Akshay Khanna

The World of Indicators: The Making of Government Knowledge through Quantification
Edited by Richard Rottenburg, Sally E. Merry, Sung-Joon Park, and Johanna Mugler

Contesting Immigration Policy in Court: Legal Activism and Its Radiating Effects in the United States and France
Leila Kawar

The Quiet Power of Indicators: Measuring Governance, Corruption, and Rule of Law
Edited by Sally Engle Merry, Kevin E. Davis, and Benedict Kingsbury

Investing in Authoritarian Rule: Punishment and Patronage in Rwanda's Gacaca Courts for Genocide Crimes
Anuradha Chakravarty

Contractual Knowledge: One Hundred Years of Legal Experimentation in Global Markets
Edited by Grégoire Mallard and Jérôme Sgard

Iraq and the Crimes of Aggressive War: The Legal Cynicism of Criminal Militarism
John Hagan, Joshua Kaiser, and Anna Hanson

Culture in the Domains of Law
Edited by René Provost

China and Islam: The Prophet, the Party, and Law
Matthew S. Erie

Diversity in Practice: Race, Gender, and Class in Legal and Professional Careers
Edited by Spencer Headworth, Robert L. Nelson, Ronit Dinovitzer, and David B. Wilkins

A Sociology of Constitutions: Constitutions and State Legitimacy in Historical-Sociological Perspective
Chris Thornhill

A Sociology of Transnational Constitutions: Social Foundations of the Post-National Legal Structure
Chris Thornhill

Genocide Never Sleeps: Living Law at the International Criminal Tribunal for Rwanda
Nigel Eltringham

Shifting Legal Visions: Judicial Change and Human Rights Trials in Latin America
Ezequiel A. González-Ocantos

The Demographic Transformations of Citizenship
Heli Askola

Criminal Defense in China: The Politics of Lawyers at Work
Sida Liu and Terence C. Halliday

Contesting Economic and Social Rights in Ireland: Constitution, State and Society, 1848–2016
Thomas Murray

Buried in the Heart: Women, Complex Victimhood and the War in Northern Uganda
Erin Baines

Palaces of Hope: The Anthropology of Global Organizations
Edited by Ronald Niezen and Maria Sapignoli

The Politics of Bureaucratic Corruption in Post-Transitional Eastern Europe
Marina Zaloznaya

Revisiting the Law and Governance of Trafficking, Forced Labor and Modern Slavery
Edited by Prabha Kotiswaran

Incitement on Trial: Prosecuting International Speech Crimes
Richard Ashby Wilson

Criminalizing Children: Welfare and the State in Australia
David McCallum

Global Lawmakers: International Organizations in the Crafting of World Markets
Susan Block-Lieb and Terence C. Halliday

Duties to Care: Dementia, Relationality and Law
Rosie Harding

Insiders, Outsiders, Injuries, and Law: Revisiting "The Oven Bird's Song"
Edited by Mary Nell Trautner

Hunting Justice: Displacement, Law, and Activism in the Kalahari
Maria Sapignoli

Injury and Injustice: The Cultural Politics of Harm and Redress
Edited by Anne Bloom, David M. Engel, and Michael McCann

Ruling Before the Law: The Politics of Legal Regimes in China and Indonesia
William Hurst

The Powers of Law: A Comparative Analysis of Sociopolitical Legal Studies
Mauricio García-Villegas

A Sociology of Justice in Russia
Edited by Marina Kurkchiyan and Agnieszka Kubal

Constituting Religion: Islam, Liberal Rights, and the Malaysian State
Tamir Moustafa

The Invention of the Passport: Surveillance, Citizenship and the State, Second Edition
John C. Torpey

Law's Trials: The Performance of Legal Institutions in the US "War on Terror"
Richard L. Abel

Law's Wars: The Fate of the Rule of Law in the US "War on Terror"
Richard L. Abel

Transforming Gender Citizenship: The Irresistible Rise of Gender Quotas in Europe
Edited by Eléonore Lépinard and Ruth Rubio-Marín

Muslim Women's Quest for Justice: Gender, Law and Activism in India
Mengia Hong Tschalaer

Children as 'Risk': Sexual Exploitation and Abuse by Children and Young People
Anne-Marie McAlinden

The Legal Process and the Promise of Justice: Studies Inspired by the Work of Malcolm Feeley
Jonathan Simon, Rosann Greenspan, Hadar Aviram

Gift Exchanges: The Transnational History of a Political Idea
Grégoire Mallard

Measuring Justice: Quantitative Accountability and the National Prosecuting Authority in South Africa
Johanna Mugler

Negotiating the Power of NGOs: Women's Legal Rights in South Africa
Reem Wael

Indigenous Water Rights in Law and Regulation: Lessons from Comparative Experience
Elizabeth Jane Macpherson

The Edge of Law: Legal Geographies of a War Crimes Court
Alex Jeffrey

Everyday Justice: Law, Ethnography, and Injustice
Sandra Brunnegger

The Uncounted: Politics of Data in Global Health
Sara L. M. Davis

Transnational Legal Ordering of Criminal Justice
Gregory Shaffer and Ely Aaronson

Five Republics and One Tradition
Pablo Ruiz-Tagle

The Law Multiple: Judgment and Knowledge in Practice
Irene van Oorschot

Health as a Human Right: The Politics and Judicialisation of Health in Brazil
Octávio Luiz Motta Ferraz

Shari'a, Inshallah: Finding God in Somali Legal Politics
Mark Fathi Massoud

Policing for Peace: Institutions, Expectations, and Security in Divided Societies
Matthew Nanes

Rule of Law Intermediaries: Brokering Influence in Myanmar
Kristina Simion

Lactation at Work: Expressed Milk, Expressing Beliefs, and the Expressive Value of Law
Elizabeth A. Hoffmann

The Archival Politics of International Courts
Henry Redwood

Global Pro Bono: Causes, Context, and Contestation
Edited by Scott L. Cummings, Fabio de Sa e Silva and Louise G. Trubek

The Practice and Problems of Transnational Counter-Terrorism
Fiona de Londras

Decoupling: Gender Injustice in China's Divorce Courts
Ethan Michelson

Anti-Constitutional Populism
Martin Krygier, Adam Czarnota and Wojciech Sadurski

Lawyers in Conflict and Transition
Kieran McEvoy, Louse Mallinder and Anna Bryson

The Ghostwriters: Lawyers and the Politics behind the Judicial Construction of Europe
Tommaso Pavone

The Sentimental Court: The Affective Life of International Criminal Justice
Jonas Bens

Practices of Reparations in International Criminal Justice
Christoph Sperfeldt

Seeking Supremacy: The Pursuit of Judicial Power in Pakistan
Yasser Kureshi

The Power of the Jury: Transforming Citizens into Jurors
Nancy S. Marder

Undue Process: Persecution and Punishment in Autocratic Courts Fiona
Feiang Shen-Bayh

Discounting Life: Necropolitical Law, Culture, and the Long War on Terror
Jothie Rajah

Clean Air at What Cost? The Rise of Blunt Force Regulation in China
Denise Sienli van der Kamp

Law and Precarity: Legal Consciousness and Daily Survival in Vietnam
Tu Phuong Nguyen

Prosecutors, Voters and The Criminalization of Corruption in Latin America: The Case of Lava Jato
Ezequiel A. Gonzalez-Ocantos and Paula Muñoz Chirinos

Entangled Domains: Empire, Law and Religion in Northern Nigeria
Rabiat Akande

The Social Constitution: Embedding Social Rights Through Legal Mobilization
Whitney K. Taylor

Out of Place: Fieldwork and Positionality in Law and Society
Edited by Lynette J. Chua and Mark Fathi Massoud

Negotiating Legality: Chinese Companies in the U.S. Legal System
Ji Li

Law and Jewish Difference: Ambivalent Encounters
Mareike Riedel